# MATHEMATICS FOR BIOMEDICAL APPLICATIONS

# MATHEMATICS
# FOR
# BIOMEDICAL
# APPLICATIONS

## STANTON A. GLANTZ

UNIVERSITY OF CALIFORNIA PRESS

BERKELEY • LOS ANGELES • LONDON

University of California Press
Berkeley and Los Angeles, California

University of California Press, Ltd.
London, England

ISBN 0-520-03599-2
Library of Congress Catalog Card Number: 77-20320
Printed in the United States of America

1 2 3 4 5 6 7 8 9

To FRIEDA and LOUIS GLANTZ

# CONTENTS

# PREFACE

This text has its origins in an applied mathematics course I developed in 1973 while a postdoctoral fellow in the Stanford University Cardiology Division. Like that course, this text builds on the student's (perhaps distant) exposure to introductory calculus to develop applied differential equations and linear systems theory motivated by biomedical problems. I have sought to include enough mathematical theory to provide a sense of the structure and unity that mathematics can bring to other sciences, while always remembering that a biomedical audience is most interested in learning how to use mathematics to solve practical problems.

Because this audience is traditionally skeptical about the value of mathematics, the first two chapters formulate more-or-less real problems in terms of differential equations, but defer solving these equations until Chapter 3. Chapter 3 summarizes direct methods to solve linear ordinary differential equations and works the problems formulated in Chapter 2. Chapter 2 also constructs the exponential function from a power series solution to a first-order differential equation to show the reader why this function appears so often. Chapter 3 does the same thing for sines and cosines. My students have found this approach a useful complement to their original exposure to these functions in introductory courses. The next three chapters on the Laplace transform, properties of linear systems, and Fourier analysis introduce impulse and step functions with applications to biological signal processing. In many cases, I re-solve problems that were solved by direct methods in Chapter 3, so the reader can compare the relative difficulty of the different methods. Finally, Chapter 7 introduces numerical techniques for integration, solving differential equations, and curve fitting. The emphasis is on providing a context for reading more advanced texts or using library subroutines; no attempt is made to make the reader an expert computer programmer. Chapter 7 shows that one can use what would be perfectly acceptable logic in the algebra of real numbers to produce unreliable algorithms in floating point arithmetic.

To help the rusty reader remember the relevant portions of calculus, Appendix A contains a brief review of these topics. Appendix C presents the properties of complex numbers which are necessary to understand the Fourier transform (Chapter 6) and a few other topics. Appendices B and D contain tables of integrals and Laplace transforms to save the reader the trouble of evaluating complicated integrals.

In a formal course meeting three hours per week, one can reasonably expect to cover a brief review of calculus and the first three chapters in one quarter and the remainder of the book in a second quarter.

I thank Donald Harrison, Chief of the Cardiology Division at Stanford University, for providing the resources to start this project, and William Parmley, Chief of the Cardiology Division at the University of California at San Francisco, for providing the resources to finish it. I completed the manuscript while a Senior Research Fellow of the San Francisco Bay Area Heart Research Committee and put the finishing touches on it while holding a Research Career Development Award from the National Institutes of Health. A. Lawrence Spitz wrote the computer programs to generate the power spectra of human cardiac pressure waves included in Chapter 6. I am especially grateful to Gail Hayes, Margaret Tidd, Kathleen Hecker, and Marilyn Gruen for typing the original manuscript, David Toy, Mary Helen Stull, and Norma Riffle for preparing the illustrations, Anne Holly for helping get the manuscript ready to send to the publisher, Douglas Bullis for editing it, and Michael Bass for doing the book design and layout. Harry Miller, who helped overcome many administrative difficulties at Stanford, and Grant Barnes, my sponsor at U.C. Press, deserve special thanks. Most of all, I am grateful to Robert Goldman, Peter Renz, and my students for providing insightful criticism which helped me tailor this work for its intended audience.

S.A.G.

*San Francisco, California*
*November, 1977*

# 1

# INTRODUCTION

A qualitative understanding of physiological processes comes from the integration of knowledge of several factors which span many orders of magnitude in space, time, and energy. These factors include behavior exhibited by the entire body, performance of organ systems, histologic structure of the organs, and biochemical reactions inside cells. When one integrates these different perspectives on a problem in an attempt to understand a biological process or to reach a practical decision about how to manage a disease, one often slips from one set of assumptions to another, even though taken as a whole these assumptions might not be logically consistent. In contrast, a quantitative understanding of biological processes, based on mathematics, requires logical consistency above all. Although theoretically it may be possible to consider several factors which span many orders of magnitude, in practice it is often difficult to obtain numerical solutions when the variables which quantify these factors differ by more than a few orders of magnitude. Thus, successful mathematical analysis generally requires a consistent scale of events. This requirement sometimes restricts use of prior knowledge, but it can help avoid unimportant details.

One's prior knowledge of the structure of a process under consideration determines the questions one asks and the mathematical tools one applies to answer them. With little prior knowledge, one is limited to the description of general patterns of available observations. Quantitative methods are used to answer relatively simple questions, such as the estimation of a parameter's value or the probability that two samples were drawn from the same population. We use statistical tools to answer these questions. In contrast, if one knows (or can hypothesize) the underlying structure and mechanisms which produce the observed patterns, one can use the deterministic mathematics developed in this text to predict behavior and to draw deductive conclusions from mathematical manipulation.

For example, cardiologists often prescribe drugs from the digitalis family, which improve the heart's pumping action in patients with heart failure or slow the heart rate in patients with abnormal rhythms. To study why children require larger doses of these drugs to achieve the same serum concentrations as adults, my colleagues and I administered the same dose (per kilogram of body weight) of ouabain to adult dogs and puppies and

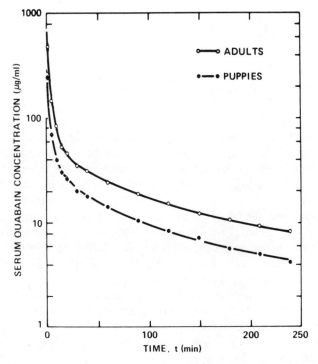

**FIGURE 1.1:** After an ouabain dose of 0.05 mg/kg, serum ouabain concentrations in adult dogs remained significantly higher than in puppies given the same dose, although the curves for both groups had the same shape. (Adapted with permission of the American Heart Association, Inc., from S. A. Glantz, R. Kernoff, and R. H. Goldman, Age-Related Changes in Ouabain Pharmacology, *Circ. Res.* 39 (1976): 407.)

measured the resulting concentrations* (Fig. 1.1). With no prior knowl-edge—or hypotheses—about ouabain distribution, we applied statistical tests and found that, for the same dose, puppies had significantly lower serum ouabain concentrations than adult dogs. This observation was inter-esting but provided no direct insight into the underlying mechanism which produced it.

The mathematical tools this text develops will permit us, among other things, to propose and verify a theoretical description for ouabain distribu-tion. Suppose that some of the ouabain present in the body remains dissolved in the plasma, some is reversibly bound in the body, and some is irreversibly removed (Fig. 1.2). The constants $k_{12}$, $k_{21}$, and $k_{10}$ describe how quickly ouabain is bound $(k_{12})$ and released $(k_{21})$ from reversible binding sites or removed from the body $(k_{10})$. The equations which describe this system show that these constants determine the shape of the curve for serum concentration versus time, whereas the dose and the volume in which the drug is distributed determine the magnitude of the concentration but not the way in which it changes with time. (This fact follows from the important mathematical property of linearity, which we will discuss at length.) Since both adult dogs and puppies received the same dose and since their curves had the same shape, we concluded that

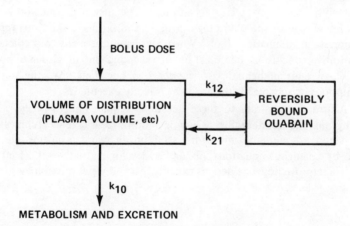

BOLUS DOSE

$$
\begin{array}{ccc}
\boxed{\begin{array}{c}\text{VOLUME OF DISTRIBUTION}\\\text{(PLASMA VOLUME, etc)}\end{array}} & \xrightarrow{k_{12}} & \boxed{\begin{array}{c}\text{REVERSIBLY}\\\text{BOUND}\\\text{OUABAIN}\end{array}}
\end{array}
$$

$k_{21}$

$k_{10}$

METABOLISM AND EXCRETION

**FIGURE 1.2:** One way to picture the distribution of ouabain in a dog. This picture, called a two-compartment model, will lead to equations that describe how ouabain concentration changes with time. We will see that the constants that describe how the drug is reversibly bound ($k_{12}$ and $k_{21}$) and eliminated from the body ($k_{10}$) determine the shape, but not the magnitude, of the concentration versus time curve.

* Chapter 3 treats this problem in detail.

the only difference between puppies and adult dogs was that the effective volume in which the drug was distributed was larger in puppies. This mathematical result suggested additional experiments, which confirmed that the puppies had larger physiological fluid spaces per kilogram of body weight than the adult dogs, a finding which accounts for the greater volume of distribution in the puppies. Thus, the techniques this text develops permitted us to draw much stronger conclusions from our experiments than would have been possible if we had been limited to a statistical approach.

Sometimes, however, one should spurn a mathematical approach. The value of any analysis depends heavily on the initial assumptions, and often one cannot translate them into convenient mathematical expressions. Some workers, with glib disregard for the violence done to known underlying physiology, recast their assumptions to make the problem workable. Perhaps the most common such offense is the assumption, often implicit, of linearity. Linear equations are relatively easy to solve; indeed, often one cannot solve nonlinear equations analytically. But since biological systems often exhibit nonlinear behavior, assumptions of linearity require careful scrutiny and, if necessary, rejection. Rejection may preclude solving the problem and restrict one to qualitative arguments. The question then arises whether to trust precise analysis based on imprecise assumptions or imprecise analysis based on precise assumptions. The answer depends both on one's knowledge of the physiology involved and on one's ability to apply appropriate mathematical tools. When mathematical analysis predicts a nonintuitive conclusion, one must be secure enough in knowledge of both physiology and mathematics to answer two questions: Are the initial assumptions reasonable? Is the analysis correctly executed?

Affirmative answers to these questions require one to accept new conclusions and reorient his or her intuition. As the reader comes to understand the common underlying structure in many problems, illuminated by analogous equations, his or her developing mathematical intuition will improve how one designs experiments and views physiology.

# 2

# WRITING DIFFERENTIAL EQUATIONS

Most problems in physiology and medicine concern dynamic processes which involve the rates of change of several variables, as well as their values. With derivatives to describe a variable's rate of change, we will describe dynamic processes with equations containing derivatives, which are called *differential equations*. After understanding differentiation, translating physiological statements into mathematical statements provides the key to writing useful differential equations. The formulation and solution of a dynamic problem includes three distinct phases. First, one must use knowledge and intuition to write one or more differential equations and an equal number of uniqueness conditions which describe the physiological situation. Second, one must manipulate these mathematical expressions to solve the differential equations. Finally, one must interpret the mathematical solution in physiological terms. Typical examples best illustrate this process, so the bulk of this chapter consists of examples which highlight different approaches to the translation of physiological statements into differential equations.

Most cases present and verify the solutions, but we defer discussion of the formal procedures for solving differential equations to Chapters 3, 4, and 7. Before we study these examples, however, we must address the theoretical question: What is a solution to a differential equation and when does it exist? We begin with four *definitions*.

> *Differential equation:* an equation containing one or more ordinary or partial derivatives.

*Ordinary differential equation:* an equation containing only ordinary derivatives, all with respect to the same variable.

*Partial differential equation:* an equation which contains one or more partial derivatives. (It may also contain ordinary derivatives.)

The *order* of a differential equation is the order of the highest derivative that appears in the equation.

For example,

$$F = m \frac{d^2 x}{dt^2} \qquad m = \text{constant} \tag{2.1}$$

and

$$\ddot{q} + \dot{q} + q + 1 = 0 \tag{2.2}$$

are second-order ordinary differential equations. In contrast,

$$\frac{\partial Q(x, y)}{\partial x} = kx \tag{2.3}$$

is a first-order partial differential equation. Partial differential equations are much harder to solve than ordinary differential equations. Luckily, ordinary differential equations suffice for most applications we will encounter, so we will concentrate on writing and solving them.

Many applications, such as multiple-compartment descriptions for drug distribution, give rise to a set of first-order ordinary differential equations. Such a set of $n$ first-order differential equations is equivalent to a single $n$th-order differential equation. Suppose a problem led to the two first-order ordinary differential equations

$$\dot{x}_1 = x_2 \tag{2.4}$$

and

$$\dot{x}_2 = x_1 \tag{2.5}$$

To convert (2.4) and (2.5) to a single equivalent second-order differential equation, differentiate (2.4) with respect to time,

$$\ddot{x}_1 = \dot{x}_2 \tag{2.6}$$

and eliminate $\dot{x}_2$ from (2.6) with (2.5):

$$\ddot{x}_1 = x_1 \tag{2.7}$$

Thus, we have converted the set of two first-order differential equations in the variables $x_1$ and $x_2$ into a single equivalent second-order differential equation in $x_1$. One could use (2.4) and (2.5) simultaneously to find $x_1$ and $x_2$ or find $x_1$ from the single equation (2.7), then differentiate the result to get $x_2$. This process of differentiation and substitution permits the conversion of any set of $n$ first-order ordinary differential equations into a single $n$th-order differential equation. Therefore, *a set of n first-order differential equations is nth order.* Conversely, an $n$th-order ordinary differential equation may be transformed into a set of $n$ first-order differential equations by reversing this process.

## PROBLEM SET 2.1

What order are these differential equations?

1. $\dfrac{dy}{dx} = kx^2$

2. $y'' + y' + y = x$

3. $\dfrac{\partial Q}{\partial x} = e^z + z$

4. $\dot{x}_1 = x_1 + x_2$        $\dot{x}_2 = x_2 + x_3$        $\dot{x}_3 = x_1^2$

5. $\dot{x}_1 = x_1 + x_2$        $\dot{x}_2 = x_2 + x_3$        $x_3 = x_1^2$

Write each system of differential equations as a single differential equation in terms of the first variable.

6. $\dot{x}_1 = x_1 + x_2$                                 $x_1(0) = x_{10}$

    $\dot{x}_2 = x_2$                                      $x_2(0) = x_{20}$

7. $\dot{x}_1 = x_1 - x_2$                                 $x_1(0) = x_{10}$

    $\dot{x}_2 = x_2$                                      $x_2(0) = x_{20}$

8. $\dot{c}_1 = \dfrac{I}{V} + k_{21}c_2 - (k_{12} + k_{10})c_1$        $c_1(0) = c_{10}$

    $\dot{c}_2 = k_{12}c_1 - k_{21}c_2$                        $c_2(0) = 0$

**9.** $\dfrac{dy}{dx} = y + z$ $\qquad\qquad\qquad\qquad$ $y(0) = 1$

$\dfrac{dz}{dx} = w$ $\qquad\qquad\qquad\qquad$ $z(0) = 0$

$\dfrac{dw}{dx} = x$ $\qquad\qquad\qquad\qquad$ $w(0) = 0$

**10.** $\dot{x}_1 = x_1 + x_2$ $\qquad\qquad\qquad$ $x_1(0) = x_{10}$

$\dot{x}_2 = x_2 + x_3$ $\qquad\qquad\qquad$ $x_2(0) = x_{20}$

$x_3 = x_1^2$ $\qquad\qquad\qquad\qquad$ $x_3(0) = x_{10}^2$

## SOLUTIONS OF ORDINARY DIFFERENTIAL EQUATIONS

Before discussing what the word *solution* means in reference to differential equations, let us examine solutions to algebraic equations. We say that $x = 4$ is the solution of $x - 4 = 0$ because replacing the symbol $x$ with the value 4 satisfies the equation, i.e., $4 - 4 = 0$. Algebraic equations may have more than one solution or no solution at all. For example, both $x = +2$ and $x = -2$ solve $x^2 - 4 = 0$, and $x^2 = -1$ has no solution if $x$ must be a real number. Thus, the solution of an algebraic equation is the set of values which, when substituted into the equation, satisfy it.

Later in this chapter we will construct the exponential function,

$$y(x) = e^x \qquad\qquad (2.8)$$

to have the property of equaling its own derivative. In other words, the exponential function will be defined so that

$$\frac{d(e^x)}{dx} = e^x \qquad\qquad (2.9)$$

Substitute from (2.8) into (2.9) to obtain

$$\frac{dy}{dx} = y \qquad\qquad (2.10)$$

a first-order differential equation. This equation says that $y$'s rate of change equals its magnitude. We say that

$$y = Ae^x \qquad A = \text{any constant} \qquad (2.11)$$

is the solution of (2.10) because *it is the function which, when substituted into the differential equation, satisfies it.*

To demonstrate that (2.11) satisfies (2.10) compute $dy/dx$ from (2.11), then substitute into (2.10):

$$Ae^x = \frac{dy}{dx} = y = Ae^x \qquad (2.12)$$

Note that we have introduced the arbitrary constant $A$, which has no effect on whether or not (2.11) solves (2.10). Additional conditions determine $A$'s value. This example illustrates one important way of solving differential equations: guess a solution, then substitute into the original equation to see if the equation is satisfied. We use this process to solve a differential equation which often arises in connection with natural phenomena:

$$\frac{dy}{dx} = ky \qquad k = \text{constant} \qquad (2.13)$$

$y$'s rate of change is directly proportional to its magnitude. The previous example, (2.12), suggests that

$$y = Ae^{kx} \qquad A = \text{constant} \qquad (2.14)$$

is a solution. Differentiate (2.14) with respect to $x$ and substitute into (2.13) to show that (2.14) is a solution of (2.13).

Given a differential equation, does a solution *exist*? And is it *unique*? These questions motivate much advanced mathematical theory of differential equations and become very important when analyzing complex problems which require substantial time and energy to seek a solution. Fortunately, we deal with problems simple enough to show a unique solution exists simply by finding it! While we will not discuss the mathematical details, the concepts of existence and uniqueness highlight two important points:

*If a meaningful problem is correctly formulated mathematically as a differential equation, then the mathematical problem should have a solution.*

and

> *If a given differential equation has more than one solution,*
> *additional conditions must be specified to define a single unique*
> *solution.*

For example, Equation (2.14) represents an infinite number of different solutions, corresponding to the infinite number of possible values for *A* (Fig. 2.1). A single point on each curve, say the value at $x = 0$, distinguishes each solution from the others. Thus, to define a solution uniquely for (2.13), one must specify a condition which indicates which curve to use. The most common specification for ordinary differential equations is the so-called *initial condition**

$$y(0) = y_0 \qquad\qquad (2.15)$$

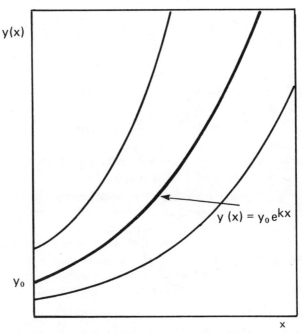

**FIGURE 2.1:** The initial condition $y(0) = y_0$ specifies which of the infinite different functions that satisfy the differential equation is the unique solution.

---

\* The uniqueness condition for partial differential equations generally requires entire functions, not just the value of a function at a point. We will not discuss the so-called *boundary conditions* for partial differential equations.

where $y_0$ is given. Substitute $x = 0$ into (2.14) and compare the result with (2.15) to show

$$y(0) = Ae^{k \cdot 0} = A \cdot 1 = y_0 \qquad (2.16)$$

Therefore, the unique solution to (2.14) is

$$y(x) = y_0 e^{kx} \qquad (2.17)$$

A physiological problem correctly formulated and translated into differential equations should have a unique solution. If no solution exists, the physiological problem was not correctly translated into mathematical statements. If many solutions exist, additional uniqueness conditions must be specified to define a unique solution. In general, one must provide one uniqueness condition (generally an initial condition) for each order of an ordinary differential equation.

Now, let us turn our attention to translating physiological statements into differential equations.

## ONE-COMPARTMENT DRUG DISTRIBUTION

When the body distributes a drug or hormone so that all of the drug-containing fluid acts as a single entity with respect to the drug's dynamic behavior, we say that it is immediately diluted and distributed in a single *compartment* with a constant *volume of distribution* (Fig. 2.2). Suppose metabolism removes a fixed fraction of the total quantity of drug present per unit time. We can use three different, yet equivalent, ways to develop a differential equation which describes this phenomenon.

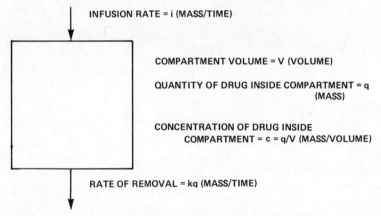

INFUSION RATE = i (MASS/TIME)

COMPARTMENT VOLUME = V (VOLUME)

QUANTITY OF DRUG INSIDE COMPARTMENT = q (MASS)

CONCENTRATION OF DRUG INSIDE COMPARTMENT = c = q/V (MASS/VOLUME)

RATE OF REMOVAL = kq (MASS/TIME)

**FIGURE 2.2:** One-compartment description for drug distribution and metabolism. The mass removal rate increases in direct proportion to the mass of drug inside the compartment. ($k$'s units are time$^{-1}$.)

Most directly, conservation of mass requires that the rate at which material accumulates in the compartment equals the difference between the rate at which it enters and leaves the compartment. Let:

$i$ = rate at which drug is infused or secreted into the compartment,

$q$ = quantity of drug in the compartment,

$V$ = compartment volume (volume of distribution),

$c = q/V$ = drug concentration in compartment,

$k$ = constant of proportionality for metabolic removal,

$t$ = time.

Then

$$\frac{dq}{dt} = i(t) - kq \qquad (2.18)$$

| Rate at which mass builds up in the compartment | Rate at which mass flows into the compartment (infusion and secretion) | Rate at which mass flows out of the compartment (metabolism) |

$k$ has units of time$^{-1}$; hence $k = 0.05$ min$^{-1}$ means that 5% of the drug mass ($q$) in the compartment is metabolized every minute. To work with concentration, not absolute quantity, divide (2.18) by the constant $V$ to obtain

$$\frac{d\left(\frac{q}{V}\right)}{dt} = \frac{i}{V} - k\left(\frac{q}{V}\right) \qquad (2.19)$$

But $c = q/V$, so

$$\frac{dc}{dt} = \frac{i}{V} - kc \qquad (2.20)$$

To complete the problem specification, we specify a uniqueness condition, the initial concentration:

$$c(0) = c_0 \qquad (2.21)$$

Alternately, one could approximate the change in mass of drug in the compartment, $\Delta q$, during time increment $\Delta t$ with

$$\Delta q = \frac{i(t) + i(t + \Delta t)}{2} \cdot \Delta t - k\frac{q(t) + q(t + \Delta t)}{2} \cdot \Delta t \qquad (2.22)$$

$[i(t) + i(t + \Delta t)]/2$ and $[q(t) + q(t + \Delta t)]/2$ approximate average drug inflow and amount of drug in the compartment during the interval from time $t$ to $t + \Delta t$, respectively. Divide (2.22) by $\Delta t$, then take the limit as $\Delta t \rightarrow 0$ to obtain (2.18). As before, (2.21) provides the uniqueness condition.

In a similar vein, we could think of incremental changes as differentials. In this case, the differential drug quantity change, $dq$, during small time change, $dt$, equals the infusion rate times $dt$, minus the removal rate times the same differential change in time,

$$dq = i \cdot dt - kq \cdot dt \qquad (2.23)$$

Divide through by (the number) $dt$ to obtain (2.18) again and continue as before.

These three approaches to the translation of a physiological statement into a differential equation proceed along slightly different lines but result in the same equation and uniqueness condition. The method used to write the differential equation does not affect the final result; in fact, deriving the differential equation or equations which describe a situation more than one way provides a good check for correct problem formulation.

The remaining examples develop equations using one of these three methods. Rework them using different approaches than those presented. In practice, one's selection of approach will depend on personal preference and, to a lesser degree, the specific problem.

## THE FUNCTION WHICH IS ITS OWN DERIVATIVE: THE EXPONENTIAL

We have already seen a number of equations of the form

$$\frac{dy}{dx} = ky \qquad (2.24)$$

Now, let us construct a function, $y = y(x)$, to solve (2.24). For convenience, we will take $k = 1$.

Mathematicians have proven that a wide class of functions can be represented as a *power series*:

$$y(x) = a_0 + a_1 x + a_2 x^2 + a_3 x^3 + a_4 x^4 + \ldots \qquad (2.25)$$

in which the $a_i$'s are constants whose specific values depend on $y(x)$. Note that this sum contains an infinite number of terms; it is known as an *infinite series*. For this sum to exist, the series must *converge,* that is, after some term in the series, each additional term must add less and less to the sum so that it exists as a finite number. There are strict mathematical standards used to prove whether or not an infinite series converges, but we will not dwell on them.

Rather, we shall see if (2.25) is a solution to (2.24) by differentiating (2.25) term by term,

$$y'(x) = a_1 + 2a_2 x + 3a_3 x^2 + 4a_4 x^3 + \ldots \qquad (2.26)$$

and substituting from (2.26) and (2.25) into (2.24):

$$a_1 + 2a_2 x + 3a_3 x^2 + 4a_4 x^3 + \ldots = a_0 + a_1 x + a_2 x^2 + a_3 x^3 + \ldots$$

$$(2.27)$$

For (2.27) to be a true statement regardless of $x$'s value, the coefficients of like-powered terms must be equal. Therefore,

$$a_1 = a_0$$

$$2a_2 = a_1 \qquad a_2 = \frac{1}{2} a_1 = \frac{1}{2} a_0$$

$$3a_3 = a_2 \qquad a_3 = \frac{1}{3} a_2 = \frac{1}{3 \cdot 2} a_0 \qquad (2.28)$$

$$4a_4 = a_3 \qquad a_4 = \frac{1}{4} a_3 = \frac{1}{4 \cdot 3 \cdot 2} a_0$$

Therefore, (2.25) is a solution to (2.24) when the $a_i$'s are given by (2.28):

$$y(x) = a_0 \left( 1 + x + \frac{x^2}{2} + \frac{x^3}{3 \cdot 2} + \frac{x^4}{4 \cdot 3 \cdot 2} + \ldots \right) \qquad (2.29)$$

Note that $a_0$ is a constant yet to be defined; its value depends on the initial condition.

Define the function

$$E(x) = \frac{x^0}{1} + \frac{x^1}{1} = \frac{x^2}{2 \cdot 1} + \frac{x^3}{3 \cdot 2 \cdot 1} + \frac{x^4}{4 \cdot 3 \cdot 2 \cdot 1} + \dots \qquad (2.30)$$

Figure 2.3 shows a plot of $E(x)$. From (2.30), the solution to (2.24) with $k = 1$ is

$$y(x) = a_0 E(x) \qquad (2.31)$$

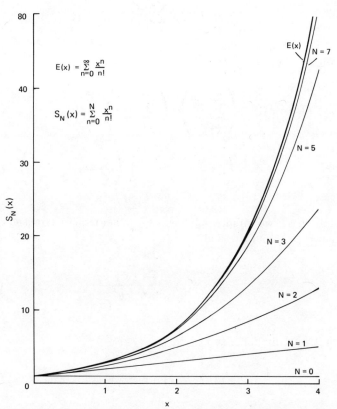

**FIGURE 2.3:** Each successive term added to the infinite sum in equation (2.30) adds progressively less to the sum, so that it approaches $E(x)$ as $n \to \infty$. Note also that as one adds more terms to the sum, the range (of $x$ values) over which $S_N(x)$ closely approximates $E(x)$ increases. This observation will be very important later when we discuss applications with approximate solutions to complicated problems.

Now, let us examine some of $E(x)$'s properties. To write (2.30) more compactly, introduce the *factorial function*

$$n! = \begin{cases} 1 & n = 0 \\ n(n-1)(n-2)\ldots 1 & n \geqslant 1 \end{cases} \tag{2.32}$$

where $n$ is a non-negative integer. Now, we can rewrite (2.30) using the factorial function and summation notation:

$$E(x) = \sum_{n=0}^{\infty} \frac{x^n}{n!} \tag{2.33}$$

What is $E(x) \cdot E(y)$? Use (2.33) to obtain

$$E(x) \cdot E(y) = \left( \sum_{n=0}^{\infty} \frac{x^n}{n!} \right) \cdot \left( \sum_{m=0}^{\infty} \frac{y^m}{m!} \right) \tag{2.34}$$

$$= \left( 1 + \frac{x}{1} + \frac{x^2}{2} + \ldots \right) \left( 1 + \frac{y}{1} + \frac{y^2}{2} + \ldots \right) \tag{2.35}$$

Multiply these two infinite polynomials together term by term and collect like powers of $x$ and $y$ to find

$$E(x) \cdot E(y) = \sum_{k=0}^{\infty} \frac{(x + y)^k}{k!} \tag{2.36}$$

which is, by definition, $E(x + y)$, so

$$E(x) \cdot E(y) = E(x + y) \tag{2.37}$$

Next we show that $e = 2.718\ldots$ and that $E(x) = e^x$. From (2.33)

$$E(1) = \sum_{n=0}^{\infty} \frac{1}{n!} = 2.718\ldots = e \tag{2.38}$$

and, if $n$ is a positive integer, (2.38) says

$$E(n) = \underbrace{E(1) \cdot E(1) \cdot E(1) \cdot \ldots \cdot E(1)}_{n \text{ times}} \qquad (2.39)$$

Substitute from (2.38) into (2.39)

$$E(n) = \underbrace{e \cdot e \cdot e \cdot \ldots \cdot e}_{n \text{ times}} = e^n \qquad (2.40)$$

Thus $E(n) = e^n$ where $n$ is a positive integer. Similar, though more advanced, arguments show that

$$E(x) = e^x \qquad (2.41)$$

for all $x$.

In sum, we have:

1. Defined a function,

$$E(x) = \sum_{n=0}^{\infty} \frac{x^n}{n!} \qquad (2.42)$$

which is its own derivative, i.e.,

$$\frac{dE(x)}{dx} = E(x) \qquad (2.43)$$

2. Defined a constant, $e = 2.718281828459045\ldots$
3. Shown that $E(x) = e^x$, so that

$$\frac{d(e^x)}{dx} = e^x \qquad (2.44)$$

Chapter 3 will continue to show why the exponential function appears so frequently when dealing with natural phenomena.

## THE NATURAL LOGARITHM FUNCTION

The exponential function always increases as its argument increases, so it is possible to construct an inverse function, $f$, such that

$$f(e^x) = x \tag{2.45}$$

Recall that the common logarithm, used as a computational aid, is defined by

$$y = \log x \qquad \text{if and only if} \qquad x = 10^y \tag{2.46}$$

We analogously define the *natural logarithm* so that

$$y = \ln x \qquad \text{if and only if} \qquad x = e^y \tag{2.47}$$

Thus $\ln e^x = x$ and $e^{\ln x} = x$, so the exponential and natural logarithm are inverse functions. (See Fig. 2.4.)

Note that while the exponential function is defined for all real numbers, it only takes on positive values. Therefore, the natural logarithm function is defined only for positive numbers even though its value can be any number, positive or negative.

What is the derivative of the natural logarithm? From (2.47)

$$\frac{dx}{dy} = \frac{d(e^y)}{dy} = e^y = x. \tag{2.48}$$

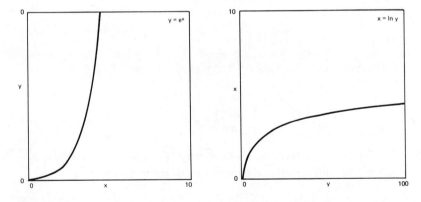

**FIGURE 2.4:** The exponential and natural logarithm are inverse functions.

According to the chain rule

$$\frac{dy}{dx}\frac{dx}{dy} = \frac{dx}{dx} = 1 \qquad (2.49)$$

so

$$\frac{dy}{dx} = 1 \bigg/ \frac{dx}{dy} \qquad (2.50)$$

Therefore, combining (2.48) and (2.50) produces

$$\frac{dy}{dx} = \frac{d(\ln x)}{dx} = 1 \bigg/ \frac{dx}{dy} = \frac{1}{x} \qquad (2.51)$$

$$\frac{d(\ln x)}{dx} = \frac{1}{x} \qquad (2.52)$$

## TIME CONSTANTS AND HALF-TIMES

Consider the one-compartment description for drug distribution and metabolism with these additional restrictions: no infusion or secretion occurs after $t = 0$ (so $i(t) = 0$), and just before $t = 0$ a quantity of drug, $q_0$, is injected into a compartment previously empty of drug. Then the dynamic equation

$$\frac{dc}{dt} = -kc \qquad (2.53)$$

describes this situation, with the initial (uniqueness) condition

$$c(0) = c_0 = \frac{q_0}{V} \qquad (2.54)$$

The solution of this differential equation is

$$c(t) = c_0 e^{-kt} \qquad (2.55)$$

which may be verified by substituting from (2.55) into (2.53) and (2.54).

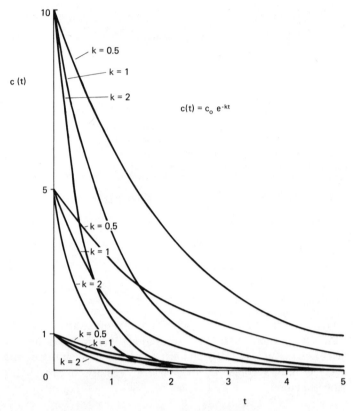

**FIGURE 2.5:** Graph of Equation (2.55) for three values of $c_0$ and $k$. Notice that changes in $c_0$ merely scale the curve without affecting its shape and that changes in $k$ change the curve's shape. As $c_0$ increases the curve moves up, and as $k$ increases it decays faster.

Figure 2.5 shows (2.55) plotted for various values of $c_0$ and $k$. $c_0$ alone determines $c(t)$'s relative magnitude and $k$ determines its shape. As $k$ increases, the curve decays faster. In particular, note that when $t = 1/k$, $c(t)$ equals $e^{-1} \simeq 0.367$ of its original value *no matter what the original value*. Thus, $1/k$ tells how long it takes to decay to 0.367 of the original value. In light of this property, one often writes (2.55) as

$$c(t) = c_0 e^{-t/\tau} \qquad \tau = \frac{1}{k} \qquad (2.56)$$

$\tau$, called the *time constant*, tells how long it takes the exponential to drop to 0.367 of its initial value; the shorter the time constant the faster the decay. Figure 2.6 shows that all solutions of this problem for all $k$ and $c_0$ may be displayed on a single graph of fraction of original concentration, $c(t)/c_0$, as a function of time measured in multiples of the time constant, $t/\tau$. We will see later how time constants relate to fundamental descriptors of many dynamic processes called *eigenvalues*, but for now we shall simply think of them as telling us how fast the exponential decays or grows.

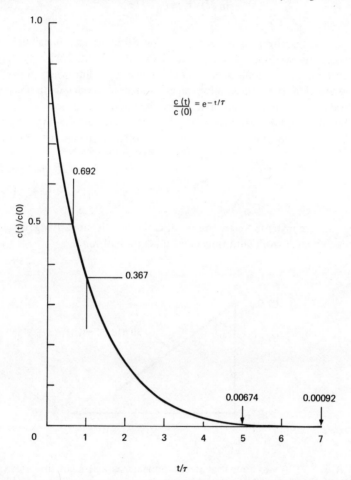

**FIGURE 2.6:** Any dynamic process that proceeds as a single exponential decay drops to 0.367 of its initial value when time equals one time constant. After five time constants, the decay is effectively complete, the function having dropped to less than 0.007 of its original value. The function drops to half its original value after 0.692 time constant.

Another useful representation of (2.55) follows by computing its natural logarithm:

$$\ln c(t) = \ln c_0 e^{-kt} = \ln c_0 + \ln e^{-kt} \qquad (2.57)$$

$$\ln c(t) = \ln c_0 - kt \qquad (2.58)$$

The natural logarithm of the concentration decreases as a linear function of time, with a slope $-k$ (Fig. 2.3). Thus, if presented with measured concentrations over time which fall along a straight line when plotted as $\ln c$ versus time (i.e., on semi-log paper), one could conclude that a single first-order differential equation describes the underlying process.

Finally, experimental workers often use results such as Figure 2.7 to measure the time required to decay to 0.5 of the original concentration, the half-time, $t_{1/2}$. $t_{1/2}$ and $\tau$ are simply related by

$$t_{1/2} \simeq .692 \, \tau^* \qquad (2.59)$$

Since time constants relate more directly to the underlying dynamic process, we shall work with time constants, not half-times.

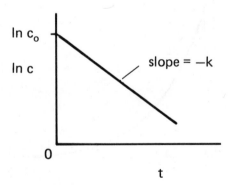

FIGURE 2.7: An exponential decay appears as a straight line when the natural logarithm is plotted versus time (i.e., on semi-log graph paper).

* To derive this result, note that, by definition, $c(t_{1/2}) = 1/2 c_0$ and from (2.56) $c(t_{1/2}) = 1/2 c_0 = c_0 e^{-t_{1/2}/\tau}$; $e^{t_{1/2}/\tau} = 2$; $t_{1/2}/\tau = \ln 2$; $t_{1/2} = (\ln 2)\tau$; and $\ln 2 \simeq 0.692$.

## METABOLIC TURNOVER

Consider a constant pool of $M$ moles of metabolite which is metabolized (and replenished) at the rate of $R$ moles/second. Furthermore, suppose we inject a small quantity, $m$ moles, of radioactively-labeled metabolite to study this process. Assuming that the radioactive metabolite behaves exactly as the native metabolite, what happens to the radioactive metabolite?

In an increment of time, $dt$, the quantity of radioactive metabolite decreases in proportion to the fraction of total metabolite plus radioactively-labeled metabolite, $m/(M + m)$, and the overall rate at which the metabolite is metabolized:

$$dm = - \frac{m(t)}{M + m(t)} R \, dt \tag{2.60}$$

$$\frac{dm}{dt} = \frac{-Rm(t)}{M + m(t)} \tag{2.61}$$

with initial condition

$$m(0) = m_0 \tag{2.62}$$

Solving this equation exactly requires methods which we will develop later, but if $m \ll M$, we approximate the fraction in (2.61) with

$$\frac{dm}{dt} = - \frac{R}{M} m \tag{2.63}$$

which describes the same simple exponential decay (with $\tau = M/R$) as the one-compartment drug distribution problem.

In addition to illustrating how one moves from physiology to mathematics, this example illustrates how two quite different situations can lead to the same differential equation. Such occurrences demonstrate how mathematics illuminates the common underlying structure which many problems share.

## PROBLEM SET 2.2

**1.** Show that $x(t) = t^2 + 1$ is the solution to $dx/dt = 2\sqrt{x - 1}$; $x(0) = 1$.

**2.** Show that $y(t) = (e^t - e^{-t})/2$ is the solution to $\ddot{y} - y = 0$; $y(0) = 0$.

3. Show that $y(t) = (e^t - e^{-t})/2$ is the solution to $\ddot{y} - y = 0; y(0) = 1$.
4. Show that $c(t) = 1/k(t + 1)$ is the solution to $dc/dt = -kc^2$; $c(0) = 1/k$.
5. Show that $y(x) = 3e^x + 2(x - 1)e^2$ is the solution to $y' - y = 2xe^{2x}$; $y(0) = 1$.
6. Guess and verify the solution to

$$\ddot{y} - y = 0 \qquad y(0) = 0 \qquad \dot{y}(0) = c \qquad c = \text{constant}$$

7. Convert these half-times, $t_{1/2}$, to the equivalent time constants, $\tau$.

   a.   1 min
   b.   1 hr
   c.   5 min
   d.   12 hr

8. Suppose that after administering 250 mg/kg of a drug as a bolus, the following concentrations in plasma are measured:

| Time (min) | Concentration (ng/ml) |
|:---:|:---:|
| 5 | 2.24 |
| 10 | 2.00 |
| 20 | 1.60 |
| 30 | 1.28 |
| 45 | 0.92 |
| 60 | 0.66 |
| 90 | 0.34 |
| 120 | 0.17 |

What is the time constant of the decay? Can one describe these data with a one-compartment model? If so, what are its parameters? (Note: 1 mg = $10^6$ ng.)

9. Suppose that after administering the same bolus as in Problem 8, these concentrations are measured:

| Time (min) | Concentration (ng/ml) |
|:---:|:---:|
| 5 | 1.79 |
| 10 | 1.36 |
| 20 | 0.90 |
| 30 | 0.67 |
| 45 | 0.46 |
| 60 | 0.33 |
| 90 | 0.17 |
| 120 | 0.09 |

Can these data be described with a one-compartment model? If so, what are its parameters?

10. On a single sheet of paper, graph these functions:
    a. $f_1(t) = e^{-t/2}$
    b. $f_2(t) = e^{-t/10}$
    c. $f_3(t) = e^{-t/2} + e^{-t/10}$

11. On a single sheet of semi-log paper, graph the following functions:
    a. $f_1(t) = e^{-t/2}$
    b. $f_2(t) = e^{-t/10}$
    c. $f_3(t) = e^{-t/2} + e^{-t/10}$

12. How could one find the steady-state solution (i.e., when none of the variables is changing) to a differential equation without solving the differential equation itself?

13. Use an infinite series to show that $y = aE(kx) = ae^{kx}$ is the solution to $y' = ky$.

## ONE-COMPARTMENT DRUG DISTRIBUTION WITH CONSTANT INFUSION

Begin with the same one-compartment description for drug distribution as before, but add a constant infusion into an initially empty compartment beginning at time zero. In this case, the dynamic equation (2.18) becomes

$$\frac{dc}{dt} = \frac{I}{V} - kc \qquad (2.64)$$

where $I$ = the constant infusion mass flow rate and $V$ = the volume of distribution. With no drug in the compartment at $t = 0$ the initial condition is

$$c(0) = 0 \qquad (2.65)$$

Unlike the differential equations developed so far, the solution to (2.64) is not $c(t) = c_0 e^{-kt}$. (Substitute it into (2.64) and (2.65) to convince yourself.)

We could solve (2.64) using the formal methods developed later, but for the moment it exemplifies how to guess the solution to a differential equation. First, the same compartment exhibits an exponentially-decaying concentration after a sudden injection, so one might expect the concentration to increase exponentially to some steady-state value during a constant infusion. (Of course, we have no a priori assurance that the concentration reaches a steady-state value.) Since $c(0) = 0$, the solution must begin with zero concentration, the increase to the steady-state value. $e^{-kt}$ equals 1 when $t = 0$ and approaches 0 as $t$ approaches infinity. Therefore, the expression $(1 - e^{-kt})$—called the *inverted exponential*—begins at 0 and approaches 1 as time approaches infinity. Therefore suppose $c(t)$ begins equal to zero at time zero (satisfying (2.65)) and approaches concentration $c_\infty$ as time approaches infinity:

$$c(t) = c_\infty (1 - e^{-kt}) \qquad (2.66)$$

Does (2.66) satisfy the differential equation (2.64) with the initial condition (2.65)?

To see, differentiate (2.66) with respect to time:

$$\frac{dc}{dt} = c_\infty k e^{-kt} \qquad (2.67)$$

then substitute from (2.66) and (2.67) into (2.64):

$$c_\infty k e^{-kt} = \frac{I}{V} - k c_\infty (1 - e^{-kt}) \qquad (2.68)$$

So (2.66) satisfies (2.64) and (2.65) if

$$c_\infty = \frac{I}{kV} \qquad (2.69)$$

Finally, substitute from (2.69) into (2.66) to obtain the solution to the one-compartment constant infusion problem:

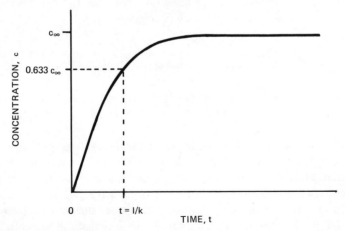

**FIGURE 2.8:** One-compartment drug distribution with constant infusion responds as an inverted exponential with the same time constant as it exhibits during washout following an injection.

$$c(t) = \frac{I}{kV}(1 - e^{-t/\tau}) \tag{2.70}$$

Figure 2.8 shows this solution graphically. Note that even though we have added a constant infusion to our compartment, the time constant of the response (in this case, time to reach $(1 - 0.367)c_\infty$) still equals $1/k$. We will see later that the time constant(s) of a process depends solely on its structure, not the input.

## TWO-COMPARTMENT DRUG DISTRIBUTION

Many drugs do not behave as if the fluid containing them acted as a single entity; therefore the mathematical expressions derived assuming a one-compartment description fail. Plotting the natural logarithm of concentration versus time (Fig. 2.9) demonstrates this failure: following an injection

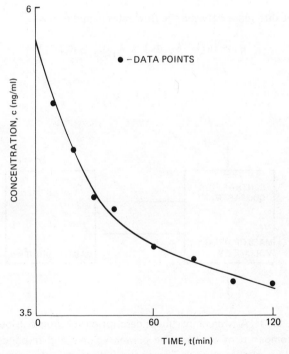

**FIGURE 2.9:** Washout of digoxin plotted on semi-log paper following a 0.2 mg/kg injection at time zero. The solid line shows that (2.82), the solution to (2.80) and (2.81), describes these data. If a one-compartment description would have sufficed, the data would have fallen along a single straight line.

at time zero, the measured concentration does not fall along a straight line as it does when the drug behaves in accordance with a one-compartment description. To describe this situation, we assume the drug distribution occurs as if it were distributed in two connected compartments (Fig. 2.10). Compartment 1, called the central compartment, contains the plasma volume and the tissues are in rapid equilibrium with it. The drug is infused into and metabolically removed from compartment 1 in direct proportion to the quantity of drug there. Compartment 2, called the outer compartment, represents those tissues which temporarily remove drug from compartment 1 by reversible binding. In addition, mass flows between the compartments in direct proportion to the quantity of mass in each compartment.

To translate this situation into differential equations, let $q_1$ and $q_2$ be the mass of drug in compartments 1 and 2, respectively, and let $i(t)$ be the infusion rate (mass flow) of drug into compartment 1. Conservation of mass for each compartment requires that the rate at which mass increases equals the difference between the flow rates in and out, so

$$\dot{q}_1 = (i(t) + k_{21}q_2) - (k_{12}q_1 + k_{10}q_1) \tag{2.71}$$

and

$$\dot{q}_2 = k_{12}q_1 - k_{21}q_2 \tag{2.72}$$

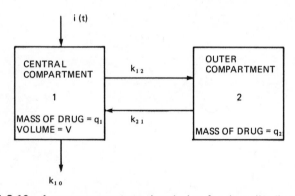

**FIGURE 2.10:** A two-compartment description for drug distribution. The central compartment contains the plasma volume and responds to infusions and metabolic removal. The arrows indicate that the mass flow rates between the two outer compartments and out of the central compartment are directly proportional to the absolute mass in each compartment. (The $k_{ij}$'s units are time$^{-1}$.)

where $k_{10}$ is the rate constant for metabolic removal and $k_{12}$ and $k_{21}$ are rate constants for transfer between the two compartments (see Fig. 2.10). Rearrange (2.71) and (2.72):

$$\dot{q}_1 = -(k_{12} + k_{10})q_1 + k_{21}q_2 + i(t) \qquad (2.73)$$

$$\dot{q}_2 = k_{12}q_1 - k_{21}q_2 \qquad (2.74)$$

To complete the problem specification, we need two initial conditions:

$$q_1(0) = q_{10} \qquad q_2(0) = q_{20} \qquad (2.75)$$

We can sample only compartment 1 (because it includes the plasma volume), so we may wish to eliminate $q_2$ from explicit consideration by transforming the two first-order differential equations, (2.73) and (2.74), into a single second-order differential equation in $q_1$. To do so, first differentiate (2.73) with respect to time,

$$\ddot{q}_1 = (k_{12} + k_{10})\dot{q}_1 + k_{21}\dot{q}_2 + \dot{i}(t) \qquad (2.76)$$

then use (2.74) to eliminate $\dot{q}_2$ from (2.76)

$$\ddot{q}_1 = -(k_{12} + k_{10})\dot{q}_1 + k_{21}(k_{11}q_1 - k_{21}q_2) + \dot{i}(t) \qquad (2.77)$$

Solve (2.73) for $q_2$ and use the result to eliminate $q_2$ from (2.77). Algebraic manipulation yields the desired differential equation:

$$\ddot{q}_1 + (k_{12} + k_{10} + k_{21})\dot{q}_1 + k_{10}k_{21}q_1 = \dot{i}(t) + k_{21}i(t) \qquad (2.78)$$

From (2.75) and (2.73), the appropriate initial conditions are

$$q_1(0) = q_{10} \qquad \dot{q}_1(0) = -(k_{12} + k_{10})q_{10} + k_{21}q_{20} + i(0)$$

$$(2.79)$$

Finally, we may wish to work in terms of concentration rather than quantity, so let $c = q_1/V$, where $V$ is the volume of distribution of the central compartment. We then divide (2.78) and (2.79) by $V$ to obtain

$$\ddot{c} + (k_{12} + k_{10} + k_{21})\dot{c} + k_{10}k_{21}c = \frac{\dot{i}(t) + k_{21}i(t)}{V} \qquad (2.80)$$

$$c(0) = \frac{q_{10}}{V} = c_0 \qquad \dot{c}(0) = -(k_{12} + k_{10})c_0 + \frac{k_{21}q_{20}}{V} + \frac{i(0)}{V}$$

$$(2.81)$$

Note that $q_2/V \neq c_2$ since $V$ is not compartment 2's volume.

We will see later that if we inject a mass, $B$, of a drug into compartment 1 just before time zero when there is no drug in compartment 2, i.e., if $q_1(0) = B, q_2(0) = 0$ and $i(t) = 0$, the solution to (2.80) and (2.81) is

$$c(t) = C_1 e^{\lambda_1 t} + C_2 e^{\lambda_2 t} \qquad (2.82)$$

where the constants $C_1$ and $C_2$ depend on $B$, $V$, and the $k_{ij}$'s, and the constants $\lambda_1$ and $\lambda_2$ (the eigenvalues) depend only on the $k_{ij}$'s. The solid line on Figure 2.9 shows that (2.82) describes the experimental data.


## FLUID-FILLED CATHETER DYNAMICS

Physicians and physiologists often need to measure pressure inside the body. Pressure transducers are often too large to conveniently insert into a heart, blood vessel, or other physiological space, so one must transmit the pressure signal to a transducer outside the body. A long fluid-filled tube, called a catheter, which extends from the pressure measuring site to the pressure transducer outside serves this purpose (Fig. 2.11). The fluid in the catheter has mass. Friction between the fluid in the catheter and the catheter wall resists motion as the fluid moves in response to pressure changes at the catheter tip. These mechanical effects distort the shape of the pressure signal which reaches the transducer. Chapter 5 develops the concept of frequency response to precisely quantify these distortions, but here we shall derive an equation to describe the fluid column's motion.

We assume that the catheter wall is perfectly rigid, even though in reality its diameter increases slightly as pressure increases. This assumption introduces relatively small errors, as evidenced by the fact that the frequency response computed from the resulting dynamic equation (in Chapter 5) accurately describes the observed response. By assuming perfectly rigid walls we can think of the catheter as a fixed cylinder containing a solid piston (since water and blood are essentially incompressible) which moves in response to the pressure force (Fig. 2.12). In addition to the pressure force, the diaphragm in the pressure transducer exerts an

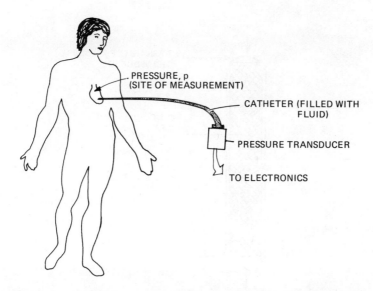

**FIGURE 2.11:** A tube filled with fluid, called a catheter, transmits pressure, $p$, from inside the body to a transducer outside. Since the fluid inside the catheter has mass and friction with the catheter walls, the pressure signal is distorted as it is transmitted to the pressure transducer.

elastic force which resists fluid motion in the same manner as do friction (viscous) forces between the fluid and the catheter wall.

To translate these statements into an equation, we begin with Newton's third law of motion: the force acting on a body equals the body's mass times the acceleration produced. Here, $d$ denotes the piston displacement from its position with zero pressure, $\dot{d}$ equals its velocity, and $\ddot{d}$, its acceleration. For the piston, Newton's law says

$$F = m\ddot{d} \tag{2.83}$$

where $F$ equals the net force acting on the fluid piston of mass $m$. For a fluid piston with density $\rho$, cross-sectional area $A$, and length $L$,

$$m = \rho A L \tag{2.84}$$

The force due to pressure, $p$, acting on the fluid piston is

$$F_p = pA \tag{2.85}$$

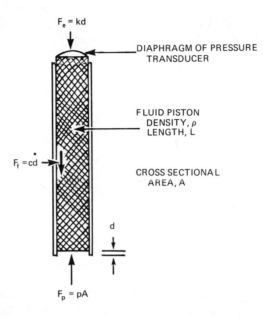

**FIGURE 2.12:** The forces acting on the fluid piston inside a catheter.

Assume that both an elastic force directly proportional to the displacement,

$$F_e = kd \qquad k = \text{constant} \tag{2.86}$$

and a viscous force directly proportional to fluid column velocity,

$$F_f = c\dot{d} \qquad c = \text{constant} \tag{2.87}$$

resist piston motion. Substitute from (2.84) – (2.87) into (2.83) to obtain the dynamic equation which describes the piston's motion in the catheter:

$$F_p - F_e - F_f = pA - kd - c\dot{d} = \rho AL\ddot{d} = m\ddot{d} \tag{2.88}$$

$$\ddot{d} + \frac{c}{\rho LA}\dot{d} + \frac{k}{\rho LA}d = \frac{p(t)}{\rho L} \tag{2.89}$$

The column displacement, $d$, is no longer directly proportional to the applied pressure, $p$. Therefore, the output of the pressure transducer will no longer be proportional to the pressure applied at the catheter tip. The voltage output, $E$, from the pressure transducer is proportional to the displacement of the sensing diaphragm, $d$:

$$E = Kd \qquad K = \text{constant} \qquad (2.90)$$

Substitute from (2.90) into (2.89) to obtain the dynamic relationship between the pressure, $p$, applied at the catheter tip and the output voltage, $E$, of the pressure transducer:

$$\ddot{E} + \frac{c}{\rho LA}\, \dot{E} + \frac{k}{\rho LA}\, E = \frac{K}{\rho L}\, p(t) \qquad (2.91)$$

Note that $E$ is no longer proportional to $p$, as it would be if we considered the pressure transducer without the catheter. How accurately the catheter transmits changes in pressure depends on the nature of the pressure signal and numerical values of the collections of constants in (2.91). We will see that by varying these constants—for example by changing catheter area or length—one can change its transmission characteristics.

To complete the problem specification we require two initial conditions, since (2.89) is a second-order ordinary differential equation. Suppose the column is initially at rest, i.e.:

$$d(0) = 0 \qquad \dot{d}(0) = 0 \qquad (2.92)$$

so, from (2.90)

$$E(0) = 0 \qquad \dot{E}(0) = 0 \qquad (2.93)$$

Equation (2.91) has the identical form as the equation for a two-compartment description of drug distribution (equation 2.80):

$$\ddot{x} + a\dot{x} + bx = f(t) \qquad (2.94)$$

in which $a$ and $b$ are constants and $f(t)$ is some specified function. Many different physical problems lead to this equation and we will devote considerable energy to its solution and the implications of this solution in Chapter 3.

## PROBLEM SET 2.3

1. Write a differential equation to describe $c(t)$ in a one-compartment model when the drug is administered as follows:

At $t = 0$: a bolus "loading dose" of magnitude $B$ (ng/kg).

Following the bolus: A constant infusion at $I$ [(ng/kg)/min].

2. Solve the differential equation from Problem 1.
3. Find the bolus size and constant infusion rate necessary to instantly achieve and hold the steady-state plasma concentration of drug, $c_\infty$. Why is it possible to instantly reach and hold $c_\infty$?
4. After administering a bolus of drug, the washout curve, when plotted on semi-log paper, exhibits three linear regions. Propose a compartment description for this drug's distribution and write the necessary differential equations and initial conditions. What form will the solution take?
5. What is the steady-state concentration, $c_\infty$, of a drug which is distributed in a two-compartment model if it is infused at constant rate $I$?
6. Write differential equations to describe the two models in Figure 2.13.
7. What is $c_\infty$ for each model in Figure 2.13 following a constant infusion? Why?

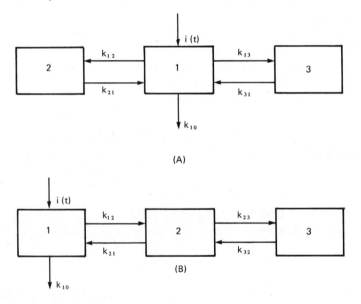

FIGURE 2.13: Three-compartment models for Problem 6 in Problem Set 2.3.

## INDICATOR-DILUTION METHODS TO MEASURE PHYSIOLOGICAL FLOW

The use of the indicator-dilution method to measure flow consists of the injection of a marker, such as a dye, radioactive tracer, or packet of thermal energy, into the blood flow, then watching when and how the marker passes a downstream point. Consider, for example, the problem of measuring blood flow from the heart into the aorta. Since blood moves quickly in large arteries and veins but slowly through longer, smaller parts of the vasculature, different blood particles—and the indicator moving with them—require different times to move between different points. This effect disperses the injected indicator marker as it moves through the vascular system with the blood (Fig. 2.14). For simplicity's sake, imagine the vasculature as a single tube into which at time zero the indicator substance is injected. It moves along the tube with the average blood flow and also disperses over a progressively longer segment of the tube. Thus, as it moves forward in time and space, the concentration at any point decreases (Fig. 2.15).

Figure 2.15's vertical axis represents the indicator concentration at any given time and location, its horizontal axis the distance through the vascular bed, and the axis coming out of the paper the time since injection. The rectangles to the left represent the indicator distributions as time progresses. The underlying flow (the cardiac output) moves the indicator forward with time to produce the general trend away from the point of injection. Since the indicator moves through the vascular bed at varying speeds, it is also distributed in space, and the concentration curve flattens out as the indicator disperses over a range of distances through the vascular bed at any given time.

Suppose that we inject the indicator at a point through which all the blood passes and locate a sensor at a point downstream from the injection site, through which all the blood also must pass. What will the sensor

## DISPERSION

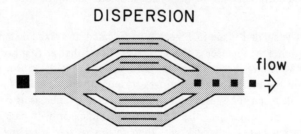

**FIGURE 2.14:** Since the circulation has many branches within which blood flows at different velocities, a single injection of indicator appears downstream at a variety of times. This process is known as dispersion.

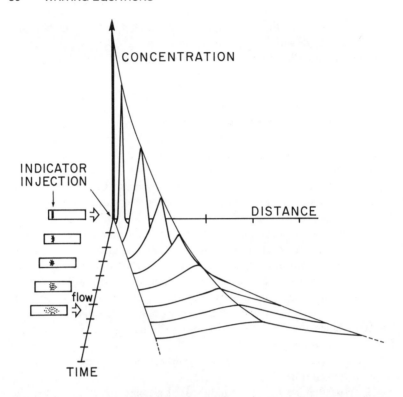

**FIGURE 2.15:** If we imagine the circulation as a single tube within which the indicator moves and disperses, we can picture concentration as a function of time since injection and distance along the tube. Initially, all the dye is located at a single point, the injection site. As time progresses, the cardiac output carries the dispersing indicator along the tube.

detect? The shaded plane in Figure 2.16 (located at a fixed distance from the injection site) represents the sensor. It shows that at first none of the indicator will have reached the sensor's location; thus the sensor will read zero. Soon the indicator which moves through the vasculature faster than average will reach the sensor and will be detected by increasing concentration. As time progresses, the bulk of the indicator will pass and the concentration curve will peak and then return to zero after the slowest-moving indicator-carrying blood passes the sensor. The exact form of the curve depends on the cardiac output, the distribution of transit times between the injection site and the sensing site, and the vascular geometry between these two points. Differences in the curve's exact shape due to

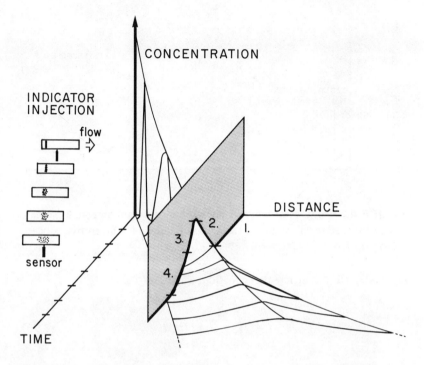

**FIGURE 2.16:** The location of a sensor at a fixed distance (through the circulation) can be thought of as passing a plane through the concentration-time-distance surface at a fixed distance. The sensed curve (1-2-3-4) is the intersection of the two surfaces.

differences in the vascular beds do not affect cardiac output calculations. Figure 2.17 shows a curve obtained following an injection of indocyanine green dye.

We can compute cardiac output from this measured curve. The indicator flow rate past the sensor at any given time, $t$, will equal its concentration, $c(t)$, times the blood flow rate, $F(t)$. Therefore, $dI$, the mass of indicator passing the sensor during a short time interval, $dt$, will approximately equal

$$dI(t) \quad = \quad c(t) \quad \cdot \quad F(t) \quad \cdot \quad dt \quad (2.95)$$

$$\text{indicator} \atop \text{mass} \quad = \quad \frac{\text{indicator mass}}{\text{ml blood}} \quad \cdot \quad \frac{\text{ml blood}}{\text{min}} \quad \cdot \quad \text{min}$$

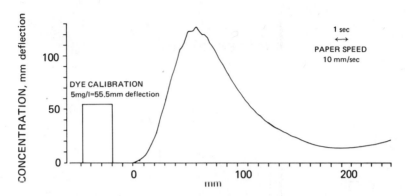

**FIGURE 2.17:** Indicator-dilution curve obtained from an actual patient. Notice that recirculation keeps the sensed indocyanine green dye concentration from returning to zero.

If we integrate this differential equation, we obtain

$$I = \int_0^\infty c(t)\, F(t)\, dt \tag{2.96}$$

where $I$ represents the amount of indicator initially injected. If the cardiac output remains constant, $F(t) = F$ (a constant), the integral becomes

$$I = F \int_0^\infty c(t)\, dt \tag{2.97}$$

so

$$F = \frac{I}{\displaystyle\int_0^\infty c(t)\, dt} \tag{2.98}$$

which is the equation for computing cardiac output using the indicator-dilution method. Since a definite integral equals the area under the curve of the function being integrated, this equation says: the cardiac output equals the quantity of indicator injected divided by the area under the concentration versus time curve. The accuracy of this equation depends on the cardiac output remaining constant from the time of indicator injection until the curve has been measured.

The inherent complication in this method arises from the fact that the circulation is a closed system. Before the indicator concentration curve returns to zero (i.e., all the indicator has passed the sensor), the indicator concentration exhibits a secondary peak due to *recirculation.* There are two ways to evaluate cardiac output in the face of recirculation. One could develop theoretical equations to explicitly account for recirculation; but while of theoretical interest, this approach is quite cumbersome, since it requires detailed analysis of the indicator washout curve rather than simply finding the area under the curve. A simpler—and generally satisfactory—method to account for recirculation is to remove its effect from the observed indicator washout curve. This correction follows from the observation that, as with a drug distributed in a single compartment, once the indicator concentration curve starts dropping, it drops according to $e^{-kt}$ until recirculation begins. Therefore, during this period concentration follows a straight line on semi-log graph paper (Fig. 2.18). On the basis of

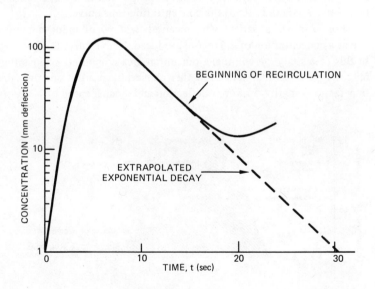

**FIGURE 2.18:** One can use a semi-log plot of the concentration versus time curve to extrapolate how the indicator concentration would have changed had there been no recirculation.

these observations, laboratory technicians replot the indicator concentration curve on semi-log paper, then extrapolate the straight-line concentration drop which occurs before recirculation begins down to negligible concentrations, then assuming they would obtain the same curve without recirculation. Under this assumption, one may read the extrapolated values off the semi-log plot and replot them on the actual indicator curve, then find the area under the corrected curve and proceed with the original formula that did not allow for recirculation (Fig. 2.19). This method presents serious practical difficulties only when recirculation begins so soon after the peak of the indicator curve as to prohibit confident linear extrapolation on the semi-log plot. Such a situation generally arises with low cardiac output.

From a practical point of view, one injects the dye or other indicator into the pulmonary artery or right side of the heart (through which all the blood must flow) by means of a catheter, then takes samples from another catheter in the central aorta, brachial, or femoral artery (which have the same indicator concentration as the central aorta). The sampling procedure for a dye indicator requires the withdrawal of a continuous blood sample through a densitometer—an optical device which detects the dye's presence (the blood being optically denser in proportion to the dye concentration)—and which thus yields the concentration-time curve.

For example, a patient who received 2.27 ml of indocyanine green dye at a concentration of 2.5 mg/ml produced the dye curve in Figure 2.17. In this case study we will make our initial area computations in terms of millimeters of recorder deflection, then convert the results using the calibration factor 5 mg/l = 55.5 mm deflection and a paper speed of 10 mm/sec.

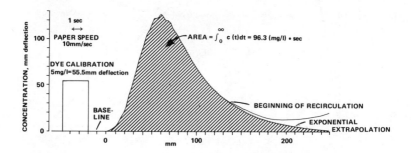

**FIGURE 2.19:** Using the concentration versus time curve corrected for recirculation, one can compute $\int_0^\infty c\,dt$ graphically by measuring the shaded area.

Replotting the washout curve on semi-log paper (Fig. 2.18) permits us to identify and extrapolate the exponential decay to negligible concentrations and then plot the resulting extrapolation on the original washout curve (Fig. 2.19). The area under the resultant corrected curve is

$$\int_0^\infty c(t)\, dt = \text{Area} = 10{,}690 \text{ mm}^2 \cdot \frac{5 \text{ mg dye/l}}{55.5 \text{ mm}} \cdot \frac{\text{sec}}{10 \text{ mm}}$$

$$= 96.3 \frac{\text{mg sec}}{1} \tag{2.99}$$

The total mass of dye injected is:

$$I = 2.5 \frac{\text{mg}}{\text{ml}} \cdot 2.27 \text{ ml} = 5.68 \text{ mg} \tag{2.100}$$

Hence, the cardiac output using (2.98) is:

$$F = \frac{I}{\displaystyle\int_0^\infty c(t)\, dt} = \frac{5.68 \text{ mg l}}{96.3 \text{ mg sec}} \cdot \frac{60 \text{ sec}}{\text{min}} = 3.60 \text{ l/min} \tag{2.101}$$

## FORMULA FOR COMPUTING VALVE AREAS IN THE HEART

The formula

$$A = \frac{F}{44.5 \sqrt{p_1 - p_2}} \tag{2.102}$$

is used to compute the area of a heart valve, $A$, using the measured flow, $F$, through the valve, and $p_1$ and $p_2$, the pressures on either side of the valve. This equation follows from a classical law of fluid mechanics called the *Bernoulli equation*, which relates the pressure and velocity of a flowing fluid, assuming that (1) the fluid is incompressible, (2) the fluid exhibits no viscosity, and (3) the flow remains constant over time. Consider a flowing stream of fluid (Fig. 2.20) and in particular the forces acting on a moving slice of it. The slice is a mass being acted upon by pressure forces, so we can write Newton's third law for the slice as

$$F = m \frac{dV}{dt}, \tag{2.103}$$

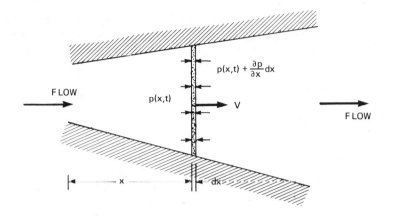

**FIGURE 2.20:** Pressure forces acting on a slice of fluid as it moves down an expanding tube.

where $F$ = net force acting on the fluid slice, $m$ = mass of the slice and $V$ = velocity of the center of the slice, so that $dV/dt$ = the acceleration of the slice. Next, replace the terms in (2.103) with the specific variables of our problem.

Since the density, $\rho$, remains constant, the fluid slice's mass is approximately

$$m = \rho A(x) \, dx \tag{2.104}$$

where $A(x)$ is the tube's cross-sectional area. Note that as $dx \to 0$, equation (2.104) approaches the actual slice mass. The mass-center velocity depends on the slice's position, $x$, so $V = V(x)$, and since $x$ varies with time,

$$\frac{dV}{dt} = \frac{dV}{dx} \cdot \frac{dx}{dt} \tag{2.105}$$

by the chain rule. But $dx/dt = V$, so

$$\frac{dV}{dt} = \frac{dV}{dx} \cdot V \tag{2.106}$$

The flow is inviscid, so that neither friction nor turbulence gives rise to any force on the fluid slice. Pressure, a function of position and time, produces the only external force on the slice, and is:

$$F = p(x, t) \cdot A(x) - \left[ p(x, t) + \frac{\partial p}{\partial x} dx \right] A(x)^* \qquad (2.107)$$

$$F = -A \frac{\partial p}{\partial x} dx \qquad (2.108)$$

Substituting from (2.104), (2.106), and (2.108) into (2.103),

$$-A \frac{\partial p}{\partial x} dx = \rho A\, dx \left( \frac{dV}{dx} \cdot V \right) \qquad (2.109)$$

Since the flow is by assumption steady, and $p = p(x, t) = p(x)$ so $\partial p/\partial x = dp/dx$, (2.109) becomes

$$-\frac{dp}{dx} = \rho V \frac{dV}{dx} \qquad (2.110)$$

But,

$$\frac{d}{dx}(V^2) = 2V \frac{dV}{dx}$$

so (2.110) can be written

$$-\frac{dp}{dx} = \frac{1}{2}\rho \frac{dV^2}{dx} = \frac{d}{dx}\left( \frac{1}{2}\rho V^2 \right) \qquad (2.111)$$

$$\frac{d}{dx}\left( p + \frac{1}{2}\rho V^2 \right) = 0 \qquad (2.112)$$

Therefore

$$p + \frac{1}{2}\rho V^2 = \text{constant} \qquad (2.113)$$

which is the Bernoulli equation. It states that for an incompressible, inviscid, and steady flow, the pressure plus kinetic energy per unit volume remains constant. How well do these assumptions apply to blood being pumped through a heart valve?

---

* To be completely proper, the second $A(x)$ should be replaced with $A(x) + A'(x)dx$, but the addition of this term does not help show how the four assumptions lead to the Bernoulli equation, and furthermore makes the derivations much more difficult. For a complete derivation for three-dimension flow, see any introductory fluid mechanics text.

Suppose we have fluid moving through a valve (Fig. 2.21), and we write the Bernoulli equation for a particle of fluid which moves from the left ventricle to the center of the aortic valve. Then

$$p_1 + \frac{1}{2}\rho V_1{}^2 = p_2 + \frac{1}{2}\rho V_2{}^2 = \text{constant} \qquad (2.114)$$

Assume $V_1 = 0$, i.e., the fluid starts from rest, so (2.114) becomes

$$2(p_1 - p_2) = \rho V_2{}^2 \qquad (2.115)$$

As before, we must ask ourselves how reasonable is the assumption that $V_1 = 0$ for a beating heart?

The mass flow rate through the valve is

$$q = \rho A V_2 \qquad (2.116)$$

and the volume flow rate is

$$F = \frac{q}{\rho} \qquad (2.117)$$

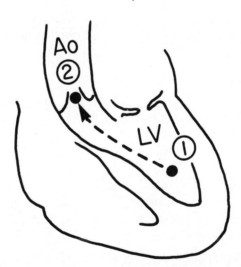

**FIGURE 2.21:** The dotted line indicates the path of a hypothetical blood particle from rest inside the left ventricle (LV) through the aortic valve (Ao).

Substitute from (2.116) and (2.117) into (2.115) to obtain the equation for the valve area

$$A = \frac{F}{\sqrt{\frac{2}{\rho}(p_1 - p_2)}} \tag{2.118}$$

Equation (2.118) is not quite equation (2.102). To obtain (2.102), assume that $p_1$ and $p_2$ are measured in mm Hg and $F$ in ml/sec, and that $\rho = 1.055$ gm/cm$^3$ (the density of blood). Then (2.118) becomes

$$A = \frac{F}{53.0\sqrt{p_1 - p_2}} \text{ cm}^2 \tag{2.119}$$

Finally, we multiply 53.0 by 0.84, which is an empirically derived correction factor that deals with errors introduced by the initial simplifying assumptions, to obtain (2.102).

## THE MICHAELIS-MENTEN MECHANISM FOR AN ENZYME-CATALYZED REACTION

L. Michaelis and M. Menten proposed that an enzyme acts on its substrate first by reversibly forming an intermediate enzyme-substrate complex which then irreversibly produces the product and releases the enzyme. In other words, they proposed the chemical mechanism

$$E + S \underset{k_2}{\overset{k_1}{\rightleftharpoons}} ES \xrightarrow{k_3} E + P$$

in which $E$ is the enzyme, $S$ the substrate, $ES$ the enzyme-substrate complex, and $P$ the product. They assumed that the reactions proceed in direct proportion to the product of the concentrations of the reactants. This assumption followed from the fact that a certain fraction of molecular collisions between reactants produce reactions, and the probability of a collision increases in proportion to the concentrations. $k_1$, $k_2$, and $k_3$ are the rate constants (constants of proportionality) for the three reactions.

Using the chemist's convention of indicating a substance's concentration by enclosing its symbol in brackets, we can translate this reaction into a set of four simultaneous nonlinear differential equations by writing expressions for the rate of change of each substance.

$$\frac{d[E]}{dt} = -k_1[E][S] + k_2[ES] + k_3[ES] = -k_1[E][S] + (k_2 + k_3)[ES]$$

$$(2.120)$$

$$\frac{d[S]}{dt} = -k_1[E][S] + k_2[ES] \tag{2.121}$$

$$\frac{d[ES]}{dt} = k_1[E][S] - k_2[ES] - k_3[ES] = k_1[E][S] - (k_2 + k_3)[ES]$$

$$(2.122)$$

$$\frac{d[P]}{dt} = k_3[ES] \tag{2.123}$$

The total quantity of enzyme, $E_T$, never changes; so any solution of equations (2.120)–(2.123) must also satisfy the condition that

$$E_T = [E] + [ES] = \text{constant} \tag{2.124}$$

If $S_0$ is the initial substrate concentration and $[P]$ is initially equal to zero,

$$S_0 = [S] + [ES] \tag{2.125}$$

at all times.

These equations, like many nonlinear differential equations, have not yet been solved for the general case. However, in Chapter 3 we will show how to solve them for some useful special cases, and in Chapter 7 we will present numerical methods which can be used with a digital computer to solve them for any given case.

## PROBLEM SET 2.4

1. In the steady state, the concentrations of enzyme, substrate, and product all remain constant in the Michaelis-Menten reaction. Find the steady-state concentrations of all these substances.

## ADDITIONAL READINGS

*Compartment Analysis for Drug Distribution*

Jacquez, J. A. *Compartment Analysis in Biology and Medicine.* Amsterdam, London, New York: Elsevier, 1972.

*Catheter Dynamics*

Falsetti, H. L., R. E. Mates, R. J. Carroll, R. J. Gupta, and A. C. Bell. Analysis and correction of pressure wave distortion in fluid-filled catheter systems, *Circulation* 49 (1974): 165-172.

*Formula for Valve Areas*

Hammermeister, K. E., J. A. Murray, and J. R. Blackman. Revision of Gorlin constant for calculation of mitral valve area from left heart pressures, *Brit. H. J.* 35 (1973): 392. ·

Sabersky, R. H., and A. J. Acosta. *Fluid Flow: A First Course in Fluid Mechanics.* New York: Macmillan, 1964. Chapter 3: Bernoulli equation.

Yang, S. Y., L. G. Bentiuglio, V. Maranhao, and H. Goldberg. *From Cardiac Catheterization Data to Hemodynamic Parameters.* Philadelphia: F. A. Davis, 1972. Chapter 2: Formulas for valve orifice.

*Indicator-Dilution Method*

Guyton, A. C., C. E. Jones, and T. G. Coleman. *Circulatory Physiology: Cardiac Output and Its Regulation.* Philadelphia: W. B. Saunders Co., 1973. Chapter 3: Indicator-dilution methods for determining cardiac output.

Bloomfield, D. A. *Dye Curves: The Theory and Practice of Indicator Dilution.* Baltimore: University Park Press, 1974. Chapter 2: Foundations of indicator dilution theory; Chapter 3: A method for performing an indicator-dilution curve to measure cardiac output.

Zierler, K. L. Circulation times and the theory of indicator-dilution methods for determining blood flow and volume. In *Handbook of Physiology,* Vol. I, pp. 585-615. Washington, D.C.: Am. Phys. Soc., 1962.

*Michaelis-Menten Kinetics*

Bartholomay, A. F. Chemical Kinetics and Enzyme Kinetics. In *Foundations of Mathematical Biology. Vol. I: Subcellular Systems,* ed. Robert Rosen. New York: Academic Press, 1972.

# DIRECT METHODS TO SOLVE
# DIFFERENTIAL EQUATIONS

Thus far we have made use of the fact that an exponential function equals its derivative in order to guess solutions to differential equations. While useful in its place, this approach often fails with the complicated equations which frequently arise in physiology and medicine. Therefore we must now develop formal methods to solve differential equations, to find the function which satisfies the differential equation and the initial conditions. We will first study first-order equations, then discuss the property of linearity and some of its important ramifications. We will then construct the sine and cosine functions, solve higher-order linear differential equations, and finally, discuss nonlinear equations. With this new knowledge, we will solve the differential equations which we wrote in Chapter 2, and study the practical implications of the solutions.

## SEPARABLE FIRST-ORDER EQUATIONS

Suppose the first-order differential equation

$$y' = f(x,y) \qquad y(x_0) = y_0 \tag{3.1}$$

has the form

$$g(y)\, y' = h(x) \tag{3.2}$$

In this case, we say that (3.1) is a *separable equation*, because we can separate the functional dependence on $x$ and $y$. We can consider $y' = dy/dx$ as a ratio of differentials, and multiply (3.2) by $dx$ to obtain

$$g(y)\, dy = h(x)\, dx \tag{3.3}$$

Integrate (3.3):*

$$\int g(y)\, dy = \int h(x)\, dx + C \tag{3.4}$$

and use the initial condition $y(x_0) = y_0$ to evaluate the constant of integration in (3.1)'s solution. Alternatively, integrate from the initial point $(x_0, y_0)$ to a general point $(x, y)$ to solve (3.1):

$$\int_{x_0}^{x} g(y)\, dy = \int_{y_0}^{y} h(x)\, dx \tag{3.5}$$

Equations (3.4) and (3.5) represent the solution in the form $G(y) = H(x)$, rather than with $y$ as an explicit function of $x$, $y = y(x)$. Often one can solve (3.4) or (3.5) for $y(x)$, but sometimes not. Failure to find $y(x)$ explicitly may complicate interpretation of the solution, but there is little one can do to simplify this situation.

As an example, let us solve

$$y' = xy + x \qquad y(0) = 0 \tag{3.6}$$

This differential equation separates to

$$\frac{1}{y+1}\frac{dy}{dx} = x \tag{3.7}$$

so

$$\int \frac{dy}{y+1} = \int x\, dx + C \tag{3.8}$$

Evaluating the integrals yields

$$\ln(y+1) = \frac{x^2}{2} + C \tag{3.9}$$

* Appendix B contains a table of integrals.

Use the initial condition $y(0) = 0$ to evaluate $C$:

$$\ln (0 + 1) = \ln 1 = 0 = \frac{0^2}{2} + C = C \tag{3.10}$$

Thus

$$\ln (y + 1) = \frac{x^2}{2} + 0 \tag{3.11}$$

$$\ln (y + 1) = \frac{x^2}{2} \tag{3.12}$$

$$y + 1 = e^{x^2/2} \tag{3.13}$$

$$y = e^{x^2/2} - 1 \tag{3.14}$$

Verify that (3.14) satisfies (3.6).
  As a second example, solve

$$y^2 y' + x^2 = 0 \qquad y(1) = 2 \tag{3.15}$$

This equation separates to

$$y^2 \, dy = -x^2 \, dx \tag{3.16}$$

Integrate (3.16) from the initial point (1,2) to the general point $(x,y)$:

$$\int_2^y y^2 \, dy = - \int_1^x x^2 \, dx \tag{3.17}$$

$$\frac{1}{3}y^3 - \frac{1}{3}2^3 = -\frac{1}{3}x^3 + \frac{1}{3}1^3 \tag{3.18}$$

$$y^3 + x^3 - 9 = 0 \tag{3.19}$$

$$y = \sqrt[3]{9 - x^3} \tag{3.20}$$

The reader may verify this.

## ONE-COMPARTMENT DRUG DISTRIBUTION WITH CONSTANT INFUSION: THE FORMAL SOLUTION

In Chapter 2 we derived a differential equation which describes the concentration $c(t)$, of a drug infused at constant rate $I$, metabolized at rate $k$, and distributed in a volume of distribution $V$:

$$\frac{dc}{dt} = \frac{I}{V} - kc \qquad c(0) = 0 \qquad (3.21)$$

We guessed the solution, and verified it by substitution into the original equation.

Now we can solve (3.21) directly because it is separable. We can integrate it directly:

$$\int_0^c \frac{dc}{\frac{I}{V} - kc} = \int_0^t dt \qquad (3.22)$$

Let $u = I/V - kc$; then $du = -k\,dc$, and the left side of (3.22) becomes

$$\int_0^c \frac{dc}{\frac{I}{V} - kc} = -\frac{1}{k}\int_0^c \frac{-k\,dc}{\frac{I}{V} - kc} = -\frac{1}{k}\int_{u(0)}^{u(c)} \frac{du}{u} = -\frac{1}{k}\ln u \,\Bigg|_{u(0)}^{u(c)}$$

$$= -\frac{1}{k}\ln\left(\frac{I}{V} - kc\right)\Bigg|_0^c = -\frac{1}{k}\ln\left(\frac{I}{V} - kc\right) + \frac{1}{k}\ln\frac{I}{V}$$

$$(3.23)$$

$$= \frac{1}{k}\ln\left(\frac{\frac{I}{V}}{\frac{I}{V} - kc}\right) \qquad (3.24)$$

Substitute from (3.24) into (3.22) to obtain

$$\frac{1}{k}\ln\left(\frac{\frac{I}{V}}{\frac{I}{V} - kc}\right) = t \qquad (3.25)$$

$$c(t) = \frac{I}{kV} [1 - e^{-kt}] \qquad (3.26)$$

This is the same result which we obtained before. (Solve this problem with $c(0) = c_0 \neq 0$.)

## THE OPERATIVE PRINCIPLE OF THE PACEMAKER

Artificial pacemakers, which supplement or replace the heart's natural pacing mechanism, require sophisticated electronic circuitry, yet their operational principle is simple. Figure 3.1 illustrates the key elements of a pacemaker: a battery, a capacitor to store electrical energy and deliver it in short, intense pulses to the heart, and a switch to alternately charge the capacitor from the battery and discharge it through the heart. When switched from the battery to the heart, the capacitor discharges, providing a sudden electrical stimulus to the heart. The sophisticated electronics of modern pacemakers control and maintain the power supply and operate the switch to mimic a healthy heart's natural pacemaker.

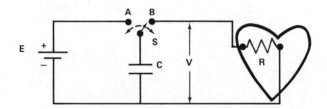

**FIGURE 3.1:** Equivalent circuit diagram for a pacemaker. When the switch $S$ is in position $A$, the battery charges the capacitor $C$. When the switch moves to $B$, the capacitor rapidly discharges its stored energy through the heart, thus stimulating it.

To mathematically describe the simple pacemaker in Figure 3.1, recall that the electrical current $i$ passing through a capacitor is directly proportional to the charge rate of voltage $V$ across the capacitor:

$$i = C \frac{dV}{dt} \qquad C = \text{constant} \qquad (3.27)$$

and the voltage drop across a resistor is directly proportional to the current passing through it:

$$V = -iR \qquad R = \text{constant} \qquad (3.28)$$

With the switch in position $B$, current through the capacitor equals the current through the heart, which acts as a resistor:

$$i = C\frac{dV}{dt} = -\frac{V}{R} \tag{3.29}$$

Hence the differential equation

$$\frac{dV}{dt} + \frac{1}{RC}V = 0 \tag{3.30}$$

describes this process. Since the voltage across the capacitor equals the battery voltage $E$ with the switch in position $A$, the initial condition is

$$V(0) = E \tag{3.31}$$

Equation (3.30) is separable, so we integrate it from the initial point $(0, E)$ to a general point $(t, V)$:

$$\int_E^V \frac{dV}{V} = \int_0^t -\frac{1}{RC}dt \tag{3.32}$$

$$\ln V - \ln E = \ln \frac{V}{E} = \left(\frac{1}{RC}\right)t \tag{3.33}$$

$$V = Ee^{-t/\tau} \qquad \tau = RC \tag{3.34}$$

When the switch swings to position $B$, the voltage applied to the heart jumps to the battery voltage $E$, then decreases exponentially with time constant $\tau = 1/RC$. This decay would continue indefinitely if the switch were left in position $B$, but as soon as it is swung back to position $A$ (to stop stimulating the heart and permit the capacitor to recharge), the pacemaker current stops flowing through the heart, so according to Equation (3.28), the applied voltage immediately drops to zero (Figure 3.2).

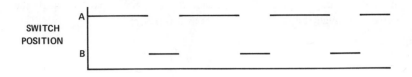

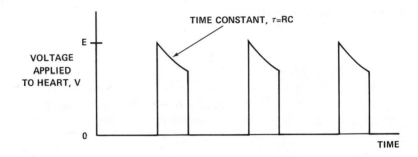

**FIGURE 3.2:** When the pacemaker switch is in position $A$, no voltage is applied to the heart. When the switch is in position $B$, the electrical energy stored in the capacitor produces a voltage across the heart to stimulate it to contract. As the capacitor discharges, the voltage drops exponentially.

## PROBLEM SET 3.1

Solve these differential equations. ($a$, $b$, $c$, $k$, etc., are constants.)

1. $y' = 2xy$            $y(0) = 1$
2. $s' = ae^{bt}$          $s(0) = 0$
3. $s' = ae^{bs}$          $s(0) = 0$
4. $(x + 1)yy' = 1$      $y(0) = 0$
5. $e^y y' = xe^{x^2}$       $y(0) = 1/2$
6. $x^2 yy' = 1$         $y(1) = 0$
7. Solve the metabolic turnover problem (page 23) without assuming $m \ll M$. Show that the result reduces to our earlier solution when $m \ll M$.
8. Suppose a drug which is distributed in a single compartment affects the kidneys in such a way that the clearance coefficient $k$ is proportional to the concentration $c$. What would $c(t)$ be:
   a. Following a bolus into a previously empty compartment?
   b. Following a constant infusion into a previously empty compartment?

## EXACT FIRST-ORDER EQUATIONS AND INTEGRATING FACTORS*

One can write the differential equation

$$y' = f(x, y) \qquad (3.35)$$

in the form

$$0 = M(x, y) \, dx + N(x,y) \, dy \qquad (3.36)$$

(for example, $M = -f$ and $N = 1$; other forms may be possible). Next, consider a function $u = u(x, y)$. Its total differential equals

$$du = \frac{\partial u}{\partial x} \, dx + \frac{\partial u}{\partial y} \, dy \qquad (3.37)$$

Compare terms in (3.36) and (3.37) to see that (3.37) exactly equals a total differential $du$ when

$$M(x, y) = \frac{\partial u}{\partial x} \qquad (3.38)$$

and

$$N(x, y) = \frac{\partial u}{\partial y} \qquad (3.39)$$

If $M$ and $N$ have continuous derivatives over the $x$ and $y$ values of interest, (3.38) and (3.39) can be differentiated again:

$$\frac{\partial M}{\partial y} = \frac{\partial^2 u}{\partial y \partial x} \qquad (3.40)$$

$$\frac{\partial N}{\partial x} = \frac{\partial^2 u}{\partial x \partial y} \qquad (3.41)$$

Since the derivatives are continuous, the order of differentiation does not matter, and if (3.36) represents an exact differential, (3.40) equals (3.41), so that

* The reader can skip this section with no loss of continuity.

$$\frac{\partial M}{\partial y} = \frac{\partial N}{\partial x} \qquad (3.42)$$

Thus (3.42) provides the test of whether or not a differential equation is exact.* If it is, we can integrate (3.38) and (3.39) directly to obtain the solution to (3.35).

Comparing terms in (3.36) and (3.37) shows that for an exact differential equation,

$$du = 0 \qquad (3.43)$$

therefore

$$u(x, y) = \int du = C \qquad (3.44)$$

From (3.38) and (3.44):

$$u(x, y) = \int M(x, y)\, dx + F(y) = C \qquad (3.45)$$

similarly, from (3.39) and (3.44):

$$u(x, y) = \int N(x, y)\, dy + G(x) = C \qquad (3.46)$$

We must include the functions of integration, $F(y)$ and $G(x)$, because (3.45) and (3.46) represent integrals of partial derivatives. Both (3.45) and (3.46) equal $C = u(x, y)$; we equate them to evaluate $F$ and $G$, and obtain the solution $u(x, y) = C$.

As an example, we show

$$\frac{dy}{dx} = -\frac{x}{y} \qquad y(0) = 1 \qquad (3.47)$$

to be an exact differential equation, and solve it. From (3.47):

$$x\, dx + y\, dy = 0 \qquad (3.48)$$

so $M = x$ and $N = y$. Thus

$$\frac{\partial M}{\partial y} = 0 = \frac{\partial N}{\partial x} \qquad (3.49)$$

---

* We have simply shown (3.42) to be *necessary* in order for (3.36) to be an exact differential. Equation (3.42) is also the *sufficient* condition, but proving so is beyond the scope of this text.

Therefore (3.47) is exact. From (3.45):

$$u(x, y) = \int x \, dx + F(y) = \frac{x^2}{2} + F(y) = C \qquad (3.50)$$

and from (3.46):

$$u(x, y) = \int y \, dy + G(x) = \frac{y^2}{2} + G(x) = C \qquad (3.51)$$

Comparing terms in (3.50) and (3.51) shows $F(y) = y^2/2$ and $G(x) = x^2/2$, so

$$u(x, y) = 1/2x^2 + 1/2y^2 = C \qquad (3.52)$$

Finally, the initial condition, $y(0) = 1$ requires that $C = 1/2$ and produces the solution to (3.47):

$$x^2 + y^2 = 1 \text{ (or } y = \pm\sqrt{1 - x^2}) \qquad (3.53)$$

Note that as it stands, (3.53) is not a function. Why not?

Equation (3.47) is also separable and could have been solved by using the methods previously shown. We now solve the nonseparable exact equation

$$\frac{dy}{dx} = \frac{x - 2y}{2x + y} \qquad y(0) = 0 \qquad (3.54)$$

From (3.54):

$$(x - 2y) \, dx - (2x + y) \, dy = 0 \qquad (3.55)$$

Since $M = (x - 2y)$ and $N = -(2x + y)$,

$$\frac{\partial M}{\partial y} = -2 = \frac{\partial N}{\partial x} \qquad (3.56)$$

and (3.55) represents an exact differential. From (3.45) and (3.46):

$$u = \int (x - 2y) \, dx + F(y) = \frac{x^2}{2} - 2xy + F(y) = C \qquad (3.57)$$

$$u = \int -(2x + y)\, dy + G(x) = -2xy - \frac{y^2}{2} + G(x) = C \qquad (3.58)$$

Comparing terms in (3.57) and (3.58) shows that $F(y) = -y^2/2$ and $G(x) = -x^2/2$, so

$$\frac{x^2}{2} - \frac{y^2}{2} - 2xy = C \qquad (3.59)$$

Again, use the initial condition, $y(0) = 0$, to evaluate $C$ and obtain (3.54)'s solution:

$$x^2 - 4xy - y^2 = 0 \qquad (3.60)$$

We can now solve all differential equations of the form

$$y' + p(x)\, y = r(x) \qquad y(x) = y_0 \qquad (3.61)$$

Is (3.61) an exact differential equation? From (3.35):

$$[p(x)\, y - r(x)]\, dx + dy = 0 \qquad (3.62)$$

thus $M(x, y) = py - r$ and $N(x, y) = 1$. As it stands, (3.62) represents an exact differential only if $p(x) = 0$ for all $x$, which is hardly an interesting case. However, we can convert (3.62) to an exact differential by multiplying it by a yet-to-be-determined function, $\mu(x)$, called an *integrating factor*. Multiply it by $\mu$ to obtain

$$\mu(x)[p(x)y - r(x)]\, dx + \mu(x)\, dy = 0 \qquad (3.63)$$

which is exact when

$$\frac{\partial}{\partial y}\, [\mu(py - r)] = \mu p = \frac{\partial \mu}{\partial x} \qquad (3.64)$$

Furthermore, since $\mu$ is a function only of $x$, $\partial\mu/\partial x = d\mu/dx$, and (3.64) becomes the separable differential equation

$$\mu p = \mu' \qquad (3.65)$$

whose solution is

$$\ln \mu = \int p(x)\, dx \qquad (3.66)$$

$$\mu = e^{\int p(x)\, dx} \qquad (3.67)$$

Now multiply (3.61) by $\mu$ to make it the exact differential equation

$$\mu y' + \mu p y = \mu r \qquad (3.68)$$

and solve it using the methods developed above. Use (3.65) to eliminate $\mu p$ from (3.68):

$$\mu y' + \mu' y = \mu r$$

Since the expression on the left equals the derivative of $(\mu y)$ with respect to $x$,

$$\frac{d(\mu y)}{dx} = \mu r \qquad (3.69)$$

which integrates to

$$\mu y = \int \mu r\, dx + C \qquad C = \text{constant} \qquad (3.70)$$

Thus the solution to all differential equations of the form of (3.61) is

$$y(x) = \frac{1}{\mu(x)} \left[ \int \mu(x) r(x)\, dx + C \right] \qquad (3.71)$$

where (3.67) gives $\mu(x)$, and $y(x_0) = y_0$ determines $C$.
 Here are two examples:

1. $y' + y = x \qquad y(0) = 0 \qquad (3.72)$

From (3.67):

$$\mu(x) = e^{\int 1\, dx} = e^x \qquad (3.73)$$

So from (3.71):

$$y(x) = e^{-x} \left[ \int e^x \cdot x \, dx + C \right] \tag{3.74}$$

Appendix B, Formula 68, evaluates the integral in (3.74), showing

$$y(x) = e^{-x} [xe^x - e^x + C] \tag{3.75}$$

$$y(x) = x - 1 + Ce^{-x} \tag{3.76}$$

The initial condition, $y(0) = 0$, requires $C = 1$, so (3.72)'s solution is

$$y(x) = x - 1 + e^{-x} \tag{3.77}$$

2. $y' + y/x = e^{x^2}$     $y(1) = 0$ $\qquad\qquad$ (3.78)

From (3.67):

$$\mu(x) = e^{\int dx/x} = e^{\ln x} = x \tag{3.79}$$

So (3.71) yields

$$y(x) = \frac{1}{x} \left[ \int xe^{x^2} \, dx + C \right] \tag{3.80}$$

To evaluate the integral, let $u = x^2$, then $du = 2x \, dx$ and the integral becomes

$$\int xe^{x^2} \, dx = 1/2 \int 2xe^{x^2} \, dx = 1/2 \int e^u \, du = 1/2 e^u = 1/2 e^{x^2} \tag{3.81}$$

and (3.81) becomes

$$y(x) = \frac{1}{x} [1/2 \, e^{x^2} + C] \tag{3.82}$$

Finally, since $y(1) = 0$, $C = -e/2$ and the solution is

$$y(x) = \frac{e^{x^2} - e}{2x} \tag{3.83}$$

It is theoretically possible to use integrating factors to solve any first-order differential equation by first writing it in the form

$$M(x, y) \, dx + N(x, y) \, dy = 0$$

and then seeking, as before, an integrating factor, $\mu = \mu(x, y)$, which makes

$$\mu(M \, dx + N \, dy) = 0 \tag{3.85}$$

an exact differential. This will be the case when

$$\frac{\partial(\mu M)}{\partial y} = \frac{\partial(\mu N)}{\partial x} \tag{3.86}$$

One obtains $\mu(x, y)$ by solving this partial differential equation. Unfortunately, solving (3.86) is generally harder than solving the original differential equation, so the use of integrating factors is generally restricted to equations of the form of (3.61).

## PROBLEM SET 3.2

Test to see if the following equations are exact; if so, solve them.

1. $(x + 3) + 4(y - 1)y' = 0$

2. $xy^2 + x^2yy' = 0$

3. $\dfrac{dy}{dx} = \dfrac{ax + by}{ax + cy}$

4. $x^2 + y^2y' = 0$

## LINEAR TRANSFORMATIONS AND THEIR PROPERTIES

Before continuing with our discussion of methods used to solve ordinary differential equations, we must pause to study two key concepts: *linearity* and *transformation*.

The property of linearity not only lies at the heart of solving a large class of differential equations, but provides the structure which supports important techniques, such as frequency response and Fourier analysis,* which help specify and design instruments for obtaining undistorted measurements. We will study linear transformations in general, then use the results to guide us in solving the wide class of differential equations which act as linear transformations.

Transformations represent Alice's looking-glass. Consider the process represented in Figure 3.3. The transformation operates on an input function, $u(x)$, to transform it to the output function, $g(x)$. We say that Figure 3.3 represents a transformation of $u$ to $g$ and write:

$$\mathscr{T}\{u\} = g \qquad (3.87)$$

For example, a transformation could operate on a photograph to produce a magnified, rotated, moved, and systematically distorted image; another could transform input to output by integrating it. Other mathematical transformations change a problem's outward form in order to simplify it. For example, the Laplace transform, discussed in Chapter 4, converts linear constant-coefficient differential equations into more easily solved algebraic equations. After solving these algebraic equations, one steps back through the looking-glass by transforming the algebraic solution back to the original variables to obtain the final solution.

FIGURE 3.3: A transformation of input $u$ to output $g$.

We will focus on the specific class of transformations called *linear transformations*. A transformation is linear when it has the properties of *homogeneity*:

$$\mathscr{T}\{cu\} = c\,\mathscr{T}\{u\} \qquad c = \text{any constant} \qquad (3.88)$$

and *additivity*:

$$\mathscr{T}\{u_1 + u_2\} = \mathscr{T}\{u_1\} + \mathscr{T}\{u_2\} \qquad (3.89)$$

---

* Discussed in Chapters 5 and 6.

All other transformations are *nonlinear*. A single equivalent statement of linearity is:

$$\mathscr{T}\{c_1 u_1 + c_2 u_2\} = c_1\,\mathscr{T}\{u_1\} + c_2\,\mathscr{T}\{u_2\}$$

$$c_1,\, c_2 = \text{constants}$$

(3.90)

Thus, for a linear transformation, scaling the input by a constant factor scales the output by the same constant factor, and the response to added inputs equals the sum of the responses to each input applied separately. Linear transformations thus obey the *superposition principle*, which states that one can superimpose (add) the individual responses to multiple simultaneous inputs in order to obtain the response to the summed inputs. (Only linear transformations exhibit this property; it makes no sense to apply the superposition principle to nonlinear transformations.) Suppose $\mathscr{T}$ represents a linear transformation, and

$$\mathscr{T}\{u_1(x)\} = g_1(x)$$

(3.91)

$$\mathscr{T}\{u_2(x)\} = g_2(x)$$

(3.92)

Then if $\mathscr{T}$ operates on $u(x) = c_1 u_1(x) + c_2 u_2(x)$, the superposition principle says the result will be $g(x) = c_1 g_1(x) + c_2 g_2(x)$, because

$$\mathscr{T}\{u\} = \mathscr{T}\{c_1 u_1 + c_2 u_2\} = c_1\,\mathscr{T}\{u_1\} + c_2\,\mathscr{T}\{u_2\}$$

$$= c_1 g_1 + c_1 g_2 = g$$

(3.93)

In short, the superposition principle states that applying a linear transformation to a weighted sum of inputs produces the same output as one would obtain by transforming each element of the sum separately, then adding the results (see Figure 3.4).

We have viewed transformations as operating on an input function to generate an output function. Now let us reverse our perspective and solve the linear equation: given $g(x)$, find $u(x)$ that satisfies

$$\mathscr{T}\{u(x)\} = g(x)$$

(3.94)

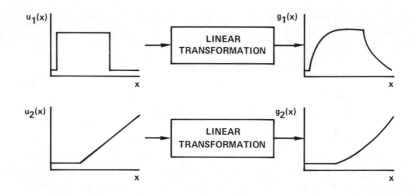

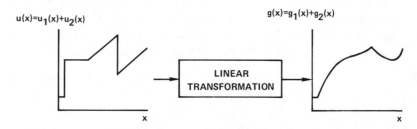

**FIGURE 3.4:** A linear transformation obeys the superposition principle: The result of a linear transformation acting on a sum of inputs is the same as the sum of the results of the transformation acting on each of the inputs individually.

The next section shows that solving (3.94) is equivalent to solving the wide class of linear differential equations. The solution of this problem proceeds in three steps: (1) solve the related *homogeneous equation*

$$\mathcal{T}\{u\} = 0 \qquad (3.95)$$

(2) find any solution to (3.94) called a *particular solution*, and (3) add the results of these two problems. One must solve the homogeneous equation (3.95) to obtain all solutions to (3.94), because linear transformations obey the superposition principle. Specifically, let $u_p$ be any particular solution to (3.94) and let $u_h$ be a solution to (3.95); then $u_p + cu_h$ ($c$ = any constant) also solves (3.94), because

$$\mathcal{T}\{u_p + cu_h\} = \mathcal{T}\{u_p\} + c\,\mathcal{T}\{u_h\} = g + c \cdot 0 = g \qquad (3.96)$$

But what if either (3.94) or (3.95) has two or more solutions? To answer this, we must understand the properties of *linear dependence* and *linear independence*. Two functions are linearly dependent when they are proportional to one another. In other words, if it is possible to obtain one function from the other by simply multiplying it by a constant, the two functions are linearly dependent. Otherwise they are linearly independent. For example, $u_1(x) = x^2$ and $u_2(x) = 5x^2$ are linearly dependent, but $u_1(x)$ and $u_3(x) = x$ are linearly independent, because simply multiplying $u_1$ by a constant will never produce $u_3$. Figure 3.5 illustrates pairs of linearly dependent and independent functions. For more than two functions we define a set of functions $\{u_1(x), u_2(x), \ldots, u_n(x)\}$ as *linearly dependent* when at least one set of constants $\{c_1, c_2, \ldots, c_n\}$, not all zero, exists such that

$$c_1 u_1 + c_2 u_2 + \ldots + c_n u_n = 0 \qquad (3.97)$$

Otherwise the functions are *linearly independent*.

In other words, when a set of functions is linearly dependent it is possible to construct at least one of them by forming a linear combination of the others. For example, $u_1 = x$, $u_2 = x^2$, and $u_3 = x^2 - x$ are linearly dependent, because $u_3 = -u_1 + u_2$. On the other hand, if the functions are linearly independent, one cannot construct any one function from a linear combination of the others.

Now we can prove an important theorem about linear transformations:

*If $u_p$ is any particular solution to the linear equation $\mathcal{T}\{u\} = g$ and if $u_{h1}, u_{h2}, \ldots, u_{hn}$ are all of the linearly independent solutions to the homogeneous linear equation $\mathcal{T}\{u\} = 0$, then*

$$u = u_p + c_1 u_{h1} + c_2 u_{h2} + \ldots + c_n u_{hn} \qquad (3.98)$$

*in which $c_1, c_2, \ldots, c_n$ are arbitrary constants, represents all solutions to the linear equation.*

First we show that (3.98) solves the linear equation

$$\mathcal{T}\{u\} = \mathcal{T}\{u_p + c_1 u_{h1} + c_2 u_{h2} + \ldots + c_n u_{hn}\}$$

$$= \mathcal{T}\{u_p\} + c_1 \mathcal{T}\{u_{h1}\} + c_2 \mathcal{T}\{u_{h2}\}$$

$$+ \ldots + c_n \mathcal{T}\{u_{hn}\} \qquad (3.99)$$

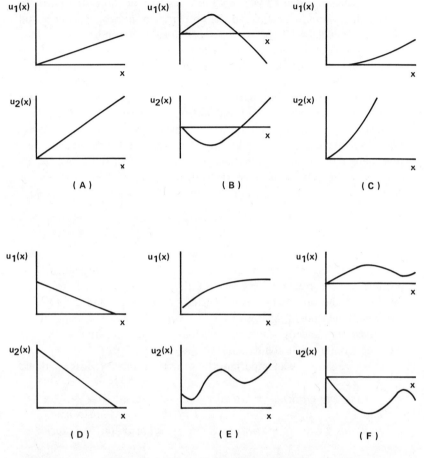

**FIGURE 3.5:** Two functions are linearly dependent when one can be obtained by multiplying the other by a constant. Thus the pairs of functions in panels A, B, and F are linearly dependent and the others are linearly independent.

$$\mathscr{T}\{u\} = g + c_1 \cdot 0 + c_2 \cdot 0 + \ldots + c_n \cdot 0 = g \qquad (3.100)$$

Next we show that (3.98) represents all possible solutions. Let $u_h$ be a solution to the homogeneous problem, not equal to $u_{h1}, u_{h2}, \ldots,$ or $u_{hn}$. Since $u_{h1}, u_{h2}, \ldots, u_{hn}$ are *all* linearly independent solutions to the homogeneous problem, it must be possible to represent $u_h$ as the linear combination

$$u_h = a_1 u_{h1} + a_2 u_{h2} + \ldots + a_n u_{hn} \qquad (3.101)$$

where $a_1, a_2, \ldots, a_n$ are the appropriate constants. Thus, since (3.98) is a solution to the linear equation, so are

$$u + u_h = (u_p + c_1 u_{h1} + c_2 u_{h2} + \ldots + c_n u_{hn})$$

$$+ (a_1 u_{h1} + a_2 u_{h2} + \ldots + a_n u_{hn}) \qquad (3.102)$$

and

$$u + u_h = u_p + (c_1 + a_1) u_{h1} + (c_2 + a_2) u_{h2} + \ldots$$

$$+ (c_n + a_n) u_{hn} \qquad (3.103)$$

But since $c_1, c_2, \ldots, c_n$ are arbitrary constants, so are $C = c_1 + a_1$, $C_2 = c_2 + a_2, C_n = c_n + a_n$; and thus

$$u + u_h = u_p + C_1 u_{h1} + C_2 u_{h2} + \ldots + C_h u_{hn} \qquad (3.104)$$

represents the same solution as (3.98). Thus, any set of linearly independent solutions to the homogeneous equation suffices for solving the linear equation.

Finally, we show that one need only include any one particular solution of the linear equation. Suppose $u_{p1}$ and $u_{p2}$ are any two particular solutions. Then

$$\mathcal{T}\{u_{p1} - u_{p2}\} = \mathcal{T}\{u_{p1}\} - \mathcal{T}\{u_{p2}\} = g - g = 0 \qquad (3.105)$$

The difference between any two particular solutions is a solution to the homogeneous equation. We just showed that (3.98) already includes *all* linearly independent solutions to the homogeneous problem—and hence, the difference between any two particular solutions. Therefore (3.98) represents all possible solutions to the linear problem $\mathcal{T}\{u\} = g$ (Eq. 3.87).

The next section shows that many differential equations represent linear transformations. We will use this theorem and the superposition principle to develop techniques for solving and interpreting them.

## PROBLEM SET 3.3

Which of these transformations are linear?

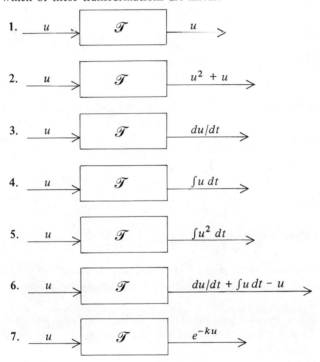

1.    $u$    $\mathcal{T}$    $u$

2.    $u$    $\mathcal{T}$    $u^2 + u$

3.    $u$    $\mathcal{T}$    $du/dt$

4.    $u$    $\mathcal{T}$    $\int u\, dt$

5.    $u$    $\mathcal{T}$    $\int u^2\, dt$

6.    $u$    $\mathcal{T}$    $du/dt + \int u\, dt - u$

7.    $u$    $\mathcal{T}$    $e^{-ku}$

Which collections of functions are linearly independent?

8. $t, t^2, t^3$

9. $t, -t, 2t, 2t - t$

10. $t^2, t, t^2 + t$

11. $e^x, e^{2x}, e^{3x}, e^x/2$

12. $e^x, e^{2x}$

## LINEAR DIFFERENTIAL EQUATIONS ARE LINEAR TRANSFORMATIONS

We can now use the theory of linear transformations to guide us in the solution of $n$th-order differential equations of the form

$$\frac{d^n y}{dx^n} + p_{n-1}(x)\frac{d^{n-1}y}{dx^{n-1}} + \ldots + p_1(x)\frac{dy}{dx} + p_0(x)y = g(x) \qquad (3.106)$$

where $p_{n-1}(x)$, $p_{n-2}(x)$, ..., $p_0(x)$—often called the coefficients—and $g(x)$ are given functions. In some applications the nonhomogeneous term $g(x)$ is known as the *forcing function*, or *input*. For example, if (3.106) describes the motion of a mass in which $y$ represents displacement, $g$ represents force. Equations of this form are known as *linear differential equations*, because they represent linear transformations. For a differential equation to be linear, the dependent variable and its derivatives must appear only to the first power and there must be no products of $y$ with its derivatives. For example,

$$y'' + y = x^2 \qquad (3.107)$$

$$y'' + e^x y = \ln x \qquad (3.108)$$

and

$$y' + x^3 y = 0 \qquad (3.109)$$

are linear differential equations, while

$$y'' + y^2 = 0 \qquad (3.110)$$

$$y'' + e^y = x, \qquad (3.111)$$

and

$$y'' + yy' = 0 \qquad (3.112)$$

are not. Differential equations which are not of the form of equation (3.106) are *nonlinear* differential equations. Since (3.106) represents a linear transformation, we can use the theory of linear transformations to help solve it.

First we must show that (3.106) represents a linear transformation. To do this we define the transformation $\mathcal{T}\{y\}$,

$$\mathcal{T}\{y\} = \frac{d^n y}{dx^n} + p_{n-1}\frac{d^{n-1}y}{dx^{n-1}} + \ldots + p_1\frac{dy}{dx} + p_0 y \qquad (3.113)$$

and examine

$$\mathcal{T}\{\alpha y_1 + \beta y_2\} = \frac{d^n(\alpha y_1 + \beta y_2)}{dx^n} + p_{n-1}\frac{d^{n-1}(\alpha y_1 + \beta y_2)}{dx^{n-1}} + \ldots$$

$$+ p_1\frac{d(\alpha y_1 + \beta y_2)}{dx} + p_0(\alpha y_1 + \beta y_2) \qquad (3.114)$$

Since the derivative of a sum equals the sum of the derivatives, and the derivative of a constant times a function equals the constant times the derivative of the function,

$$\mathcal{T}\{\alpha y_1 + \beta y_2\} = \left(\alpha\frac{d^n y_1}{dx^n} + \beta\frac{d^n y_2}{dx^n}\right) + p_{n-1}\left(\alpha\frac{d^{n-1}y_1}{dx^{n-1}} + \beta\frac{d^{n-1}y_2}{dx^{n-1}}\right) + \ldots$$

$$+ p_1\left(\alpha\frac{dy_1}{dx} + \beta\frac{dy_2}{dx}\right) + p_0(\alpha y_1 + \beta y_2) \qquad (3.115)$$

Rearrange terms to obtain

$$\mathcal{T}\{\alpha y_1 + \beta y_2\} = \alpha\left(\frac{d^n y_1}{dx^n} + p_{n-1}\frac{d^{n-1}y_1}{dx^{n-1}} + \ldots + p_1\frac{dy_1}{dx} + p_0 y_1\right)$$

$$+ \beta\left(\frac{d^n y_2}{dx^n} + p_{n-1}\frac{d^{n-1}y_2}{dx^{n-1}} + \ldots + p_1\frac{dy_2}{dx} + p_0 y_2\right) \qquad (3.116)$$

But the expressions on the right in parentheses are simply $\mathcal{T}\{y_1\}$ and $\mathcal{T}\{y_2\}$, so

$$\mathcal{T}\{\alpha y_1 + \beta y_2\} = \alpha \mathcal{T}\{y_1\} + \beta \mathcal{T}\{y_2\} \qquad (3.117)$$

Therefore, (3.113) is a linear transformation.

Since (3.113) is a linear transformation, (3.106) has a solution of the form $y(x) = y_p(x) + y_h(x)$, where $y_p$ is any particular solution to (3.106) and $y_h(x)$ is any sum of all linearly independent solutions $y_{h1}$, $y_{h2}, \ldots$ to the corresponding homogeneous problem

$$\frac{d^n y}{dx^n} + p_{n-1} \frac{d^{n-1} y}{dx^{n+1}} + \ldots + p_1 \frac{dy}{dx} + p_0 y = 0 \qquad (3.118)$$

The linearly independent solutions to (3.118) which comprise the homogeneous solution $y_{h1}(x)$, $y_{h2}(x)$, $\ldots$ are called its *fundamental* solutions. Therefore the solution to equation (3.106) is

$$y(x) = y_p(x) + c_1 y_{h1}(x) + c_2 y_{h2}(x) + \ldots + c_n y_{hn}(x) \qquad (3.119)$$

where $c_1, c_2, \ldots, c_n$ are arbitrary constants. Finally, we will use the $n$ initial conditions that must be specified for an $n$th-order differential equation to solve for the $n$ arbitrary constants which appear in the homogeneous solution.

But how many fundamental solutions are there to the homogeneous problem? An important theorem tells us:

*If $p_{n-1}(x)$, $p_{n-2}(x), \ldots, p_0(x)$ are all continuous functions, the nth-order homogeneous ordinary differential equation (3.118) has precisely n linearly independent solutions, $y_{h1}(x), y_{h2}(x), \ldots, y_{hn}(x)$.*

The proof of this theorem is beyond our scope. Another theorem insures that a solution does exist:

*If $p_{n-1}(x)$, $p_{n-2}(x), \ldots, p_0(x)$ and $g(x)$ are continuous functions of x for $x_1 \leqslant x \leqslant x_2$, then a unique function $y(x)$ exists which satisfies the linear differential equation (3.106) and the n initial conditions*

$$y(x_0) = y_0 \qquad y'(x_0) = y_0', \ldots, y^{(n-1)}(x_0) = y_0^{(n-1)} \qquad (3.120)$$

*with $x_1 \leqslant x_0 \leqslant x_2$.*

In sum, to solve the linear differential equation (3.106), we first find the linearly independent fundamental solutions of the homogeneous equation, then add a linear combination of them to a particular solution, and use the $n$ initial conditions to evaluate the $n$ arbitrary constants present in the solution. The next four sections show how to carry out this process.

## OTHER FUNCTIONS USED TO SOLVE DIFFERENTIAL EQUATIONS: THE SINE AND COSINE

In Chapter 2 we constructed the exponential function to equal its own derivative, then showed that this function solved first-order differential equations of the form

$$y' - ky = 0 \qquad (3.121)$$

Now we will construct two new functions to be two fundamental solutions of the second-order linear differential equation

$$y'' + y = 0 \qquad (3.122)$$

These two functions are the *sine* and *cosine*, and will complete our arsenal of functions which solve linear differential equations.

But why not use exponential functions to construct (3.122)'s fundamental solutions? Specifically, why not assume

$$y(x) = Ae^{\lambda x} \qquad A, \lambda = \text{constants} \qquad (3.123)$$

then substitute into (3.122) to find $A$ and $\lambda$? This process yields

$$A\lambda^2 e^{\lambda x} + Ae^{\lambda x} = 0 \qquad (3.124)$$

Factor out the common term $Ae^{\lambda x}$ to obtain

$$(\lambda^2 + 1)Ae^{\lambda x} = 0 \qquad (3.125)$$

But $Ae^{\lambda x} \neq 0$ regardless of $x$, so (3.125) requires that

$$\lambda^2 + 1 = 0 \qquad (3.126)$$

Therefore $\lambda = \pm\sqrt{-1} = \pm i^*$ and thus $y_{h1}(x) = A_1 e^{ix}$ and $y_{2h}(x) = A_2 e^{-ix}$ (where $A_1$ and $A_2$ are arbitrary constants) are solutions to (3.122). Furthermore, $e^{ix}$ and $e^{-ix}$ do not differ by a multiplicative constant, so they are linearly independent, and hence $y_{1h}$ and $y_{2h}$ are (3.122)'s two fundamental solutions. Thus,

$$y(x) = y_{h1}(x) + y_{h2}(x) = A_1 e^{ix} + A_2 e^{-ix} \qquad (3.127)$$

is the solution. ($y_p(x) = 0$ is a particular solution.) But what do $e^{ix}$ and $e^{-ix}$ mean? After all, we have only defined the exponential function for real numbers, not the imaginary number $i = \sqrt{-1}$. To resolve this dilemma—indeed, to give $e^{ix}$ and $e^{-ix}$ meaning—we must construct two functions, which form two different, but equivalent, fundamental solutions to (3.122). Just as with the exponential function, we represent (3.122)'s solution with the infinite sum

$$y(x) = \sum_{n=0}^{\infty} a_n x^n \qquad a_n = \text{constants} \qquad (3.128)$$

then select the $a_n$ to satisfy (3.122). (As before, we need not prove that the resulting infinite sums converge. They do.) Differentiate (3.128) term by term:

$$y'(x) = \sum_{n=0}^{\infty} a_n \cdot n x^{n-1} \qquad (3.129)$$

$$y''(x) = \sum_{n=0}^{\infty} a_n \cdot n \cdot (n-1) x^{n-2} \qquad (3.130)$$

$$= a_0 \cdot 0 \cdot (-1) x^{-2} + a_1 \cdot 1 \cdot 0 \cdot x^{-1} + a_2 \cdot 2 \cdot 1 x^0$$

$$+ a_3 \cdot 3 \cdot 2 \cdot x^1 + a_4 \cdot 4 \cdot 3 \cdot x^2 + \ldots \qquad (3.131)$$

$$y''(x) = \sum_{n=0}^{\infty} a_{n+2}(n+2)(n+1) x^n \qquad (3.132)$$

---

* Appendix C summarizes properties of complex numbers.

Substitute from (3.128) and (3.132) into (3.122):

$$\sum_{n=0}^{\infty} a_{n+2}(n + 2)(n + 1)x^n + \sum_{n=0}^{\infty} a_n x^n = 0 \tag{3.133}$$

$$\sum_{n=0}^{\infty} [a_{n+2}(n + 2)(n + 1) + a_n]x^n = 0 \tag{3.134}$$

Since (3.134) must hold for any $x$,

$$a_{n+2}(n + 2)(n + 1) + a_n = 0 \tag{3.135}$$

for all $n$. This relationship permits us to compute all $a_n$ except the two constants $a_0$ and $a_1$ by successive substitutions into

$$a_{n+2} = -\frac{a_n}{(n + 2)(n + 1)} \tag{3.136}$$

$n = 0$    $a_2 = \dfrac{a_0}{1 \cdot 2}$

$n = 1$    $a_3 = -\dfrac{a_1}{2 \cdot 3}$

$n = 2$    $a_4 = -\dfrac{a_2}{3 \cdot 4} = +\dfrac{a_0}{1 \cdot 2 \cdot 3 \cdot 4}$

$n = 3$    $a_5 = -\dfrac{a_3}{4 \cdot 5} = +\dfrac{a_0}{1 \cdot 2 \cdot 3 \cdot 4 \cdot 5}$    (3.137)

$n = 4$    $a_6 = -\dfrac{a_4}{5 \cdot 6} = -\dfrac{a_0}{1 \cdot 2 \cdot 3 \cdot 4 \cdot 5 \cdot 6}$

$n = 5$    $a_7 = -\dfrac{a_5}{6 \cdot 7} = -\dfrac{a_1}{1 \cdot 2 \cdot 3 \cdot 4 \cdot 5 \cdot 6 \cdot 7}$

Substitute from (3.137) into (3.128):

$$y(x) = a_0 x^0 + a_1 x^1 - \frac{a_0}{2 \cdot 1} x^2 - \frac{a_1}{3 \cdot 2 \cdot 1} x^3 + \frac{a_0}{4 \cdot 3 \cdot 2 \cdot 1} x^4$$

$$+ \frac{a_1}{5 \cdot 4 \cdot 3 \cdot 2 \cdot 1} x^5 - \frac{a_0}{6 \cdot 5 \cdot 4 \cdot 3 \cdot 2 \cdot 1} x^6$$

$$- \frac{a_1}{7 \cdot 6 \cdot 5 \cdot 4 \cdot 3 \cdot 2 \cdot 1} x^7 + \ldots \tag{3.138}$$

Use the factorial function to write (3.137) more compactly:

$$y(x) = a_0 \left( \frac{x^0}{0!} - \frac{x^2}{2!} + \frac{x^4}{4!} - \frac{x^6}{6!} + \ldots \right)$$

$$+ a_1 \left( \frac{x^1}{1!} - \frac{x^3}{3!} + \frac{x^5}{5!} - \frac{x^7}{7!} + \ldots \right) \tag{3.139}$$

$$y(x) = a_0 \left( \sum_{n=0}^{\infty} \frac{(-1)^n x^{2n}}{(2n)!} \right) + a_1 \left( \sum_{n=0}^{\infty} \frac{(-1)^n x^{2n+1}}{(2n+1)!} \right) \tag{3.140}$$

Since the two sums in parentheses involve *different* powers of $x$, they do not differ by a constant multiplicative factor; hence they are two linearly independent solutions of (3.122) and therefore represent two *fundamental* solutions to (3.122). Thus (3.140) is *the* solution to (3.122), and $a_0$ and $a_1$ are the two arbitrary constants whose values follow from the two initial conditions associated with the second-order differential equation.

   The two infinite sums in (3.140) often arise. What functions do they represent? Figures 3.6 and 3.7 show the functions obtained by taking more and more terms in these two sums. The infinite sums represent functions whose values smoothly vary between $-1$ and $+1$, repeating every $2\pi$ along the $x$ axis. Functions which repeat indefinitely are known as *periodic* functions, and the minimum change in the value of the independent variable which occurs before the function begins repeating is its *period*, $T$. Thus, for these functions, $T = 2\pi$ $x$-axis units. One could obtain the function which the second sum represents by

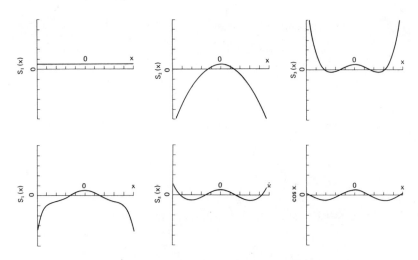

**FIGURE 3.6:** Functions obtained by adding more and more terms to Equation (3.141). As the number of terms in the truncated series is increased, the actual function, cos $x$, is approximated over a progressively wider range of $x$. $S_N(x)$ represents the sum of the first $N$ terms in (3.141).

shifting the function which the first represents by $\pi/2$ along the $x$-axis. Like exponential functions, these sums have been named and their values tabulated. They are:

$$\sum_{n=0}^{\infty} \frac{(-1)^n x^{2n}}{(2n)!} = \cos x \qquad \text{(Fig. 3.6)} \qquad (3.141)$$

and

$$\sum_{n=0}^{\infty} \frac{(-1)^n x^{2n+1}}{(2n+1)!} = \sin x \qquad \text{(Fig. 3.7)} \qquad (3.142)$$

These definitions permit the solution to (3.140) to be written compactly:

$$y(x) = a_0 \cos x + a_1 \sin x \qquad (3.143)$$

Thus, the cosine and sine functions encountered in geometry appear now as functions which can solve a second-order linear differential equation!

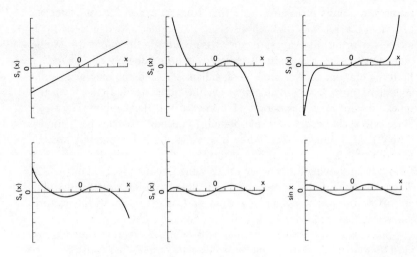

**FIGURE 3.7:** Functions obtained by adding progressively more terms to Equation (3.142). The infinite sum defines sin $x$. $S_N(x)$ represents the sum of the first $N$ terms in (3.142).

The cosine and sine functions repeat when their arguments change by $2\pi$, so the function sin $\omega t$ has the period $T = 2\pi/\omega$. As the parameter $\omega = 2\pi/T$–called the *frequency*–increases, the period shortens (Figure 3.8). The sine and cosine arguments must be dimensionless; thus the frequency has the inverse dimensions of the period. For example, if the units of $t$ are

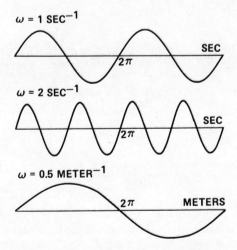

**FIGURE 3.8:** Sine functions with various frequencies.

seconds, the units of $\omega$ are $\sec^{-1}$. Therefore, $\sin (1 \sec^{-1})t$ completes one period in $2\pi$ seconds and $\sin (2 \sec^{-1})t$ completes two periods in $2\pi$ seconds. Written this way, frequency has no units in the numerator. Sometimes this unitless numerator is replaced by a pseudo-unit called a *radian.* In this notation, $\omega = 2 \sec^{-1} = 2$ radians/sec, and the sine and cosine arguments must have radian units. On the other hand, frequency sometimes appears as cycles/period (1 cycle/sec = 1 Hertz, abbreviated Hz). Since one cycle occurs over one period, frequency in cycles per period is simply $f = 1/T$ and $\omega = 2\pi f$. While this representation commonly arises in experimental work, it must be converted to the dimensionless-numerator form by multiplying by $2\pi$ when one is using Equation (3.141) or (3.142). When the dimensions of frequency are clear from the context, the units are often dropped and simply written $\sin t$ or $\sin 2t$. We will henceforth indicate radian frequency by $\omega$ and cycle frequency by $f$.

Since sine and cosine functions will be encountered frequently, we must find their derivatives and integrals. The cosine's derivative is found by differentiating (3.141) term by term:

$$\frac{d(\cos x)}{dx} = \frac{d}{dx}\left(\frac{x^0}{0!} - \frac{x^2}{2!} + \frac{x^4}{4!} - \frac{x^6}{6!} + \ldots\right) \qquad (3.144)$$

$$= 0 - 2\frac{x^1}{2!} + 4\frac{x^3}{4!} - 6\frac{x^5}{6!} + \ldots \qquad (3.145)$$

$$= -\left(\frac{x^1}{1} - \frac{x^3}{3!} + \frac{x^5}{5!} + \ldots\right) \qquad (3.146)$$

But the sum in parentheses is, by definition, $\sin x$, so

$$\frac{d(\cos x)}{dx} = -\sin x \qquad (3.147)$$

Similarly,

$$\frac{d(\sin x)}{dx} = \cos x \qquad (3.148)$$

The reader may also show that $y_1 = a_0 \cos x$ and $y_2 = a_1 \sin x$ each satisfies (3.122). Since the integral is the antiderivative, (3.142) and (3.148) require that

$$\int \sin x \, dx = - \cos x + c \qquad (3.149)$$

$$\int \cos x \, dx = \sin x + c \qquad (3.150)$$

Finally, we return to the question: what does $e^{ix}$ mean? Both (3.127) and (3.143) represent (3.122)'s unique solution, so they must be equivalent. We now derive the formula which relates $e^{ix}$, $\sin x$, and $\cos x$ and show that (3.127) and (3.143) are different ways to write the same function. By definition,

$$E(x) = \sum_{n=0}^{\infty} \frac{x^n}{n!} = e^x \qquad (3.151)$$

where $x$ represents any real $x$. Therefore, we define

$$E(ix) = \sum_{n=0}^{\infty} \frac{(ix)^n}{n!} = e^{ix} \qquad (3.152)$$

expand the sum in (3.152), taking note of the fact that $i^0 = 1$, and since $i = \sqrt{-1}, i^2 = -1, i^3 = -i, i^4 = +1, i^5 = i, \ldots$

$$e^{ix} = \frac{x^0}{0!} + \frac{ix}{1!} - \frac{x^2}{2!} - \frac{ix^3}{3!} + \frac{x^4}{4!} + \frac{ix^5}{5!} - \frac{x^6}{6!} - \frac{ix^7}{7!} + \ldots \qquad (3.153)$$

Rearranging terms:

$$e^{ix} = \left( \frac{x^0}{0!} - \frac{x^2}{2!} + \frac{x^4}{4!} - \frac{x^6}{6!} + \ldots \right)$$

$$+ i \left( \frac{x^1}{1!} - \frac{x^3}{3!} + \frac{x^5}{5!} - \frac{x^7}{7!} + \ldots \right) \qquad (3.154)$$

The sums in parentheses equal $\cos x$ and $\sin x$ respectively, so (3.154) yields the Euler formula:*

$$e^{ix} = \cos x + i \sin x \qquad (3.155)$$

---

* Also called Cauchy's formula or de Moivre's formula.

Similar logic shows that

$$e^{-ix} = \cos x - i \sin x \qquad (3.156)$$

Now, we show equivalence of (3.127) and (3.143). Substitute from (3.155) and (3.156) into (3.127):

$$y(x) = (A_1 + A_2) \cos x + i(A_1 - A_2) \sin x \qquad (3.157)$$

$A_1$ and $A_2$ are arbitrary constants, therefore so are $(A_1 + A_2)$ and $i(A_1 - A_2)$, and we may write (3.157) as:

$$y(x) = a_0 \cos x + a_1 \sin x \qquad (3.158)$$

which is identical to (3.143).*

In sum, we have defined two new functions, the sine and cosine, to conveniently write two fundamental solutions to the second-order linear differential equation (3.122). These functions oscillate values between $-1$ and $+1$, and are similar in that, by shifting one function $\pi/2$ units along the $x$-axis, the other is produced. Finally, we have expanded our definition of the exponential function to include complex values, and have related the result to the cosine and sine functions. We are now able to solve linear differential equations which have constant coefficients.

## PROBLEM SET 3.4

1. Graph the following functions from $t = -10$ to $t = +10$ (note the arguments are *not* in degrees):

   a. $\sin 2t$
   b. $2 \sin 2t$
   c. $\sin (2t - 1)$
   d. $\sin (t/2\pi)$
   e. $\cos (2t - 2\pi)$

2. Solve
   $$\dot{x}_1 = -x_2 \qquad x_1(0) = 1$$
   $$\dot{x}_2 = x_1 \qquad x_2(0) = 0$$

---

* Note that for $y(x)$ to take on real values, $a_0$ and $a$ are also real numbers. Therefore $A_1$ and $A_2$ in (3.157) represent the complex numbers $(a_0 + ia_1)/2$ and $(a_0 - ia_1)/2$, respectively.

then plot $x_2$ against $x_1$ and use the resulting graph to show that the sine and cosine functions which we constructed to solve a second-order differential equation are the same sine and cosine which arise in geometry and trigonometry.

3. Draw a circle with radius 1 centered on the origin. What is its circumference? What is the circumference of the upper half? Define the angle $\theta$ as the counterclockwise angle between the $x$-axis and any line extending out from the origin. What is the length of the arc on the unit circle between the intersection of the circle with the positive $x$-axis and the line? This arc length could be used to measure angle; in such case the angle is given in *radians*.

## LINEAR DIFFERENTIAL EQUATIONS WITH CONSTANT COEFFICIENTS: FINDING EIGENVALUES AND FUNDAMENTAL SOLUTIONS

We study the $n$th-order linear differential equation

$$a_n y^{(n)} + a_{n-1} y^{(n-1)} + \ldots + a_1 y' + a_0 y = g(x) \qquad (3.159)$$

with the $n$ initial conditions

$$y^{(n-1)}(x_0) = y_0^{(n-1)} \qquad y^{(n-2)}(x_0) = y_0^{(n-2)}, \ldots, y(x_0) = y_0$$

$$(3.160)$$

and in which all the coefficients of $y$ and its derivatives are the constants $a_n, a_{n-1}, \ldots, a_0$. This restriction seems to be substantial, but most practical problems which involve ordinary differential equations either lead directly to (3.159) (or the equivalent set of $n$ first-order differential equations) or can be approximated by (3.159). Constant-coefficient equations such as (3.159) are substantially easier to solve than the general linear differential equation in which functions of $x$ replace the constants $a_n, a_{n-1}, \ldots, a_0$. This section explains how to find (3.159)'s fundamental solutions by solving the homogeneous equation obtained by replacing $g(x)$ with zero. The next section presents one method to find a particular solution. The complete solution follows by adding a linear combination of $n$ linearly independent fundamental solutions (and hence introducing $n$ arbitrary constants) to a particular solution, then using the $n$ initial conditions to evaluate the $n$ arbitrary constants.

To find the $n$ fundamental solutions of

$$a_n y^{(n)} + a_{n-1} y^{(n-1)} + \ldots + a_1 y' + a_0 y = 0 \qquad (3.161)$$

assume

$$y(x) = A e^{\lambda x} \qquad A, \lambda = \text{constants} \qquad (3.162)$$

is the solution. Since

$$\frac{d^m}{dx^m} (A e^{\lambda x}) = \lambda^m A e^{\lambda x} \qquad (3.163)$$

substituting (3.162) into (3.161) produces

$$A(a_n \lambda^n + a_{n-1} \lambda^{n-1} + \ldots + a_1 \lambda + a_0) e^{\lambda x} = 0 \qquad (3.164)$$

Since $e^{\lambda x} \neq 0$, (3.164) requires that

$$a_n \lambda^n + a_{n-1} \lambda^{n-1} + \ldots + a_1 \lambda + a_0 = 0 \qquad (3.165)$$

This polynomial, called the *fundamental equation,* has $n$ solutions, $\lambda_1$, $\lambda_2, \ldots, \lambda_n$, each of which is called a fundamental value or *eigenvalue* of equation (3.159). For the moment, assume the $n$ eigenvalues are real and distinct. Then, the $n$ linearly independent functions $e^{\lambda_1 x}, e^{\lambda_2 x}, \ldots, e^{\lambda_n x}$ are (3.161)'s fundamental solutions. Hence, the homogeneous solution is

$$y_h(x) = A_1 e^{\lambda_1 x} + \ldots + A_n e^{\lambda_n x} \qquad A_1, A_2, \ldots, A_n = \text{any constants}$$

$$(3.166)$$

Thus we have reduced the problem of solving the differential equation (3.161) to solving the algebraic equation (3.165).

But what if some eigenvalues are not real, or if some values repeat? To answer these questions, let us examine the second-order differential equation

$$ay'' + by' + cy = 0 \qquad (3.167)$$

In addition to helping us answer our questions, this relatively simple equation is in itself one of the most important differential equations. For example, it frequently appears in mechanics, electronics, and studies of drug distribution using compartment analysis (as we saw in Chapter 2). Its fundamental equation is

$$a\lambda^2 + b\lambda + c = 0 \qquad (3.168)$$

The general quadratic formula gives the two eigenvalues directly:

$$\lambda_1 = \frac{-b + \sqrt{b^2 - 4ac}}{2a} \qquad \lambda_2 = \frac{-b - \sqrt{b^2 - 4ac}}{2a} \qquad (3.169)$$

There are three possible cases, which we examine individually:

1. $b^2 - 4ac > 0$     $\lambda_1$ and $\lambda_2$ are real and distinct
2. $b^2 - 4ac = 0$     $\lambda_1$ and $\lambda_2$ are real and equal
3. $b^2 - 4ac < 0$     $\lambda_1$ and $\lambda_2$ are complex conjugates*

If the eigenvalues are real and distinct, the functions $e^{\lambda_1 x}$ and $e^{\lambda_2 x}$ are linearly independent real-value functions, and thus are fundamental solutions to (3.167). The homogeneous solution is

$$y_h(x) = A_1 e^{\lambda_1 x} + A_2 e^{\lambda_2 x} \qquad (3.170)$$

If the eigenvalues are equal, $\lambda_1 = \lambda_2 = \lambda$, hence $e^{\lambda_1 x} = e^{\lambda_2 x}$. These two functions are linearly dependent and therefore do not include all linearly independent fundamental solutions. Advanced theory of linear transformations shows that the fundamental solutions are $e^{\lambda x}$ and $xe^{\lambda x}$. Rather than derive $y = xe^{\lambda x}$ as a fundamental solution to (3.167), we can simply verify it by substituting it, along with

$$y' = \lambda x e^{\lambda x} + e^{\lambda x} \qquad (3.171)$$

and

$$y'' = \lambda^2 x e^{\lambda x} + 2e^{\lambda x} \qquad (3.172)$$

into (3.167):

---

* Complex conjugates are a pair of complex numbers of the form $\zeta + i\omega$ and $\zeta - i\omega$. Complex solutions to fundamental equations always appear as conjugate pairs. See Appendix C for details.

$$ay'' + by' + cy = a(\lambda^2 xe^{\lambda x} + 2\lambda e^{\lambda x}) + b(\lambda xe^{\lambda x} + e^{\lambda x}) + cxe^{\lambda x}$$

$$(3.173)$$

$$ay'' + by' + cy = [(a\lambda^2 + b\lambda + c)x + (2\lambda a + b)]e^{\lambda x} \quad (3.174)$$

Equation (3.168) shows that the first term in parentheses equals zero, and since $b^2 - 4ac = 0$, $\lambda = -b/2a$, so $2\lambda a + b = 0$. Therefore (3.174)'s left side equals zero and $y = xe^{\lambda x}$ is one of (3.168)'s fundamental solutions. Since $e^{\lambda x}$ and $xe^{\lambda x}$ are two linearly independent fundamental solutions to (3.168),

$$y_h(x) = A_1 e^{\lambda x} + A_2 xe^{\lambda x} \quad (3.175)$$

is (3.168)'s homogeneous solution.

If $\lambda_1$ and $\lambda_2$ are the two complex conjugate numbers $\lambda_1 = \zeta + i\omega$ and $\lambda_2 = \zeta - i\omega$, the two linearly independent fundamental solutions are $e^{\lambda_1 x}$ and $e^{\lambda_2 x}$, so (3.168)'s homogeneous solution is:

$$y_h(x) = \hat{A}_1 e^{(\zeta + i\omega)x} + \hat{A}_2 e^{(\zeta - i\omega)x} \quad (3.176)$$

$$= \hat{A}_1 e^{\zeta x} e^{i\omega x} + \hat{A}_2 e^{\zeta x} e^{-i\omega x} \quad (3.177)$$

$$= e^{\zeta x}(\hat{A}_1 e^{i\omega x} + \hat{A}_2 e^{-i\omega x}) \quad (3.178)$$

But the last section showed we could replace the sum in parentheses with $(A_1 \cos \omega x + A_2 \sin \omega x)$, so that

$$y_h(x) = e^{\zeta x}(A_1 \cos \omega x + A_2 \sin \omega x) \quad (3.179)$$

is the homogeneous solution to (3.168).

For the $n$th-order case, the $n$ eigenvalues lead to the fundamental system according to these rules:

1. Each real distinct eigenvalue $\lambda_i$ is associated with the fundamental solution $e^{\lambda_i x}$.

2. Any eigenvalue $\lambda_i$ repeated $m$ times is associated with the $m$ fundamental solutions $e^{\lambda_i x}, xe^{\lambda_i x}, x^2 e^{\lambda_i x}, \ldots, x^{m-1} e^{\lambda_i x}$.

3. Each pair of complex conjugate eigenvalues, $\lambda_1 = \zeta + i\omega$ and $\lambda_2 = \zeta - i\omega$, is associated with the two fundamental solutions $e^{\zeta x} \cos \omega x$ and $e^{\zeta x} \sin \omega x$.

The eigenvalues contain important information about the phenomenon the differential equation describes. If any eigenvalue is real and positive, $y$ grows exponentially without bound as $x$ increases. If an eigenvalue is negative (which they generally are for phenomena commonly encountered in medicine, such as drug distribution dynamics), $y$'s value decays exponentially as $x$ increases. When complex eigenvalues are present, $y$ oscillates as $x$ increases. This oscillation grows exponentially in amplitude if the real part $\zeta$ of the eigenvalues is positive, remains constant if $\zeta = 0$, and decays exponentially if $\zeta$ is negative. When the real parts of all eigenvalues are negative, we say the system is *stable,* since regardless of the initial conditions, the dependent variable in the homogeneous equation eventually returns to zero. On the other hand, if at least one eigenvalue has a positive (or zero) real part, we say the system is *unstable,* since a disturbance (represented by nonzero initial conditions) makes the value of the dependent variable either grow without bound or oscillate indefinitely.

Below are five examples of finding eigenvalues and the associated fundamental solutions to linear constant-coefficient differential equations. In each case, note that the homogeneous solution contains one arbitrary constant for each order of the equation. After combining the homogeneous and particular solutions, we will use the initial conditions to evaluate these constants.

1. $y' + ky = 0$. $\qquad\qquad\qquad\qquad\qquad\qquad\qquad$ (3.180)

The fundamental equation is

$$\lambda + k = 0 \qquad\qquad\qquad\qquad (3.181)$$

The one real distinct eigenvalue $\lambda = -k$ leads to the homogeneous solution

$$y_h(x) = Ae^{\lambda x} = Ae^{-kx} \qquad\qquad\qquad (3.182)$$

2. $y'' + y = 0$. $\qquad\qquad\qquad\qquad\qquad\qquad\qquad$ (3.183)

The fundamental equation is

$$\lambda^2 + 1 = 0 \tag{3.184}$$

so $\lambda_1 = +i$, $\lambda_2 = -i$, and the homogeneous solution is

$$y_h(x) = e^{0x}(A_1 \cos x + A_2 \sin x) = A_1 \cos x + A_2 \sin x$$

$$\tag{3.185}$$

3. $y'' + 3y' + 2y = 0.$  $\hspace{2cm}$ (3.186)

The fundamental equation

$$\lambda^2 + 3\lambda + 2 = 0 \tag{3.187}$$

has roots $\lambda_1 = -1$ and $\lambda_2 = -2$, so

$$y_h(x) = A_1 e^{-x} + A_2 e^{-2x} \tag{3.188}$$

4. $y''' - y = 0.$  $\hspace{2cm}$ (3.189)

The fundamental equation

$$\lambda^3 - 1 = 0 \tag{3.190}$$

produces the three identical eigenvalues: $\lambda_1 = 1$, $\lambda_2 = 1$, $\lambda_3 = 1$. Therefore the homogeneous solution is

$$y_h(x) = A_1 e^x + A_2 x e^x + A_3 x^2 e^x \tag{3.191}$$

5. $\ddot{y} + 2\zeta\omega_n\dot{y} + \omega_n^2 y = 0$  $\hspace{1cm}$ $\zeta < 1$  $\hspace{1cm}$ (3.192)

The fundamental equation

$$\lambda^2 + 2\zeta\omega_n\lambda + \omega_n^2 = 0 \tag{3.193}$$

has solutions

$$\lambda_1 = -\zeta\omega_n - \omega_n\sqrt{\zeta^2 - 1}$$

$$\tag{3.194}$$

$$\lambda_2 = -\zeta\omega_n + \omega_n\sqrt{\zeta^2 - 1}$$

Since $\zeta < 1, \zeta^2 - 1 < 0$, so $\sqrt{\zeta^2 - 1} = i\sqrt{1 - \zeta^2}$ and the eigenvalues are

$$\lambda_1 = -\zeta\omega_n - i\omega_n\sqrt{1 - \zeta^2}$$

$$\lambda_2 = -\zeta\omega_n + i\omega_n\sqrt{1 - \zeta^2}$$

(3.195)

The homogeneous solution is

$$y_h(t) = e^{-\zeta\omega_n t}[A_1 \cos (\omega_n\sqrt{1 - \zeta^2}t) + A_2 \sin (\omega_n\sqrt{1 - \zeta^2}t)]$$

(3.196)

We can write (3.196) more compactly by defining the time constant $\tau = 1/(\zeta\omega_n)$ and frequency $\omega_d = \omega_n\sqrt{1 - \zeta^2}$ :

$$y_h(t) = e^{-t/\tau}(A_1 \cos \omega_d t + A_2 \sin \omega_d t)$$

(3.197)

## PROBLEM SET 3.5

Find the eigenvalues and fundamental solutions.

1. $y'' - 4y = 0$
2. $y'' - 4y = 6x$
3. $y'' - 4y' + 8y = e^x + e^{2x} + 1$
4. $y'' + 4y = 6x$
5. $3y'' + 12y' - 48y = 0$
6. $y'' + y' = 0$
7. $y'' - y' - 12y = 0$
8. $y'' - y = 0$
9. $y'' + 4y' + 4y = 0$
10. $y' - ky = 0$
11. $y''' = 0$
12. Prove that the eigenvalues for a two-compartment drug distribution system are always real, negative, and distinct. What does this result say about stability?

## LINEAR DIFFERENTIAL EQUATIONS WITH CONSTANT COEFFICIENTS: FINDING A PARTICULAR SOLUTION

In this section we continue our study of the $n$th-order constant-coefficient linear differential equation

$$a_n y^{(n)} + a_{n-1} y^{(n-1)} + \ldots + a_1 y' + a_0 y = g(x) \qquad (3.198)$$

by finding a *particular* solution to combine with the *homogeneous* solution to yield a *complete* solution. Of the methods available to find this particular solution, we will concentrate here on the *method of undetermined coefficients*. This method consists of guessing a particular solution which includes one or more undefined constants, substituting it into (3.198), then adjusting the coefficients to satisfy the resulting equation. This is a process analogous to that we used in the previous section to find the eigenvalues and associated fundamental solutions to the homogeneous problem. This is a procedure generally limited to problems in which one can guess from experience the particular solution's form by studying $g(x)$—i.e., when $g(x)$ is a sum of powers of $x$, exponential functions, or sines and cosines.* Fortunately, many practical problems can be solved by the use of this method. In each case note that, unlike the *homogeneous* solution, the *particular* solution contains no arbitrary constants and thus does not depend on the initial conditions.

We begin with two simple examples. Suppose

$$y' + ky = K \qquad (3.199)$$

Guess $y_p = c$, where $c$ is a constant yet to be determined. Since $y'_p = 0$, (3.199) becomes

$$0 + kc = K \qquad (3.200)$$

so

$$y_p = c = \frac{K}{k} \qquad (3.201)$$

On the other hand, this solution would not satisfy

$$y' + ky = Kx \qquad (3.202)$$

---

* We will solve more general problems using Laplace transform methods in the next chapter.

because no value of the constant $c$ satisfies

$$0 + kc = Kx \qquad (3.203)$$

for all $x$. Since this simple guess failed, guess $y_p = cx$. Then $y'_p = c$ and (3.201) becomes

$$c + ckx = Kx \qquad (3.204)$$

For this equation to hold for all $x$, the coefficients of like powers of $x$ must be equal:

$$x^0 \text{ coefficient} \qquad c = 0 \qquad (3.205)$$

$$x^1 \text{ coefficient} \qquad kc = K \qquad (3.206)$$

But (3.205) and (3.206) cannot hold simultaneously, so $y_p \neq cx$. Equations (3.205) and (3.206) do, however, point the way to solve (3.202): we need to choose a function which will contribute both a constant value and multiple of $x$ to (3.202)'s left side. Therefore, we guess $y_p(x) = c_1 x + c_0$. Then $y'_p = c_1$ and (3.201) becomes

$$c_1 + k(c_1 x + c_0) = Kx \qquad (3.207)$$

Equating coefficients of like powers of $x$:

$$x^0 \text{ coefficients} \qquad c_1 + kc_0 = 0 \qquad (3.208)$$

$$x^1 \text{ coefficients} \qquad kc_1 = K \qquad (3.209)$$

Solve (3.208) and (3.209) for $c_1$ and $c_0$ to obtain $c_1 = K/k$ and $c_0 = -K/k^2$. Therefore,

$$y_p(x) = \frac{K\left(x - \frac{1}{k}\right)}{k} \qquad (3.210)$$

(Verify this solution by substitution into (3.202).)

As another example, find a particular solution to

$$y'' + \alpha y = Be^{\beta x} \qquad \alpha, \beta, B = \text{constants} \qquad (3.211)$$

Since the exponential is its own derivative, and since after the substitution of the guessed particular solution into (3.211) we will equate coefficients, we guess

$$y_p(x) = Ce^{\beta x} \qquad (3.212)$$

Substitute from (3.212) into (3.211) to obtain

$$C\beta^2 e^{\beta x} + \alpha Ce^{\beta x} = Be^{\beta x} \qquad (3.213)$$

$$(C\beta^2 + \alpha C)e^{\beta x} = Be^{\beta x} \qquad (3.214)$$

So $C = B/(\alpha + \beta^2)$ and

$$y_p(x) = \frac{B}{\alpha + \beta^2}\, e^{\beta x} \qquad (3.215)$$

Verify that (3.215) satisfies (3.212).

As a final example find a particular solution to

$$\ddot{y} + 2\zeta\omega_n\dot{y} + \omega_n^2 y = A \sin \omega t \qquad (3.216)$$

Since differentiating sines and cosines produces cosines and sines of the same frequency, one would guess that (3.216)'s particular solution should be a sine or a cosine. But which? With no prior knowledge, why not use both and guess

$$y_p(t) = C \sin \omega t + D \cos \omega t \qquad (3.217)$$

Then

$$y_p'(t) = C\omega \cos \omega t - D\omega \sin \omega t \qquad (3.218)$$

and

$$y_p''(t) = -C\omega^2 \sin \omega t - D\omega^2 \cos \omega t \qquad (3.219)$$

Substitute from (3.217) through (3.219) into (3.216):

$$(-C\omega^2 \sin \omega t - D\omega^2 \cos \omega t) + 2\zeta\omega_n(C\omega \cos \omega t - D\omega \sin \omega t)$$

$$+ \omega_n^2(C \sin \omega t + D \cos \omega t) = A \sin \omega t \qquad (3.220)$$

and collect terms

$$[(\omega_n^2 - \omega^2)C - 2\zeta\omega_n\omega D] \sin \omega t + [2\zeta\omega_n\omega C + (\omega_n^2 - \omega^2)D] \quad \cos \omega t$$

$$= A \sin \omega t \qquad (3.221)$$

Equate coefficients of $\sin \omega t$ and $\cos \omega t$, and solve the two resulting equations for $C$ and $D$:

$$(\omega_n^2 - \omega^2)C - 2\zeta\omega_n\omega D = A \qquad (3.222)$$

$$2\zeta\omega_n\omega C + (\omega_n^2 - \omega^2)C = 0 \qquad (3.223)$$

Therefore

$$C = \frac{(\omega_n^2 - \omega^2)A}{(\omega_n^2 - \omega^2)^2 + (2\zeta\omega_n\omega)^2} \qquad D = -\frac{2\zeta\omega_n\omega A}{(\omega_n^2 - \omega^2)^2 + (2\zeta\omega_n\omega)^2}$$

$$(3.224)$$

So a particular solution is

$$y_p(t) = \frac{A}{(\omega_n^2 - \omega^2)^2 + (2\zeta\omega_n\omega)^2} [(\omega_n^2 - \omega^2) \sin \omega t - 2\zeta\omega_n\omega \cos \omega t)]$$

$$(3.225)$$

We can use the trigonometric identity

$$\sin \alpha \cos \beta - \cos \alpha \sin \beta = \sin (\alpha - \beta) \qquad (3.226)$$

to simplify (3.225). Consider a right triangle whose sides are $(\omega_n^2 - \omega^2)$ and $2\zeta\omega_n\omega$ long (Figure 3.9). According to the Pythagorean theoreom, the hypotenuse is $\sqrt{(\omega_n^2 - \omega^2)^2 + (2\zeta\omega_n\omega)^2}$. Rewrite (3.225):

$$y_p(t) = \frac{A}{\sqrt{(\omega_n^2 - \omega^2)^2 + (2\zeta\omega_n\omega)^2}} \left[ \frac{\omega_n^2 - \omega^2}{\sqrt{(\omega_n^2 - \omega^2)^2 + (2\zeta\omega_n\omega)^2}} \sin \omega t \right.$$

$$\left. - \frac{2\zeta\omega_n\omega}{\sqrt{(\omega_n^2 - \omega^2)^2 + (2\zeta\omega_n\omega)^2}} \cos \omega t \right] \qquad (3.227)$$

But, from Figure 3.9, the coefficient of $\sin \omega t$ equals $\cos \phi$ and the coefficient of $\cos \omega t$ equals $\sin \phi$. Therefore (3.227) can be written

$$y_p(t) = \frac{A}{\sqrt{(\omega_n^2 - \omega^2)^2 + (2\zeta\omega_n\omega)^2}} (\sin \omega t \cos \phi - \cos \omega t \sin \phi) \qquad (3.228)$$

Finally, use (3.226) to rewrite the term in parentheses:

$$y_p(t) = \frac{A}{\sqrt{(\omega_n^2 - \omega^2)^2 + (2\zeta\omega_n\omega)^2}} \sin (\omega t - \phi) \qquad (3.229)$$

Since

$$\tan \phi = \frac{2\zeta\omega_n\omega}{\omega_n^2 - \omega^2} \qquad (3.230)$$

$$\phi = \tan^{-1} \frac{2\zeta\omega_n\omega}{\omega_n^2 - \omega^2} \qquad (3.231)$$

Thus, the particular solution is another sinusoid of frequency $\omega$ whose amplitude is proportional to the amplitude of the forcing function $A$,

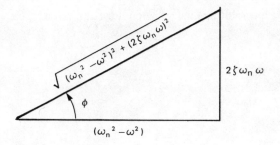

**FIGURE 3.9:** Definition of $\phi$.

which lags by an amount $\phi$ behind the forcing function. This difference is called the *phase lag* (Fig. 3.10).

In sum, the method of undetermined coefficients involves looking at the form of the forcing function ($g(x)$ in (3.158)) and making an educated guess at the form of a particular solution to the differential equation. We substitute this guess into the differential equation and determine values of the coefficients which make the particular solution satisfy the equation. If this procedure succeeds, we have one particular solution to add to the set of linearly independent fundamental solutions to the homogeneous equation.

The principle of superposition allows us to generalize the method of undetermined coefficients developed above to solve equations in which $g(x)$ in (3.158) is a sum of functions. Suppose

$$\mathcal{T}\{y\} = g_1(x) + g_2(x) \tag{3.232}$$

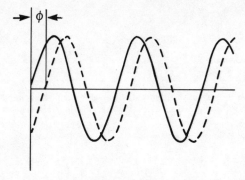

**FIGURE 3.10:** The dotted sinusoid lags behind the solid sinusoid by an amount $\phi$.

represents a linear differential equation. Furthermore, suppose

$$\mathcal{T}\{y_{1p}\} = g_1(x) \tag{3.233}$$

and

$$\mathcal{T}\{y_{2p}\} = g_2(x) \tag{3.234}$$

In other words, suppose $y_{1p}(x)$ and $y_{2p}(x)$ are particular solutions to (3.233) and (3.234). The principle of superposition requires that a particular solution to (3.232) be $y_p = y_{1p} + y_{2p}$, because

$$\mathcal{T}\{y_p\} = \mathcal{T}\{y_{1p} + y_{2p}\} = \mathcal{T}\{y_{1p}\} + \mathcal{T}\{y_{2p}\} = g_1 + g_2$$

$$\tag{3.235}$$

In other words, when $g(x)$ is a sum of functions, one can use the method of undetermined coefficients to find the particular solution associated with each additive term, then add these solutions to obtain a particular solution to the original problem. Table 3.1 suggests educated guesses for a given $g(x)$.

**TABLE 3.1**    Educated Guesses for $y_p(x)$

| $g(x)$ | Guess for $y_p(x)$ | $\lambda$* |
|--------|---------------------|-----------|
| $x^n$ | $K_n x^n + K_{n-1}x^{n-1} + \ldots + K_1 x + K_0$ | $0$ |
| $e^{kx}$ | $Ke^{kx}$ | $k$ |
| $\cos \omega x$ | $K_1 \cos \omega x + K_2 \sin \omega x$ | $\pm i\omega$ |
| $\sin \omega x$ | $K_1 \cos \omega x + K_2 \sin \omega x$ | $\pm i\omega$ |

* If the number in the last column is an eigenvalue of the associated homogeneous equation, and it is repeated $m$ times, multiply the suggested $y_p$ by $x^m$.

PROBLEM SET 3.6

Find particular solutions to these differential equations:

1. $y'' + ay' + by = 0$
2. $y'' + y = 2e^x$

3. $y'' + y = \sin 2x$
4. $y'' + y = 2e^x + \sin 2x$
5. $y'' + ay' + by = x^2 + 3b$
6. $y''' + y = \cos 3x$

## LINEAR DIFFERENTIAL EQUATIONS: FINDING THE COMPLETE SOLUTION

Now that we can find the homogeneous solution and one particular solution to a differential equation, we are ready to find the complete solution* by adding these two solutions and then using the initial conditions to evaluate the arbitrary constants the homogeneous equation contributes to the complete solution. This procedure should be followed with all linear differential equations. To find homogeneous and particular solutions for linear differential equations in which the coefficients of $y$ and its derivatives are functions of $x$ is quite involved. Identical procedures should be followed for using the homogeneous solution, particular solution, and initial conditions to find the complete solution for both constant-coefficient and variable-coefficient linear differential equations. Therefore we will illustrate this process with the same examples we used in the last two sections.

The procedure is straightforward. We will add the homogeneous and particular solutions, then use the $n$ initial conditions which must accompany an $n$th-order differential equation to compute appropriate values for the $n$ arbitrary constants which appear in the homogeneous solution.

As a first example, consider

$$y' + ky = mx + b \qquad y(0) = 0 \qquad (3.236)$$

We have seen that the solution to the associated homogeneous equation,

$$y' + ky = 0 \qquad (3.237)$$

is

$$y_h = Ae^{-kx} \qquad (3.238)$$

To find the particular solution, we apply the method of undetermined coefficients to the two differential equations

---

* The complete solution is also called the *general* or *total* solution.

$$y' + ky = mx \qquad (3.239)$$

and

$$y' + ky = b \qquad (3.240)$$

then apply the principle of superposition and add the two particular solutions to obtain a particular solution for (3.236). The particular solution to (3.236) is

$$y_p(x) = \frac{m\left(x - \frac{1}{k}\right)}{k} + \frac{b}{k} \qquad (3.241)$$

(Verify by substitution into (3.236).) Therefore (3.236)'s solution is

$$y(x) = y_h(x) + y_p(x) = Ae^{-kx} + \left[\frac{m\left(x - \frac{1}{k}\right)}{k} + \frac{b}{k}\right] \qquad (3.242)$$

To find $A$—and hence complete the solution—substitute the initial condition, $y(0) = 0$, into (3.242):

$$y(0) = 0 = Ae^{-k \cdot 0} + \frac{m\left(0 - \frac{1}{k}\right)}{k} + \frac{b}{k} \qquad (3.243)$$

$$A = \frac{\left(\frac{m}{k} - b\right)}{k} \qquad (3.244)$$

So (3.236)'s complete solution is

$$y(x) = \frac{\left[\left(\frac{m}{k} - b\right)(e^{-kx} - 1) + mx\right]}{k} \qquad (3.245)$$

which the reader may verify.

As a second example, consider

$$y'' + y = e^x \qquad y(0) = 0 \qquad y'(0) = 1 \qquad (3.246)$$

The solution to the associated homogeneous equation

$$y'' + y = 0 \tag{3.247}$$

has been shown to be

$$y_h(x) = A_1 \cos x + A_2 \sin x \tag{3.248}$$

and a particular solution is

$$y_p(x) = \frac{e^x}{2} \tag{3.249}$$

Therefore

$$y(x) = y_h(x) + y_p(x) = A_1 \cos x + A_2 \sin x + \frac{e^x}{2} \tag{3.250}$$

To evaluate the arbitrary constants $A_1$ and $A_2$, differentiate (3.250):

$$y'(x) = -A_1 \sin x + A_2 \cos x + \frac{e^x}{2} \tag{3.251}$$

and use the initial conditions with (3.250) and (3.251):

$$y(0) = 0 = A_1 \cos 0 + A_2 \sin 0 + \frac{e^0}{2} \tag{3.252}$$

$$0 = A_1 + \frac{1}{2} \tag{3.253}$$

$$y'(0) = 1 = -A_1 \sin 0 + A_2 \cos 0 + \frac{e^0}{2} \tag{3.254}$$

$$1 = A_2 + \frac{1}{2} \tag{3.255}$$

Therefore $A_1 = -1/2$ and $A_2 = 1/2$, so the complete solution is

$$y(x) = \frac{(\sin x - \cos x + e^x)}{2} \tag{3.256}$$

In sum, we have developed a formal technique for solving linear differential equations with constant coefficients, including those we wrote in Chapter 2 to describe physiological processes. First, we find the eigenvalues and linearly independent fundamental solutions to the associated homogeneous equation. Second, we find one particular solution to the specific problem at hand. Finally, we add these solutions together and use the initial conditions to evaluate the arbitrary constants contained in the homogeneous solution.

Now, let us apply this technique to biomedical problems.

## TWO-COMPARTMENT DRUG DISTRIBUTION FOLLOWING A BOLUS INJECTION OR CONSTANT INFUSION AND ITS APPLICATION TO LIDOCAINE

We now have the tools to solve the two-compartment drug-distribution problem which we formulated in Chapter 2. We will study separately the two most important types of drug administration: bolus injection and constant infusion. After predicting the drug concentration to be expected following these two types of administration, we will use the superposition principle to predict drug levels following a bolus loading dose *combined* with a constant infusion. In every case, note that the two time constants for the approach to steady-state concentration are the same.

In Chapter 2 we derived a second-order linear differential equation and two initial conditions to describe the dynamics of a drug which behaves as if it were distributed in two compartments:

$$\ddot{c} + (k_{12} + k_{21} + k_{10})\dot{c} + k_{10}k_{21}c = \frac{\left[\dot{i}(t) + k_{21}i(t)\right]}{V} \quad (3.257)$$

$$c(0) = \frac{q_{10}}{V} = c_0 \qquad \dot{c}(0) = -(k_{12} + k_{10})c_0 + \frac{k_{21}q_{20}}{V} + \frac{i(0)}{V}$$

$$(3.258)$$

where

$$c = \text{drug concentration in compartment 1,}$$

$$i = \text{drug infusion rate (into compartment 1),}$$

$$V = \text{central compartment}$$

$$q_{10} = \text{quantity of drug in compartment 1 at } t = 0,$$

$q_{20}$ = quantity of drug in compartment 2 at $t = 0$,

$k_{10}, k_{12}, k_{21}$ = transfer coefficients.

See Fig. 2.10.

Before solving the two particular problems of finding drug concentration as a function of time following a bolus or constant infusion, we must solve the associated homogeneous problem:

$$\ddot{c} + (k_{12} + k_{21} + k_{10})\dot{c} + k_{10}k_{21}c = 0 \qquad (3.259)$$

The fundamental equation,

$$\lambda^2 + (k_{12} + k_{21} + k_{10})\lambda + k_{10}k_{21} = 0 \qquad (3.260)$$

has roots

$$\lambda_1 = \frac{-(k_{10} + k_{12} + k_{21}) - \sqrt{(k_{10} + k_{12} + k_{21})^2 - 4k_{10}k_{21}}}{2}$$

$$(3.261)$$

$$\lambda_2 = \frac{-(k_{10} + k_{12} + k_{21}) + \sqrt{(k_{10} + k_{12} + k_{21})^2 - 4k_{10}k_{21}}}{2}$$

$$(3.262)$$

Since $k_{10}$, $k_{12}$, and $k_{21}$ are all real, positive numbers, $\lambda_1$ and $\lambda_2$ are real, negative, and distinct; therefore, the homogeneous solution is

$$c_h(t) = C_1 e^{\lambda_1 t} + C_2 e^{\lambda_2 t} \qquad (3.263)$$

To solve (3.257) for $c(t)$ following a bolus injection of mass $B$ into a subject with no prior drug present, we take the initial conditions $q_{10} = B$ and $q_{20} = 0$. Since we infuse no drug after administering the bolus, $i(t) = 0$, and (3.257) becomes

$$\ddot{c} + (k_{12} + k_{21} + k_{10})\dot{c} + k_{10}k_{21}c = 0 \qquad (3.264)$$

and the initial conditions of (3.258) become

$$c(0) = \frac{B}{V} \qquad \dot{c}(0) = -(k_{12} + k_{10})\frac{B}{V} \qquad (3.265)$$

We have already found the homogeneous solution associated with (3.264), so we need only find a particular solution. From the method of undetermined coefficients, guess $c_p(t) = 0$ and substitute into (3.265) to verify that it is a particular solution. Therefore, we can add $c_h$ and $c_p$ and use the initial conditions of (3.265) to find the complete solution:

$$c(t) = c_h(t) + c_p(t) = C_1 e^{\lambda_1 t} + C_2 e^{\lambda_2 t} + 0 \qquad (3.266)$$

and

$$\dot{c}(t) = C_1 \lambda_1 e^{\lambda_1 t} + C_2 \lambda_2 e^{\lambda_2 t} \qquad (3.267)$$

Substitute from (3.265) into (3.266) and (3.267):

$$c(0) = \frac{B}{V} = C_1 + C_2 \qquad (3.268)$$

$$\dot{c}(0) = -(k_{12} + k_{10})\frac{B}{V} = \lambda_1 C_1 + \lambda_2 C_2 \qquad (3.269)$$

Solve (3.268) and (3.269) for $C_1$ and $C_2$:

$$C_1 = \frac{B(\lambda_1 + k_{12} + k_{10})}{V(\lambda_1 - \lambda_2)} \qquad C_2 = \frac{-B(\lambda_2 + k_{12} + k_{10})}{V(\lambda_1 - \lambda_2)} \qquad (3.270)$$

Finally, we can use (3.261) and (3.262) to eliminate $\lambda_1$ and $\lambda_2$ from (3.270) to obtain

$$c(t) = \frac{B}{V}\left[ \frac{(k_{10} + k_{12} - k_{21}) + \sqrt{(k_{10} + k_{12} + k_{21})^2 - 4k_{10}k_{21}}}{2\sqrt{(k_{10} + k_{12} + k_{21})^2 - 4k_{10}k_{21}}} e^{-t/\tau_f} \right.$$
$$\left. + \frac{(k_{10} + k_{12} - k_{21}) - \sqrt{(k_{10} + k_{12} + k_{21})^2 - 4k_{10}k_{21}}}{2\sqrt{(k_{10} + k_{12} + k_{21})^2 - 4k_{10}k_{21}}} e^{-t/\tau_s} \right]$$

$$(3.271)$$

in which

$$\tau_f = -\frac{1}{\lambda_1} = \frac{2}{(k_{10} + k_{12} + k_{21}) + \sqrt{(k_{10} + k_{12} + k_{21})^2 - 4k_{10}k_{21}}}$$

(3.272)

and

$$\tau_s = -\frac{1}{\lambda_2} = \frac{2}{(k_{10} + k_{12} + k_{21}) - \sqrt{(k_{10} + k_{12} + k_{21})^2 - 4k_{10}k_{21}}}$$

(3.273)

The concentration begins at $B/V$ at time zero and decreases to zero according to this bi-exponential function. Notice that the transfer coefficients, not the size of the dose or volume of distribution, determine the shape of the concentration versus time curve (i.e., the expression in brackets). This situation reflects the fact that the drug distribution exhibits linear dynamics. By the principle of superposition, one would expect doubling the dose (input) to simply double the concentration (output) at all times without affecting the form of the response (shape of the curve). It does.

Figure 3.11 illustrates (3.271), using $k_{12}$, $k_{21}$, $k_{10}$, and $V$ values for ouabain distribution in adult dogs. Figure 3.11B shows that, unlike drugs that behave as if distributed in one compartment, a plot of ouabain concentration versus time does not follow a single straight line on a semi-logarithmic plot. Rather, it exhibits two straight-line regions with notably different slopes. Just as when discussing one-compartment drug distribution, we can talk about the time constants of each phase of the decay.

We call $\tau_f$ and $\tau_s$ the time constants for the *fast* and *slow phases* of the decay, respectively. This is because each exponential term in (3.272) drops to 0.37 of its original value in an interval equal to the associated time constant. People often simply associate the slow time constant $\tau_s$ with the drug's metabolic clearance, i.e., the constant $k_{10}$. Equations (3.272) and (3.273) show the inaccuracy of this view. Unlike a one-compartment distribution in which the fractional transfer coefficient representing metabolic removal determines the time constant, both time constants depend on all three fractional transfer coefficients, $k_{10}$, $k_{12}$, and $k_{21}$.

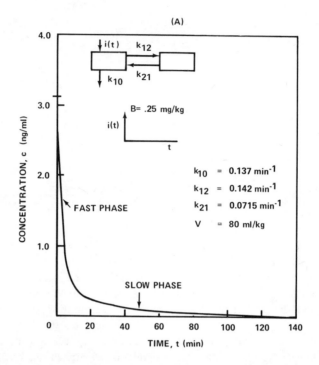

**FIGURE 3.11A:** Typical concentrations of ouabain administered to an adult dog. The curve is given by

$$c(t) = 31.2\ (0.859e^{-t/3.13\ \text{min}} + 0.141e^{-t/32.7\ \text{min}})\ \text{ng/ml}.$$

If $\tau_f \ll \tau_s$, then the effect of the slow phase will be relatively constant while the fast phase dominates (3.271); hence one can use the slope of the fast phase curve in Figure 3.11B to estimate $\tau_f$. Likewise, for $t > 5\tau_f$ the fast phase's contribution to $c(t)$ will be negligible, so the slope of the curve in Figure 3.11B at large times can be used to estimate $\tau_s$. The intercepts can be used to estimate $C_1$ and $C_2$. Figure 3.12 illustrates this process.

Now let us move to the problem of predicting drug concentrations during a constant infusion. Let $I$ = the constant infusion (drug mass flow) rate, and suppose $q_{10} = q_{20} = 0$. Then (3.257) and (3.258) become

$$\ddot{c} + (k_{12} + k_{21} + k_{10})\dot{c} + k_{10}k_{21}c = k_{21}\frac{I}{V} \qquad (3.274)$$

**(B)**

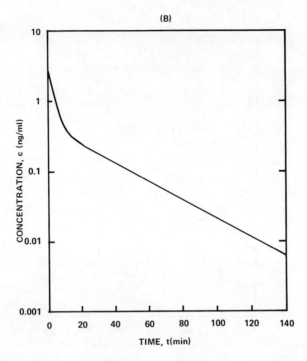

**FIGURE 3.11B:** When the concentration history shown in Figure 3.11A is plotted on semi-log paper, the bi-exponential decay appears as two connected straight line segments.

and

$$c(0) = 0 \qquad \dot{c}(0) = \frac{I}{V} \qquad (3.275)$$

We have already found the homogeneous solution. By use of the method of undetermined coefficients, a particular solution is $c_p(t) = I/(k_{10}V)$, so

$$c(t) = c_h(t) + c_p(t) = C_1 e^{\lambda_1 t} + C_2 e^{\lambda_2 t} + \frac{I}{(k_{10}V)} \qquad (3.276)$$

Finally, substitute the initial conditions (3.275) into (3.276) and its derivative, to find

$$C_1 = \frac{-I(\lambda_2 + k_{10})}{k_{10}V(\lambda_2 - \lambda_1)} \qquad (3.277)$$

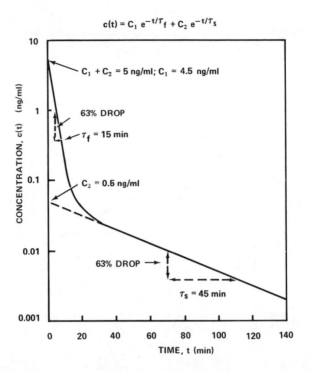

$$c(t) = C_1 e^{-t/\tau_f} + C_2 e^{-t/\tau_s}$$

**FIGURE 3.12:** A semi-logarithmic plot of $c(t)$ versus $t$ can be used to estimate $\tau_f$, $\tau_s$, $C_1$, and $C_2$ from experimental measurements when $\tau_s > 5\tau_f$. Given $B$, one could then use these $\tau_f$, $\tau_s$, $C_1$, and $C_2$ to compute $k_{12}$, $k_{21}$, $k_{10}$, and $V$. The procedure is often used to compute the parameters which describe a drug's distribution. $\tau_f$ and $\tau_s$ are the time required for a 63% drop in concentration along each linear phase; $C_1$ and $C_2$ follow from extrapolating the two linear phases back to $t = 0$.

and

$$C_2 = \frac{I(\lambda_1 + k_{10})}{k_{10}V(\lambda_2 - \lambda_1)} \qquad (3.278)$$

As before, we use (3.261) and (3.262) to eliminate $\lambda_1$ and $\lambda_2$ from (3.277) and (3.278), to find that the concentration begins at zero and increases to $c_\infty = I/(k_{10}V)$ according to

$$c(t) = \frac{I}{k_{10}V}\left[1 - \frac{(k_{10}-k_{12}-k_{21}) + \sqrt{(k_{10}+k_{12}+k_{21})^2 - 4k_{10}k_{21}}}{2\sqrt{(k_{10}+k_{12}+k_{21})^2 - 4k_{10}k_{21}}}e^{-t/\tau_f}\right.$$

$$\left. + \frac{(k_{10}-k_{12}-k_{21}) - \sqrt{(k_{10}+k_{12}+k_{21})^2 - 4k_{10}k_{21}}}{2\sqrt{(k_{10}+k_{12}+k_{21})^2 - 4k_{10}k_{21}}}e^{-t/\tau_s}\right]$$

$$(3.279)$$

This two-phase exponential increase to $c_\infty$ has the same two time constants as the decrease following a bolus injection (Fig. 3.13). The time constants (i.e., the eigenvalues) follow directly from the properties of the drug-distribution dynamics, independent of the type or magnitude of infusion, so long as the basic dynamic equation, (3.257), holds.

Now let us apply this analysis to predict how to administer the drug lidocaine, which is used widely to treat irregular heartbeats (arrhythmias).* Generally, a bolus washes out so quickly that the plasma level remains in the therapeutic range only a short time ($\tau_f$ dominates), while a constant infusion takes substantial time to build up therapeutic plasma levels ($\tau_s$ dominates). See Figures 3.14 and 3.15.

One can, however, rapidly achieve and maintain therapeutic concentrations by administering a bolus loading dose followed by a constant infusion. So long as the kinetics remain linear and the principle of superposition holds, one can keep plasma levels in the therapeutic range by simply adding the bolus response to the infusion response (Fig. 3.16). Note that the concentration begins above the steady-state level, dips below it, then approaches steady-state from below. If arrhythmias recur at the time of minimum drug concentration, one may administer a second, smaller bolus (Fig. 3.17) and use the principle of superposition to obtain the plasma concentration by adding the effect of the second bolus to the combined effects of the initial bolus and constant infusion. Note that this additional bolus does not change the final steady-state concentration.

After reaching steady-state, it may be necessary to further increase plasma concentration. An increase of infusion rate accomplishes this, but the approach to the new steady-state is dominated by the same slow-time

---

* For more details, see Winkle, R. A., Glantz, S. A., and Harrison, D. C., Pharmacologic Therapy of Ventricular Arrhythmias, *Am. J. Cardiol.* 36 (1975): 629.

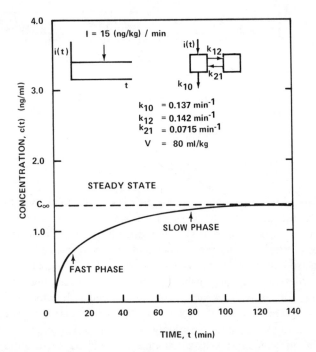

**FIGURE 3.13:** Response of two-compartment drug distribution model to a constant infusion. The concentration exponentially increases from zero to its steady-state value with the same two time constants which it exhibited in the decreasing concentration following a bolus injection. $I = 15$(ng/kg)/min, and $k_{10}, k_{12}, k_{21}, V$ are the same as in Figure 3.11. The curve is given by

$$c(t) = 1.36 \left[ 1 - 0.368e^{-t/3.13 \text{ min}} - 0.632e^{-t/32.7 \text{ min}} \right] \text{ ng/ml}$$

constant, $\tau_s$, as was the buildup to the original steady-state. Administering another bolus at the time the infusion rate is increased avoids a delay in achieving the new therapeutic level (Fig. 3.18).

Following a bolus, the fast time constant generally reflects drug movement into the initially empty outer compartment and the slow time constant reflects drug movement from the outer compartment to the central compartment and subsequent removal. Similarly, with a constant infusion, the fast-time constant usually reflects the drug's initial rapid buildup in the central compartment, and the slow-time constant represents the outer compartment's slower filling as plasma level increases. When a constant infusion is stopped, the plasma levels decline with the same two time

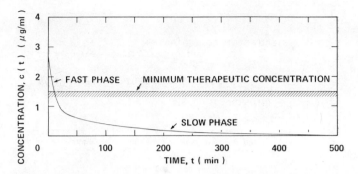

**FIGURE 3.14:** The response of a two-compartment model which describes lidocaine distribution in an individual following a 100-mg bolus. The lidocaine concentration remains in the therapeutic range only for about ten minutes. The transfer coefficients, $k_{10}$ = 0.024 min$^{-1}$, $k_{21}$ = 0.038 min$^{-1}$, and $k_{12}$ = 0.066 min$^{-1}$ determine the time constants for the fast and slow phases of the decay, $\tau_f$ = 8.3 min and $\tau_s$ = 130 min, following the bolus, as well as the relative importance of each phase in determining the actual plasma concentration at any given time while the bolus magnitude $B$ = 100 mg and the volume of distribution $V$ = 44 ml/kg scale the actual concentration magnitude. The kinetic parameters are from M. Rowland et al. Disposition Kinetics of lidocaine in normal subjects. *Ann. N.Y. Acad. Sci.* 179 (1971): 383–397. [Figures 3.14 through 3.19 reproduced with permission from R. A. Winkle, S. A. Glantz, and D. C. Harrison, Pharmacologic therapy of ventricular arrhythmias, *Am. J. Cardiol.* 36 (1975): 629.]

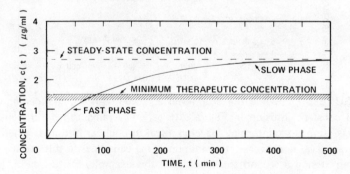

**FIGURE 3.15:** Response of the same individual as in Figure 3.14 to a constant infusion of 2 mg/min of lidocaine. A two-phase exponential characterizes the increase to steady-state with the same two time constants as the bolus washout. It takes about 90 minutes to reach the minimum therapeutic concentration of lidocaine.

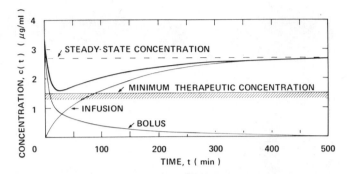

**FIGURE 3.16:** Response of the same individual as in Figures 3.14 and 3.15 to a 100 mg bolus loading dose followed by a 2 mg/min constant infusion. Since lidocaine obeys the principle of superposition, we can simply add the bolus and infusion responses (Figs. 3.14 and 3.15) to obtain the net plasma concentration of lidocaine. Since the bolus is washing out while the constant infusion is building up, the net effect is to keep plasma concentration in the therapeutic range. By combining a bolus loading dose with a constant infusion, one can quickly achieve and indefinitely maintain therapeutic plasma concentrations.

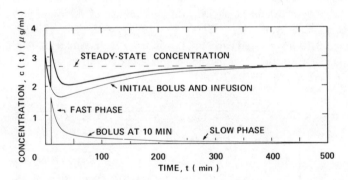

**FIGURE 3.17:** While the drug levels achieved with a single loading dose and constant infusion in Figure 3.16 generally remain in the therapeutic range, some patients may develop breakthrough arrhythmias when the plasma level approaches its minimum. One can alleviate this problem by administering a second small bolus, in this example, 50 mg administered 10 minutes after the first bolus. By the principle of superposition, one only need add the effect of the second bolus to the result depicted in Figure 3.16. The washout due to the second bolus exhibits the same fast and slow phases as the initial bolus.

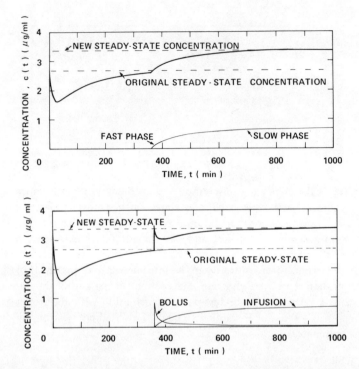

**FIGURE 3.18:** (A) If the steady-state blood level initially obtained from the constant infusion is not adequate, one can obtain a higher steady-state concentration simply by increasing the infusion rate (in this example, from 2 mg/min to 2.5 mg/min). The principle of superposition states that the net effect will simply be to add the effect of a 0.5 mg/min infusion (depicted at the bottom of the graph) to the result of the initial loading dose and infusion. The effect of the additional infusion exhibits the same two time constants as the initial infusion, and hence requires about 300 minutes to approach the new steady-state concentration.

(B) One can instantly achieve higher plasma levels by administering a small bolus loading dose at the same time one increases the infusion rate. The example shows a 25 mg bolus given when the infusion rate is increased by 25%. The second bolus is 25% of the original loading dose.

constants which describe the washout following a bolus and the buildup to steady-state during a constant infusion (Fig. 3.19). In fact, all changes in plasma concentration proceed according to a two-phase exponential with the same two time constants, $\tau_f$ and $\tau_s$.

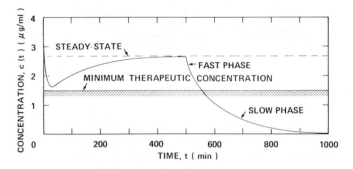

**FIGURE 3.19:** When one discontinues drug therapy, plasma concentrations decrease with the same two time constants which describe the increase following a constant infusion or decrease following a bolus. The relative importance of the fast and slow phases (i.e., the relative magnitudes of the two exponential terms) depends on how close to steady-state the plasma concentration was when the infusion was terminated. If plasma concentration is near steady-state, the washout at the end of the infusion will have a relatively minor fast-phase contribution with the slow phase dominating. If the drug is terminated quickly after administration, the fast phase dominates.

While $V$, $k_{10}$, $k_{12}$, and $k_{21}$ do not represent specific physiological entities, they may change value with physiological changes. For example, depressed renal or hepatic function effectively decreases $k_{10}$, changing the time constants and increasing steady-state concentration. When a drug exhibits saturable binding or metabolism, the parameters $V$, $k_{10}$, $k_{12}$, and $k_{21}$ no longer remain constant, so drug distribution becomes nonlinear and the principle of superposition no longer applies.

### EXPLAINING AGE-RELATED DIFFERENCES IN OUABAIN PHARMACOKINETICS*

Chapter 1 used the example of serum ouabain concentration changes over time in adult dogs and puppies in order to show how mathematical analysis can provide insight into physiological processes. We will now work with this example in more detail. The experiments we will analyze have as their goal a better understanding of why one must in general administer nearly twice the ouabain dose to children and immature animals in order to obtain the same serum concentrations as one obtains in adults (Fig. 3.20).

* For more details, see Glantz, S. A., Kernoff, R., and Goldman, R. H., "Age-Related Changes in Ouabain Pharmacology: Ouabain Exhibits Different Volumes of Distribution in Adult and Puppy Dogs," *Circ. Res.* 39 (1976): 407.

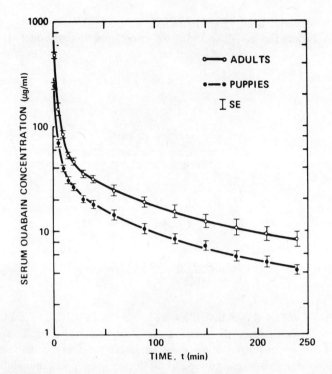

**FIGURE 3.20:** Following the same 0.05 mg/kg dose of ouabain, serum concentration in adult dogs remains significantly higher than in puppies, although both curves have the same shape and merely differ by a multiplicative constant. (The vertical error bars quantify the uncertainty in the estimate of the mean values of concentration for each group of dogs.) (Figures 3.20 through 3.22 reproduced with permission of the American Heart Association, Inc., from S. A. Glantz, R. Kernoff, and R. H. Goldman, Age-Related Changes in Ouabain Pharmacology, *Circ. Res.* 39 (1976): 407).

The observed serum concentrations following a single 0.05 mg/kg bolus behaved according to the two-compartment linear drug distribution model we just solved:

$$c(t) = C_1 e^{\lambda_1 t} + C_2 e^{\lambda_2 t} \tag{3.280}$$

After fitting the serum ouabain concentration which was observed in each dog with (3.280) to find the values of $C_1, C_2, \lambda_1$, and $\lambda_2$ for each dog, we can then use equations (3.261), (3.262), and (3.270) to derive expressions for the parameters associated with the two-compartment model for each dog.

$$V = \frac{B}{(C_1 + C_2)} \tag{3.281}$$

$$k_{10} = \frac{-\lambda_1 \lambda_2 (C_1 + C_2)}{(\lambda_1 C_2 + \lambda_2 C_1)} \tag{3.282}$$

$$k_{12} = \frac{-C_1 C_2 (\lambda_1 - \lambda_2)^2}{(C_1 + C_2)(\lambda_1 C_2 + \lambda_2 C_1)} \tag{3.283}$$

$$k_{21} = \frac{-(\lambda_1 C_2 + \lambda_2 C_1)}{(C_1 + C_2)} \tag{3.284}$$

Figure 3.21A shows that the transfer coefficients $k_{10}$, $k_{12}$, and $k_{21}$ did not differ significantly between the young and old dogs. This result should not be surprising, since these parameters define the shape of the concentration versus time curve, and the curves for puppies and adult dogs are parallel. However, the volume of distribution is significantly higher per kilogram of body weight in the puppies than in the adults (Fig. 3.21B). Thus the puppies exhibit lower concentrations at all times, not because they distribute or metabolize the drugs differently than adult dogs, but because they dilute in a greater volume the drug in the central compartment. This mathematical result led to additional experiments to identify the source of this greater distribution volume, which showed that the puppies had significantly higher plasma, interstitial, and other physiological fluid spaces than the adults (Fig. 3.22). Notably, the puppies' fluid spaces were greater than the adults in the same ratio as one would predict from the ratio of the volumes of distribution.*

In fact, this conclusion derives not from the two-compartment model which we had assumed for the drug distribution, but a much less restrictive hypothesis in which the drug distribution kinetics are simply linear. We have seen that the shape of the response depends only on the transfer coefficients, not on the dose or distribution volume. This situation would

---

* More precisely, the ratios were not significantly different in a statistical sense.

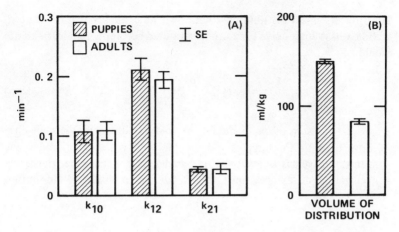

**FIGURE 3.21:** (A) The transfer coefficients which describe the change in serum ouabain concentration following a single injection are not significantly different in adult and puppy dogs. (B) Puppies do, however, have significantly larger volumes of distribution for ouabain than adults. This difference leads to the puppies having lower concentrations of the drug in their serum than the adults, but has no effect on the shape of the concentration versus time curve.

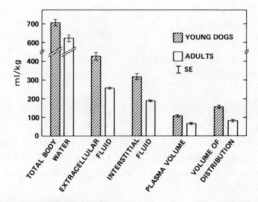

**FIGURE 3.22:** The physiological fluid spaces in the puppy are significantly larger per kilogram than in the adult by about the same proportion as the distribution volume, suggesting that the distribution volume represents the plasma volume plus a fraction of the interstitial space. (Adapted with permission of the American Heart Association, Inc., from S. A. Glantz, R. Kernoff, and R. H. Goldman, Age-Related Changes in Ouabain Pharmacology, *Circ. Res.* 39 (1976): 407).

hold for any linear distribution kinetics, so we could say that the concentration versus time curve for a drug distributed according to linear kinetics would be

$$c(t) = \frac{B}{V} f(t) \tag{3.285}$$

where $f(t)$ is a sum of exponentials. Hence if we administer the same dose of drug to both the puppies and the adults, $B$ is the same, and if the concentration versus time curves are parallel, $f(t)$ is the same. Hence the concentration differences must follow from distribution volume differences.

## PROBLEM SET 3.7

Solve these differential equations:

1. $y'' + 3y' + 2y = 2(1 - \cos 2x)$     $y(0) = 1$     $y'(0) = 0$
2. $y' - ky = K$     $y(0) = 0$     $k, K$ = constants
3. $y'' + 6y' + 9y = 9t + 1$     $y(0) = 1$     $y'(0) = 1$
4. $y'' + y = x^2 + 2$     $y(0) = 0$     $y'(0) = 2$
5. $x'' + \omega_0^2 x = \cos \omega t$   $\omega \neq \omega_0$     $x(0) = 1$     $\dot{x}(0) = 0$
6. $x'' + \omega_0^2 x = \cos \omega_0 t$     $x(0) = 1$     $\dot{x}(0) = 0$
7. $y'' + 2y' + y = e^t \cos t$     $y(0) = 0$     $\dot{y}(0) = 0$
8. $x'' + \omega_0^2 x = 0$     $x(0) = 0$     $\dot{x}(0) = 0$

9. Figure 3.23 shows the plasma concentration of a drug measured after a 2.5 mg/kg bolus injection. Since it follows a bi-exponential decay,

$$c(t) = C_1 e^{-t/\tau_f} + C_2 e^{-t/\tau_s}$$

its pharmacokinetic behavior can be described with a two-compartment model. If $C_1 = 419$ ng/ml, $C_2 = 31.4$ ng/ml, $\tau_f = 2.39$ min, $\tau_s = 57.6$ min, and $B = 0.05$ mg/kg, find $k_{10}, k_{12}, k_{21}$, and $V$ in such a model.

10. Find a loading dose and constant infusion which will immediately bring the concentration of drug in a one-compartment distribution model to steady-state value, $c_\infty$, and keep it there.

11. Find $c(t)$ for a drug distributed in two compartments when it is administered according to the following regime: At time $t = 0$ administer a bolus of magnitude $B$ followed by an infusion according to $Bk_{12}e^{-k_{12}t}$ combined with a constant infusion of magnitude $Bk_{10}$.

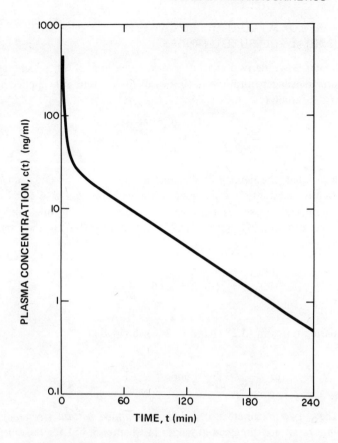

**FIGURE 3.23:** Plasma concentration of a drug following a 2.5 mg/kg dose.

12. Show that it is impossible to use a simple loading dose followed by a constant infusion to bring the concentration of drug in the central compartment of a two-compartment model immediately to its steady-state value and hold it there. (Hint: Show that it is only possible if $\lambda_1 = \lambda_2$, then show that $\lambda_1$ never equals $\lambda_2$.)

13. Propose a compartment model for an orally administered drug which behaves in accordance with a one-compartment model when administered intravenously. Write equations for this model and solve for plasma concentration as a function of time, assuming a single dose of drug into an initially drug-free patient.

## RESPONSE OF A FLUID-FILLED CATHETER TO STEP AND SINUSOIDAL PRESSURE CHANGES

In Chapter 2 we derived the differential equation (2.91), which related pressure transducer output voltage $E(t)$ to the pressure $p(t)$ applied at the end of the catheter:

$$\ddot{E} + \frac{c}{\rho LA} \dot{E} + \frac{k}{\rho LA} E = \frac{K}{\rho L} p(t) \qquad (3.286)$$

where $\rho$ equals the density of the fluid in the catheter, $k$ and $c$ quantify the effective elasticity and damping of the catheter, $L$ and $A$ equal catheter length and cross-sectional area, and $K$ describes the pressure transducer. We can simplify our analysis by rewriting (3.286) in the standard form:

$$\ddot{E} + 2\zeta\omega_n\dot{E} + \omega_n^2 E = \frac{K}{\rho L} p(t) \qquad (3.287)$$

Comparing terms in (3.287) and (3.286) shows that

$$\omega_n = \sqrt{\frac{k}{\rho LA}} \quad \text{and} \quad \zeta = \frac{c}{2}\sqrt{\frac{1}{\rho k LA}} \qquad (3.288)$$

These two parameters, called the *undamped natural frequency* and *damping ratio,* are discussed at length in Chapter 5, but for our purposes here the undamped natural frequency is the frequency at which the catheter would oscillate if there were no friction, and the damping ratio tells us the nature of the response. If $\zeta < 1$, the catheter will tend to respond with oscillatory responses; if $\zeta > 1$, it will respond with exponential growth and decay. In each case we assume the catheter is initially at rest; $p(0) = \dot{p}(0) = 0$; in other words, $E(0) = 0$ and $\dot{E}(0) = 0$.

Now, let us compute the response to a step change in pressure:

$$p(t) = \begin{cases} 0 & t \leq 0 \\ P = \text{constant} & t > 0 \end{cases} \qquad (3.289)$$

*First*, we must solve the associated homogeneous problem

$$\ddot{E} + 2\zeta\omega_n\dot{E} + \omega_n^2 E = 0 \qquad (3.290)$$

The fundamental equation is

$$\lambda^2 + 2\zeta\omega_n\lambda + \omega_n^2 = 0 \qquad (3.291)$$

so the eigenvalues are

$$\lambda_1 = -\zeta\omega_n - \omega_n\sqrt{\zeta^2 - 1}$$
$$\lambda_2 = -\zeta\omega_n + \omega_n\sqrt{\zeta^2 - 1} \qquad (3.292)$$

There are three possible cases, depending on $\zeta$'s value. (Compare this discussion with the discussion of equation (3.168).)

1. If $\zeta > 1$, then $\zeta^2 - 1 > 0$; so the square root has a real value, and the two eigenvalues are real, negative, and distinct. The solution to the homogeneous equation is thus a sum of decaying exponentials:

$$E_h(t) = A_1 e^{\lambda_1 t} + A_2 e^{\lambda_2 t} = A_1 e^{-t/\tau_1} + A_2 e^{-t/\tau_2} \qquad (3.293)$$

This situation is called *overdamped*.

2. If $\zeta = 1$, the two eigenvalues are equal,

$$\lambda_1 = \lambda_2 = \lambda = \zeta\omega_n = -\omega_n \qquad (3.294)$$

so the solution to the homogeneous equation is

$$E_h(t) = (B_1 + B_2 t)e^{\lambda t} = (B_1 + B_2 t)e^{-t/\tau} \qquad (3.295)$$

This situation is called *critical damping*.

3. If $\zeta < 1$, then $\zeta^2 - 1 < 0$, so the square root has an imaginary value and the eigenvalues are a complex conjugate pair. The solution to the homogeneous equation is thus (see equation (3.192)) a decaying sinusoidal oscillation:

$$E_h(t) = e^{-\zeta\omega_n t}[C_1 \cos(\omega_n\sqrt{1 - \zeta^2}t) + C_2 \sin(\omega_n\sqrt{1 - \zeta^2}t)] \qquad (3.296)$$

This situation is called *underdamped*.

*Second,* we must find a particular solution. Since the right side of (3.287) is a constant for $t > 0$, guess

$$E_p(t) = E_\infty = \text{constant} \qquad (3.297)$$

and substitute into (3.287)

$$0 + 0 + \omega_n^2 E_\infty = \frac{PK}{(\rho L)} \qquad (3.298)$$

$$E_\infty = \frac{PK}{(\omega_n^2 \rho L)} \qquad (3.299)$$

So (3.297) is a particular solution when (3.299) defines $E_\infty$. Note that the particular solution does not depend on the eigenvalues or value of the damping coefficient.

*Third,* we add the homogeneous and particular solutions and use the initial conditions to evaluate the arbitrary constants in the homogeneous solution. We will repeat this step for each of the three homogeneous solutions developed above.

1. *Overdamping ($\zeta > 1$):*

Add (3.293) and (3.297) to obtain the complete solution

$$E(t) = A_1 e^{\lambda_1 t} + A_2 e^{\lambda_2 t} + E_\infty \qquad (3.300)$$

Then

$$\dot{E}(t) = \lambda_1 A_1 e^{\lambda_1 t} + \lambda_2 A_2 e^{\lambda_2 t} \qquad (3.301)$$

Now use the initial conditions

$$E(0) = 0 = A_1 + A_2 + E_\infty$$

$$\dot{E}(0) = 0 = \lambda_1 A_1 + \lambda_2 A_2 \qquad (3.302)$$

So

$$A_1 = \frac{-E_\infty \lambda_2}{(\lambda_2 - \lambda_1)} \quad \text{and} \quad A_2 = \frac{E_\infty \lambda_1}{(\lambda_2 - \lambda_1)}$$

and

$$E(t) = E_\infty \left( 1 - \frac{\lambda_2}{\lambda_2 - \lambda_1} e^{-t/\tau_1} + \frac{\lambda_1}{\lambda_2 - \lambda_1} e^{-t/\tau_2} \right) \quad (3.303)$$

in which $\tau_1 = -1/\lambda_1$ and $\tau_2 = -1/\lambda_2$. Finally, from (3.292) and (3.299):

$$E(t) = E_\infty \left( 1 + \frac{\zeta - \sqrt{\zeta^2 - 1}}{2\sqrt{\zeta^2 - 1}} e^{-t/\tau_1} - \frac{\zeta + \sqrt{\zeta^2 - 1}}{2\sqrt{\zeta^2 - 1}} e^{-t/\tau_2} \right)$$

$$(3.304)$$

Figure 3.24 illustrates two typical overdamped responses. The transducer output $E$ increases exponentially to the steady-state value $E_\infty$. As the damping ratio $\zeta$ decreases, $E$ approaches $E_\infty$ more quickly. (Compare this response to the two-compartment drug-distribution model with a constant infusion, Figures 3.11–3.13.)

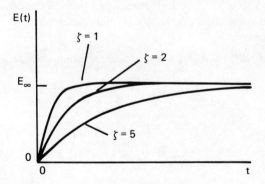

**FIGURE 3.24:** Responses of overdamped and critically damped systems. As the damping ratio $\zeta$ decreases toward 1, the system responds faster. (For this illustration, $\omega_n = 40 \text{ sec}^{-1}$; the $t$ axis is 0.8 sec long.)

2. *Critical Damping* ($\zeta = 1$):

Add (3.295) and (3.297) to obtain the complete solution:

$$E(t) = (B_1 + B_2 t)e^{\lambda t} + E_\infty \qquad (3.305)$$

Then

$$\dot{E}(t) = \lambda(B_1 + B_2 t)e^{\lambda t} + B_2 e^{\lambda t} \qquad (3.306)$$

Substitute the initial conditions into (3.305) and (3.306):

$$0 = B_1 + E_\infty$$

$$0 = \lambda B_1 + B_2 \qquad (3.307)$$

So $B_1 = -E_\infty$ and $B_2 = \lambda E_\infty$ and, since $\lambda = -\omega_n$,

$$E(t) = E_\infty[1 + (-1 + \lambda t)e^{\lambda t}] = E_\infty[1 - (1 + \omega_n t)e^{-t/\tau}] \quad (3.308)$$

Figure 3.24 shows that while a critically damped response looks similar to an exponential increase, it approaches steady-state more quickly than an overdamped system. Many instruments are designed to exhibit critical damping to provide the fastest response without overshooting the steady-state value.

3. *Underdamping* ($\zeta < 1$):

Add (3.296) and (3.297) to obtain the complete solution,

$$E(t) = e^{-\zeta\omega_n t}[C_1 \cos(\omega_n\sqrt{1 - \zeta^2}\,t)$$

$$+ C_2 \sin(\omega_n\sqrt{1 - \zeta^2}\,t)] + E_\infty \qquad (3.309)$$

Then

$$\dot{E}(t) = e^{-\zeta\omega_n t}[(-\zeta\omega_n C_1 + \omega_n\sqrt{1 - \zeta^2}\,C_2) \cos(\omega_n\sqrt{1 - \zeta^2}\,t)$$

$$+ (-\omega_n\sqrt{1 - \zeta^2}\,C_1 - \omega_n C_2) \sin(\omega_n\sqrt{1 - \zeta^2}\,t)] \qquad (3.310)$$

Substitute the initial conditions into (3.309) and (3.310):

$$E(0) = 0 = C_1 + E_\infty$$

$$\dot{E}(0) = 0 = -\zeta\omega_n C_1 + \omega_n\sqrt{1 - \zeta^2}C_2$$

(3.311)

So, $C_1 = -E_\infty$ and $C_2 = -E_\infty\zeta/\sqrt{1 - \zeta^2}$. To simplify the notation, let $\tau = 1/(\zeta\omega_n)$ and $\omega_d = \omega_n\sqrt{1 - \zeta^2}$; then

$$E(t) = E_\infty[1 - e^{-t/\tau}\cos\omega_d t + (\zeta/\sqrt{1 - \zeta^2}\sin\omega_d t)]$$    (3.312)

To further simplify (3.312), define $\theta$ with the triangle in Figure 3.25 and rewrite (3.312) as:

$$E(t) = E_\infty\left[1 - \frac{e^{-t/\tau}}{\sqrt{1 - \zeta^2}}(\sqrt{1 - \zeta^2}\cos\omega_d t + \zeta\sin\omega_d t)\right]$$    (3.313)

But from Figure 3.25, $\cos\theta = \sqrt{1 - \zeta^2}$ and $\sin\theta = \zeta$, so

$$E(t) = E_\infty\left[1 - \frac{e^{-t/\tau}}{\sqrt{1 - \zeta^2}}\cos\omega_d t\cos\theta + \sin\omega_d t\sin\theta\right]$$    (3.314)

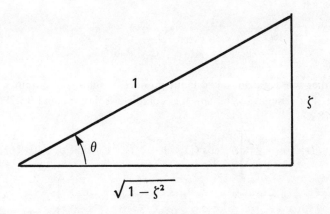

**FIGURE 3.25:** Definition of $\theta$.

But $\cos (x - y) = \cos x \cos y + \sin x \sin y$, so

$$E(t) = E_\infty \left[ 1 - \frac{e^{-t/\tau}}{\sqrt{1 - \zeta^2}} \cos (\omega_d t - \theta) \right] \qquad (3.315)$$

in which

$$\theta = \sin^{-1} \zeta \qquad (3.316)$$

Underdamped systems exhibit a decaying oscillation following a step change in input. Figure 3.26 shows the response of an underdamped catheter (the most typical case) for three different damping ratios. As the damping decreases, the catheter responds faster, but with more overshoot.

Now let us examine the response of an underdamped catheter to a sinusoidally varying pressure of amplitude $P$ and frequency $\omega$. In this case the differential equation is

$$\ddot{E} + 2\zeta\omega_n \dot{E} + \omega_n^2 E = \frac{PK}{\rho L} \sin \omega t \qquad (3.317)$$

To simplify the notation, let $(PK)/(\rho L) = A$. In Equation (3.229) we found a particular solution to this equation is

$$E_p(t) = \frac{A}{\sqrt{(\omega_n^2 - \omega^2)^2 + (2\zeta\omega_n\omega)^2}} \sin (\omega t - \phi) \qquad (3.318)$$

in which

$$\phi = \tan^{-1} \frac{2\zeta\omega_n\omega}{\omega_n^2 - \omega^2} \qquad (3.319)$$

In other words, a sinusoidal input produces a sinusoidal output with the same frequency. To obtain the complete solution, add (3.296) and (3.318):

$$E(t) = e^{-\zeta\omega_n t} \left[ C_1 \cos (\omega_n\sqrt{1 - \zeta^2}t) + C_2 \sin (\omega_n\sqrt{1 - \zeta^2}t) \right.$$

$$\left. + \frac{A}{\sqrt{(\omega_n^2 - \omega^2)^2 + (2\zeta\omega_n\omega)^2}} \sin (\omega t - \phi) \right] \qquad (3.320)$$

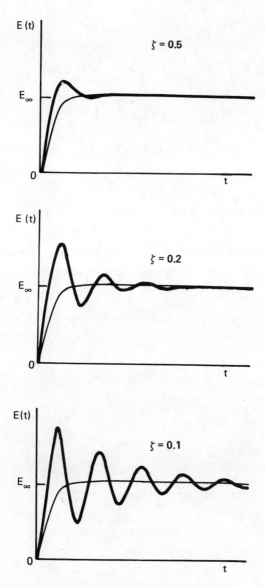

**FIGURE 3.26:** As the damping ratio decreases below 1, the system response continues to speed up and exhibits increasing oscillations. For this illustration, $\omega_n = 40 \text{ sec}^{-1}$ and the $t$-axis is 0.8 sec long. The light line shows the solution with critical damping, $\zeta = 1$.

To evaluate $C_1$ and $C_2$, differentiate (3.320):

$$\dot{E}(t) = e^{-\zeta\omega_n t}\left[(\omega_n\sqrt{1 - \zeta^2}C^2 - \omega_n C_1)\cos(\omega_n\sqrt{1 - \zeta^2}t)\right.$$

$$\left. - (\zeta\omega_n C_2 + \omega_n\sqrt{1 - \zeta^2}C_1)\sin(\omega_n\sqrt{1 - \zeta^2}t)\right]$$

$$+ \frac{A\omega\cos(\omega t - \phi)}{\sqrt{(\omega_n^2 - \omega^2)^2 + (2\zeta\omega_n\omega)^2}} \tag{3.321}$$

then substitute in the initial conditions

$$E(0) = 0 = C_1 + \frac{A}{\sqrt{(\omega_n^2 - \omega^2)^2 + (2\zeta\omega_n\omega)^2}}\sin(-\phi) \tag{3.322}$$

$$\dot{E}(0) = 0 = (\omega_n\sqrt{1 - \zeta^2}C_2 - \zeta\omega_n C_1) + \frac{A\omega}{\sqrt{(\omega_n^2 - \omega^2) + (2\zeta\omega_n\omega)^2}}\cos(-\phi)$$

$$\tag{3.323}$$

But

$$\sin(-\phi) = -\sin\phi = \frac{-2\zeta\omega_n\omega}{\sqrt{(\omega_n^2 - \omega^2)^2 + (2\zeta\omega_n\omega)^2}} \tag{3.324}$$

$$\cos(-\phi) = \cos\phi = \frac{\omega_n^2 - \omega^2}{\sqrt{(\omega_n^2 - \omega^2)^2 + (2\zeta\omega_n\omega)^2}} \tag{3.325}$$

so (3.322) and (3.323) can be written

$$C_1 + 0 \cdot C_2 = \frac{2\zeta\omega_n\omega A}{(\omega_n^2 - \omega^2)^2 + (2\zeta\omega_n\omega)^2} \tag{3.326}$$

$$\zeta\omega_n C_1 - \omega_n\sqrt{1 - \zeta^2}C^2 = \frac{(\omega_n^2 - \omega^2)A\omega}{(\omega_n^2 - \omega^2)^2 + (2\zeta\omega_n\omega)^2} \tag{3.327}$$

Solve (3.326) and (3.327) for $C_1$ and $C_2$:

$$C_1 = \frac{2\zeta\omega_n\omega A}{(\omega_n^2 - \omega^2)^2 + (2\zeta\omega_n\omega)^2} \qquad (3.328)$$

$$C_2 = \frac{[\omega_n^2(2\zeta^2 - 1) + \omega^2]\omega A}{\omega_n\sqrt{1 - \zeta^2}\,[(\omega_n^2 - \omega^2)^2 + (2\zeta\omega_n\omega)^2]} \qquad (3.329)$$

Finally, the complete solution is

$$E(t) = \frac{PK}{\rho L}\left[\frac{\omega e^{-t/\tau}}{(\omega_n^2 - \omega^2)^2 + (2\zeta\omega_n\omega)^2}\left(2\zeta\omega_n\cos\omega_d t\right.\right.$$

$$\left.+ \frac{\omega_n^2(2\zeta^2 - 1) + \omega^2}{\omega_n\sqrt{1 - \zeta^2}}\sin\omega_d t\right)$$

$$\left.+ \frac{1}{\sqrt{(\omega_n^2 - \omega^2)^2 + (2\zeta\omega_n\omega)^2}}\sin(\omega t - \phi)\right] \qquad (3.330)$$

This response to a sinusoidal forcing function consists of two parts, one which decays exponentially to zero and which is called the *transient response*, and another which continues indefinitely, which is called the *steady-state response* (Fig. 3.27).

The eigenvalues determine the transient response's rate of decay and frequency, and the initial conditions determine its magnitude. On the other hand, the forcing function's frequency, $\omega$, equals the steady-state response's frequency; $\omega$ and the parameters which describe the physical system ($\omega_n$ and $\zeta$) define both the steady-state solution's amplitude and *phase angle* $\phi$, the amount it lags behind the forcing function (Figure 3.10). Whenever all real parts of the eigenvalues are negative, the transient response (i.e., the initial conditions' effect) dies away and the steady-state response depends only on the forcing function, not the initial conditions. Furthermore, if one is interested only in the steady-state response, one need only show that all the eigenvalues have negative real parts (i.e., that the process is stable), then proceed directly to finding the particular (i.e., steady-state) solution.

## FORCING FUNCTION

$\omega = 30 \text{ sec}^{-1}$        $\omega = 50 \text{ sec}^{-1}$

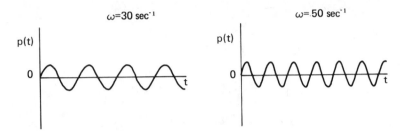

## STEADY STATE RESPONSE (PARTICULAR SOLUTION)

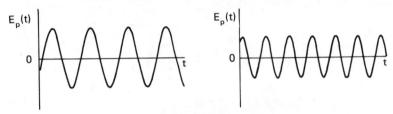

## TRANSIENT RESPONSE (HOMOGENEOUS SOLUTION)

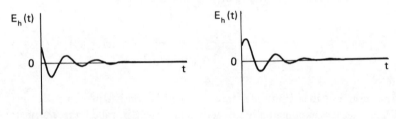

## TOTAL RESPONSE (COMPLETE SOLUTION)

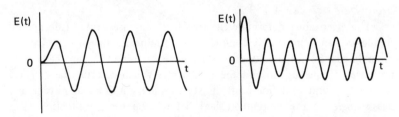

**FIGURE 3.27:** The response of a linear constant-coefficient differential equation (such as the second-order equation used to represent a fluid-filled catheter) to a sinusoidal forcing function is the sum of a steady-state response with the same frequency of the input sinusoid but which lags behind it (the particular solution), plus the transient response which

## PROBLEM SET 3.8

1. Suppose we had a catheter with an undamped natural frequency of 30 Hz ($188 \text{ sec}^{-1}$) and a damping ratio of 0.7. Plot the response to a sudden change in pressure from $p = 0$ to 15 mm Hg, assuming $K/(\rho L) = 10 \text{ volt/mmHg-sec}^2$ and that the catheter was in steady-state prior to the sudden pressure change.

2. Repeat Problem 1 for a sudden change from 5 to 20 mmHg, and compare the results. Explain the similarities and differences from both a mathematical and physical standpoint.

3. The *settling time* of a second-order system such as a fluid-filled catheter is often defined as the time following a step change in input required for the transducer output to reach 5% of its steady-state value. Estimate the settling time for such a system, given $\omega$ and $\zeta$.

4. Plot the ratio of the amplitude of sinusoidally varying pressure input to the amplitude of the steady-state voltage output (i.e., particular solution for a range of frequencies from 0 to $2\omega_n$).

## APPROACHES TO NONLINEAR DIFFERENTIAL EQUATIONS

The principle of superposition is the foundation on which the theory of linear ordinary differential equations rests. This theory leads directly to solutions of a wide class of problems. Unfortunately, biological problems often give rise to *nonlinear* differential equations, for which there is no general theory. Some first-order nonlinear differential equations are separable or exact and can be solved using the methods presented at the beginning of this chapter. But the nonlinear differential equation which can be solved in closed form is the exception rather than the rule, and by and large one must use approximate methods to analyze nonlinear differential equations.

---

depends on the initial conditions and the eigenvalues (homogeneous solution). The two columns show the response of such a second-order system with $\omega_n = 40 \text{ sec}^{-1}$ and $\zeta = 0.2$ to two different input sinusoids of the same amplitude, one of frequency $30 \text{ sec}^{-1}$ and the other with frequency $50 \text{ sec}^{-1}$. Note that the amplitude of the steady-state response to the faster sinusoid is smaller than the steady-state amplitude of the faster sinusoid. This illustration demonstrates the common fact that forcing a second-order system at a frequency much above $\omega_n$ produces a diminished response. (The time axis is 0.8 sec long; compare these figures with Figure 3.24.)

There are three general approaches to the analysis of nonlinear equations:

1. Find only steady-state solutions.
2. Make assumptions which convert the nonlinear equation to a linear equation which approximates the nonlinear equation.
3. Solve the nonlinear equation using numerical techniques.

To take the first method above, one could abandon the effort to find the *dynamic* response of a process under consideration, and simply find the potential steady-state solutions. This approach is accomplished by simply setting all the derivatives equal to zero, then solving the resulting algebraic equations. Such an approach, however, gives no information about the *nature* of the equilibrium points, in particular whether or not the points of equilibrium are stable, i.e., whether or not the process will return to the same point if slightly displaced.

For example, the equation for the angular displacement of the pendulum in Figure 3.28 is:

$$\ddot{\theta} + \dot{\theta} + \sin \theta = 0 \qquad (3.331)$$

When the pendulum is in equilibrium $\dot{\theta} = \ddot{\theta} = 0$ and (3.331) becomes

$$0 + 0 + \sin \theta = 0 \qquad (3.332)$$

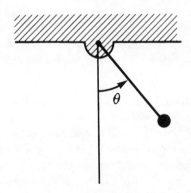

**FIGURE 3.28:** Friction at the hub and air resistance produce forces resisting a pendulum's motion in proportion to the angular speed $\dot{\theta}$.

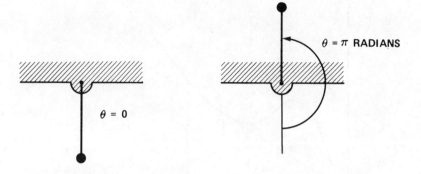

**FIGURE 3.29:**  The pendulum's two equilibrium points.

Hence, the equilibrium points are $\theta = 0$ or $\pi$ radians (180°). Figure 3.29 shows these equilibrium points.

To show that only one is stable we use the second approach—linearization. We make simplifying assumptions which allow us to approximate (3.332) with a linear differential equation, which we can then easily solve, so long as the result is consistent with the simplifying assumptions. This linearization will at least indicate whether or not the equilibrium points are stable, and may provide a complete solution. We assume that the value of the dependent variable $\theta$ remains small, so that the nonlinear function $\sin \theta$ may be replaced with a linear approximation based on its derivative at the equilibrium points (Fig. 3.30). The range over which this common approximation holds depends on the nature of the nonlinear function, how sensitive the differential equation is to the error which the approximation introduces, and how much inaccuracy one will accept in the final solution. The magnitude of this error—of obvious importance—is often difficult to assess. To continue the analysis, let us linearize (3.331) twice—once about each equilibrium point.

We assume that, for some range near $\theta = 0$,

$$\sin \theta \simeq \sin 0 + \left. \frac{d \sin \theta}{d\theta} \right|_{\theta=0} (\theta - 0) = \theta \qquad (3.333)$$

and substitute this result for $\sin \theta$ in (3.331) to obtain the linearized equation

$$\ddot{\theta} + \dot{\theta} + \theta = 0 \qquad (3.334)$$

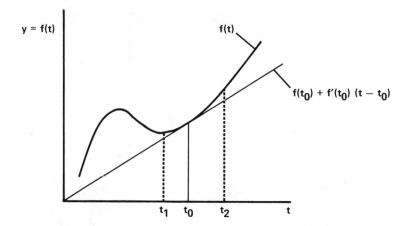

**FIGURE 3.30:** A nonlinear function can be approximated over some range by a straight line whose slope equals the function's derivative at a point within the range. In this case, the linear approximation is reasonably accurate from $t_1$ to $t_2$.

This equation holds as long as (3.333) holds, i.e., as long as $\theta$ is small. Now suppose we displace the pendulum from the equilibrium point $\theta = 0$ by small angle $\theta_0$ and release it. Using the methods of linear differential equations, we easily solve this linear differential equation with the initial conditions

$$\theta(0) = \theta_0 \qquad \dot{\theta}(0) = 0 \qquad\qquad (3.335)$$

to find that

$$\theta(t) = \sqrt{\frac{4}{3}}\,\theta_0 e^{-t/2} \, \sin\left(\sqrt{\frac{3}{4}}t + \phi\right) \qquad \phi = \tan^{-1}\sqrt{3} = 60°$$

$$(3.336)$$

The maximum excursion, however, is the small angle $\sqrt{4/3}\,\theta_0$, so our linearizing assumption holds and (3.335) is an approximate solution to the nonlinear differential equation (Fig. 3.31). Furthermore, since the sine function value never exceeds 1 and the exponential term decays toward zero as time increases, the pendulum eventually returns to $\theta = 0$. Thus, $\theta = 0$ is a stable equilibrium point.

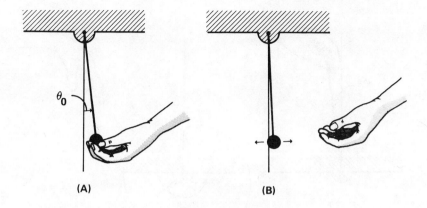

**FIGURE 3.31:** The displacement of the pendulum by a small angle $\theta_0$ from the equilibrium point $\theta = 0$ leads to an oscillation about $\theta = 0$ according to equation (3.336). Hence $\theta = 0$ is a stable equilibrium point. Since the maximum excursion is $\theta_0$, a small number, our linearizing assumption that $\theta$ remains small holds and the solution to the linearized equation (3.334) closely approximates the solution to the original nonlinear equation, (3.331).

Now let us linearize (3.331) about the other equilibrium point, $\theta = \pi$:

$$\sin \theta \simeq \sin \pi + \frac{d(\sin \theta)}{d\theta}\bigg|_{\theta=\pi} (\theta - \pi) = \sin \pi + (\cos \pi)(\theta - \pi) = \pi - \theta$$

$$(3.337)$$

Substitute from (3.337) into (3.331) to obtain the differential equation linearized about the point $\theta = \pi$:

$$\ddot{\theta} + \dot{\theta} + (\pi - \theta) = 0 \qquad (3.338)$$

Since the linearization holds so long as $\theta$ remains near $\pi$ radians, let $\phi = \pi - \theta$, in which case (3.338) becomes

$$\ddot{\phi} + \dot{\phi} - \phi = 0 \qquad (3.339)$$

which holds so long as $\phi$ remains small. If we now displace the pendulum (Fig. 3.32) from the equilibrium point at $\theta = \pi$ ($\phi = 0$) by the small

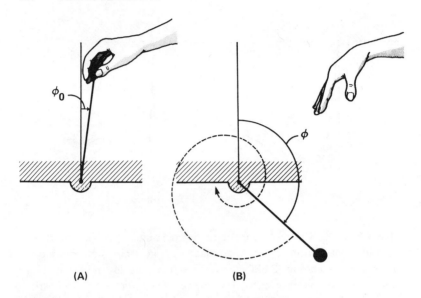

**(A)**                                  **(B)**

**FIGURE 3.32:** Displacement of the pendulum a small distance $\phi_0$ ($\phi =$ $\pi - \theta$) from the equilibrium point $\phi = 0$ leads to continued motion away from $\phi = 0$; hence a linearized solution shows that this equilibrium point is not stable. The resulting solution predicts ever-increasing (and hence large) values of $\phi$, which violates the assumption that $\phi$ remains small which permitted our linearization. Therefore, while the linearized solution does allow us to determine that the equilibrium point is unstable, it does not accurately approximate the original nonlinear differential equation's solution.

angle $\phi_0$ so that $\phi(0) = \phi_0$ and $\dot{\phi}(0) = 0$ and then release it, (3.339) predicts

$$\phi(t) = \frac{\phi_0}{\sqrt{5}} (be^{-at} + ae^{-bt}) \qquad (3.340)$$

in which $a = (1 - \sqrt{5})/2 \simeq -0.62$ and $b = (1 + \sqrt{5})/2 \simeq 1.62$, so

$$\phi(t) = 0.72e^{0.62t} - 0.28e^{-1.62t} \qquad (3.341)$$

Thus $\phi = 0$ (or $\theta = \pi$) is not a stable equilibrium point, because $\phi$ grows without bound rather than settling back to zero following the small displacement to $\phi_0$. In addition, $\phi$ does not remain small, thus violating our linearization assumption and (3.341) is *not* an accurate approximation to (3.331)'s true solution.

The exact nature of the linearization assumptions which one makes depends strongly on the specific physiological problem under study and on the nature of the nonlinear equations to which it leads. Hence one can offer little by way of instruction on what constitutes a generally acceptable linearization technique. In light of the techniques for solving linear differential equations, there is often a strong impulse to linearize a problem regardless of the violence being done to the underlying physiology. Beware of linearizations. Further, *after solving the linearized version of a differential equation, always go back and verify that the initial assumptions remain valid.* When in doubt, solve the problem numerically, using the methods in Chapter 7.

## PSEUDO-STEADY-STATE SOLUTION FOR THE MICHAELIS-MENTEN ENZYME-CATALYZED REACTION

In Chapter 2 we derived the nonlinear differential equations which describe the enzyme-catalyzed reaction

$$E + S \underset{k_2}{\overset{k_1}{\rightleftharpoons}} ES \overset{k_3}{\longrightarrow} P + E$$

They are:

$$\frac{d[E]}{dt} = -k_1 [E] [S] + (k_2 + k_3)[ES] \qquad (3.342)$$

$$\frac{d[S]}{dt} = -k_1 [E] [S] + k_2 [ES] \qquad (3.343)$$

$$\frac{d[ES]}{dt} = k_1 [E] [S] - (k_2 + k_3)[ES] \qquad (3.344)$$

$$\frac{d[P]}{dt} = k_3 [ES] \qquad (3.345)$$

where the total amount of enzyme present, $E_T$, remains constant:

$$E_T = [E] + [ES] = \text{constant} \qquad (3.346)$$

We cannot solve this system of nonlinear differential equations as they stand, but we can still obtain useful information about the rate at which product is formed,

$$v = \frac{d[P]}{dt} \qquad (3.347)$$

To obtain this result, assume that equilibrium is so rapidly established between $E$, $S$, and $ES$ that the reaction essentially remains in a steady-state, so that

$$\frac{d[ES]}{dt} \simeq 0 \qquad (3.348)$$

Use (3.348) with (3.344) and (3.346) to obtain

$$[ES] = \frac{k_1 E_T [S]}{(k_2 + k_3) + k_1 [S]} \qquad (3.349)$$

Now substitute from (3.349) into (3.345) to obtain an expression for $v$, the rate of product formation:

$$v = \frac{k_3 k_1 E_T [S]}{(k_2 + k_3) + k_1 [S]} \qquad (3.350)$$

If all the enzyme was bound to substrate, $[ES]$ would equal $E_T$ and, according to (3.345), product would be formed at the maximum rate. Therefore, define

$$v_{max} = k_3 E_T \qquad (3.351)$$

By defining the (generalized) Michaelis constant

$$K_m = \frac{k_2 + k_3}{k_1} \qquad (3.352)$$

we obtain the classic Michaelis-Menten equation. For the rate of product formation in an enzyme-catalyzed reaction (Fig. 3.33),

$$v = \frac{v_{max} [S]}{K_m + [S]} \qquad (3.353)$$

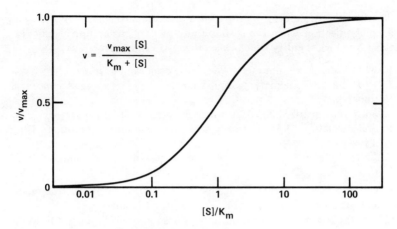

**FIGURE 3.33:** At low concentrations of substrate $S$, the product is formed slowly from lack of substrate. As substrate concentration increases, the rate at which the product forms also increases. The maximum rate of product formation $v_{max}$ would occur if all the enzyme were combined with substrate to form the intermediate enzyme-substrate complex $ES$.

Notice that when the substrate concentration $S$ equals $K_m$,

$$v = \frac{v_{max} K_m}{K_m + K_m} = \frac{1}{2} v_{max} \tag{3.354}$$

This equation has found wide use among biochemists, but it should be applied only in those cases in which the simplifying assumption can be made that the intermediate complex formation proceeds so quickly as to remain in a pseudo-steady-state.* Note that we obtained useful information from our mathematical formulation of this reaction even though we did not actually solve the nonlinear differential equations.

PROBLEM SET 3.9

The differential equation

$$\dot{c}(t) = -b(1 - e^{-ac}) \tag{3.355}$$

---

* For a discussion of the limitations of this assumption, see Bartholomay, A. F., "Chemical Kinetics and Enzyme Kinetics," in *Foundations of Mathematical Biology, Vol. I. Subcellular Systems*, ed. by Robert Rosen. New York: Academic Press, 1972. See especially pp. 160-164.

describes the washout of a drug from a one-compartment model following a bolus injection when the absolute rate of drug has an upper limit (i.e., the physiological entity which clears the drug can be saturated).

1. What is the maximum rate at which the drug can be removed?
2. What linearized equation approximates (3.355) for small concentrations?
3. Solve the linearized equation with the initial condition $c(0) = c_0$.
4. Solve equation (3.355) directly with the same initial condition. (Hint: it is separable.)

For the following problems, assume $a = 1(mg/kg)^{-1}$ and $b = 0.05$ $(mg/kg)/min$.

5. Plot the clearance rate $-\dot{c}$ against concentration $c$ for the true model and the linearized model for $c$ between 0 and 10 mg/kg.
6. Plot the actual concentration (using the solution to Problem 4) and the approximate solution (using the solution to Problem 3) for times between 0 and 120 minutes, when the initial concentration, $c_0$, equals
   a. 0.05 mg/kg
   b. 0.1 mg/kg
   c. 0.5 mg/kg
   d. 1.0 mg/kg


## ADDITIONAL READINGS

*Compartment Analysis for Drug Distribution*

Glantz, S. A., R. Kernoff, and R. H. Goldman. Age-Related Changes in Ouabain Pharmacology: Ouabain Exhibits Different Volumes of Distribution in Adult and Puppy Dogs. *Circ. Res.* 39 (1976): 407.

Jacquez, J. A. *Compartment Analysis in Biology and Medicine.* Amsterdam, London, and New York: Elsevier, 1972.

Winkle, R. A., S. A. Glantz, and D. C. Harrison. Pharmacologic Therapy of Ventricular Arrhythmias, *Am. J. Cardiol.* 36 (1975): 629.

*Nonlinear Differential Equations Applied to Biological Problems*

Riggs, D. S. *Control Theory and Physiological Feedback Mechanisms.* Chapter 6, Nonlinear Systems, and Chapter 7, The Analysis of Nonlinear Feedback Systems in the Steady State. Baltimore: Williams and Wilkins, 1970.

*Michaelis-Menten Reaction*

Bartholomay, A. F. Chemical Kinetics and Enzyme Kinetics. In *Foundations of Mathematical Biology, Volume I: Subcellular Systems,* ed. R. Rosen. New York: Academic Press, 1972.

# 4

# LAPLACE TRANSFORM METHODS
# FOR SOLVING LINEAR
# DIFFERENTIAL EQUATIONS

The methods used to solve constant-coefficient linear differential equations introduced in Chapter 3 can be quite involved, especially when a set of first-order equations most simply describes the phenomena under study or when discontinuous or impulsive inputs occur. For example, to solve the two-compartment drug distribution problem, we had to combine into one second-order differential equation the two first-order equations which described each compartment's mass balance, find two fundamental solutions and a particular solution, add them, and finally, evaluate two arbitrary constants. In addition, since we lacked a mathematical formalism for a bolus (impulse) injection, we had to place the drug in the central compartment as an initial condition rather than considering it as part of the forcing function (i.e., an impulse injection into a previously empty compartment). This procedure worked, but would prove cumbersome for predicting concentrations following multiple injections. In contrast, the Laplace transform, which converts linear constant-coefficient ordinary differential equations into algebraic equations, easily treats these problems. We will solve the resulting algebraic equations, then transform the result back to the original variables to obtain the final answer. This straightforward process finds and adds the homogeneous and particular solutions, and incorporates the initial conditions in a single step. In addition, Laplace transform methods easily treat problems with impulsive or discontinuous forcing functions or phenomena best described by a set of differential equations, such as drug-distribution problems.

By definition*, the *Laplace transform* of a piecewise-continuous function $f(t)$ is

$$\mathscr{L}\{f(t)\} = F(s) = \int_0^\infty e^{-st} f(t)\, dt \tag{4.1}$$

where $s$ is a complex variable. (Strictly speaking, since Equation (4.1) requires integration to infinity, it may not have a finite value for all $s$, so one must restrict its use to those $s$ for which it exists as a finite-valued function. Such $s$ values comprise (4.1)'s *region of convergence*. We will later specify this region for completeness, but it presents no practical restriction in solving the problems which we will now address. (One may always assume that one is in the region of convergence.) Equation (4.1) also illustrates the convention of denoting a function with a small letter and its Laplace transform with the corresponding capital letter.

One can show that a Laplace transform's *inverse* is

$$f(t) = \mathscr{L}^{-1}\{F(s)\} = \frac{1}{2\pi i} \int_{a-i\infty}^{a+i\infty} e^{st} F(s)\, ds \tag{4.2}$$

The computation of this integral requires advanced techniques, so rather than finding inverse transforms with (4.2), we will compute forward transforms with (4.1) and tabulate them, then use this table to look up inverses.

## BASIC PROPERTIES OF THE LAPLACE TRANSFORM

Four theorems insure that a unique Laplace transform exists for all but one function we will encounter (the impulse, which we will treat separately), and these set the stage for our use of transforms to solve differential equations.

> *If $f(t)$ has a most finite number of discontinuities in the interval $0 < t < t_A$ for any positive $t_A$, and if $|f(t)| < Me^{at}$ when $t > t_B$, where $t_A, t_B$, and $M$ are real constants, the Laplace transform $\mathscr{L}\{f(t)\} = F(s)$, defined by*
>
> $$\mathscr{L}\{f(t)\} = F(s) = \int_0^\infty e^{-st} f(t)\, dt \tag{4.3}$$
>
> *exists and is unique for all $s > a$.*

---

\* Chapter 6 derives the Laplace transform and its inverse from the Fourier transform, which may be interpreted as a spectrum.

We will not prove this theorem, but note that this integral exists for increasing (or decreasing) functions so long as they do not increase too fast; such functions are of *exponential order*. Except for the impulse, all functions which we will encounter are of exponential order.

*The Laplace transform is a linear transformation.*

To prove this theorem, we show that it obeys the superposition principle.

$$\mathscr{L}\{\alpha f_1(t) + \beta f_2(t)\} = \int_0^\infty e^{-st}[\alpha f_1(t) + \beta f_2(t)] \; dt \tag{4.4}$$

$$= \alpha \int_0^\infty e^{-st} f_1(t) \; dt + \beta \int_0^\infty e^{-st} f_2(t) \; dt \tag{4.5}$$

$$\mathscr{L}\{\alpha f_1(t) + \beta f_2(t)\} = \alpha \mathscr{L}\{f_1(t)\} + \beta \mathscr{L}\{f_2(t)\} \tag{4.6}$$

To transform derivatives we prove

*If $f(t)$ is continuous and of exponential order for all $t > 0$, and if $f'(t)$ is Laplace-transformable for $t > 0$, then, for $s > a$,*

$$\mathscr{L}\{f'(t)\} = s\mathscr{L}\{f(t)\} - f(0) \tag{4.7}$$

By definition,

$$\mathscr{L}\{f'(t)\} = \int_0^\infty e^{-st} f'(t) \; dt \tag{4.8}$$

Let $u = e^{-st}$ and $v = f$ in Formula 3 of Appendix B; then $du = -se^{st} \, dt$ and $dv = f'(t) \, dt$, so (4.8) becomes

$$\mathscr{L}\{f'(t)\} = e^{-st} \cdot f \Big|_0^\infty + s \int_0^\infty e^{-st} f(t) \; dt \tag{4.9}$$

$$= \lim_{t \to \infty} e^{-st} f(t) - e^{-0} f(0) + s\mathscr{L}\{f(t)\} \tag{4.10}$$

The fact that $f(t)$ is of exponential order insures that, for $s > a$, $e^{-st}$ decreases faster than $f(t)$ increases, so $\lim_{t \to \infty} e^{-st} f(t) = 0$, and (4.10) becomes

$$\mathcal{L}\{f'(t)\} = s\mathcal{L}\{f(t)\} - f(0) \qquad (4.11)$$

This theorem permits transforming higher-order derivatives. For example,

$$\mathcal{L}\{f''(t)\} = \mathcal{L}\{[f'(t)]'\} = s\,\mathcal{L}\{f'(t)\} - f'(0) \qquad (4.12)$$

$$= s\{s\mathcal{L}[f(t)] - f(0)\} - f'(0) \qquad (4.13)$$

$$\mathcal{L}\{f''(t)\} = s^2\,\mathcal{L}\{f'(t)\} - sf(0) - f'(0) \qquad (4.14)$$

Similarly,

$$\mathcal{L}\{f'''(t)\} = s^3\,\mathcal{L}\,\{f(t)\} - s^2 f(0) - sf'(0) - f''(0) \qquad (4.15)$$

To transform integrals, we prove

*If f(t) is Laplace-transformable,*

$$\mathcal{L}\left\{\int_0^t f(\tau)\,d\tau\right\} = \frac{1}{s}\mathcal{L}\{f(t)\} \qquad \text{when } s > 0 \text{ and } s > a \qquad (4.16)$$

Let

$$g(t) = \int_0^t f(\tau)\,d\tau \qquad (4.17)$$

To show that its Laplace transform exists, we must show that $g(t)$ is piecewise-continuous and of exponential order. Since $f(t)$ is piecewise-continuous, $g(t)$ is continuous. To show that $g(t)$ is of exponential order,

$$g(t) = \int_0^t f(\tau)\,d\tau \leqslant \int_0^t |f(\tau)|\,d\tau \leqslant \int_0^t Me^{at}\,dt$$

$$= \frac{M}{a}(e^{at} - 1) < \frac{M}{a}e^{at} \qquad (4.18)$$

if $a > 0$. Thus, $g(t)$ is of exponential order. Furthermore $g'(t) = f(t)$ except where $f(t)$ is discontinuous, so $g(t)$ is piecewise-continuous and hence Laplace-transformable. Finally,

$$\mathscr{L}\{g'(t)\} = \mathscr{L}\{f(t)\} \tag{4.19}$$

and, by the previous theorem,

$$s\mathscr{L}\{g(t)\} - g(0) = \mathscr{L}\{f(t)\} \tag{4.20}$$

But $g(t) = \int_0^t f(\tau)\,d\tau$, so $g(0) = 0$ and (4.20) yields

$$\mathscr{L}\left\{\int_0^t f(\tau)\,d\tau\right\} = \frac{1}{s}\,\mathscr{L}\{f(t)\} \tag{4.21}$$

Now, suppose we wish to solve

$$a_2 y'' + a_1 y' + a_0 y = f(t) \qquad a_2, a_1, a_0 = \text{constants} \tag{4.22}$$

with initial conditions

$$y(0) = y_0 \qquad y'(0) = y_0' \tag{4.23}$$

Apply the Laplace transform to both sides of (4.22):

$$\mathscr{L}\{a_2 y'' + a_1 y' + a_0 y\} = \mathscr{L}\{f(t)\} \tag{4.24}$$

Since the Laplace transform is linear,

$$a_2\,\mathscr{L}\{y''\} + a_1\,\mathscr{L}\{y'\} + a_0\,\mathscr{L}\{y\} = \mathscr{L}\{f(t)\} \tag{4.25}$$

and, using the rules for transforms of derivatives,

$$a_2 s^2\,\mathscr{L}\{y\} - a_2 s y(0) - a_2 y'(0) + a_1 s\,\mathscr{L}\{y\} - a_1 y(0) + a_0\,\mathscr{L}\{y\}$$

$$= \mathscr{L}\{f(t)\} = F(s) \tag{4.26}$$

Substitute from (4.23) into (4.26) and rearrange:

$$\mathscr{L}\{y\} = \frac{F(s) + (a_2 s + a_1)y_0 + a_2 y_0'}{a_2 s^2 + a_1 s + a_0} \tag{4.27}$$

Therefore,

$$y(t) = \mathcal{L}^{-1}\left\{\frac{F(s) + (a_2 s + a_1)y_0 + a_2 y_0'}{a_2 s^2 + a_1 s + a_0}\right\} \tag{4.28}$$

(Note the fundamental equation, with $s$ replacing $\lambda$, in the denominator.) Since $f(t)$ is a known function of $t$, $\mathcal{L}\{f(t)\} = F(s)$ is a known function of $s$, and $y_0$ and $y_0'$ are given; therefore the expression in brackets is a known function of $s$. Thus, we could look up the function in brackets in a table of transforms to find its inverse transform $y(t)$. This result is (4.22)'s solution with the initial conditions in (4.23). Note that the Laplace transform reduced the problem to one of algebra and automatically included the initial conditions without having first to find the fundamental and particular solutions and evaluate the arbitrary constants with the initial conditions. Now, let us develop a table of Laplace transforms.

## IMPORTANT LAPLACE TRANSFORM PAIRS

We can readily compute the Laplace transforms for several important functions. Each function and its transform constitute a transform *pair*.

*Pair 1*

$$\mathcal{L}\{e^{-at}\} = \frac{1}{s+a} \qquad s > a \tag{4.29}$$

By definition,

$$\mathcal{L}\{e^{-at}\} = \int_0^\infty e^{-st}e^{-at}\,dt = \int_0^\infty e^{-(s+a)t}\,dt \tag{4.30}$$

$$= -\frac{1}{s+a}e^{-(s+a)t}\Big|_0^\infty$$

if $s > a$, $-(s+a) < 0$ and $\lim_{t \to \infty} e^{-(s+a)t} = 0$, so (4.30) becomes

$$\mathcal{L}\{e^{-at}\} = \frac{1}{s+a} \tag{4.31}$$

*Pair 2*

$$\mathscr{L}\{\sin \omega t\} = \frac{\omega}{s^2 + \omega^2} \tag{4.32}$$

In Chapter 3 we derived the Cauchy formulae ($e^{ix} = \cos x + i \sin x$, and $e^{-ix} = \cos x - i \sin x$) which show that $\sin x = (e^{ix} - e^{-ix})/(2i)$, so

$$\mathscr{L}\{\sin \omega t\} = \mathscr{L}\left\{\frac{e^{i\omega t} - e^{-i\omega t}}{2i}\right\} = \frac{1}{2i} \mathscr{L}\{e^{i\omega t}\} - \frac{1}{2i} \mathscr{L}\{e^{-i\omega t}\}$$

$$\tag{4.33}$$

Use (4.29) with (4.33) to obtain

$$\mathscr{L}\{\sin \omega t\} = \frac{1}{2i} \frac{1}{s - i\omega} - \frac{1}{2i} \frac{1}{s + i\omega} = \frac{1}{2i} \frac{2i\omega}{s^2 + \omega^2} = \frac{\omega}{s^2 + \omega^2}$$

$$\tag{4.34}$$

*Pair 3*

$$\mathscr{L}\{\cos \omega t\} = \frac{s}{s^2 + \omega^2} \tag{4.35}$$

The Cauchy formulae show that $\cos x = (e^{ix} + e^{-ix})/2$, so

$$\mathscr{L}\{\cos \omega t\} = \mathscr{L}\left\{\frac{e^{i\omega t} + e^{-i\omega t}}{2}\right\} = \frac{1}{2}\left(\frac{1}{s - i\omega} + \frac{1}{s + i\omega}\right) \tag{4.36}$$

$$= \frac{1}{2} \frac{2s}{s^2 + \omega^2} = \frac{s}{s^2 + \omega^2} \tag{4.37}$$

*Pair 4*

$$\mathscr{L}\{1\} = \frac{1}{s} \tag{4.38}$$

Since $1 = e^0 = e^{0t}$,

$$\mathscr{L}\{1\} = \mathscr{L}\{e^{0t}\} = \frac{1}{s + 0} = \frac{1}{s} \tag{4.39}$$

*Pair 5*

$$\mathcal{L}\{t^n\} = \frac{n!}{s^{n+1}} \qquad n = \text{nonnegative integer} \qquad (4.40)$$

By definition,

$$\mathcal{L}\{t^n\} = \int_0^\infty t^n e^{-st}\, dt \qquad s > 0 \qquad (4.41)$$

Let $\omega = st$, then (4.41) becomes

$$\mathcal{L}\{t^n\} = \int_0^\infty \left(\frac{\omega}{s}\right)^n e^{-\omega} \frac{d\omega}{s} = \frac{1}{s^{n+1}} \int_0^\infty \omega^n e^{-\omega}\, d\omega \qquad s > 0$$

$$(4.42)$$

This integral frequently arises and, like the infinite series which often represent solutions to second-order differential equations (the sine and cosine), has been named and tabulated. By definition, the *gamma function* (or *generalized factorial function*) (Fig. 4.1) is

$$\Gamma(n) = \int_0^\infty \omega^{n-1} e^{-\omega}\, d\omega \qquad (4.43)$$

Thus

$$\mathcal{L}\{t^n\} = \frac{\Gamma(n+1)}{s^{n+1}} \qquad (4.44)$$

When $n$ is a positive integer $\Gamma(n+1) = n!$,* in which case

$$\mathcal{L}\{t^n\} = \frac{n!}{s^{n+1}} \qquad n = \text{nonnegative integer} \qquad (4.45)$$

* From (4.43),

$$\Gamma(1) = \int_0^\infty \omega^0 e^{-\omega}\, d\omega = \int_0^\infty e^{-\omega}\, d\omega = -e^{-\omega}\,\Big|_0^\infty = 1$$

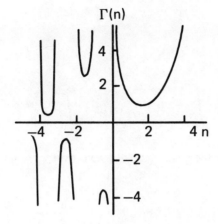

$\Gamma(n)$

**FIGURE 4.1:** The gamma (or generalized factorial) function.

*Pair 6*

If $\mathscr{L}\{f(t)\} = F(s)$ when $s > \alpha$, then $\mathscr{L}\{e^{-\alpha t}f(t)\} = F(s - \alpha)$

$$(4.46)$$

This pair, called the *first shifting theorem,* states that substituting $(s - \alpha)$ for $s$ in a transform corresponds to multiplying the original function by $e^{-\alpha t}$. By definition

---

To find $\Gamma(n + 1)$, use Formula 3 of Appendix B with $u = e^{-\omega}$ and $v = \dfrac{1}{n + 1}\,\omega^{n+1}$. In this case $du = e^{-\omega}\,d\omega$ and $dv = \omega^n\,d\omega$, so

$$\int_0^{\infty} \omega^n e^{-\omega}\,d\omega = \int u\,dv = uv - \int v\,du = e^{-\omega}\,\frac{\omega^{n+1}}{n+1}\,\bigg|_0^{\infty} + \int_0^{\infty} \frac{\omega^{n+1}}{n+1}\,e^{-\omega}\,d\omega$$

$$= 0 - 0 + \frac{1}{n+1}\int_0^{\infty} \omega^{n+1} e^{-\omega}\,d\omega$$

Use (4.43) with this equation to obtain the recursive relationship

$$\Gamma(n + 1) = \frac{1}{n + 1}\,\Gamma(n + 2)$$

Let $N = n + 1$, then $\Gamma(N + 1) = N \cdot \Gamma(N)$, and since $\Gamma(1) = 1$

$$\Gamma(1) = 1 = 0!$$
$$\Gamma(2) = 1 \cdot \Gamma(1) = 1 \cdot 1 = 1 = 1!$$
$$\Gamma(3) = 2 \cdot \Gamma(2) = 2 \cdot 1 = 2 = 2!$$
$$\Gamma(4) = 3 \cdot \Gamma(3) = 3 \cdot 2! = 3!$$
$$\Gamma(5) = 4 \cdot \Gamma(4) = 4 \cdot 3! = 4!$$
$$\Gamma(n + 1) = n!$$

$$\mathcal{L}\{f(t)\} = F(s) = \int_0^\infty e^{-st} f(t)\, dt \tag{4.47}$$

so

$$F(s + \alpha) = \int_0^\infty e^{-(s+\alpha)t} f(t)\, dt = \int_0^\infty e^{-st} e^{-\alpha t} f(t)\, dt \tag{4.48}$$

The first shifting theorem, combined with pairs 2, 3, and 5, yields these useful results:

$$\mathcal{L}\{e^{-\alpha t} \sin \omega t\} = \frac{\omega}{(s + \alpha)^2 + \omega^2} \tag{4.49}$$

$$\mathcal{L}\{e^{-\alpha t} \cos \omega t\} = \frac{s + \alpha}{(s + \alpha)^2 + \omega^2} \tag{4.50}$$

$$\mathcal{L}\{t^n e^{-\alpha t}\} = \frac{n!}{(s + \alpha)^{n+1}} \tag{4.51}$$

Table 4.1 summarizes our results. (Appendix D is a more extensive table.) Now, let us use Table 4.1 to solve two differential equations. (Re-solve each problem using the methods in Chapter 3, and compare the amount of work involved.)

1. $\ddot{y} + 3y = 0$   $y(0) = -1,$   $\dot{y}(0) = 1$   (4.52)

$$\mathcal{L}\{\ddot{y} + 3y\} = \mathcal{L}\{0\} \tag{4.53}$$

$$s^2 Y(s) - sy(0) - y'(0) + 3Y(s) = 0 \tag{4.54}$$

so

$$Y(s) = \frac{-s + 1}{s^2 + 3} \tag{4.55}$$

and

$$y(t) = \mathcal{L}^{-1}\{Y(s)\} = \mathcal{L}^{-1}\left\{\frac{-s + 1}{s^2 + 3}\right\} \tag{4.56}$$

**TABLE 4.1**  Laplace Transform Pairs

| $f(t) = \mathcal{L}^{-1}\{F(s)\}$ | $F(s) = \mathcal{L}\{f(t)\}$ | |
|---|---|---|
| 1. $1$ | $\dfrac{1}{s}$ | |
| 2. $e^{-\alpha t}$ | $\dfrac{1}{s + \alpha}$ | |
| 3. $\sin \omega t$ | $\dfrac{\omega}{s^2 + \omega^2}$ | |
| 4. $\cos \omega t$ | $\dfrac{s}{s^2 + \omega^2}$ | |
| 5. $t^n$ | $\begin{cases} \dfrac{n!}{s^{n+1}} \\[2mm] \dfrac{\Gamma(n+1)}{s^{n+1}} \end{cases}$ | $\begin{array}{l} n = \text{non-negative integer} \\[2mm] n > -1 \end{array}$ |
| 6. $t^n e^{-\alpha t}$ | $\dfrac{n!}{(s+\alpha)^{n+1}}$ | $n = \text{non-negative integer}$ |
| 7. $e^{-\alpha t} \sin \omega t$ | $\dfrac{\omega}{(s+\alpha)^2 + \omega^2}$ | |
| 8. $e^{-\alpha t} \cos \omega t$ | $\dfrac{s + \alpha}{(s + \alpha)^2 + \omega^2}$ | |
| 9. $f'(t)$ | $s\,F(s) - f(0)$ | |
| 10. $f^{(n)}(t)$ | $s^n F(s) - s^{n-1} f(0) - \ldots - f^{(n-1)}(0)$ | |
| 11. $\displaystyle\int_0^t f(\tau)\,d\tau$ | $\dfrac{1}{s}F(s)$ | |

To use Table 4.1, break (4.56) down into a sum of fractions included in the table.

$$y(t) = \mathcal{L}^{-1}\left\{\frac{-s + 1}{s^2 + 3}\right\} = -\mathcal{L}^{-1}\left\{\frac{s}{s^2 + 3}\right\} + \frac{1}{\sqrt{3}}\,\mathcal{L}^{-1}\left\{\frac{\sqrt{3}}{s^2 + 3}\right\}$$

$$(4.57)$$

$$y(t) = -\cos 3t + \frac{\sqrt{3}}{3}\sin 3t \qquad (4.58)$$

2. $\dddot{c} + 5\ddot{c} + 8\dot{c} + 6c = 4e^{-t/2}$ $\qquad$ $c(0) = \dot{c}(0) = \ddot{c}(0) = 0$ $\qquad$ (4.59)

Transforming the equation yields

$$[s^3 C(s) - s^2 c(0) - s\dot{c}(0) - \ddot{c}(0)]$$

$$+ 5[s^2 C(s) - sc(0) - \dot{c}(0)] + 8[sC(s) - c(0)] + 6C(s) = 4\frac{1}{s + \dfrac{1}{2}}$$

(4.60)

Substitute in the initial conditions and rearrange terms to obtain

$$C(s) \cdot [s^3 + 5s^2 + 8s + 6] = \frac{4}{s + \dfrac{1}{2}} \qquad (4.61)$$

hence

$$C(s) = \frac{4}{(s^3 + 5s^2 + 8s + 6)\left(s + \dfrac{1}{2}\right)} \qquad (4.62)$$

To use Table 4.1 we must break (4.62) into entries which appear in the table. To do so, first factor the denominator,

$$C(s) = \frac{4}{(s + 1)(s + 2)(s + 3)\left(s + \dfrac{1}{2}\right)} \qquad (4.63)$$

then find the sum of fractions of the form $a_1/(s + a_2)$ which equals (4.62). (Since the first polynomial in (4.62)'s denominator is the fundamental equation associated with this problem, finding its factors is equivalent to finding the differential equation's eigenvalues.)

$$C(s) = \frac{4}{(s + 1)(s + 2)(s + 3)\left(s + \dfrac{1}{2}\right)} = \frac{-4}{s + 1} + \frac{\dfrac{8}{3}}{s + 2} + \frac{\dfrac{-4}{5}}{s + 3} + \frac{\dfrac{32}{15}}{s + \dfrac{1}{2}}$$

(4.64)

Since $\mathscr{L}\{e^{-\alpha t}\} = 1/(s + \alpha)$,

$$c(t) = \mathscr{L}^{-1}\{C(s)\} = -8e^{-t} + \left(\frac{8}{3}\right)e^{-2t} - \left(\frac{4}{5}\right)e^{-3t} + \left(\frac{16}{15}\right)e^{-t/2}$$

$$(4.65)$$

Since expanding (4.64) into *partial fractions* is a key computational step, we next turn to developing a simple, systematic way to do it.

## PROBLEM SET 4.1

Find the Laplace transforms of these functions:

1. $5t + 3$

2. $at + b$

3. $t^2 + 2t + 1$

4. $7e^{2t}$

5. $c_0 e^{-t/\tau}$

6. $\sin t$

7. $Ae^{-\zeta\omega_n t} \sin(\omega_n \sqrt{1 - \zeta^2}\, t)$

8. $B \cos(\omega t - \phi)$

9. $\displaystyle\int_0^t x^n \, dx$

10. $\dfrac{t^{n+1}}{(n + 1)}$

11. Show that $\mathscr{L}^{-1}\{F(s)\}$ is a linear transformation.

Invert these Laplace transforms:

12. $\dfrac{1}{s^3}$

13. $\dfrac{2}{(s - 3)^2 + 4}$

14. $\dfrac{3s + 5}{(s + 1)(s + 3)}$

15. $\dfrac{100}{s^2 + 25}$

16. $\dfrac{2(s + 6)}{s^2 + 12s + 37} - \dfrac{1}{s + 1}$

## PARTIAL FRACTIONS

When solving differential equations with Laplace transforms, one commonly encounters the form

$$Y(s) = \frac{N(s)}{D(s)} \tag{4.66}$$

where $N(s)$ and $D(s)$ are polynomials in $s$, with $N(s)$ of lower order than $D(s)$. To use a table of transforms to find $y(t) = \mathscr{L}^{-1}\{Y(s)\}$, one must generally break $N(s)/D(s)$ into an equivalent sum of partial fractions which appear in the table. In essence, this process is the reverse of finding the least common denominator in fraction addition. For example, to compute the sum

$$Y(s) = \frac{N(s)}{D(s)} = \frac{1}{s} + \frac{1}{s + 1} + \frac{3}{s + 4} + \frac{4}{(s + 4)^2} \tag{4.67}$$

one would first find that $s(s + 1)(s + 4)^2$ is the common denominator, then rewrite each fraction as a fraction of $s(s + 1)(s + 4)^2$ and add the numerators:

$$Y(s) = \frac{1(s + 1)(s + 4)^2}{s(s + 1)(s + 4)^2} + \frac{1(s)(s + 4)^2}{s(s + 1)(s + 4)^2} + \frac{3(s)(s + 1)(s + 4)}{s(s + 1)(s + 4)^2}$$

$$+ \frac{4(s)(s + 1)}{s(s + 1)(s + 4)^2} \tag{4.68}$$

$$Y(s) = \frac{5s^3 + 41s^2 + 56s + 16}{s(s + 1)(s + 4)^2} \tag{4.69}$$

$$Y(s) = \frac{5s^3 + 41s^2 + 56s + 16}{s^4 + 8s^3 + 24s^2 + 16s} \tag{4.70}$$

Equation (4.70) could well arise when solving a fourth-order differential equation using Laplace transforms. While it does not appear in our transform table, we could use the equivalent equation, (4.67), with the table to find

$$y(t) = \mathcal{L}^{-1} \left\{ \frac{1}{s} + \frac{1}{s+1} + \frac{3}{s+4} + \frac{4}{(s+4)^2} \right\} = 1 + e^{-t} + 3e^{-4t} + 4te^{-4t}$$

(4.71)

We shall now develop systematic methods for breaking equations like (4.66) into a sum of partial fractions which appear in the transform table.

The first step to finding a partial fraction for $N(s)/D(s)$ is to factor $D(s)$ into linear terms of the form $(s + \alpha_i)$. If all the factors are distinct, $D(s)$ can be factored into a product of nonrepeating linear factors, so

$$Y(s) = \frac{N(s)}{D(s)} = \frac{N(s)}{(s + \alpha_1)(s + \alpha_2) \ldots (s + \alpha_n)}$$

$$= \frac{A_1}{s + \alpha_1} + \frac{A_2}{s + \alpha_2} + \ldots + \frac{A_n}{s + \alpha_n}$$

(4.72)

where $A_1, A_2, \ldots, A_n$ are constants, which makes (4.72) an identity that holds for all values of $s$.

Suppose we wish to break

$$Y(s) = \frac{N(s)}{D(s)} = \frac{1}{s^2 + 6s + 5}$$

(4.73)

into partial fractions. Since $s^2 + 6s + 5 = (s + 5)(s + 1)$, we want to find $A_1$ and $A_2$ to make

$$Y(s) = \frac{1}{s^2 + 6s + 5} = \frac{1}{(s+5)(s+1)} = \frac{A_1}{s+5} + \frac{A_2}{s+1}$$

(4.74)

hold for all $s$. Put the sum on the right over the common denominator, $(s + 5)(s + 1)$:

$$Y(s) = \frac{1}{(s+5)(s+1)} = \frac{A_1(s+1) + A_2(s+5)}{(s+5)(s+1)} = \frac{(A_1 + A_2)s + (A_1 + 5A_2)}{(s+5)(s+1)}$$

(4.75)

For (4.75) to hold for all $s$, the coefficients of each power of $s$ must be equal, so

$$s^1 \text{ coefficient: } 0 = A_1 + A_2 \qquad (4.76)$$

$$s^0 \text{ coefficient: } 1 = A_1 + 5A_2 \qquad (4.77)$$

Equations (4.76) and (4.77) provide two linear algebraic equations in the two unknown coefficients $A_1$ and $A_2$ that require $A_1 = -1/4$ and $A_2 = 1/4$. Therefore

$$Y(s) = \frac{-\dfrac{1}{4}}{s + 5} + \frac{\dfrac{1}{4}}{s + 1} \qquad (4.78)$$

Alternatively, we could multiply both sides of (4.74) by $(s + 5)$ to obtain:

$$(s + 5) \frac{1}{(s + 5)(s + 1)} = (s + 5) \frac{A_1}{(s + 5)} + (s + 5) \frac{A_2}{(s + 1)} \qquad (4.79)$$

$$\frac{1}{s + 1} = A_1 + \frac{(s + 5)}{(s + 1)} A_2 \qquad (4.80)$$

Since (4.74), and therefore (4.80), must hold for *all* values of $s$, it must hold for $s = -5$,* in which case (4.80) becomes

$$\frac{1}{-5 + 1} = A_1 + \frac{(-5 + 5)}{(-5 + 1)} A_2 = A_1 + 0A_2 \qquad (4.81)$$

so $A_1 = -1/4$. Likewise, we could multiply both sides of (4.74) by $(s + 1)$ and set $s = -1$ to obtain $A_2 = 1/4$. (Do it.) In sum, if $D(s)$ has distinct roots, it can be factored into the form of equation (4.72) in which

$$A_i = (s + \alpha_i) \frac{N(s)}{D(s)} \bigg|_{s = -\alpha_i} \qquad (4.82)$$

---

* Strictly speaking, one cannot substitute $s = -5$ into (4.80) and proceed to equation (4.81) because we are essentially multiplying both sides of (4.79) by zero, then concluding that the numerators are equal. To be rigorous, we should talk about limits as $s \to -5$. Heaviside showed that this limiting process produces no surprises and that the direct substitution outlined here works.

As a second example, let us break

$$Y(s) = \frac{s^2 + 2s - 1}{s^3 - s} \tag{4.83}$$

into partial fractions. Since $s^3 - s = s(s + 1)(s - 1)$, the roots of the denominator are distinct, and we want to find $A_1, A_2$, and $A_3$ that satisfy

$$Y(s) = \frac{s^2 + 2s - 1}{s(s + 1)(s - 1)} = \frac{A_1}{s} + \frac{A_2}{s + 1} + \frac{A_3}{s - 1} \tag{4.84}$$

From (4.82):

$$A_1 = s \cdot \frac{s^2 + 2s - 1}{s(s + 1)(s - 1)} \bigg|_{s=0} = \frac{s^2 + 2s - 1}{(s + 1)(s - 1)} \bigg|_{s=0} = \frac{0 + 2 \cdot 0 - 1}{(0 + 1)(0 - 1)} = 1$$

$$\tag{4.85}$$

$$A_2 = (s + 1) \cdot \frac{s^2 + 2s - 1}{s(s + 1)(s - 1)} \bigg|_{s=-1} = \frac{s^2 + 2s - 1}{s(s - 1)} \bigg|_{s=-1} = -1$$

$$\tag{4.86}$$

$$A_3 = (s - 1) \frac{s^2 + 2s - 1}{s(s + 1)(s - 1)} \bigg|_{s=1} = \frac{s^2 + 2s - 1}{s + 1} \bigg|_{s=1} = 1$$

$$\tag{4.87}$$

Therefore,

$$Y(s) = \frac{s^2 + 2s - 1}{s^3 - s} = \frac{1}{s} - \frac{1}{s + 1} + \frac{1}{s - 1} \tag{4.88}$$

Factors which appear as complex conjugate pairs are still distinct, so one could use equation (4.82) to find a partial fraction expansion in terms of linear factors. This process would produce a solution (upon in-verting the Laplace transforms) which includes a pair of exponential functions with complex exponents equivalent to a sum of sine and cosine functions. Sometimes it may be convenient not to factor quadratics with complex roots, but rather to deal with them directly. When such quadratics appear as part of a larger partial-fraction expansion problem, treat the real linear terms as before, but leave the quadratics which lead to complex factors alone.

For example, we solve

$$\ddot{z} + 2\dot{z} + 2z = 0 \qquad z(0) = 1 \qquad \dot{z}(0) = 1 \qquad (4.89)$$

If $\mathcal{L}\{z(t)\} - Z(s)$

$$[s^2 Z(s) - s \cdot z(0) - z(0)] + 2[sZ(s) - z(0)] + 2Z(s) = 0 \quad (4.90)$$

so

$$Z(s) = \frac{s + 3}{s^2 + 2s + 2} \qquad (4.91)$$

Rather than expanding (4.91) in partial fractions of the form $A_i/(s + \alpha_i)$, manipulate it into the transforms of sines and cosines:

$$Z(s) = \frac{s + 1}{(s + 1)^2 + 1^2} + \frac{2}{(s + 1)^2 + 1^2} \qquad (4.92)$$

From the table of transforms,

$$z(t) = \mathcal{L}^{-1}\left\{\frac{s + 1}{(s + 1)^2 + 1^2}\right\} + 2\mathcal{L}^{-1}\left\{\frac{1}{(s + 1)^2 + 1}\right\}$$

$$= e^{-t}(\cos t + 2 \sin t) \qquad (4.93)$$

(Solve this problem by expanding (4.91) in partial fractions of the form $A_1/[s + (-1 + i)] + A_2/[s + (-1 - i)]$, and show that you get the same answer.)

When $D(s)$ contains a factor repeated $m$ times, this factor contributes $m$ terms to the partial-fraction expansion. To understand why, note that the term $(s + 4)^2$ in (4.69)'s denominator followed from both $3/(s + 4)$ and $4/(s + 4)^2$ in (4.67). In general, the term $(s - \alpha)^m$ in $D(s)$ will give use to $m$ terms in a partial-fraction expansion:

$$\frac{N(s)}{D(s)} = \frac{N(s)}{(s + \alpha)^m} = \frac{A_m}{(s + \alpha)^m} + \frac{A_{m-1}}{(s + \alpha)^{m-1}} + \ldots + \frac{A_1}{(s + \alpha)} \quad (4.94)$$

To find a simple formula for $A_m, A_{m-1}, \ldots, A$, analogous to (4.82), let us begin with an example:

$$\frac{N(s)}{D(s)} = \frac{s + 1}{(s + 2)^3} = \frac{A_3}{(s + 2)^3} + \frac{A_2}{(s + 2)^2} + \frac{A_1}{(s + 2)} \quad (4.95)$$

To follow a procedure analogous to that we used to motivate (4.82), multiply both sides of (4.95) by $(s + 2)^3$:

$$(s + 2)^3 \frac{s + 1}{(s + 2)^3} = (s + 2)^3 \frac{A_3}{(s + 2)^3} + (s + 2)^3 \frac{A_2}{(s + 2)^2} + (s + 2)^3 \frac{A_1}{(s + 2)}$$

$$(4.96)$$

$$(s + 1) = A_3 + (s + 2) A_2 + (s + 2)^2 A_1 \quad (4.97)$$

Now, set $s = -2$,

$$-1 = A_3 + 0 \cdot A_2 + 0 \cdot A_1 = A_3 \quad (4.98)$$

If, however, we used the analogous procedure to find $A_2$, we would multiply (4.95) by $(s + 2)^2$ and set $s = -2$ to obtain

$$(s + 2)^2 \frac{(s + 1)}{(s + 2)^3} = (s + 2)^2 \frac{A_3}{(s + 2)^3} + (s + 2)^2 \frac{A_2}{(s + 2)^2} + (s + 2)^2 \frac{A_1}{(s + 2)}$$

$$(4.99)$$

$$\left. \frac{s + 1}{s + 2} \right|_{s=-2} = \left. \frac{A_3}{s + 2} \right|_{s=-2} + A_2 + (s + 2)A_1 \Big|_{s=-2} \quad (4.100)$$

$$\frac{-1}{0} = \frac{A_3}{0} + A_2 + 0 \cdot A \quad (4.101)$$

and it is not permissible to divide by zero. We can reduce the order of the term in the denominator and avoid this problem by differentiating (4.97) with respect to $s$, then setting $s = -2$ in the result.

$$1 = A_2 + s(s + 2)A_1 \tag{4.102}$$

$$1 = A_2 + (-2)(0)A_1 = A_2 \tag{4.103}$$

To find $A_1$, we differentiate (4.102) with respect to $s$ and set $s = -2$

$$0 = 2A_1 \qquad A_1 = 0 \tag{4.104}$$

Therefore if a factor $(s + \alpha)$ is repeated $m$ times $D(s)$, we find the $A_i$'s in (4.94) with the formulae

$$A_m = \left[ (s + \alpha)^m \frac{N(s)}{D(s)} \right]_{s=-\alpha}$$

$$A_{m-1} = \frac{d}{ds} \left[ (s + \alpha)^m \frac{N(s)}{D(s)} \right]_{s=-\alpha} \tag{4.105}$$

$$A_{m-2} = \frac{1}{2!} \frac{d^2}{ds^2} \left[ (s + \alpha)^m \frac{N(s)}{D(s)} \right]_{s=-\alpha}$$

$$\vdots$$

or, in general,

$$A_i = \frac{1}{(m - i)!} \frac{d^{m-i}}{ds^{m-i}} \left[ (s + \alpha)^m \frac{N(s)}{D(s)} \right]_{s=-\alpha} \tag{4.106}$$

## PROBLEM SET 4.2

1. Show that $\mathscr{L}^{-1} \left\{ \dfrac{\omega}{(s^2 + \omega^2)^2} \right\} = \dfrac{1}{2\omega^2} (\sin \omega t - \omega t \cos \omega t)$.

Invert these Laplace transforms:

2. $\dfrac{3s + 5}{s^2 + 3s + 2}$

3. $\dfrac{s + 1}{s^2 + 1}$

4. $\dfrac{4s + 3}{\left(s + \dfrac{1}{2}\right)^2}$

5. $\dfrac{s^2 + 2s + 25}{(s^2 - 2s + 17)(s + 2)}$

6. $\dfrac{6s^2 + 17s + 6}{s^3 + 5s^2 + 6s}$

Solve problems 1 through 8 in Problem Set 3.7 using Laplace transforms. Compare the amount of work required with that required using the direct methods developed in Chapter 3.

## THE UNIT STEP FUNCTION

To describe processes which suddenly begin or end, such as a constant infusion, we define the *unit step* function,

$$u(t) = \begin{cases} 0 & t < 0 \\ 1 & t \geq 0 \end{cases} \qquad (4.107)$$

which equals zero until its argument reaches zero, then jumps to one and remains there (Fig. 4.2). Suppose we wish to study a problem in which $g(t) = 0$ for $t < 0$ and $g(t) = \sin t$ for $t \geq 0$. We can describe this situation compactly with $g(t) = u(t) \sin t$ (Fig. 4.3A). The unit-step function can also be used to shift another function along the time axis. Since $u(t - t_0)$ equals zero until $t = t_0$ and one thereafter, $u(t - t_0) \sin (t - t_0)$ represents Figure 4.3A's sine wave shifted by $t_0$ (Fig. 4.3B), and $[u(t) - u(t - t_0)]$ represents a rectangular pulse between time $t$ and $t_0$ (Fig. 4.4).

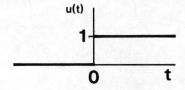

**FIGURE 4.2:** The unit step function defined by equation (4.107).

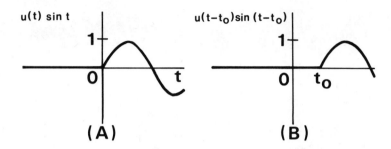

**FIGURE 4.3:** The unit step can be used to turn on or shift another function (in this case, a sinusoid).

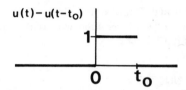

**FIGURE 4.4:** A rectangular pulse written as the sum of two unit step functions.

We now show

$$\mathscr{L}\{u(t - t_0)\} = \frac{e^{-st_0}}{s} \qquad s > 0 \qquad (4.108)$$

By definition,

$$\mathscr{L}\{u(t - t_0)\} = \int_0^\infty e^{-st} u(t - t_0)\, dt$$

$$= \int_0^{t_0} e^{-st} \cdot 0 \, dt + \int_{t_0}^\infty e^{-st} \cdot 1 \, dt \qquad (4.109)$$

$$\mathscr{L}\{u(t - t_0)\} = -\left. \frac{e^{-st}}{s} \right|_{t_0}^\infty = \frac{e^{-st_0}}{s} \qquad (4.110)$$

Solving practical problems often requires the *second shifting theorem,* which relates a shifted function's transform to the unshifted function's transform:

*If $F(s) = \mathcal{L}\{f(t)\}$ for $s > a \geqslant 0$, and $t$ is a positive constant,*

$$\mathcal{L}\{u(t - t_0) f(t - t_0)\} = e^{-t_0 s} \mathcal{L}\{f(t)\} = e^{-t_0 s} F(s) \qquad s > a$$

(4.111)

By definition,

$$\mathcal{L}\{u(t - t_0) f(t - t_0)\} = \int_0^\infty e^{-st} u(t - t_0) f(t - t_0) \, dt$$

(4.112)

Let $\tau = t - t_0$; then (4.112) becomes

$$\mathcal{L}\{u(t - t_0) f(t - t_0)\} = \int_0^\infty e^{-s(\tau + t_0)} f(\tau) \, d\tau$$

$$= e^{-st_0} \int_0^\infty e^{-s\tau} f(\tau) \, d\tau = e^{-st_0} F(s)$$

(4.113)

To use the unit-step function, we return to the one-compartment drug-distribution problem, now assuming that we administer the drug at a constant rate $I$ (mg/min) beginning at time zero and stopping at time $t_S$, with no drug initially in the compartment. In other words, we wish to solve the differential equation

$$\dot{c} + kc = \left(\frac{I}{V}\right) [u(t) - u(t - t_S)] \qquad c(0) = 0 \qquad (4.114)$$

Equation (4.114)'s Laplace transform is

$$sC(s) - c(0) + kC(s) = \frac{I}{V}\left(\frac{1}{s} - \frac{e^{-st_S}}{s}\right)$$

(4.115)

But $c(0) = 0$, so

$$C(s) = \frac{I}{V}\left[\frac{1}{s(s+k)} - \frac{e^{-st_s}}{s(s+k)}\right]$$    (4.116)

Next, expand $1/[s(s+k)]$ in partial fractions:

$$\frac{1}{s(s+k)} = \frac{A_1}{s} + \frac{A_2}{s+k} = \frac{A_1(s+k) + A_2 s}{s(s+k)} = \frac{\frac{1}{k}}{s} + \frac{\frac{-1}{k}}{s+k}$$    (4.117)

Therefore

$$\mathscr{L}^{-1}\left\{\frac{1}{s(s+k)}\right\} = \frac{1}{k}(1 - e^{-kt})$$    (4.118)

and, by the second shifting theorem,

$$\mathscr{L}^{-1}\left\{\frac{e^{-st_s}}{s(s+k)}\right\} = u(t - t_s)\left\{\frac{1}{k}\left(1 - e^{-k(t-t_s)}\right)\right\}$$    (4.119)

so

$$c(t) = \mathscr{L}^{-1}\{C(s)\} = \frac{I}{kV}(1 - e^{-kt}) - u(t - t_s)\frac{I}{kV}(1 - e^{kt_s}e^{-kt})$$    (4.120)

$$c(t) = \frac{I}{kV}([1 - u(t - t_s)] - e^{-kt}[1 - u(t - t_s)e^{kt_s}])$$    (4.121)

Figure 4.5 shows the solution. (Solve this problem using Chapter 3's methods.)

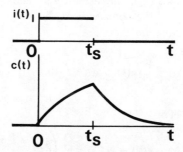

**FIGURE 4.5:** Response of a single compartment to a constant infusion beginning at time zero and stopping at time $t_s$.

## THE UNIT IMPULSE

We shall now develop a mathematical formalism to describe brief, intense phenomena such as the mass-flow rate during a drug bolus injection. We will treat this formalism as if it were a function like the others we have used, even though it is not. The detailed theory required to justify our behavior follows from generalized function theory. Mathematicians have shown that the steps we will take (rather naively, from their point of view) make sense. The result will be a useful *unit impulse* or *delta function.** 

To *define* the unit impulse, suppose (Fig. 4.6A):

$$\delta(t, \tau) = \begin{cases} 1/\tau & 0 < t < \tau \\ \\ 0 & \text{otherwise} \end{cases} \qquad (4.122)$$

Note that

$$\int_{-\infty}^{\infty} \delta(t, \tau)\, dt = \int_{-\infty}^{0} 0\, dt + \int_{0}^{\tau} \frac{1}{\tau}\, dt + \int_{\tau}^{\infty} 0\, dt = \frac{1}{\tau}\tau = 1$$

$$(4.123)$$

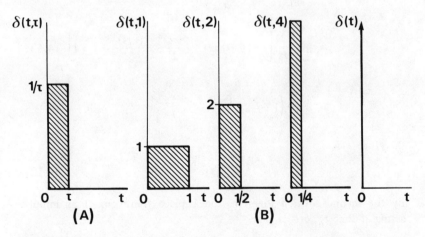

**FIGURE 4.6:** As we make a pulse of fixed-unit area $\delta(t, \tau)$ narrower and narrower and higher and higher, it approaches the unit impulse $\delta(t)$.

* Also called the Dirac delta function, or sampling function.

independent of $\tau$. Now let $\tau$, the time over which $\delta(t, \tau) \neq 0$, decrease toward zero. The rectangle in Figure 4.6A gets narrower and narrower and higher and higher (Fig. 4.6B). In the limit the pulse becomes infinitely high and infinitesimally short. Specifically, define

$$\delta(t) = \lim_{\tau \to 0} \delta(t, \tau) \tag{4.124}$$

Thus $\delta(t) = 0$ for all $t \neq 0$, while $\int_{-\infty}^{\infty} \delta(t)\, dt = 1$.

Since $\delta(t)$ is not of exponential order—it increases too fast—we cannot conclude immediately that it has a unique Laplace transform. However, $\delta(t, \tau)$ is of exponential order, so we can compute

$$\mathcal{L}\{\delta(t, \tau)\} = \int_0^\infty e^{-st}\, \delta(t, \tau)\, dt = \frac{1}{\tau}\int_0^\tau e^{-st}\, dt = \frac{1}{\tau s}(1 - e^{-\tau s})$$

$$\tag{4.125}$$

Since the unit impulse is the limit of a sequence of narrower and narrower finite pulses, we will define its Laplace transform to be the corresponding limit of the sequence of transforms of the finite pulses.

$$\mathcal{L}\{\delta(t)\} = \lim_{\tau \to 0} \mathcal{L}\{\delta(t, \tau)\}\ \lim_{\tau \to 0} \frac{1}{\tau s}(1 - e^{-\tau s}) \tag{4.126}$$

$$= \lim_{\tau \to 0} \frac{1}{\tau s}\left[1 - \left(1 + (-\tau s) + \frac{(-\tau s)^2}{2!} + \frac{(-\tau s)^3}{3!} + \ldots\right)\right] \tag{4.127}$$

$$= \lim_{\tau \to 0} \left(1 - \frac{\tau s}{2!} + \frac{(\tau s)^2}{3!} - \ldots\right) \tag{4.128}$$

therefore

$$\mathcal{L}\{\delta(t)\} = 1 \tag{4.129}$$

By the second shifting theorem, the Laplace transform of an impulse acting at time $t_0$, $\delta(t - t_0)$ is

$$\mathcal{L}\{\delta(t - t_0)\} = e^{-st_0}\ \mathcal{L}\{\delta(t)\} = e^{-st_0} \qquad t_0 \geq 0$$

$$\tag{4.130}$$

$\delta(t)$ can also be used to *sample* the value of another function:

$$\int_{-\infty}^{\infty} \delta(t - t_0) f(t)\, dt = f(t_0) \tag{4.131}$$

To prove (4.131), refer to the definition of $\delta$ as a limit:

$$\int_{-\infty}^{\infty} \delta(t - t_0) f(t)\, dt = \int_{-\infty}^{\infty} \lim_{\tau \to 0} \delta(t, \tau) f(t)\, dt$$

$$= \lim_{\tau \to 0} \int_{t_0}^{t_0 + \tau} \frac{1}{\tau} f(t)\, dt = \lim_{\tau \to 0} \frac{1}{\tau} \int_{t_0}^{t_0 + \tau} f(t)\, dt \tag{4.132}$$

Let $\overline{f}$ and $\underline{f}$ be $f(t)$'s maximum and minimum values in the interval $t_0 \leqslant t \leqslant t_0 + \tau$; then

$$\underline{f} = \lim_{\tau \to 0} \frac{1}{\tau} \underline{f} \int_{t_0}^{t_0 + \tau} dt \leqslant \lim_{\tau \to 0} \frac{1}{\tau} \int_{t_0}^{t_0 + \tau} f(t)\, dt$$

$$\leqslant \lim_{\tau \to 0} \frac{1}{\tau} \overline{f} \int_{t_0}^{t_0 + \tau} dt = \overline{f} \tag{4.133}$$

But $f(t)$ is continuous at $t_0$, so $\lim_{\tau \to 0} (\overline{f} - \underline{f}) = 0$, and $\underline{f}$ and $\overline{f}$ approach $f(t_0)$, and

$$\lim_{\tau \to 0} \int_{t_0}^{t_0 + \tau} f(t)\, dt = f(t_0) = \int_{-\infty}^{\infty} \delta(t - t_0) f(t)\, dt \tag{4.134}$$

Now, let us solve the one-compartment distribution problem following a bolus into an initially empty compartment. The differential equation is

$$\dot{c} + kc = \left(\frac{B}{V}\right) \delta(t) \qquad c(0) = 0 \tag{4.135}$$

Notice that now we can represent the bolus explicitly, rather than having to manipulate the initial conditions to account for it. If we transform (4.135) and substitute in the initial condition,

$$sC(s) + kC(s) = \left(\frac{B}{V}\right) \cdot 1 \qquad (4.136)$$

Therefore

$$C(s) = \frac{B}{V} \frac{1}{s + k} \qquad (4.137)$$

and

$$c(t) = \frac{B}{V} e^{-kt} \qquad (4.138)$$

as before.

No real phenomenon strictly obeys (4.124), so we are led to the question: how short must a change be to be considered an "impulse" for analytical purposes? The answer is that it must be much faster than the shortest time constant which characterizes the phenomena. Thus, if studying a drug-distribution problem with a 100-minute fast-time constant, administration of the dose over a few minutes could be considered an impulse. On the other hand, if the fastest time constant were 5 minutes, the bolus would have to be administered over a few seconds in order to be considered an impulse.

PROBLEM SET 4.3

1. Equation (4.121) in the section on the unit step showed that if one infuses drug at a constant rate $I$ into an initially empty one-compartment model from time zero to time $t_S$, the resulting concentration is (equation (4.121))

$$c(t) = \frac{I}{kV}([1 - u(t - t_S)] - e^{-kt}[1 - u(t - t_S) e^{kt_S}])$$

Consider an individual whose volume of distribution $V$ is 5 liters and whose clearance coefficient $k$ is 0.05 min$^{-1}$. We wish to administer a total dose of 1000 mg of drug to this individual.

a. What is the time constant of this individual's response to the drug?

Plot the concentration against time if the 1000 mg is administered in a constant infusion lasting

b. 200 minutes
c. 100 minutes
d.   60 minutes
e.   30 minutes
f.   20 minutes
g.   10 minutes
h.     5 minutes
i.     1 minute
j.   30 seconds

2. Suppose one administers the same dose as a bolus of 1000 mg of drug at time zero. Plot the concentration as a function of time. By comparing this result with Problem 1, estimate how "fast" the infusion must be in order to be considered an impulse.
3. Solve Problem 1 of Problem Set 3.8 using Laplace transforms.
4. Find and plot the response of the catheter in the above problem to a pressure pulse of magnitude 100 mm Hg.
5. Use Laplace transforms to find the concentration in an initially empty two-compartment model to a bolus of magnitude $B$ applied at time zero.

## THE DIRECT SOLUTION OF SYSTEMS OF DIFFERENTIAL EQUATIONS

We used the equivalence of a set of $n$ first-order differential equations with a single $n$th-order differential equation to solve physiological problems such as the $n$-compartment drug-distribution problem. The Laplace transform, however, permits dealing with the set of $n$ first-order equations directly, and often simplifies the search for a solution by bypassing the cumbersome step of combining the $n$ equations into a single $n$th-order equation and recomputing the initial conditions in terms of that equation's variable. In essence, one transforms each of $n$ simultaneous first-order differential equations to obtain a set of $n$ simultaneous algebraic equations, which are then solved for the transform of the desired variable, then invert that transform.

To illustrate this process, let us rework the two-compartment drug distribution following a bolus into initially empty compartments without combining the two first-order differential equations which describe each compartment into a single second-order differential equation. From Equation (2.73):

$$\dot{q}_1 = -(k_{12} + k_{10})q_1 + k_{21}q_2 + B\delta(t) \qquad q_1(0) = 0 \qquad (4.139)$$

$$\dot{q}_2 = k_{12}q_1 - k_{21}q_2 \qquad\qquad q_2(0) = 0$$

$$(4.140)$$

where $q_1$ and $q_2$ are the drug mass in each compartment and $k_{12}, k_{21}$, and $k_{10}$ are the transfer coefficients. Note that we can now represent the bolus directly with $B\delta(t)$. If we apply the Laplace transform to (4.139) and (4.140),

$$sQ_1(s) = -(k_{12} + k_{10})Q_1(s) + k_{21}Q_2(s) + B \cdot 1 \qquad (4.141)$$

$$sQ_2(s) = k_{12}Q_1(s) - k_{21}Q_2(s) \qquad (4.142)$$

or

$$[s + (k_{12} + k_{10})]\, Q_1 - k_{21}Q_2 = B \qquad (4.143)$$

$$-k_{12}Q_1 + (s + k_{21})Q_2 = 0 \qquad (4.144)$$

Solve (4.143) and (4.144) for $Q_1(s)$:

$$Q_1(s) = \frac{B(s + k_{21})}{s^2 + (k_{12} + k_{21} + k_{10})s + k_{10}k_{21}} \qquad (4.145)$$

and expand it in partial fractions.

$$Q_1(s) = \frac{B(s + k_{21})}{(s - \lambda_1)(s - \lambda_2)} = \frac{A_1}{s - \lambda_1} + \frac{A_2}{s - \lambda_2} = \frac{(s - \lambda_2)A_1 + (s - \lambda_1)A_2}{(s - \lambda_1)(s - \lambda_2)}$$

$$(4.146)$$

where

$$\lambda_1 = \frac{-(k_{12} + k_{21} + k_{10}) - \sqrt{(k_{12} + k_{21} + k_{10})^2 - 4k_{10}k_{21}}}{2}$$

$$(4.147)$$

and

$$\lambda_2 = \frac{-(k_{12} + k_{21} + k_{10}) + \sqrt{(k_{12} + k_{21} + k_{10})^2 - 4k_{10}k_{21}}}{2}$$

(4.148)

Thus $A_1 = \dfrac{B(\lambda_1 + k_{21})}{\lambda_1 - \lambda_2}$ and $A_2 = \dfrac{-B(\lambda_2 + k_{21})}{\lambda_1 - \lambda_2}$, so

$$c(t) = \frac{1}{V}q_1(t) = \frac{1}{V}\mathscr{L}^{-1}\{Q_1(s)\}$$

$$= \frac{B}{V}\left[\frac{\lambda_1 + k_{21}}{\lambda_1 - \lambda_2}\mathscr{L}^{-1}\left\{\frac{1}{s - \lambda_1}\right\} - \frac{\lambda_2 + k_{21}}{\lambda_1 - \lambda_2}\mathscr{L}^{-1}\left\{\frac{1}{s - \lambda_2}\right\}\right]$$

(4.149)

Thus,

$$c(t) = \frac{B}{V}\left[\frac{\lambda_1 + k_{21}}{\lambda_1 - \lambda_2}e^{-\lambda_1 t} - \frac{\lambda_2 + k_{21}}{\lambda_1 - \lambda_2}e^{-\lambda_2 t}\right]$$

(4.150)

where $c$ = central-compartment drug concentration and $V$ = volume of distribution. Let $\tau_f = -1/\lambda_1$ and $\tau_s = -1/\lambda_2$ and eliminate $\lambda_1$ and $\lambda_2$ from (4.150) to obtain:

$$c(t) = \frac{B}{V}\left[\frac{(k_{10} + k_{12} - k_{21}) + \sqrt{(k_{10} + k_{12} + k_{21})^2 - 4k_{10}k_{21}}}{2\sqrt{(k_{10} + k_{12} + k_{21})^2 - 4k_{10}k_{21}}}e^{-t/\tau_f}\right.$$

$$\left. - \frac{(k_{10} + k_{12} - k_{21}) - \sqrt{(k_{10} + k_{12} + k_{21})^2 - 4k_{10}k_{21}}}{2\sqrt{(k_{10} + k_{12} + k_{21})^2 - 4k_{10}k_{21}}}e^{-t/\tau_s}\right]$$

(4.151)

Compare the effort required to solve this problem using Laplace transforms with that required by the direct method.

## PROBLEM SET 4.4

Solve each of the following systems of differential equations for the first variable.

1. $\dot{x}_1 = x_1 + x_2$          $x_1(0) = x_{10}$

   $\dot{x}_2 = -x_2$          $x_2(0) = x_{20}$

2. $\dot{x}_1 = x_1 - x_2$          $x_1(0) = x_{10}$

   $\dot{x}_2 = -x_2$          $x_2(0) = x_{20}$

3. $\dfrac{dy}{dx} = y + z$          $y(0) = 1$

   $\dfrac{dz}{dx} = y - z$          $z(0) = 0$

4. Suppose one takes a pill of mass $P$, all of which is absorbed into the blood from the gastrointestinal tract at a rate $k_A$ and metabolized out of the blood at a rate $k_M$. If the blood acts as a single compartment, find

   a. The differential equation(s) which describe this process.

   b. The blood concentration as a function of time.

## DRUG DISTRIBUTION FOLLOWING AN ORAL OR INTRAMUSCULAR DOSE

One- and two-compartment models provide useful descriptions for drug concentrations over time following intravenous administration when the drug directly enters the plasma volume (and, hence, the central compartment). If one administers a drug orally or intramuscularly, however, it rarely mixes instantly with the central compartment, so we must add another compartment to account for absorption into the plasma from either the gastrointestinal tract or muscle. We now write equations to describe this situation and use Laplace transforms to solve them for drugs which, when administered intravenously, behave according to a one- or two-compartment model.

We denote this compartment which represents the gastrointestinal tract or muscle (and tissues in rapid kinetic equilibrium with it) as the initial compartment, or compartment 3. Generally, a drug moves from compartment 3 to the central compartment with little or no reverse transfer, so one typically characterizes the drug transfer with the single transfer coefficient $k_{31}$ (Fig. 4.7). In addition, sometimes a substantial fraction of an orally administered dose appears in the feces, making it necessary to add another fractional transfer coefficient $k_{30}$ to represent direct excretion. If all drug eventually appears in the plasma, $k_{30} = 0$.

First, let us study drugs distributed in a single compartment when administered intravenously (Fig. 4.7A). Let $q_3$ = drug mass in the initial compartment, $q_1$ = drug mass in the central compartment, $c$ = central compartment drug concentration, and $V$ = volume of distribution of the central compartment. Conservation of mass for each compartment requires

$$\dot{q}_3 = i(t) - k_{30}q_3 - k_{31}q_3 \qquad q_3(0) = 0 \qquad (4.152)$$

$$\dot{q}_1 = k_{31}q_3 - k_{10}q_1 \qquad q_1(0) = 0 \qquad (4.153)$$

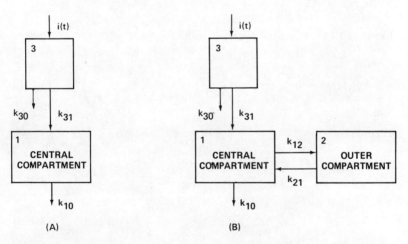

(A)                    (B)

FIGURE 4.7: Standard one- and two-compartment models must be modified to treat orally or intramuscularly administered drugs by adding a third compartment which represents the gastrointestinal tract or muscle. Concentration and volume of distribution still refer to the central compartment. If a substantial part of the original dose does not eventually appear in the central compartment, the transfer coefficient $k_{30}$ is used to quantify direct removal from the initial compartment.

where $i(t)$ = mass flow rate of administered drug. To solve (4.152) and (4.153) for $c(t) = q_1(t)/V$, first compute their Laplace transforms:

$$sQ_3 = I(s) - (k_{30} + k_{31})Q_3 \tag{4.154}$$

$$sQ_1 = k_{31}Q_3 - k_{10}Q_1 \tag{4.155}$$

Solve these two equations in the two unknowns $Q_1(s)$ and $Q_2(s)$ for $Q_1(s)$:

$$Q_1(s) = \frac{k_{31}I(s)}{(s + k_{10})(s + k_{30} + k_{31})} \tag{4.156}$$

If we administer the drug as a pill, $i(t) = B\delta(t)$. Therefore, $I(s) = B$ and (4.156) becomes

$$Q_1(s) = \frac{Bk_{31}}{(s + k_{10})(s + k_{30} + k_{31})} \tag{4.157}$$

Expand (4.157) in partial fractions to find

$$Q_1(s) = \frac{Bk_{31}}{k_{30} + k_{31} - k_{10}}\left(\frac{1}{s + k_{10}} - \frac{1}{s + k_{30} + k_{31}}\right) \tag{4.158}$$

Therefore

$$c(t) = \frac{q_1(t)}{V} = \frac{\mathcal{L}^{-1}\{Q_1(s)\}}{V} = \frac{Bk_{31}}{V(k_{30} + k_{31} - k_{10})}(e^{-t/\tau_1} - e^{-t/\tau_2}) \tag{4.159}$$

where $k_{10} \neq k_{30} + k_{31}$ (Why?) and $\tau_1 = 1/k_{10}$ and $\tau_2 = 1/(k_{30} + k_{31})$. The two compartments lead to two first-order differential equations and hence a second-order system characterized by two time constants (eigenvalues) and two exponentials. Since the solution is given by the difference of two exponential functions with different time constants (Fig. 4.8A), plasma concentration begins at zero, increases to a peak value at $t_p = [\tau_1\tau_2/(\tau_2 - \tau_1)] \ln(\tau_2/\tau_1)$, then drops back to zero (Fig. 4.8B). The

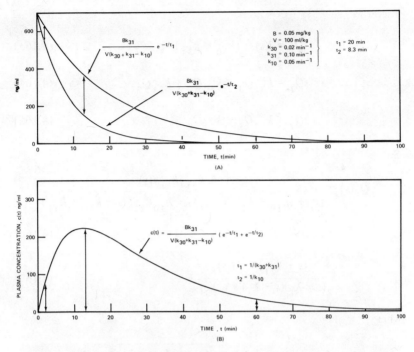

**FIGURE 4.8:** Equation (4.159) gives the response to an oral dose of a hypothetical drug which is distributed in one compartment following intravenous administration. Since there are two compartments there are two time constants, and plasma concentration equals the difference of two exponentials. This difference begins at zero (first arrow), increases to a peak (second arrow), then decays to zero as the drug is removed from the body (third arrow).

increasing part of the curve shows the drug entering the central compartment faster than it is metabolized or excreted; the falling part reflects the opposite situation.

For a drug distributed in two compartments when administered intravenously, we again add a third compartment (Fig. 4.7B). As before, conservation of mass requires

$$\dot{q}_3 = i(t) - k_{30}q_3 - k_{31}q_3 \qquad q_3(0) = 0 \qquad (4.160)$$

$$\dot{q}_1 = k_{31}q_3 - k_{12}q_1 + k_{21}q_2 \qquad q_1(0) = 0 \qquad (4.161)$$

$$\dot{q}_2 = k_{12}q_1 - k_{21}q_2 \qquad q_2(0) = 0 \qquad (4.162)$$

Therefore

$$sQ_3 = I(s) - (k_{30} - k_{31})Q_3 \qquad (4.163)$$

$$sQ_1 = k_{31}Q_3 - k_{12}Q_1 + k_{21}Q_2 \qquad (4.164)$$

$$sQ_2 = k_{12}Q_1 - k_{21}Q_2 \qquad (4.165)$$

So

$$Q_1(s) = \frac{(s + k_{21})k_{31} I(s)}{[s^2 + (k_{10} + k_{12} + k_{21})s + k_{10}k_{21}](s + k_{30} + k_{31})}$$

$$(4.166)$$

$$= \frac{(s + k_{21})k_{31} I(s)}{(s - \lambda_1)(s - \lambda_2)(s - \lambda_3)} \qquad (4.167)$$

where

$$\lambda_1 = \frac{-(k_{10} + k_{12} + k_{21}) - \sqrt{(k_{10} + k_{12} + k_{21})^2 - 4k_{10}k_{21}}}{2}$$

$$(4.168)$$

$$\lambda_2 = \frac{-(k_{10} + k_{12} + k_{21}) + \sqrt{(k_{10} + k_{12} + k_{21})^2 - 4k_{10}k_{21}}}{2}$$

$$(4.169)$$

and

$$\lambda_3 = -(k_{30} + k_{31}) \qquad (4.170)$$

For a bolus (pill) of mass $B$, $i(t) = B\delta(t)$, so $I(s) = B$ and

$$Q_1(s) = \frac{(s + k_{21})k_{31}B}{(s - \lambda_1)(s - \lambda_2)(s - \lambda_3)} = \frac{A_1}{s - \lambda_1} + \frac{A_2}{s - \lambda_2} + \frac{A_3}{s - \lambda_3} \qquad (4.171)$$

Equation (4.171) requires

$$A_1 = \frac{(\lambda_1 + k_{21})k_{31}}{(\lambda_1 - \lambda_2)(\lambda_1 - \lambda_3)}$$

$$A_2 = \frac{(\lambda_2 + k_{21})k_{31}}{(\lambda_2 - \lambda_1)(\lambda_2 - \lambda_3)} \qquad (4.172)$$

$$A_3 = \frac{(\lambda_3 + k_{21})k_{31}}{(\lambda_3 - \lambda_1)(\lambda_3 - \lambda_2)}$$

Thus

$$c(t) = \frac{q_1(t)}{V} = \mathscr{L}^{-1}\frac{\{Q_1(s)\}}{V} = \frac{B}{V}\left[\frac{k_{31}(\lambda_1 + k_{21})}{(\lambda_1 - \lambda_2)(\lambda_1 - \lambda_3)}e^{-t/\tau_1}\right.$$

$$\left. + \frac{k_{31}(\lambda_2 - k_{21})}{(\lambda_2 - \lambda_1)(\lambda_2 - \lambda_3)}e^{-t/\tau_2} + \frac{k_{31}(\lambda_3 + k_{21})}{(\lambda_3 - \lambda_1)(\lambda_3 - \lambda_2)}e^{-t/\tau_3}\right]$$

$$(4.173)$$

where $\tau_i = -1/\lambda_i$.

Figure 4.9 illustrates Equation (4.173) with fractional transfer coefficients corresponding to orally administered lidocaine.

The three compartments comprise a third-order system and hence exhibit three time constants. The time constants and relative importance of each term in (4.173) depend only on the fractional transfer coefficients, with the dose $B$ and the volume of distribution $V$ acting as scaling factors. Note that the two time constants $\tau_1$ and $\tau_2$ are the same as we obtained with the two-compartment model following intravenous administration ($\tau_f$ and $\tau_s$). This situation arises because there is no backflow from compartment 1 to compartment 3, in which case compartment 3 could be replaced with a variable infusion rate to compartment 1, independent of the other two compartments. On the other hand, if there were transfer from compartment 1 to 3 (i.e., $k_{13} \neq 0$), all three eigenvalues (and hence time constants) would depend on all three transfer coefficients.

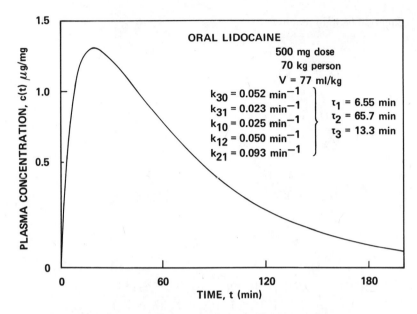

**FIGURE 4.9:** Plasma concentration following a 500 mg oral dose of the anti-arrhythmic drug lidocaine with $k_{10} = 0.025$ min$^{-1}$, $k_{12} = 0.050$ min$^{-1}$, $k_{21} = 0.093$ min$^{-1}$, $k_{30} = 0.056$ min$^{-1}$, $k_{31} = 0.023$ min$^{-1}$, and $V = 77$ ml/kg computed with (4.173). (Values of kinetic parameters from R. N. Boyes, et al., Pharmacokinetics of Lidocaine in Man, *Clin. Pharm. Therap.* 12 (1971): 105. The equation is

$$c(t) = 92.8 \, (-0.129 e^{-t/6.55\text{min}} + 0.218 e^{-t/65.7\text{min}}$$

$$- 0.089 e^{-t/13.3\text{min}}) \text{ mg/ml}.$$

## PROBLEM SET 4.5

1. Find the concentration in the central compartment of Figure 4.7A, if $k_{30} = k_{31} = k/2$ and $k_{10} = k$:
   a. Following a bolus into compartment 3.
   b. Following a constant infusion into compartment 3.

2. Prove that the maximum concentration in the drug-distribution model of Figure 4.7A occurs at $t_p = [\tau_1 \tau_2 / (\tau_2 - \tau_1)] \ln (\tau_2/\tau_1)$.

3. Plot the plasma concentration of lidocaine as a function of time for 6 hours for the individual shown in Figure 4.9, assuming he is given a 250 mg dose at time zero, and one, two, and three hours later.

# 5

# WAYS TO CHARACTERIZE
# LINEAR PROCESSES

We will consider four equivalent ways of characterizing linear behavior—
impulse response, step response, frequency response, and transfer function. All require us to regard the process of interest as one in which an
input, or forcing function, produces an output, or response (Fig. 5.1). For
example, the input might be a drug administered to a patient, or a pressure
pulse whose output is either plasma concentration or recorder deflection.
Regardless of what the input and output specifically represent, we can use
the response to a *standard* input to characterize the process. To compute
the response to any other input, we break that input into a sum of
standard inputs for each of which we know the response, then use the
principle of superposition to combine the individual responses into the
total response due to the input. Impulse response, step response, and
frequency response differ only in the standard input used: a unit impulse,
a unit step, or a unit sine function. All three of these responses contain the
same information and relate to each other through simple formulae.

We will study *time-invariant* linear processes in which a change in
input in time shifts the output by the same amount without changing the
output's shape.* Linear, ordinary differential equations that have constant
coefficients describe such processes. The nonhomogeneous term in the

---

* One can generalize the concepts developed in this chapter to apply them to non-
  constant coefficient cases. However, most practical applications deal with time-
  invariant processes, that is, ones in which the underlying mechanism described by
  the coefficients in the differential equation remain constant. For a discussion of
  *time-varying* processes, see L. K. Timothy and B. E. Bona, *State Space Analysis: An
  Introduction*, Chs. 4 & 5. New York: McGraw-Hill, 1968.

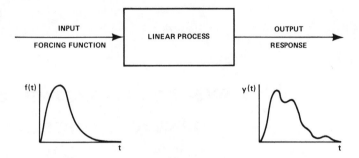

**FIGURE 5.1:** The input or forcing function $f(t)$ acts to produce an output or response $y(t)$. We will restrict ourselves to linear processes, which obey the principle of superposition. Thus we will be able to break down the input into a sum of standard functions for each of which we know the response, then sum these responses to find the output.

differential equation represents the input or forcing function. In essence, we then will examine how the system responds to the standard input, then describe the arbitrary input as a linear combination (weighted sum) of standard inputs. Since the principle of superposition states that the result of a linear transformation (such as a linear differential equation) acting on a sum of inputs will be the sum of its actions on each individual input, we can predict the resulting output in terms of the individual responses to the standard inputs. Every method discussed in this chapter grows directly out of the principle of superposition. Thus they cannot be used to characterize nonlinear phenomena, which do not exhibit superposition.

The coefficients of a linear differential equation determine its eigenvalues, and hence its response to any input, whether standard or otherwise. If this is so, why not simply use these coefficients to characterize the response? Sometimes one would do just that. For example, many mechanical vibrations and electrical devices obey the same second-order differential equation we used to describe a fluid-filled catheter. Simply knowing the magnitudes of its coefficients provides an experienced analyst with the same understanding of how the device responds as would the analysis we will develop. In contrast, many important processes involve equations which have not as yet been so thoroughly studied; the characterizations we will develop often provide a useful insight into their responses. In addition, one often does not know the equations which describe many processes (or perhaps the exact values of coefficients within an equation of known form), and the methods discussed here will permit the reader to experimentally characterize a process's dynamic behavior, then predict its response to any inputs. Equally important, these experimental characterizations often answer important practical questions, such as how to re-move noise from a signal while preserving the information the signal con-tains.

## WHY TAKE ALL INITIAL CONDITIONS EQUAL TO ZERO?

To describe the manner in which a linear process responds to any forcing function, we will study how it responds to standard forcing functions, such as a unit impulse, step, or sinusoid. However, the total response (i.e., the complete solution to the differential equation) depends not only on the forcing function (the nonhomogeneous term in the equation) and the equation's form, but also the initial conditions. To insure that the charac-teristic responses reflect only the standard forcing function, we will *always* consider the process to have been at rest prior to the application of the forcing function. This permits us to insure that the reponse reflects only the input, not a transient effect due to the initial conditions.

To assume that the process is initially at rest is equivalent to taking the output and its derivatives (the initial conditions) all equal to zero. To see why, suppose that

$$a_n y^{(n)} + a_{n-1} y^{(n-1)} + \ldots + a_1 y' + a_0 y = f(t) \tag{5.1}$$

describes the process. If we apply no forcing function $f(t) = 0$, and if $y(0) = y'(0) = \ldots = y^{(n-1)}(0) = 0$, Equation (5.1) requires that $y(t) = 0$ for all time.

But what of the *true* initial conditions? One can assume that at some time in the indefinite past the process was in fact at rest, and that the current initial conditions are simply the result of past inputs. By applying the appropriate impulse inputs at time zero, we can produce the same values of the dependent variable as would be present if the initial condi-tions had not been zero. For example, in Chapter 3, we computed drug distribution following a bolus injection by treating the mass of drug injected at time zero as an initial condition. In Chapter 4, we developed the unit impulse which permitted direct functional representation of the injection, so we considered the compartment model initially empty (and thus set all initial conditions equal to zero). Additionally, virtually every process we wish to characterize by means of these methods has negative eigenvalues, so that the transient response—the part of the solution which depends on initial conditions—eventually dies away while our interest centers on the steady-state response, which depends only on the particular solution. Finally, it is generally clearer to consider a process as initially at rest, with all changes occurring as a result of inputs or forcing functions rather than as a result of initial conditions.

## IMPULSE RESPONSE

Suppose that the response to a unit impulse applied to a process at rest at time zero $\delta(t)$ is some function of time $h(t)$. $h(t)$ is called the *impulse response* (Fig. 5.2A). We can use this knowledge to construct the response to any forcing function $f(t)$. Since the process is time-invariant, delaying the time at which we apply the impulse simply delays the response by the same time interval. Thus, if we apply our unit impulse at $t_0$ instead of time 0, the response has the same shape as in Figure 5.2A, but is shifted to $t_0$ (Fig. 5.2B). This fact, combined with the principle of superposition, forms the basis for the use of the impulse response to characterize behavior.

First we show that any process which an $n$th-order linear constant-coefficient differential equation represents is time-invariant. Suppose

$$a_n y^{(n)} + a_{n-1} y^{(n-1)} + \ldots + a_1 y' + a_0 y = \sum_{j=0}^{n} a_j \frac{d^j y}{dt^j} = f(t)$$

(5.2)

which, with the appropriate initial conditions, has some solution, $y_1(t)$. Now, suppose we keep the dynamic relationship the same, but shift the forcing function in time by an amount $t_0$ and examine the solution to the equation

$$\sum_{j=0}^{n} a_j \frac{d^j y}{dt^j} = f(t - t_0)$$

(5.3)

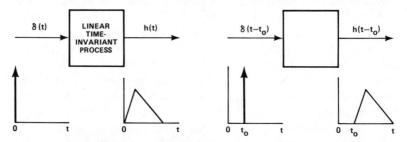

**FIGURE 5.2:** Shifting the time at which one applies an impulse to a time-invariant process merely shifts the impulse response by the same amount, without changing its shape.

If we make a change of variables and let $\tau = t - t_0$, (5.3) becomes

$$\sum_{j=0}^{n} a_j \frac{d^j y}{d\tau^j} = f(\tau) \tag{5.4}$$

which is identical to (5.2), and hence its solution is $y_2 = y_1(\tau)$. But $\tau = t - t_0$, so $y_2 = y_1(t - t_0)$. In short, shifting the input (forcing function) in time by $t_0$ shifts the output (response) by the same amount, $t_0$. Constant-coefficient linear differential equations thus represent time-invariant processes.

Next, let us apply two unit impulses, one at time zero and one at time $t_0$, to the processes in Figure 5.2. The two impulses $\delta(t)$ and $\delta(t - t_0)$ produce the two impulse responses $h(t)$ and $h(t - t_0)$, respectively (the light lines in Figure 5.3A), and by the principle of superposition the total response is the sum of the two individual responses (the heavy line in Fig. 5.3A). One need not simply apply unit impulses: Figure 5.3B shows that the response to $1/4\delta(t) + \delta(t - t_0) + 1/2\delta(t - t_1)$ is $1/4h(t) + h(t - t_0) + 1/2h(t - t_1)$, since superposition simply restates homogeneity and additivity.

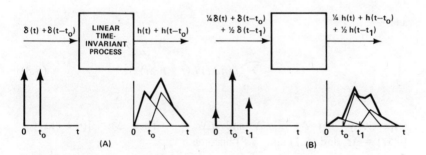

**FIGURE 5.3:** (A) If two unit impulses are applied to a linear time-invariant process, one can find the response by passing each through separately (as in Figure 5.2), then applying the principle of superposition and adding the results to get the total response (heavy line). (B) It is not necessary to simply apply a train of unit impulses to the process; in this case, the total response is obtained by shifting and scaling the impulse response to each pulse by the same amount as the impulse, then adding them to get the total response.

Now, let us extend this procedure to a train of $N$ impulses of varying magnitude (Figure 5.4A):

$$v(t) = \sum_{n=0}^{N} a_n \, \delta(t - n\Delta t) \tag{5.5}$$

Since the impulse response is $h(t)$, the response to (5.5) will be (Fig. 5.4B):

$$y(t) = \sum_{n=0}^{N} a_n h(t - n\Delta t) \tag{5.6}$$

Again, we could apply each impulse individually, then add up all the individual responses to find the net response (Fig. 5.4B). One could define a function $f(t)$ so that $f(n\Delta t) \, \Delta t = a_n$, and rewrite (5.5) and (5.6) as

$$v(t) = \sum_{n=0}^{N} f(n\Delta t) \, \delta(t - n\Delta t) \, \Delta t \tag{5.7}$$

and

$$y(t) = \sum_{n=0}^{N} f(n\Delta t) \, h(t - n\Delta t) \, \Delta t \tag{5.8}$$

respectively. Let $\Delta t = t/N$ and $n\Delta t = \tau$. Then $\Delta \tau = [(n + 1)\Delta t] - [n\Delta t] = \Delta t$, and (5.7) and (5.8) become

$$v(t) = \sum_{n=0}^{N} f(\tau) \, \delta(t - \tau) \, \Delta \tau \tag{5.9}$$

and

$$y(t) = \sum_{n=0}^{N} f(\tau) \, h(t - \tau) \, \Delta \tau \tag{5.10}$$

Now, hold $t$ fixed and let $N \to \infty$, in which case $\Delta \tau \to 0$, and (5.9) and (5.10) become

$$v(t) = \int_0^t f(\tau)\delta(t - \tau)d\tau = f(t) \tag{5.11}$$

and

$$y(t) = \int_0^t f(\tau)h(t - \tau)d\tau \tag{5.12}$$

respectively. Thus, (5.12) gives the result, $y(t)$, which we obtain by applying the input $f(t)$ to a time-invariant linear process initially at rest (zero initial conditions) in terms of the unit impulse response $h(t)$. Equation (5.12), which contains the so-called *convolution integral*,* says that the response at time $t$ represents the sum of effects of the input being applied at all times up to time $t$ (Fig. 5.4).

For example, we have shown that, following a bolus of $B$ mg of drug which is distributed in a single compartment, the concentration is

$$c(t) = \frac{B}{V}e^{-t/\tau} \qquad \text{where } \tau = \frac{1}{k} \tag{5.13}$$

The bolus is an impulsive input, therefore the impulse response is the resulting concentration following a bolus of magnitude 1. From (5.13):

$$h(t) = \frac{1}{V}e^{-t/\tau} \tag{5.14}$$

Now suppose we wish to find an individual's response to a constant infusion of $I$ mg/min. From (5.12) and (5.13), the resulting concentration will be

$$c(t) = \int_0^t \frac{I}{V} e^{-(t-\xi)/\tau} d\xi \tag{5.15}$$

$$c(t) = \frac{I}{V} \int_0^t e^{-t/\tau} e^{\xi/\tau} d\xi \tag{5.16}$$

* The convolution integral is also known as the Faltung integral, superposition integral, Duhamel integral, weighted running means, cross-correlation function, and smoothing function.

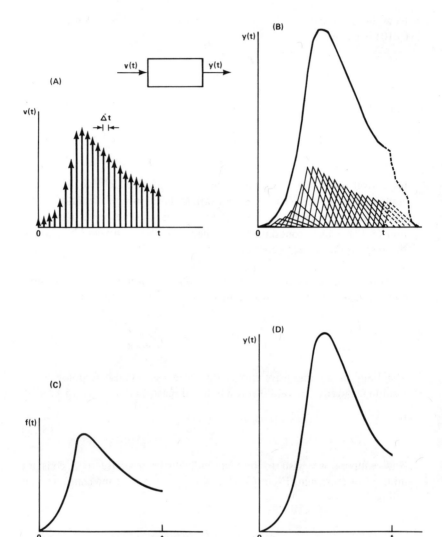

**FIGURE 5.4:** The string of 22 impulses in (A) produces the 22 responses shown as light lines in (B). The dark line in (B) shows the total response to all the pulses in (A). By moving the pulses closer and closer together, one approaches the continuous function $f(t)$ in (C), which in turn produces the response $y(t)$ shown in (D). This process of scaling, shifting, and adding up responses is called *convolution*.

But $t$ does not depend on $\xi$, so

$$c(t) = \frac{I}{V} e^{-t/\tau} \int_0^t e^{\xi/\tau} d\xi \qquad (5.17)$$

$$c(t) = \frac{I}{V} e^{-t/\tau} \left. \tau e^{\xi/\tau} \right|_0^t \qquad (5.18)$$

and since $\tau = 1/k$,

$$c(t) = \frac{I}{kV} e^{-t/\tau} (e^{t/\tau} - 1) \qquad (5.19)$$

$$c(t) = \frac{I}{kV} (1 - e^{-t/\tau}) \qquad (5.20)$$

which is the same result we obtained by approaching the problem directly.

Since its impulse response completely characterizes a linear time-invariant process, one can experimentally measure the impulse response in order to predict the response to any other input. For example, for a drug which exhibits linear kinetics, knowing how it disappears from the plasma following a bolus permits one to compute the response to any other administration regime. Thus, an empirically derived impulse response can be used to predict the response of *any* constant-coefficient linear system, by graphically convolving the response impulse with the input, as we did in Figures 5.3 and 5.4.

## PROBLEM SET 5.1

1. Figure 5.5 shows the responses of four different processes to a unit impulse input. Plot the response of each system to the input $v(t) = 1/2\, \delta(0) + \delta(1) + 2\delta(2) + 2\delta(2) + \delta(4) + 1/2\, \delta(5) + 1/4\, \delta(6)$, shown in Figure 5.4E.
2. Find the impulse response of processes described by the following differential equations. In each case $f(t)$ represents the input or forcing function. (Hint: Use Laplace transforms.)
   a. $\dot{y} + 2y = f(t)$
   b. $\ddot{y} + 2\dot{y} + y = f(t)$
   c. $\ddot{y} + 5\dot{y} + 6y = f(t)$
   d. $\ddot{x} + 4x = f(t)$

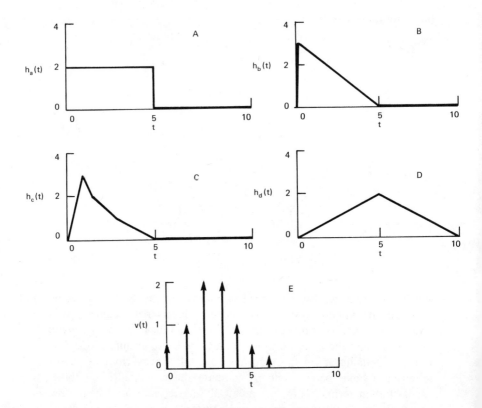

**FIGURE 5.5:** Illustration for Problem 1. A–D show the response of four different linear processes to a unit impulse, $\delta(t)$. The problem is to find the response of each system to the train of impulses in E.

e. $\dddot{c} + 6\ddot{c} + 8\dot{c} = f(t)$

f. $\ddot{E} + 2\zeta\omega_n\dot{E} + \omega_n^2 E = f(t)$

3. Use the convolution integral and impulse response to find the response of each system in Problem 2 to a unit step input $f(t) = u(t)$. Check your results by solving the differential equations directly with $f(t) = u(t)$, using Laplace transforms. What is the relationship between the step and impulse response?

4. Use the convolution integral and impulse response to find the response of each system in Problem 2 to a square pulse of magnitude and duration 1, $f(t) = u(t) - u(t - 1)$.

5. Consider a device with impulse responses $h(t) = Ae^{-t\xi}$ ($A$, $\xi$ = constants); find the response to the input $f(t) = B \sin \omega t$.

6. Equation (5.16) gives the response of a two-compartment drug-distribution model to a bolus dose. If the bolus is of magnitude 1 this equation represents the impulse response of this system. Use this impulse response and the convolution integral to find the response of a constant infusion.

## STEP RESPONSE

We can also use the unit step function to characterize linear time-invariant processes. We call the response to a unit step $u(t)$ the *step response, $A(t)$*. Figure 5.6 illustrates a step response and the effect of shifting the time at which the step occurs. As with the impulse response of a linear time-invariant process, shifting the time at which one applies the unit step merely shifts the step response by the same amount. Figure 5.7 shows how one can superimpose unit steps of varying magnitudes to form any forcing function, as well as how one uses the principle of superposition to obtain the response by adding the responses to each step. In essence, using this characterization to construct the response of the system to an arbitrary input is no different from characterizing the system with its impulse response; only the standard input and response differ.

To find the response of the linear time-invariant process in Figure 5.6 to the input function in Figure 5.8, first divide the interval between 0 and $t$ into $N$ equal increments, each $\Delta t = t/N$ wide. Next, approximate the function $f(t)$ with the sum of step functions (Fig. 5.8A):

$$v(t) = \sum_{n=0}^{N} \Delta f(n\Delta t)\, u\,(t - n\Delta t)$$

where

$$\Delta f(n\Delta t) = f(n\Delta t) - f([n-1]\,\Delta t) \tag{5.21}$$

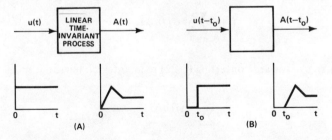

**FIGURE 5.6:** For a linear time-invariant process, shifting the time at which we apply the step change shifts the response by the same amount, without affecting its form.

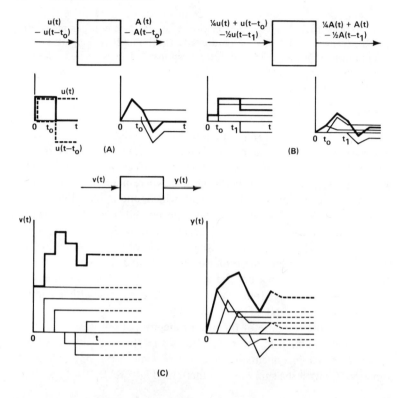

**FIGURE 5.7:** The response to multiple steps produces a response equal to the sum of the separate responses.

By the principle of superposition, the response to $v(t)$ will be

$$y(t) = \sum_{n=0}^{N} \Delta f(n\Delta t)\, A(t - n\Delta t) \qquad (5.22)$$

With an eye toward converting (5.22) to an integral, rewrite it

$$y(t) = \sum_{n=0}^{N'} \frac{\Delta f(n\Delta t)}{\Delta t}\, A(t - n\Delta t)\, \Delta t \qquad (5.23)$$

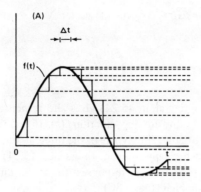

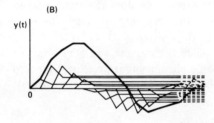

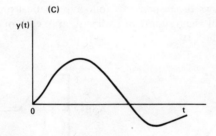

**FIGURE 5.8:** (A) One can approximate the arbitrary function $f(t)$ with a collection of steps up and down, each occurring $\Delta t$ after the last one. (B) Assuming the same step response as in Figures 5.1 and 5.2, we can compute the response to the sequence of steps by scaling and shifting the unit step response appropriately. (C) As $\Delta t \to 0$, the sum of steps more and more closely approximates the function $f(t)$ and the sum of responses approaches the convolution integral given by Equation (5.24).

Let $n\Delta t = \tau$, then $\Delta t = \Delta\tau$, and if we let $N \to \infty$ in (5.21) and (5.23), $v(t) \to f(t)$ and

$$y(t) = \int_0^t \frac{df}{d\tau} A(t - \tau) d\tau \qquad (5.24)$$

The convolution integral in (5.24) gives the response on a linear time-invariant process to any forcing function $f(t)$. If there are points at which $f(t)$ is not differentiable, simply break the integral into pieces which avoid the points at which $\dot{f}$ fails to exist. In essence, (5.24) says that the total response is the sum of the responses to an infinite number of step functions, each $\dot{f} d\tau$ high (Fig. 5.8C).

Just as the impulse response contained all the information necessary to characterize the process, so does the step response. Thus, one could empirically measure the step response (say, the response to a constant infusion of a drug), then use graphical convolution to find the response to any other input. Since the impulse and step responses both completely characterize the same phenomenon, we expect them to be closely related. Indeed, they are; later we will prove that $h(t) = dA/dt$.

PROBLEM SET 5.2

1. Figure 5.9 shows the response of four hypothetical processes to a unit step input. Plot the response of each system to each of the three inputs shown in Figure 5.10.

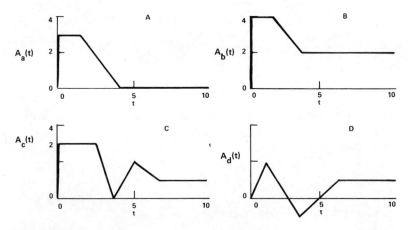

**FIGURE 5.9:** Response of four hypothetical systems to a unit step input at time zero for Problem 1.

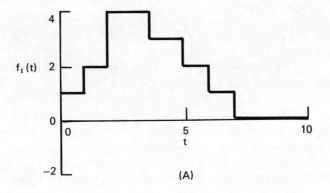

(A)

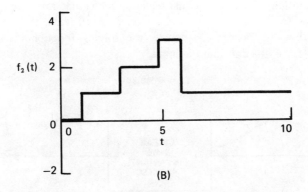

(B)

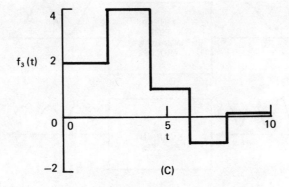

(C)

**FIGURE 5.10:** Input functions for Problem 1.

### FREQUENCY RESPONSE

Thus far we have characterized linear processes with the response to a single function (either a unit impulse or unit step) and then written other input functions with a sum of impulses or steps, each of which acted at a different time, and finally computed the total output by adding through convolution the individual responses to these impulses or steps. Now let us consider a different approach to our standard input. Instead of considering the response to one function which acts at one time and then summing shifted functions to determine the actual input, we will find the responses to many different but related functions, all of which act all the time (Fig. 5.11). Specifically, we will examine the steady-state response to forcing by unit sinusoidal functions of different frequencies. For a stable, linear, time-invariant process, the steady-state response is simply the particular solution to the differential equation which describes the process. According to the method of undetermined coefficients, the particular solution has the same frequency as the forcing function (Chapter 3, p. 125). Hence, the unit sinusoid input

$$f(t) = \sin \omega t \qquad (5.25)$$

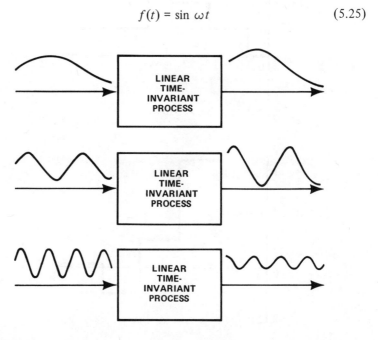

**FIGURE 5.11:** A sinusoidal input to a linear time-invariant process produces a steady output of the same frequency, although it differs in amplitude and lags behind the input.

produces a steady-state output which is sinusoidal with the same frequency

$$y(t) = R \sin (\omega t - \phi) \qquad (5.26)$$

in which the output amplitude $R$ and the angle $\phi$ depend on the input frequency $\omega$. The two functions $R = R(\omega)$ and $\phi = \phi(\omega)$ comprise the system's *frequency response* and can be used to predict the steady-state response to any applied input.

Had the input been a sinusoid of amplitude $A$ instead of 1, the resulting sinusoidal output would be of amplitude $RA$. Thus, $R$ is the *amplitude ratio,* the ratio of output to input amplitudes, and $\phi$, the *phase angle*, tells how far the response sinusoid lags behind the forcing sinusoid. Frequency-response characterizations prove especially useful for characterizing man-made linear time-invariant devices such as electronic instruments, since one can evaluate the device's frequency response empirically without knowing the equations which describe it.

Now, suppose we apply an input

$$f(t) = \sum_{j=1}^{N} b_j \sin \omega_j t \qquad (5.27)$$

to a process with a frequency response described by $R(\omega)$ and $\phi(\omega)$. By the principle of superposition, we could apply each sinusoid one at a time, then add the results to obtain the total steady-state response to (5.27), which will be

$$y(t) = \sum_{j=1}^{N} b_j R(\omega_j) \sin (\omega_j t - \phi(\omega_j)) \qquad (5.28)$$

For example, in order to find the response of a system with the frequency response shown in Figure 5.12 to the input

$$f(t) = \frac{1}{4} \sin t + \frac{1}{2} \sin 2t + \sin 3t + \frac{1}{2} \sin 4t + \frac{1}{4} \sin 5t \qquad (5.29)$$

where the units of $t$ are seconds, find the response to each sinusoid individually, then apply the principle of superposition in order to add the individual responses and obtain the total response. From Figure 5.12 the response will be

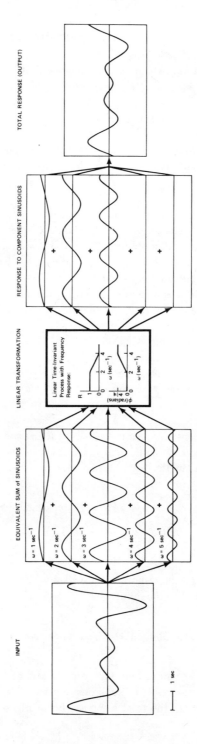

**FIGURE 5.12:** One can decompose an arbitrary signal into a set of sinusoids, then pass each sinusoid through the system independently. The resulting output signal will be a sinusoid of the same frequency, but shifted in time (phase) and amplitude. The output due to the total input signal will be the sum of these individual sinusoidal responses.

$$y(t) = 1 \cdot \frac{1}{4} \sin t + 1 \cdot \frac{1}{2} \sin 2t + \frac{1}{2} \cdot 1 \sin \left(3t - \frac{\pi}{8}\right)$$

$$+ 0 \cdot \frac{1}{2} \sin \left(4t - \frac{\pi}{4}\right) + 0 \cdot \frac{1}{4} \sin \left(5t - \frac{\pi}{4}\right) \tag{5.30}$$

$$= \frac{1}{4} \sin t + \frac{1}{2} \sin 2t + \frac{1}{2} \sin \left(3t - \frac{\pi}{8}\right) \tag{5.31}$$

Note that the higher frequency components of the input fail to affect the output because the amplitude ratio falls to zero above $\omega = 4 \text{ sec}^{-1}$.

This device functions as a *low-pass filter* because it passes the input's low-frequency components with little or no change, but does not respond to its high-frequency components. The sinusoids which describe the noise one encounters when trying to measure physical phenomena are often of significantly higher frequency than those which comprise the measurement, so electronic equipment often includes a low-pass filter to remove noise. Of course, care must be taken not to filter out significant components of the measurement signal itself.

Chapter 6 will show that any periodic function can be represented with a sum resembling (5.27), which is called a *Fourier series*. For example, the Fourier series

$$f(t) = \frac{4}{\pi} \left( \sin t + \frac{1}{3} \sin 3t + \frac{1}{5} \sin 5t + \ldots \right) \tag{5.32}$$

represents the series of rectangular pulses shown in Figure 5.13. Chapter 6 also shows how to use the Fourier transform, a generalization of the Laplace transform, to extend this analysis to include any input function and replace (5.28) with an integral equivalent to a convolution integral in order to sum over all frequencies. For the moment, however, we will concentrate on understanding what frequency response means and how to find it.

How can one determine the frequency response associated with a system? Given the equations, one could demonstrate that all the eigenvalues have negative real parts (i.e., that the system is stable), then find the steady-state solution and plot the amplitude ratio $R(\omega)$ and phase shift $\phi(\omega)$ as functions of frequency. For example, Equation 3.229 showed that the steady-state (particular) solution associated with

$$\ddot{y} + 2\zeta\omega_n\dot{y} + \omega_n^2 y = A \sin \omega t \tag{5.33}$$

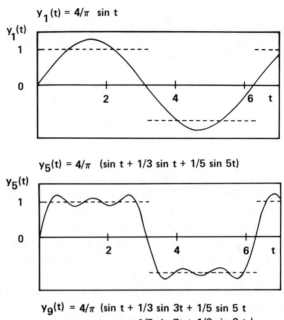

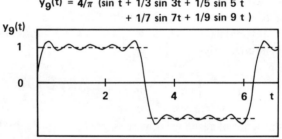

**FIGURE 5.13:** One can represent any periodic signal as a sum of sinu-soidal functions called a Fourier series. As one adds more and more terms to the series, it more and more closely approaches the actual function. When the function to be decomposed is not periodic, one replaces the sum with an integral.

is

$$y_p(t) = \frac{A}{\sqrt{(\omega_n{}^2 - \omega^2)^2 + (2\zeta\omega_n\omega)^2}} \sin(\omega t - \phi) \qquad (5.34)$$

in which

$$\phi = \tan^{-1} \frac{2\zeta\omega_n\omega}{\omega_n^2 - \omega^2} \qquad (5.35)$$

The ratio of the amplitude of the output to the amplitude of the input, from (5.33) and (5.34), is

$$R(\omega) = \frac{1}{\sqrt{(\omega_n^2 - \omega^2)^2 + (2\zeta\omega_n\omega)^2}} \qquad (5.36)$$

Thus (5.35) and (5.36) give the frequency response associated with (5.33); Figure 5.14 illustrates this response for $\omega_n = 1$ sec$^{-1}$ and $\zeta = 0.1$ sec$^{-1}$.

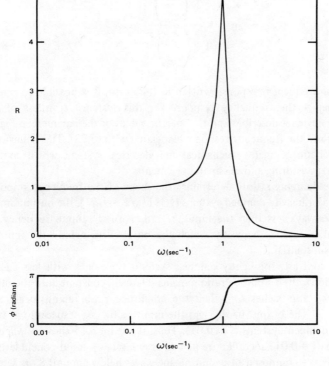

**FIGURE 5.14:** Frequency response of (5.33), with $\omega_n = 1$ sec$^{-1}$ and $\zeta = 0.1$ sec$^{-1}$.

Equation (5.33) approximately describes many mechanical systems, such as an automobile or fluid-filled catheter (Equation (3.287), which contain both energy-storing and dissipating elements. Since this equation arises so often, we will study the associated frequency response in detail. In particular, we will see that the *undamped natural frequency* $\omega_n$ is the frequency at which the system will oscillate in the absence of damping (friction), and the dimensionless *damping ratio* $\zeta$ reflects the amount of damping or other dissipation. We can further simplify our analysis by rearranging (5.35) and (5.36) to be in terms of the dimensionless damping ratio and the dimensionless *frequency ratio* $\omega/\omega_n$:

$$R(\omega) = \frac{1}{\omega_n^2 \sqrt{\left[1 - \left(\dfrac{\omega}{\omega_n}\right)^2\right]^2 + 4\zeta^2 \left(\dfrac{\omega}{\omega_n}\right)^2}} \tag{5.37}$$

$$\phi = \tan^{-1} \frac{2\zeta \left(\dfrac{\omega}{\omega_n}\right)}{1 - \left(\dfrac{\omega}{\omega_n}\right)^2} \tag{5.38}$$

With the frequency response written in this form, it is possible to graphically depict the frequency response for this system, regardless of the specific device it describes and the specific values of the parameters. Figure 5.15 shows the frequency response associated with (5.33). This behavior is characteristic of many mechanical and electrical systems which contain both energy-storing and -dissipating elements.

The damping ratio $\zeta$ determines the shape of the frequency response curves. For heavily damped systems ($\zeta > 1/\sqrt{2} \simeq 0.71$), the output amplitude is always less than the input, regardless of the input frequency. In addition, the phase angle by which the output lags behind the input is always substantial.

In contrast, for lightly damped systems (i.e., ones with less energy dissipation), the amplitude ratio remains relatively constant until the input frequency approaches $\omega_n$, then the amplitude ratio rapidly peaks and drops off. The output hardly lags the input below $\omega_n$, especially in very lightly damped systems ($\zeta < 0.01$). Thus, if Figure 5.15 showed a lightly damped ($\zeta = 0.01$) recorder frequency response, we could conclude that input signals composed of a sum of sine waves below about 0.8 $\omega_n$ would produce output that accurately mirrored the input, but that above this frequency the recorded value would differ substantially from the actual signal.

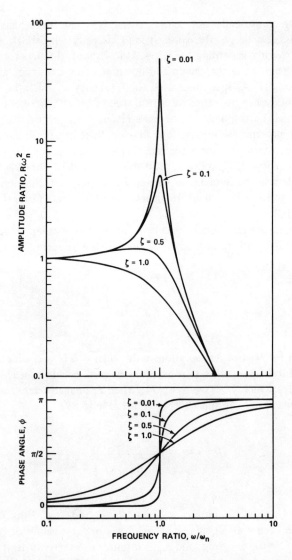

**FIGURE 5.15:** The frequency response of a second-order system depends only on the undamped natural frequency $\omega_n$ and damping ratio $\zeta$.

The peak in Figure 5.15 represents *resonance*, indicating that the sinusoidal input adds energy to the energy-storing elements faster than the dissipative elements dissipate it. One commonly feels resonance when riding down the highway in an automobile with slightly out-of-balance tires. Ignoring the car's forward motion, the rotating tires push the car up and down sinusoidally as it moves ahead. The car, a mechanical system with mass, elasticity (the springs), and viscosity (the shock absorbers), behaves roughly according to (5.33). At low speeds the tires rotate slowly, so the wheels shake the car up and down at a low frequency and the car rides smoothly. As speed increases, the frequency at which the tires shake the car increases until, at some critical speed (typically between 50 and 60 mph) which corresponds to the car's resonant frequency, the occupants suddenly become aware that it is shaking. Speeding up or slowing down diminishes the noticeable vibration. Typically, at speeds below the resonant frequency the amplitude ratio is so small that vibration cannot be felt, while near the resonant frequency the car amplifies the vibration until it is felt. Above the resonant frequency, the tires vibrate faster than the car can respond.

To find the resonant frequency $\omega_r$ of a second-order process, differentiate (5.37) with respect to $\omega$, set the derivative equal to zero, and solve to find

$$\omega_r = \omega_n \sqrt{1 - 2\zeta^2} \qquad (5.39)$$

Equation (5.39) has real solutions only when $\zeta \leqslant 1/\sqrt{2}$, which confirms our graphical observation that no resonant peak occurs in heavily damped systems for which $\zeta > 1/\sqrt{2} \approx 0.71$. When resonance occurs, we can find its peak magnitude by substituting $\omega_r$ for $\omega$ in (5.37).

$$R_r = R(\omega_r) = \frac{1}{2\zeta\omega_n^2 \sqrt{1 - \zeta^2}} \qquad (5.40)$$

Figure 5.16 shows a plot of $\omega_r$ and $R_r\omega_n^2$ against $\zeta$. Note that when resonance occurs at all, it occurs near $\omega_n$ for most values of $\zeta$. With no damping ($\zeta = 0$), $\omega_r = \omega_n$, and $R_r$ is infinite. In other words, if one adds energy to an undamped system at its natural frequency, the resulting output grows without bound.

The undamped natural frequency relates directly to the eigenvalues. When $\zeta = 0$, the fundamental equation associated with (5.33) is

$$\lambda^2 + \omega_n{}^2 = 0 \qquad (5.41)$$

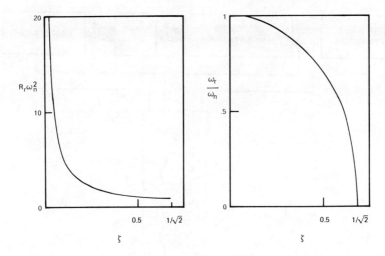

**FIGURE 5.16:** As the damping ratio approaches zero, the maximum amplitude which occurs during resonance approaches infinity. The damping ratio determines how close resonance will occur to the undamped natural frequency.

so the two eigenvalues are $\lambda_1 = i\omega_n$ and $\lambda_2 = -i\omega_n$. These eigenvalues correspond to a sinusoidal oscillation with frequency $\omega_n$. Thus, the undamped natural frequency follows directly from the eigenvalues of the undamped process.

While analytical observations are important, one often finds the frequency response experimentally, with little or no prior knowledge of the differential equations that describe the system. To do this, simply connect the input to a sinusoidal forcing function (for example, an electrical signal or mechanical perturbation), then monitor the output at a variety of frequencies to measure the amplitude ratio and phase angle associated with the frequencies of interest (Fig. 5.17). As long as the sinusoidal input produces a sinusoidal output of the same frequency, the process behaves linearly, and the concepts developed in this chapter apply. Frequency-response analysis probably finds its greatest use in the description of complex devices whose equations are not known.

All these results followed from the forcing function $A\sin \omega t$. We could, however, have obtained them by beginning with $A\cos \omega t$ or any sinusoid of frequency $\omega$, $A\sin (\omega t - \phi)$. This fact should not be surprising, since such phase shifts are equivalent to shifting the (time) origin, which does not affect the form of the response of a linear time-invariant process.

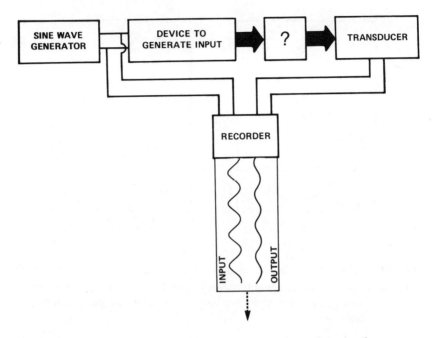

**FIGURE 5.17:** Apparatus to experimentally determine the frequency response of a device whose characteristics are unknown.

How does the frequency response relate to the other ways we have characterized linear time-invariant systems? Chapter 6 will show that the frequency response equals the Fourier transform of the impulse response.

## FREQUENCY RESPONSE OF FLUID-FILLED CATHETERS

In Chapter 3 we derived the differential equation (3.287) which related the pressure signal present at one end of a fluid-filled catheter to the electrical voltage signal produced by a strain-gauge pressure transducer at the other. We can now show that this simple description accurately describes the catheter dynamics reflected by its frequency response, and use this fact to predict catheter response. The longer and larger the catheter, the lower its resonant frequency and damping ratio, and hence the more limited the frequency range it will transmit accurately.

Equation (3.287) showed that

$$\ddot{E} + 2\zeta\omega_n\dot{E} + \omega_n{}^2E = \frac{p(t)K}{\rho L} \tag{5.42}$$

describes the dynamics of a fluid-filled catheter in which

$$\omega_n = \sqrt{\frac{k}{\rho LA}} \qquad \text{and} \qquad \zeta = \frac{c}{2}\sqrt{\frac{1}{\rho kLA}} \qquad (5.43)$$

where $k$ and $c$ quantify the effective mechanical elasticity and damping, $L$ and $A$ equal catheter length and cross-section area, $\rho$ equals the density of fluid in the catheter, and $K$ describes the pressure transducer. We predict that the catheter-transducer system should exhibit frequency response similar to that shown in Figure 5.15. Figure 5.18 shows that the catheter-transducer system indeed does exhibit this behavior.

The frequency response depends directly on the length and area of the catheter, as well as the elasticity and friction manifested as the fluid moves back and forth in the catheter in response to the pressure pulse. For example, air bubbles make the fluid in the tube appear springier, reflected

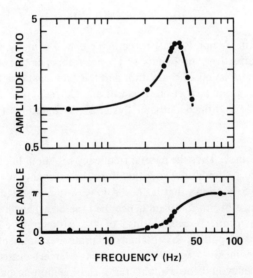

**FIGURE 5.18:** Frequency response for a typical catheter system determined experimentally by subjecting the catheter tip to a sinusoidally varying pressure of known frequency and amplitude, then measuring the resulting transducer signal. The amplitude ratio represents the ratio of recorded to applied pressure. Note that the catheter behaves like a second-order system. (Reproduced with permission of the authors and the American Heart Association, Inc., from H. L. Falsetti et al., Analysis and Correction of Pressure Wave Distortion in Fluid-filled Catheter Systems, *Circulation* 49 (1974): 165, Figure 2.)

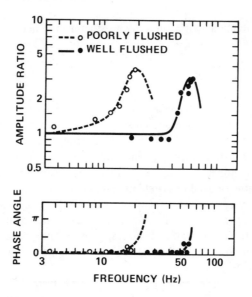

**FIGURE 5.19:** A poorly flushed catheter contains many small air bubbles, which effectively decrease $k$ and hence resonance frequency. (Reproduced with permission of the author and the American Heart Association, Inc., from H. L. Falsetti et al., Analysis and Correction of Pressure Wave Distortion in Fluid-filled Catheter Systems, *Circulation* 49 (1974): 165, Figure 5.)

as a decrease in $k$. Thus the natural frequency $\omega_n$ should decrease and the damping ratio $\zeta$ should increase; therefore the resonant frequency should drop. Figure 5.19 shows that it does. A lower resonant frequency severely limits the range of sinusoids and hence the type of signals the catheter will accurately transmit. A careful flush of the catheter to eliminate small bubbles is very important for obtaining accurate measurements.

Similarly, making the catheter longer (or larger) decreases both the natural frequency and the damping ratio, causing more resonance at lower frequencies and degrading the quality of the transmitted signal. To obtain the most accurate pressure recordings from a fluid-filled catheter system, one should seek to use a well-flushed, stiff, short, narrow catheter to maximize the range of frequencies that it accurately transmits to the recorder.

Figure 5.20 shows the actual step and computed frequency response of three tubes used to measure pressure: a small, short, stiff catheter; a longer, wider, more elastic teflon tube; and a soft polyvinyl tube. As

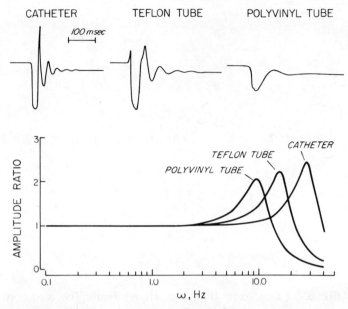

**FIGURE 5.20:** Measured step and computed frequency response of three different tubes used to transmit pressure signals. The first cycle does not look sinusoidal because of artifacts produced by the device which produces the step change in pressure.

(5.43) predicts, as the tube becomes softer and longer, the undamped natural frequency $\omega_n$ drops and the damping $\zeta$ increases. The step response reflects these changes by exhibiting slower, smaller-amplitude oscillations, while the amplitude ratio part of the frequency-response diagram exhibits a lower resonant peak at lower frequencies.

Figure 5.21 shows actual aortic and left ventricular pressure waves that were measured in dogs, using the above three tubes as catheters. Chapter 6 will show that sudden changes in a signal, such as the rapid upstroke in pressure when the heart begins to contract, reflect high-frequency components of the signal. The catheter has a high enough $\omega_n$ to reproduce both pressure signals accurately. By contrast, the teflon tube's resonant frequency falls near the frequency components of the pressure signals which represent the rapid pressure increases, so these components are amplified, producing the artifactual wiggles shown in the center panels. The $\omega_n$ of the polyvinyl tube is so low that it does not pass the high-frequency components, making the pressure changes look slower than they actually are.

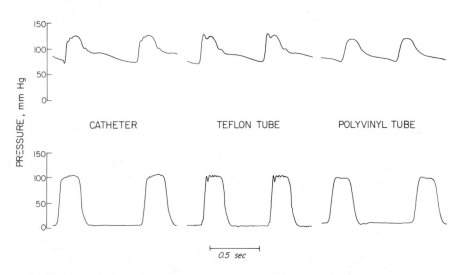

**FIGURE 5.21:** Dog aortic (top) and left ventricular (bottom) pressures measured through the three tubes illustrated in Figure 5.20.

## PROBLEM SET 5.3

1. Plot the impulse, step, and frequency response of second-order systems governed by $\ddot{x} + 2\zeta\,\omega_n\dot{x} + \omega_n^2 x = f(t)$ for
   a. $\omega_n = 20$ Hz       $\zeta = 0.1$
   b. $\omega_n = 20$ Hz       $\zeta = 0.5$
   c. $\omega_n = 20$ Hz       $\zeta = 0.8$
   d. $\omega_n = 20$ Hz       $\zeta = 1.2$
   e. $\omega_n = 10$ Hz       $\zeta = 0.1$
   f. $\omega_n = 10$ Hz       $\zeta = 0.5$
   g. $\omega_n = 10$ Hz       $\zeta = 1.2$

2. Find the response of the system shown in Figure 5.12 to the series of square waves in Figure 5.13. The equation of the input is $f(t) = 4/\pi\,(\sin t + 1/3 \sin 3t + 1/5 \sin 5t + \ldots)$. Plot the input and output.

3. Find the time response of an undamped second-order system with a sinusoidal input (of magnitude 1) applied at the natural frequency.

4. Find the undamped natural frequency and damping ratio for the second-order system whose step response is shown in Figure 5.22. (Hint: Find the time constant of decay and the damped natural frequency, then use the fact that $\tau = 1/\zeta\omega_n$ and $\omega_d = \omega_n\sqrt{1 - \zeta^2}$.)

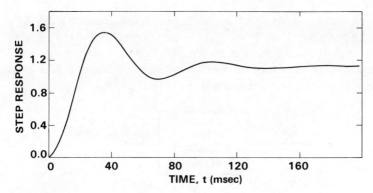

**FIGURE 5.22:** Illustration for Problem 5.4.

## TRANSFER FUNCTIONS

Impulse, step, and frequency response characterize the response of time-invariant linear processes using standard inputs. Transfer functions use Laplace transforms to represent the process as a compact mathematical expression. If the input $f(t)$ produces output $y(t)$ in accordance with the linear constant-coefficient differential equation

$$a_n y^{(n)} + a_{n-1} y^{(n-1)} + \ldots + a_1 y' + a_0 y_0 = f(t) \qquad (5.44)$$

with the initial conditions

$$y^{(n-1)}(0) = y^{(n-2)}(0) = \ldots = y'(0) = y(0) = 0 \qquad (5.45)$$

we can compute (5.44)'s Laplace transform:

$$(a_n s^n + a_{n-1} s^{n-1} + \ldots + a_0) Y(s) = F(s) \qquad (5.46)$$

Rather than solving for the output Laplace transform $Y(s)$, find the ratio of the Laplace transform of the output to the Laplace transform of the input:

$$H(s) = \frac{Y(s)}{F(s)} = \frac{1}{a_n s^n + a_{n-1} s^{n-1} + \ldots + a_1 s + a_0} \qquad (5.47)$$

This ratio of the input to the output Laplace transforms $H(s)$ is called the *transfer function*. Thus, if the transfer function associated with a linear constant-coefficient process is known, the Laplace transform of the response to any input can be found by simply multiplying its Laplace transform by the transfer function (Fig. 5.23).

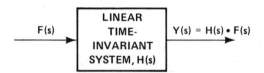

FIGURE 5.23: One can use the ratio of the Laplace transforms of the output to the input (the transfer function), $H(s)$, to describe the input-output relationship of a time-invariant linear process. Given $H(s)$, one obtains the Laplace transform of the output by multiplying the Laplace transform of the input times the transfer function.

In other words, the response of a process with transfer function $H(s)$ to input $x(t)$ is

$$y(t) = \mathcal{L}^{-1}\{X(s) \, H(s)\} \qquad \text{where } X(s) = \mathcal{L}\{x(t)\} \qquad (5.48)$$

For example, suppose we wish to find the response of a one-compartment drug distribution with the transfer function

$$H(s) = \frac{1/V}{s + k} \qquad (5.49)$$

to the constant infusion input

$$x(t) = Iu(t) \qquad (5.50)$$

First find

$$X(s) = \mathcal{L}\{x(t)\} = \frac{I}{s} \qquad (5.51)$$

then multiply it by $H(s)$, and invert the result to find

$$y(t) = \mathcal{L}^{-1}\left\{\frac{I/V}{s(s + k)}\right\} = \frac{I}{kV}(1 - e^{-kt}) \qquad (5.52)$$

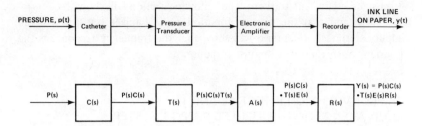

**FIGURE 5.24:** When a signal representing a measurement passes through a number of devices, each device alters the signal in accordance with its transfer function before passing it on to the next device in the chain. If the transfer functions associated with each device are known, the overall transfer function can be found. It relates the pressure signal $p(t)$ to the chart deflection $y(t)$ and is $H(s) = Y(s)/P(s) = C(s) \cdot T(s) \cdot E(s) \cdot R(s)$.

Transfer functions lend themselves especially to problems involving multiple interconnected elements, each of which has a known transfer function. Suppose, for example, that one wishes to analyze the overall response of a catheter system involving a fluid-filled catheter connected to a pressure transducer whose output passes through electronic amplifiers to a chart recorder (Fig. 5.24). Each element in the chain acts on the output of the previous element to produce the input to the next element, and each element is characterized by some dynamic response represented by its transfer function. At each stage the previous result becomes an input to the next stage, and thus is multiplied by the transfer function of that stage to produce its output, which in turn is the input to the next stage. Therefore, the pressure pulse $p(t)$ will produce a deflection $y(t)$ on the chart recorder, according to

$$y(t) = \mathscr{L}^{-1}\{Y(s)\} = \mathscr{L}^{-1}\{P(s) \cdot C(s) \cdot T(s) \cdot E(s) \cdot R(s)\}$$

$$(5.53)$$

where $P(s) = \mathscr{L}\{p(t)\}$. This representation of cascaded processes is called a *block diagram* and is especially useful for analyzing signal flows in systems with discrete components, especially when some of the components are electronic or mechanical devices.*

Since the transfer function contains the same information about a time-invariant linear process as the impulse, step, and frequency response,

---

* Block diagrams can also be useful for analyzing biologcal systems. See, for example Talbot, S. A., and Gessner, V., *Systems Physiology*. New York: Wiley, 1973.

it must be equivalent to them. The following section will show that $H(s) = \mathscr{L}\{h(t)\}$, and that the transfer function is the Laplace transform of the impulse response. Chapter 6 will show that the frequency response is the Fourier transform of the impulse response.*

## THE CONVOLUTION INTEGRAL AND THE EQUIVALENCE OF THE IMPULSE RESPONSE, STEP RESPONSE, AND TRANSFER FUNCTION

We have noted that the impulse response, step response, and transfer function all completely characterize the behavior of a linear time-invariant process described by linear constant-coefficient ordinary differential equations. Since all these representations contain the same information, they must be equivalent. In fact, we have already stated that $h(t) = \dot{A}(t)$ and $H(s) = \mathscr{L}\{h(t)\}$. We will now study the properties of the convolution integral which appeared earlier in this chapter and use these properties to logically derive the relationships between the impulse response, step response, and transfer function.

The results we wish to prove all follow from the theorem:

*If $F(s) = \mathscr{L}\{f(t)\}$, $G(s) = \mathscr{L}\{g(t)\}$, and both exist for $s < a < 0$, then*

$$h(t) = \int_0^t f(t-\tau)g(\tau)d\tau = \int_0^t f(t)g(t-\tau)d\tau \tag{5.54}$$

*where*

$$H(s) = F(s) \cdot G(s) = \mathscr{L}\{h(t)\} \qquad s > a. \tag{5.55}$$

The function $h(t)$ is called the *convolution* of the two functions $f(t)$ and $g(t)$. The convolution of these two functions can also be denoted $f(t) * g(t)$. By definition,

$$F(s) = \mathscr{L}\{f(t)\} = \int_0^\infty e^{-s\tau}f(\tau)d\tau \tag{5.56}$$

---

* Since $h(t) = dA/dt$, $H(s) = \mathscr{L}\{dA/dt\}$ and so $H(s)$ is also directly related to the step response.

and

$$G(s) = \mathcal{L}\{g(t)\} = \int_0^\infty e^{-sv} g(v) dv \qquad (5.57)$$

so

$$H(s) = F(s) \cdot G(s) = \int_0^\infty e^{-s\tau} f(\tau) d\tau \cdot \int_0^\infty e^{-sv} g(v) dv$$

$$(5.58)$$

The second integral does not depend on $\tau$, so we can move $e^{-s\tau}$ across the integral to obtain

$$H(s) = \int_0^\infty f(\tau) d\tau \int_0^\infty e^{-s\tau} e^{-sv} g(v) dv$$

$$= \int_0^\infty f(\tau) d\tau \int_0^\infty e^{-s(\tau+v)} g(v) dv \qquad (5.59)$$

Now let $\tau + v = t$, in which case $dv = dt$ for fixed $\tau$ and (5.59) becomes

$$H(s) = \int_0^\infty f(\tau) d\tau \int_\tau^\infty e^{-st} g(t - \tau) dt$$

$$= \int_0^\infty f(\tau) \left[ \int_\tau^\infty e^{-st} g(t - \tau) dt \right] d\tau \qquad (5.60)$$

Since $g(t - \tau) = 0$ for $t < \tau$ we can rewrite (5.60) as

$$H(s) = \int_0^\infty f(\tau) \left[ \int_0^\infty e^{-st} g(t - \tau) dt \right] d\tau \qquad (5.61)$$

Since $f(\tau)$ does not depend on $t$, we can move it into the inner integral without changing its value:

$$H(s) = \int_0^\infty \left[ \int_0^\infty e^{-st} f(\tau) g(t - \tau) dt \right] d\tau \qquad (5.62)$$

The conditions for the Laplace transform to exist also allow us to reverse the order of integration in (5.62) to obtain

$$H(s) = \int_0^\infty \left[ \int_0^\infty e^{-st} f(\tau) g(t - \tau) d\tau \right] dt \qquad (5.63)$$

But $e^{-st}$ does not depend on $\tau$, so we can remove it from the inner integral with no change in value. In addition, since $g(t - \tau) = 0$ for $\tau > t$, the inner integration effectively ends at $\tau = t$, and we can replace the upper limit with $t$. With these two changes, (5.63) becomes

$$H(s) = \int_0^\infty e^{-st} \left[ \int_0^t f(\tau) g(t - \tau) d\tau \right] dt \qquad (5.64)$$

According to (5.55), the integral in brackets is $h(t)$, so

$$H(s) = \int_0^\infty e^{-st} h(t) dt = \mathscr{L}\{h(t)\} \qquad (5.65)$$

The other form of the convolution integral follows by changing variables to eliminate $\tau$ rather than $v$ from (5.59).

We now use this theorem to show that the impulse response $h(t)$, step response $A(t)$, and transfer function are related according to

$$h(t) = \frac{dA(t)}{dt} \qquad (5.66)$$

and

$$H(s) = \mathscr{L}\{h(t)\} \qquad (5.67)$$

We showed that a process with impulse response $h(t)$ responds to the forcing function $f(t)$ according to

$$y(t) = \int_0^t f(\tau)\, h(t - \tau)\, d\tau \qquad (5.68)$$

A process with step response $A(t)$ responds to the same forcing function according to

$$y(t) = \int_0^t \frac{df}{dt} A(t - \tau)\, d\tau \qquad (5.69)$$

The theorem we just proved says that (5.68) and (5.69) lead to

$$\mathscr{L}\{y(t)\} = \mathscr{L}\{f(t)\} \cdot \mathscr{L}\{h(t)\} \qquad (5.70)$$

and

$$\mathscr{L}\{y(t)\} = \mathscr{L}\left\{\frac{df}{dt}\right\} \cdot \mathscr{L}\{A(t)\} \qquad (5.71)$$

$$= [s\mathscr{L}\{f(t)\} - f(0)] \cdot \{A(t)\} \qquad (5.72)$$

respectively. But since all initial conditions equal zero, (5.72) becomes

$$\mathscr{L}\{y(t)\} = [s\mathscr{L}\{f(t)\}] \cdot \mathscr{L}\{A(t)\}$$

$$= \mathscr{L}\{f(t)\} \cdot [s\mathscr{L}\{A(t)\}]$$

$$= \mathscr{L}\{f(t)\} \cdot \mathscr{L}\left\{\frac{dA}{dt}\right\} \qquad (5.73)$$

Comparing (5.70) and (5.73) reveals that

$$\mathscr{L}\{h(t)\} = \mathscr{L}\left\{\frac{dA}{dt}\right\} \qquad (5.74)$$

therefore

$$h(t) = \frac{dA}{dt} \qquad (5.75)$$

The impulse response is thus the derivative of the step response.

To show that $H(s) = \mathcal{L}\{h(t)\}$, divide both sides of (5.70) by $\mathcal{L}\{f(t)\}$:

$$\mathcal{L}\{h(t)\} = \frac{\mathcal{L}\{y(t)\}}{\mathcal{L}\{f(t)\}} = \frac{Y(s)}{F(s)} = H(s) \qquad (5.76)$$

But $Y(s)$ is the Laplace transform of the output $y(t)$, and $F(s)$ is the transform of the input $f(t)$, so $Y(s)/F(s)$ is by definition the transfer function $H(s)$. Thus the transfer function is the Laplace transform of the impulse response.

Finally, to relate the discussion in this chapter to Chapter 3, we show that a convolution integral such as (5.68) represents the particular solution to the ordinary differential equation which describes the process, even with nonzero initial conditions. For example, to solve

$$a_2\ddot{y} + a_1\dot{y} + a_0 y = f(t) \qquad y(0) = y_0 \qquad \dot{y}(0) = \dot{y}_0 \qquad (5.77)$$

begin by computing its Laplace transform:

$$(a_2 s^2 + a_1 s + a_0)\, Y(s) - (a_2 s + a_1)\, y_0 - a_2 \dot{y}_0 = F(s) \qquad (5.78)$$

Before continuing, note that taking all initial conditions equal to zero in (5.78) produces the transfer function associated with (5.77):

$$H(s) = \frac{Y(s)}{F(s)} = \frac{1}{a_2 s^2 + a_1 s + a_0} \qquad (5.79)$$

Returning to our original problem, solve (5.78) for $Y(s)$:

$$Y(s) = \frac{F(s)}{a_2 s^2 + a_1 s + a_0} + \frac{(a_2 s + a_1)y_0 + a_2 \dot{y}_0}{a_2 s^2 + a_1 s + a_0} \qquad (5.80)$$

then substitute from (5.79) into (5.80) to obtain

$$Y(s) = H(s)\, F(s) + \frac{(a_2 s + a_1)y_0 + a_2 \dot{y}_0}{a_2 s^2 + a_1 s + a_0} \qquad (5.81)$$

Therefore

$$y(t) = \mathcal{L}^{-1}\{H(s) \cdot F(s)\} + y_0 \, \mathcal{L}^{-1}\left\{\frac{a_2 s + a_1}{a_2 s^2 + a_1 s + a_0}\right\}$$

$$+ \dot{y}_0 \, \mathcal{L}^{-1}\left\{\frac{a_2}{a_2 s^2 + a_1 s + a_0}\right\} \qquad (5.82)$$

Now use our new theorem to invert the first transformation and let

$$y_1(t) = \mathcal{L}^{-1}\left\{\frac{a_2 s + a_1}{a_2 s^2 + a_1 s + a_0}\right\} \qquad (5.83)$$

and

$$y_2(t) = \mathcal{L}^{-1}\left\{\frac{a_2}{a_2 s^2 + a_1 s + a_0}\right\} \qquad (5.84)$$

both of which can be found from our table of Laplace transforms. Thus (5.83) becomes

$$y(t) = \int_0^t h(t - \tau) f(\tau) d\tau + y_0 \, y_1(t) + \dot{y}_0 \, y_2(t) \qquad (5.85)$$

The first term on the right side represents the system's response to forcing function $f(t)$. In the terminology of Chapter 3, it is the particular solution corresponding to (5.77)'s nonhomogeneous term $f(t)$. Similarly, $y_1(t)$ and $y_2(t)$ represent two linearly independent fundamental solutions to the homogeneous problem associated with (5.77), and $y_0$ and $\dot{y}_0$ represent the two arbitrary constants.

In sum, the impulse response, step response, frequency response, and transfer function are equivalent ways to describe the response of a linear system to a forcing function or input. The resulting equations represent the particular solution we obtained using the direct methods developed in Chapter 3 to solve the differential equation which describes the process.

## PROBLEM SET 5.4

Find the transfer functions associated with the systems or processes described by the following differential equations. In each case, the variable to the right of the equal sign represents the input.

1. $\dot{v} + av = e(t)$        $a$ = constant
2. $3\ddot{y} + 2\dot{y} - y = f(t)$
3. $\dddot{x} + \ddot{x} - 5\dot{x} + 2x = 2g(t) + 4\dot{g}(t)$
4. $y = 2x$
5. $\ddot{E} + 2\zeta\omega_n \dot{E} + \omega_n^2 E = p(t) \cdot K/(\rho L)$
6. a. Find the transfer function relating the central-compartment concentration $c(t)$ to the infusion rate $i(t)$ in a two-compartment drug-distribution model described by Equation (2.80):

$$\ddot{c} + (k_{12} + k_{21} + k_{10}) \dot{c} + k_{10} k_{21} c = [\dot{i}(t) + k_{21} i(t)] / V$$

b. Find the same transfer function from the two first-order equations which describe the drug flow into and out of each compartment, without combining them into a single second-order differential equation (see Chapter 2).

$$\dot{q}_1 = -(k_{12} + k_{10})q_1 + k_{21}q_2 + i(t) \qquad \text{(Eq. 2.73)}$$

$$\dot{q}_2 = k_{12}q_1 - k_{21}q_2 \qquad \text{(Eq. 2.74)}$$

$$c = \frac{q_1}{V} \qquad \text{(following Eq. 2.79)}$$

in which $q_1$ and $q_2$ represent the mass of drug in compartments 1 and 2 respectively.

7. Suppose we connect a catheter whose transfer function is given by the result of Problem 5 to a recorder whose transfer function is given by the result of Problem 1.

a. What is the transfer function of the resulting system?
b. Suppose the catheter has an undamped natural frequency of 10 Hz = 62.8 sec$^{-1}$, a damping ratio of 0.1, and $K/(\rho L)$ = 1 volt/mmHg-sec$^{-2}$, and the recorder has the property that $a$ = 50 sec$^{-1}$. What is the transfer function?
c. Plot the frequency response for the catheter from 0 to 20 Hz, using semi-log paper for the amplitude ratio segment. (Hint: Use Figure 5.15 to save some arithmetic.)

d. Using the same scale, plot the frequency response of the catheter-recorder system.

e. Repeat part (d) for a recorder with $a = 10 \text{ sec}^{-1}$ and $a = 100 \text{ sec}^{-1}$.

f. How does the recorder alter the signal?

8. Suppose that we have a device whose transfer function is $H(s)$ and whose purpose is to respond, as closely as possible, to an input $I(s) = \mathscr{L}\{i(t)\}$.

a. If we apply the input directly to the transducer as shown in Figure 5.25A, what will the response be?

b. Suppose that instead of applying $I(s)$ directly to the device, we apply the *difference* between the output and the input (Fig. 5.25B). This arrangement, called *unit feedback*, means that when the output differs greatly from the input (which, after all, is the

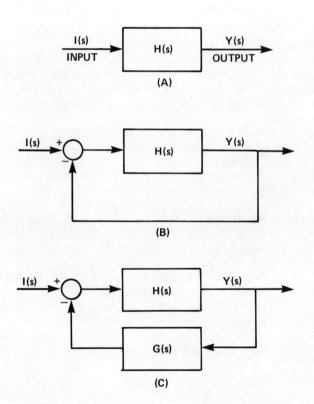

**FIGURE 5.25:** Illustrations for Problem Set 5.4.

desired output), the signal applied to the device is large, whereas when the input equals the output no adjusting signal is applied to the device. What then would be the transfer function relating output to input?

9. Find and plot the step responses of devices with the following transfer functions, at first alone, and then with unit feedback (remember that the goal of each device is to reproduce the step change as accurately as possible).

a. $\dfrac{1}{2(s + 1)}$

b. $\dfrac{1}{s^2 + 4s + 3}$

c. $\dfrac{1}{s^2 + 0.4s + 4}$

10. What does feedback do to the response?
11. What is the transfer function of the system shown in Figure 5.25C which represents a general feedback system in which one alters the output before feeding it back? This illustration describes a general *servo system* such as is used in most control systems for laboratory apparatus.
12. The simplest kind of servo system involves setting $G(s)$ = constant, i.e., multiplying the output by some constant factor (called the *gain* in electronics) before feeding the signal back. Find and plot the step response of these systems in Problem 9 if $G$ = 0.5, 2, and 10. What happens as the feedback increases?

## ADDITIONAL READINGS

Grodins, F. S. *Control Theory and Biological Systems.* New York: Columbia University Press, 1963.

Jones, R. W. *Principles of Biological Regulation: An Introduction to Feedback Systems.* New York: Academic Press, 1963.

Riggs, D. S. *Control Theory and Physiological Feedback Mechanisms,* Chapter 3. Baltimore: Williams and Wilkins, 1970.

Timothy, L. K., and Bona, B. E. *State Space Analysis: An Introduction,* Chapters 4 and 5. New York: McGraw-Hill, 1968.

# 6

# FOURIER ANALYSIS, SPECTRA, AND FILTERS

In order to make use of frequency characterizations of linear time-invariant processes, we must know which sinusoids compose the forcing function or input signal. We will now develop a method to decompose functions (signals) into sums or integrals of their constituent sinusoids of varying frequency and amplitude. Periodic signals are comprised of sinusoids with discrete frequencies and can be represented by a sum of sine and cosine functions with these frequencies; this sum is called a *Fourier series*. The *Fourier integral*—a generalization of the Fourier series—represents any function as an integral over all frequencies. In the process of computing the Fourier series or Fourier integral we will discover the magnitude, phase, and frequency of each sinusoidal component of the signal, which is called the signal's *spectrum.* If the signal contains energy of only discrete frequencies, for example, a mixture of different laser lights, its spectrum consists of a few discrete elements (lines); the signal's energy is concentrated at each line (frequency). By contrast, white light, which contains energy at all frequencies in a given range, has a continuous spectrum in which energy varies with frequency. Once a signal's spectrum is known, one can determine whether the frequency response of a device such as a transducer is adequate to reproduce the signal faithfully, and if necessary, design filters to selectively remove specified frequency components from the signal.

## THE FOURIER SERIES REPRESENTS PERIODIC FUNCTIONS

A function is *periodic* with period $T$ when

$$f(t + T) = f(t) \qquad (6.1)$$

for all $t$. Hence, $f(t + nT) = f(t)$ where $n$ is any integer (Figure 6.1A). In earlier chapters we represented functions, such as the exponential, sine, and cosine, with infinite sums of the form $\Sigma a_n x^n$. Now we shall seek to represent any periodic function $f(t)$, by selecting appropriate values of the constants in an infinite sum of the form

$$f(t) = \frac{1}{2}a_0 + a_1 \cos t + a_2 \cos 2t + a_3 \cos 3t + \ldots$$

$$+ b_1 \sin t + b_2 \sin 2t + b_3 \sin 3t + \ldots \qquad (6.2)$$

Since the cosine and sine functions have the period $2\pi$, we begin with the functions $f(t)$, having period $2\pi$, then generalize to permit the representation of any periodic function with a sum like (6.2).

To evaluate the constants in (6.2) we proceed naively, without worrying about the details of convergence. The following theorem, called the Dirichlet condition, insures that all Fourier series of practical importance converge, and that the steps we take below make strict mathematical sense:

> *If f(t) is a periodic function which has at most a finite number of maxima, minima, and discontinuities in each period, and for which $|f(t)| < M$ where M is a constant, then f(t) can be represented with a Fourier series which converges to (a) f(t) where f(t) is continuous; and (b) the average value of the left- and right-hand limits, $1/2[f(t^-) + f(t^+)]$, where f(t) is discontinuous.*

The proof of the Dirichlet condition is beyond the scope of this book. Fortunately, these details are not necessary to understand practical Fourier analysis.

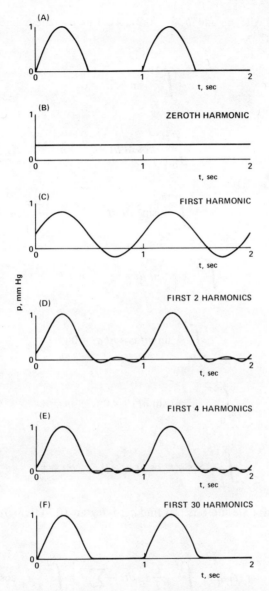

**FIGURE 6.1:** (A) A periodic function with period $T = 1$ sec. (B–F) Adding more and more terms (harmonics) to the Fourier series representation of function (A) produces closer and closer agreement with the actual function.

To find the $a_i$ and $b_i$ in (6.2), we will use these integrals from Appendix B:*

$$\int_0^{2\pi} \sin nt \, dt = 0 \tag{6.3}$$

$$\int_0^{2\pi} \cos nt \, dt = 0 \qquad n \neq 0 \tag{6.4}$$

$$\int_0^{2\pi} \sin^2 nt \, dt = \pi \tag{6.5}$$

$$\int_0^{2\pi} \cos^2 nt \, dt = \pi \qquad n \neq 0 \tag{6.6}$$

$$\int_0^{2\pi} \sin mt \cos nt \, dt = 0 \tag{6.7}$$

$$\int_0^{2\pi} \sin mt \sin nt \, dt = 0 \qquad m \neq n \tag{6.8}$$

$$\int_0^{2\pi} \cos mt \cos nt \, dt = 0 \qquad m \neq n \tag{6.9}$$

where $m$ and $n$ are integers. To find $a_0$, integrate (6.2) term by term over one period:

$$\int_0^{2\pi} f(t) \, dt = \int_0^{2\pi} \frac{1}{2} a_0 \, dt + \sum_{n=1}^{\infty} \left[ \int_0^{2\pi} a_n \cos nt \, dt \right.$$

$$\left. + \int_0^{2\pi} b_n \sin nt \, dt \right] \tag{6.10}$$

* Numbers 44, 45, 50, 53, 57, 58, and 59, respectively.

Equations (6.3) and (6.4) require that each of the integrals behind the infinite sum equal zero, so (6.10) yields

$$\int_0^{2\pi} f(t)\, dt = \frac{1}{2} a_0\, t \, \bigg|_0^{2\pi} = \pi a_0 \qquad (6.11)$$

$$a_0 = \frac{1}{\pi} \int_0^{2\pi} f(t)\, dt \qquad (6.12)$$

To find the other $a_m$, multiply (6.2) by $\cos mt$ and integrate term by term again:

$$\int_0^{2\pi} f(t) \cos mt\, dt = \int_0^{2\pi} \frac{1}{2} a_0 \cos mt\, dt$$

$$+ \sum_{n=1}^{\infty} \left[ \int_0^{2\pi} a_n \cos nt \cos mt\, dt \right.$$

$$+ \left. \int_0^{2\pi} b_n \sin nt \cos mt\, dt \right] \qquad (6.13)$$

$$= \frac{1}{2} a_0 \int_0^{2\pi} \cos mt\, dt$$

$$+ \sum_{n=1}^{m-1} a_n \int_0^{2\pi} \cos nt \cos mt\, dt$$

$$+ a_m \int_0^{2\pi} \cos^2 mt\, dt$$

$$+ \sum_{n=m+1}^{\infty} a_n \int_0^{2\pi} \cos nt \cos mt\, dt$$

$$+ \sum_{n=1}^{\infty} b_n \int_0^{2\pi} \sin nt \cos mt\, dt \qquad (6.14)$$

Equations (6.4), (6.6), (6.7), and (6.9) show that, except for the $m$th one that equals $\pi$, all the integrals in (6.14) vanish. Hence

$$a_m = \frac{1}{\pi} \int_0^{2\pi} f(t) \cos mt \, dt \qquad (6.15)$$

Multiplying (6.2) by $\sin mt$ and repeating the integration process yields

$$b_m = \frac{1}{\pi} \int_0^{2\pi} f(t) \sin mt \, dt \qquad (6.16)$$

Since $\cos(0 \cdot t) = 1$, (6.15) includes (6.12).*

To generalize this work to functions with any period $T$, let $x = (2\pi/T)t$. When $t = T, x = 2\pi$, so if $f(t)$ has period $T, f(x)$ has period $2\pi$ and

$$f(x) = \frac{1}{2}a_0 + \sum_{n=1}^{\infty} [a_n \cos nx + b_n \sin nx] \qquad (6.17)$$

where

$$a_n = \frac{1}{\pi} \int_0^{2\pi} f(x) \cos nx \, dx \qquad (6.18)$$

and

$$b_n = \frac{1}{\pi} \int_0^{2\pi} f(x) \sin nx \, dx \qquad (6.19)$$

Rather than writing (6.17) to (6.19) in terms of $x$, replace $x$ with $(2\pi/T)t$ and $dx$ with $(2\pi/T) \, dt$:

$$f(t) = \frac{1}{2}a_0 + \sum_{n=1}^{\infty} \left[ a_n \cos \frac{2\pi n}{T} t + b_n \sin \frac{2\pi n}{T} t \right] \qquad (6.20)$$

---

* If an unreasonable result occurs for $a_0$ by substituting $n = 0$ in (6.15), compute it directly by integrating $f(t)$ without the cosine term. Sometimes setting $n = 0$ after integration implicitly involves a mathematically unjustified step such as dividing by zero or invoking a relationship such as (6.3) or (6.6), which does not apply when $n = 0$.

where

$$a_n = \frac{2}{T} \int_0^T f(t) \cos \frac{2\pi n}{T} t \, dt \qquad (6.21)$$

and

$$b_n = \frac{2}{T} \int_0^T f(t) \sin \frac{2\pi n}{T} t \, dt \qquad (6.22)$$

Since $f(t)$ is periodic with period $T$, we could replace the limits of integration in (6.21) and (6.22) with $t_0$ and $t_0 + T$ where $t_0$ is any time. Equations (6.20) to (6.22) define the Fourier series representation for *any* function with period $T$, which satisfies the Dirichlet condition.

Now let us represent the periodic ($T = 1$ sec) pulse train in Figure 6.1A as a Fourier series. We first represent $p(t)$ mathematically:*

$$p(t) = \begin{cases} \sin (2\pi \text{ sec}^{-1})t \text{ mmHg} & 0 < t \leq 0.5 \text{ sec} \\ 0 & 0.5 < t \leq 1 \text{ sec} \\ p(t - nT) & \text{otherwise } (n = \text{integer}) \end{cases} \qquad (6.23)$$

Substitute from (6.23) into (6.21) and (6.22):

$$a_n = \frac{2}{1 \text{ sec}} \left[ \int_0^{0.5 \text{ sec}} \sin \frac{2\pi}{\text{sec}} t \, \cos \frac{2\pi n}{\text{sec}} t \text{ mmHg } dt \right.$$

$$\left. + \int_{0.5 \text{ sec}}^{1 \text{ sec}} 0 \cos \frac{2\pi n}{\text{sec}} t \, dt \right] \qquad (6.24)$$

$$b_n = \frac{2}{1 \text{ sec}} \left[ \int_0^{0.5 \text{ sec}} \sin \frac{2\pi}{\text{sec}} t \, \sin \frac{2\pi n}{\text{sec}} t \text{ mmHg } dt \right.$$

$$\left. + \int_0^{1 \text{ sec}} \sin \frac{2\pi n}{\text{sec}} t \, dt \right] \qquad (6.25)$$

* One often bypasses this step and integrates (6.21) and (6.22) numerically.

From Formula 56 of Appendix B:

$$a_1 = \frac{2}{\text{sec}} \int_0^{0.5 \text{ sec}} \sin (2\pi \text{ sec}^{-1})t \cos (2\pi \text{ sec}^{-1})\, t \text{ mmHg } dt$$

$$= \frac{1}{2\pi} \sin^2 (2\pi \text{ sec}^{-1})t \bigg|_0^{0.5 \text{ sec}} \quad \text{mmHg} = 0 \tag{6.26}$$

From Formula 57 of Appendix B:

$$a_n = \frac{2}{\text{sec}} \int_0^{0.5 \text{ sec}} \sin (2\pi \text{ sec}^{-1})t \cos (2\pi n \text{ sec}^{-1})t \text{ mmHg } dt$$

$$= \frac{2}{\text{sec}} \left[ -\frac{\cos (2\pi - 2\pi n) \text{ sec}^{-1} t}{2(2\pi - 2\pi n) \text{ sec}^{-1}} - \frac{\cos (2\pi + 2\pi n) \text{ sec}^{-1} t}{2(2\pi + 2\pi n) \text{ sec}^{-1}} \right]_0^{0.5 \text{ sec}} \text{mmHg} \tag{6.27}$$

$$= -\frac{1}{2\pi} \left[ \frac{\cos \pi(1 - n) - 1}{1 - n} + \frac{\cos \pi(1 + n) - 1}{1 + n} \right] \text{mmHg} \tag{6.28}$$

But $\cos (1 - n)\pi = \cos (n - 1)\pi = (-1)^{n+1}$ and $\cos (n + 1)\pi = (-1)^{n+1} = -(-1)^n$ so

$$a_n = \frac{1}{2\pi} \left[ \frac{(-1)^n + 1}{1 - n} + \frac{(-1)^n + 1}{1 + n} \right] \text{mmHg} \tag{6.29}$$

$$= \frac{1}{\pi} \frac{(-1)^n + 1}{1 - n^2} \text{mmHg} \qquad n \neq 1 \tag{6.30}$$

Thus $a_n = 2/[\pi(1 - n^2)]$ mmHg for even $n$ and zero for odd $n$.
Formula 50 of Appendix B shows that

$$b_1 = \frac{2}{\text{sec}} \int_0^{0.5 \text{ sec}} \sin^2 (2\pi \text{ sec}^{-1})t \text{ mmHg } dt$$

$$= \frac{2}{\text{sec}} \left[ \frac{1}{2}t - \frac{1}{4}\sin (4\pi \text{ sec}^{-1})t \right]_0^{0.5 \text{ sec}} \text{mmHg}$$

$$= \frac{1}{2} \text{mmHg} \tag{6.31}$$

Formula 58 of Appendix B shows that $b_n = 0$ for all $n \neq 1$.
Therefore, we can replace (6.23) with the Fourier series

$$p(t) = \left[ \frac{1}{\pi} + \frac{1}{2} \sin 2\pi t - \frac{2}{3\pi} \cos \frac{4\pi}{\sec} t - \frac{2}{15\pi} \cos \frac{8\pi}{\sec} t \right.$$

$$\left. - \frac{2}{35\pi} \cos \frac{12\pi}{\sec} t - \frac{2}{63\pi} \cos \frac{16\pi}{\sec} t - \ldots \right] \text{mmHg} \qquad (6.32)$$

Figure 6.1 (B-F) shows some partial sums of (6.32). The zeroth term (the constant $1/\pi$) gives $p(t)$'s average value. Adding more terms adds progressively more information about $p(t)$'s shape (Fig. 6.1B). The first and slowest sinusoid, $\sin \pi t$, gives $f(t)$'s period and general shape. This slowest-frequency sinusoid is the *first harmonic*, and its frequency, which is called the *fundamental frequency*, is the same as the signal itself. In our example the fundamental frequency $\omega$ is 1 cycle/sec = 1 Hz = $2\pi$ rad/sec = $2\pi \sec^{-1}$. All the other terms in the Fourier series have frequencies that are integral multiples of the fundamental frequency; the second harmonic has twice the fundamental frequency, the third three times, and so forth. The magnitude of the coefficients of each succeeding nonzero harmonic decreases (Fig. 6.2), indicating that each successive harmonic adds less and less to the sum. However, these higher harmonics contain the detailed information necessary to reconstruct sudden changes in the value of the signal. For example, while the first harmonic tells us that the signal varies with a 1-second period, it only suggests that the signal is positive more than negative (Fig. 6.1C). Adding the second harmonic (Fig. 6.1D) increases our suspicion that the signal always remains positive, but does not reveal the sudden changes in slope at the start and finish of each pulse. Adding still more harmonics (Figs 6.1E and F) produces a much better representation of the actual signal, yet even the addition of 30 harmonics still fails to distinctly show the sudden change in slope that occurs every 0.5 sec. In general, the more suddenly a function changes value, the greater the number of harmonics needed to accurately describe it.

Our example used either a sine or cosine function at each frequency (harmonic), but in general, both cosine and sine terms will appear at each harmonic.

We can also rewrite the Fourier series with a single sinusoid at each harmonic. We begin with the Fourier series, (6.20)

$$f(t) = \frac{1}{2}a_0 + \sum_{n=1}^{\infty} \left( a_n \cos \frac{2\pi n}{T} t + b_n \sin \frac{2\pi n}{T} t \right) \qquad (6.33)$$

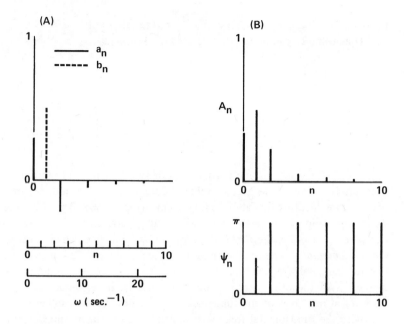

**FIGURE 6.2:** Graphical representation of the first 10 harmonics in the Fourier series representation for the function in Figure 6.1A. (A) The amplitude of each cosine $(a_n)$ and sine $(b_n)$ term. (B) The amplitude and phase of each harmonic, written as a single sinusoid. Both of these representations contain exactly the same information and are equally suitable for reconstructing the original function.

then combine the two sinusoids as we did beginning with Equation (3.226).

$$f(t) = \frac{1}{2}a_0 + \sum_{n=1}^{\infty} \sqrt{a_n^2 + b_n^2} \left( \frac{a_n}{\sqrt{a_n^2 + b_n^2}} \cos \frac{2\pi n}{T} t \right.$$

$$\left. + \frac{b_n}{\sqrt{a_n^2 + b_n^2}} \sin \frac{2\pi n}{T} t \right)$$

$$(6.34)$$

Define the angle $\psi_n$ with the triangle in Figure 6.3. Since $\sin \psi_n = b_n/\sqrt{a_n^2 + b_n^2}$ and $\cos \psi_n = a_n/\sqrt{a_n^2 + b_n^2}$, we can rewrite (6.34) as

$$f(t) = \frac{1}{2}a_0 + \sum_{n=1}^{\infty} \sqrt{a_n^2 + b_n^2}\left(\cos\frac{2\pi n}{T}t \sin \psi_n + \sin\frac{2\pi n}{T}t \cos \psi_n\right)$$

$$(6.35)$$

$$f(t) = \frac{1}{2}a_0 + \sum_{n=1}^{\infty} \sqrt{a_n^2 + b_n^2}\,\cos\left(\frac{2\pi n}{T}t - \psi_n\right) \qquad (6.36)$$

$$f(t) = A_0 + \sum_{n=1}^{\infty} A_n \cos\left(\frac{2\pi n}{T}t - \psi_n\right) \qquad (6.37)$$

where $A_0 = 1/2a_0$ is the mean value of the signal, $A_n = \sqrt{a_n^2 + b_n^2}$ is the amplitude of the $n$th harmonic, and $\psi_n = \tan^{-1} b_n/a_n$ is the phase angle by which each harmonic lags behind a pure cosine. Figure 6.2B shows the amplitudes for the function in Figure 6.1 represented by using (6.37). This representation contains no more information than Figure 6.2A, but in some contexts is more convenient. If we were trying to measure the signal in Figure 6.1, with a transducer whose frequency response permitted only observing the first harmonic of the signal, we would lose substantially more information about the signal than we would with a transducer which passed the first 30 harmonics.

Figure 6.4 shows the first six harmonics of an aortic pressure signal measured in a dog, along with the result obtained by adding more and more harmonics. The first 10 harmonics contain most of the information necessary to reconstruct the signal; the first 20 harmonics contain virtually all of it.

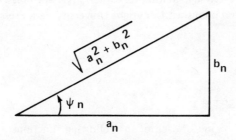

**FIGURE 6.3:** Definition of $\psi_n$. (Compare this figure with Figure 3.9.)

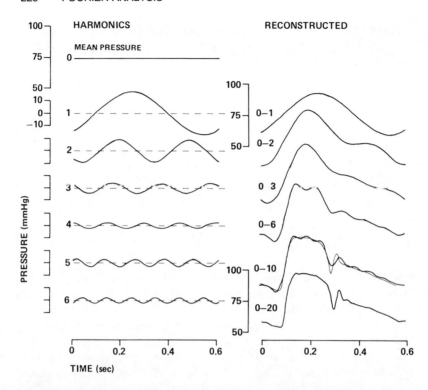

**FIGURE 6.4:** The left panel shows the first 6 harmonics of the Fourier series representing the periodic aortic pressure pulse measured in a dog. The period, *T*, is 0.6 seconds. The right panel shows the reconstructed signal obtained by adding more and more harmonics. The light line on the tracing second from the bottom shows the actual pressure signal. Adding more harmonics produces a progressively better representation of the true function. (Reproduced from N. Westerhof, *Physical Principles in Cardiology,* ed. N. Hwang, Baltimore: University Park Press. By permission of the author and publisher. Copyright University Park Press, Baltimore.)

## PROBLEM SET 6.1

1. Find the period of each of the following functions:
   a. $\sin x$
   b. $\cos 3x$
   c. $\cos 2\pi x$

### TABLE 6.1   Fourier Decomposition
### of the Dog Aortic Pressure Signal
### Shown in Figure 6.4*

| Harmonic $n$ | Amplitude (mmHg) $A_n$ | Phase (radians) $\psi_n$ |
|---|---|---|
| 0 | 74.542 | 0 |
| 1 | 10.761 | 3.763 |
| 2 | 8.975 | 2.410 |
| 3 | 3.993 | 1.007 |
| 4 | 2.010 | 0.372 |
| 5 | 3.035 | 5.738 |
| 6 | 2.280 | 3.992 |
| 7 | 0.327 | 4.201 |
| 8 | 1.485 | 2.912 |
| 9 | 1.365 | 0.489 |
| 10 | 0.352 | 3.084 |
| 11 | 1.138 | 5.978 |
| 12 | 0.779 | 3.486 |
| 13 | 0.613 | 5.774 |
| 14 | 0.863 | 2.850 |
| 15 | 0.465 | 6.018 |
| 16 | 0.527 | 2.177 |
| 17 | 0.511 | 5.630 |
| 18 | 0.196 | 2.153 |
| 19 | 0.295 | 4.917 |
| 20 | 0.232 | 1.950 |
| 21 | 0.142 | 5.146 |
| 22 | 0.112 | 1.146 |
| 23 | 0.132 | 4.899 |
| 24 | 0.047 | 0.662 |
| 25 | 0.083 | 4.888 |
| 26 | 0.026 | 5.765 |
| 27 | 0.058 | 4.709 |
| 28 | 0.022 | 6.020 |
| 29 | 0.021 | 5.335 |
| 30 | 0.019 | 5.818 |
| 31 | 0.032 | 5.121 |
| 32 | 0.023 | 5.385 |
| 33 | 0.030 | 5.368 |
| 34 | 0.024 | 5.712 |
| 35 | 0.025 | 5.696 |
| 36 | 0.022 | 5.868 |
| 37 | 0.024 | 5.497 |
| 38 | 0.024 | 5.592 |
| 39 | 0.021 | 5.478 |
| 40 | 0.021 | 5.837 |

* These data were kindly supplied by Nico Westerhof.

    d. $\sin(4\pi t - \pi/4)$

    e. $\sin(4\pi t + \pi/4)$

2. Plot enough terms of the Fourier series $x(t) = \pi^2/3 - 4 \, (\cos t - 1/4 \cos 2t + 1/9 \cos 3t - 1/16 \cos 4t + \ldots)$ to define $x(t)$ for $-5 \leqslant t \leqslant 5$.

3. Compute Fourier series representations for the following functions using both representations developed in the preceding section:

    a. $y(t) = \begin{cases} 1 & 0 \leqslant t < \pi \\ -1 & \pi \leqslant t < 2 \\ y(t - 2\pi n) & \text{otherwise}; n \text{ integer} \end{cases}$

    b. $q(t) = \begin{cases} 2 & 0 \leqslant t < \pi \\ 0 & \pi \leqslant t < 2\pi \\ q(t - 2\pi n) & \text{otherwise}; n \text{ integer} \end{cases}$

    c. $z(t) = \begin{cases} t & 0 \leqslant t < 1 \\ 0 & 1 \leqslant t < 2\pi \\ z(t - 2n) & \text{otherwise}; n \text{ integer} \end{cases}$

4. Table 6.1 presents the magnitude and phase (measured relative to the QRS wave in the electrocardiogram) of the components which make up the aortic pressure wave in Figure 6.4. Plot these data in a manner analogous to Figure 6.2B and use this plot to understand why the first 20 harmonics produce such an accurate reproduction of the actual pressure measurement. The plot also helps to understand why instruments which do not pass higher harmonics can produce the type of distortions seen in the upper parts of Figure 6.4.

## THE COMPLEX VARIABLE FORM OF THE FOURIER SERIES*

Since from Eqs. 3.155 and 3.156 we can derive $\cos x = (e^{ix} + e^{-ix})/2$ and $\sin x = (e^{ix} - e^{-ix})/2i$, we can rewrite the Fourier series as a sum of exponential functions with imaginary exponents instead of sinusoids. The resulting series has many applications, but for our purposes it is important because it bridges the gap between the Fourier series, which represents

---

* If the reader does not have a good grounding in the representation of complex variables graphically and how to manipulate them, he should study Appendix C before proceeding.

periodic functions, and the Fourier integral, which can be used to represent most functions, be they periodic or not. In addition to permitting a
frequency decomposition of nonperiodic functions, the Fourier integral
leads to theorems which indicate how different operations on a signal
change its spectrum. Before discussing these practical applications, we
must derive the complex representation of the Fourier series.

We begin by replacing the cosine and sine functions in the Fourier
series, (6.20),

$$f(t) = \frac{1}{2}a_0 + \sum_{n=1}^{\infty}\left(a_n \cos\frac{2\pi n}{T}t + b_n \sin\frac{2\pi n}{T}t\right) \qquad (6.38)$$

with the equivalent complex exponential functions.

$$f(t) = \frac{1}{2}a_0 + \sum_{n=1}^{\infty}\left(a_n\frac{e^{2\pi int/T}+e^{-2\pi int/T}}{2} + b_n\frac{e^{2\pi int/T}-e^{-2\pi int/T}}{2i}\right)$$

$$(6.39)$$

then collect terms in powers of $e$ and replace $1/i$ with $-i$:

$$f(t) = \frac{1}{2}a_0 + \frac{a_1-ib_1}{2}e^{2\pi it/T} + \ldots + \frac{a_n-ib_n}{2}e^{2\pi int/T} + \ldots$$

$$+ \frac{a_1+ib_1}{1}e^{-2\pi it/T} + \ldots + \frac{a_n+ib_n}{2}e^{-2\pi int/T} + \ldots$$

$$(6.40)$$

Define

$$c_n = \begin{cases} \dfrac{a_n-ib_n}{2} & n > 0 \\[2mm] \dfrac{1}{2}a_0 & n = 0 \\[2mm] \dfrac{a_{|n|}+ib_{|n|}}{2} & n < 0 \end{cases} \qquad (6.41)$$

in which case (6.40) becomes

$$f(t) = \sum_{n=-\infty}^{\infty} c_n e^{2\pi i n t/T} \tag{6.42}$$

the *complex form of the Fourier series.*

Since one often wishes to work with (6.42) directly, we will derive an expression for computing $c_n$ directly. From (6.41), when $n$ is positive

$$c_n = \frac{a_n - ib_n}{2} \tag{6.43}$$

Use (6.21) and (6.22) to replace $a_n$ and $b_n$ in (6.43) to obtain

$$c_n = \frac{1}{2}\left[\frac{2}{T}\int_0^T f(t)\cos\frac{2\pi n}{T}t\,dt - i\frac{2}{T}\int_0^T f(t)\sin\frac{2\pi n}{T}t\,dt\right]$$

$$= \frac{1}{T}\int_0^T f(t)\left[\cos\frac{2\pi n}{T}t - i\sin\frac{2\pi n}{T}t\right]dt \tag{6.44}$$

But $\cos x - i\sin x = e^{-ix}$, so

$$c_n = \frac{1}{T}\int_0^T f(t)e^{-2\pi i n t/T}\,dt \tag{6.45}$$

When $n$ equals zero (6.45) becomes

$$c_n = c_0 = \frac{1}{2}a_0 = \frac{1}{2}\left[\frac{2}{T}\int_0^T f(t)\,dt\right] = \frac{1}{T}\int_0^T f(t)e^0\,dt$$

$$= \frac{1}{T}\int_0^T f(t)e^{-2\pi i n t/T}\,dt$$

$$\tag{6.46}$$

Likewise, for negative $n$,

$$c_n = \frac{a_{|n|} + ib_{|n|}}{2}$$

$$= \frac{1}{2}\left[\frac{2}{T} \int_0^T f(t) \cos \frac{2\pi|n|}{T} t \, dt + i \frac{2}{T} \int_0^T f(t) \sin \frac{2\pi|n|}{T} t \, dt\right]$$

$$= \frac{1}{T} \int_0^T f(t) \left[\cos \frac{2\pi|n|}{T} t + i \sin \frac{2\pi|n|}{T} t\right] \tag{6.47}$$

Since $\cos x + i \sin x = e^{ix}$,

$$c_n = \frac{1}{T} \int_0^T f(t) e^{2\pi i |n| t/T} \, dt \tag{6.48}$$

Since $n$ is negative, $|n| = -n$,

$$c_n = \frac{1}{T} \int_0^T f(t) e^{-2\pi i n t/T} \, dt \tag{6.49}$$

Thus whether $n$ is positive, zero, or negative,

$$c_n = \frac{1}{T} \int_0^T f(t) e^{-2\pi i n t/T} \, dt \tag{6.50}$$

Since $f(t)$ is periodic, we can integrate (6.50) over any interval of length $T$. Specifically, (6.50) can be replaced with the equivalent integral

$$c_n = c(n) = \frac{1}{T} \int_{-T/2}^{T/2} f(t) e^{-2\pi i n t/T} \, dt \tag{6.51}$$

Note that the Fourier series for $f(t)$, (6.42), and the integral for $c(n)$ (6.51) have symmetric structures:

| Equation (6.42) | : | Equation (6.51) |
|:---:|:---:|:---:|
| $t$ | : | $n$ |
| $f(t)$ | : | $c(n)$ |
| $e^{2\pi i n t/T}$ | : | $e^{-2\pi i n t/T}$ |
| $\displaystyle\sum_{n=-\infty}^{\infty}(\ )$ | : | $\displaystyle\frac{1}{T}\int_{-T/2}^{T/2}(\ )\,dt$ |

This symmetry will become important as we move from dealing with infinite series to the Fourier transform and its close relative the Laplace transform. For a hint of things to come, compare the structure of the integral for $c(n)$ with the definition of the Laplace transform (Eq. 4.1) and the Fourier series with the expression for the inverse Laplace transform (Eq. 4.2).

## A COMPREHENSIVE EXAMPLE

As a case example of the foregoing, let us expand the periodic function $g(x)$ in Figure 6.5A into a Fourier series, using the three equivalent series we have developed so far, and then examine the coefficients of each harmonic in each representation.

$$g(x) = \begin{cases} e^{-x} & 0 \leqslant x \leqslant X \\ g(x - nX) & n = \text{integer} \end{cases} \tag{6.52}$$

where the units of $x$ are mm and the period $X$ is 5 mm. First let us find the values of $a_n$ and $b_n$ in a Fourier series written as a sum of cosines and sines (6.20):

$$a_n = \frac{2}{X}\int_0^X e^{-x}\cos\frac{2\pi n}{X}x\,dx = \frac{2(1 - e^{-X})}{X\left[1 + \left(\frac{2\pi n}{X}\right)^2\right]} \tag{6.53}$$

$$b_n = \frac{2}{X}\int_0^X e^{-x}\sin\frac{2\pi n}{X}x\,dx = \frac{4\pi n}{X^2}\cdot\frac{1 - e^{-X}}{1 + \left(\frac{2\pi n}{X}\right)^2} \tag{6.54}$$

EXAMPLE    235

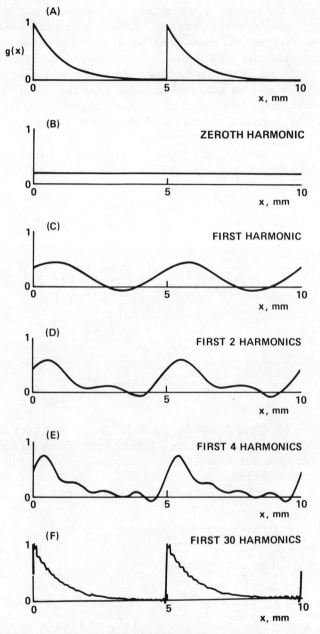

**FIGURE 6.5:** (A) A periodic function with 5 mm period. (B–F) The Fourier series representations of the function in (A) as higher and higher harmonics are added.

Figure 6.5 shows the results obtained by summing terms through the zeroth, first, second, fourth, and thirtieth harmonics in the Fourier series. Note that the series converges to the point midway in the discontinuity. Figure 6.6A shows the coefficients. Note that the more harmonics one adds, the more closely the partial sum follows $g(x)$. However, since $g(x)$ has such sudden changes, even the sum of the first 30 harmonics varies noticeably from the actual function. (Compare with Fig. 6.1.). *In general, the more suddenly a signal changes value, the more harmonics are necessary to reproduce it accurately.*

To represent the same Fourier series in terms of cosines only, with one term for each harmonic, (6.37), we compute

$$A_0 = \frac{1}{2} a_0 = \frac{(1 - e^{-X})}{X} \tag{6.55}$$

$$A_n = \sqrt{a_n^2 + b_n^2} = \frac{2(1 - e^{-X})}{X\left[1 + \left(\frac{2\pi n}{X}\right)^2\right]} \sqrt{1 + \left(\frac{2\pi n}{X}\right)^2} \tag{6.56}$$

and

$$\psi_n = \tan^{-1} \frac{b_n}{a_n} = \tan^{-1} \frac{2\pi n}{X} \tag{6.57}$$

Figure 6.6B shows $A_n$ and $\psi_n$ for (6.52), represented using the second of our three ways of writing the Fourier series. The series converges to the same function as the original trigonometric series; we have simply written it differently.

To represent (6.52) as a complex Fourier series, (6.42), we integrate

$$c_n = \frac{1}{X} \int_0^X e^{-x} e^{-2\pi i n x / X} \, dx \tag{6.58}$$

$$= \frac{1}{X} \int_0^X e^{-(2\pi i n / X + 1) x} \, dx = -\frac{1}{X\left(\frac{2\pi i n}{X} + 1\right)} e^{-(2\pi i n / X + 1) x} \Big|_0^X \tag{6.59}$$

EXAMPLE    237

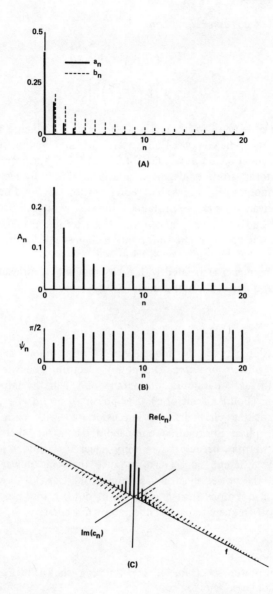

**FIGURE 6.6:** The coefficients for the Fourier series representation of (6.52). (A) Sine and cosine coefficients. (B) Amplitude and phase angle for representation as a sum of cosines. (C) Complex variable form. $Re(c_n)$ means the real part of $c_n$, and $Im(c_n)$ means its imaginary part.

Since $e^{-2\pi i n} = \cos 2\pi n - i \sin 2\pi n = 1$,

$$c_n = \frac{(1 - e^{-X})\left(1 - i\dfrac{2\pi n}{X}\right)}{X\left[1 + \left(\dfrac{2\pi n}{X}\right)^2\right]} \tag{6.60}$$

(Verify that $c_n = (a_n - ib_n)/2$ and $c_{-n} = (a_n + ib_n)/2$.) Figure 6.6C shows the coefficients in the complex Fourier series which represents (6.52).

The information on any frame of Figure 6.6 is sufficient to reconstruct $g(x)$ to an arbitrary degree of precision, simply by including high enough harmonics. Each possible representation of the Fourier series requires equivalent *pairs* of constants associated with each harmonic ($a_n$ and $b_n$, $A_n$ and $\psi_n$, or $c_{-n}$ and $c_n$) in order to describe completely its spectrum. Each pair contains information equivalent to the amplitude and phase of the sinusoid at each harmonic.

Often the power associated with each harmonic of a signal is proportional to the square of the amplitude.

$$A_n^2 = a_n^2 + b_n^2 \tag{6.61}$$

The relationship between the frequency of the $n$th harmonic and its power is called its *power spectrum*. The power spectrum associates only *one* constant with each harmonic. It contains only half the information in the spectrum (Fourier transform). The power spectrum gives the amplitude but not the phase information associated with each harmonic. Without the phase information one cannot reconstruct the signal from its power spectrum, because while every signal has a unique power spectrum, many different signals can produce the same power spectrum. However, if the power spectrum is known, one can still answer important practical questions such as whether or not a transducer has a high enough cutoff frequency to reproduce a signal accurately.

## PROBLEM SET 6.2

1. Plot the power spectrum of the function shown in Figure 6.5A. (Suggestion: Use semi-log paper.)

2. Compute the complex Fourier series representation of

$$f(t) = \begin{cases} t & 0 \leqslant t < 1 \\ 1 - t & 1 \leqslant t < 2 \\ f(t - 2n) & \text{otherwise; } n \text{ integer} \end{cases}$$

and plot the result.

3. Plot each of the following functions together with its power spectrum:

   a. $f(t) = 1 + \sin t + 1/3 \sin 3t + 1/5 \sin 5t + 1/7 \sin 7t + \ldots$
   b. $g(t) = 1 + \sin t + 1/3 \cos 3t + 1/5 \sin 5t + 1/7 \cos 7t + \ldots$

4. Plot the power spectrum of the dog aortic pressure signal shown in Figure 6.4. (Suggestion: Use semi-log paper.)

## THE FOURIER INTEGRAL REPRESENTS NONPERIODIC FUNCTIONS

We can now generalize our previous analysis to include nonperiodic functions. We will begin with a periodic function and extend its period to infinity, so that the waveform appears only once. Hence, we begin with the Fourier series (sum) representation for a periodic function and convert it to an integral by taking the limit of a sum. As before, we will not rigorously prove that the infinite sums converge, but simply describe the steps between the Fourier series and integral.

The analysis we will now develop will not apply to periodic functions, which go on forever and hence contain infinite power, but the section following generalizes the results of this section to include periodic functions. Here we will concentrate on finding the frequency content of functions which obey the Dirichlet condition and which contain finite energy—ones for which $\int_{-\infty}^{\infty} |f(x)|\, dx$ is finite.

Before developing the mathematical steps which take us from the complex representation of the Fourier series to the Fourier integral and thence the Fourier transform, let us examine what happens to the train of exponential pulses we studied in the last section. The fundamental frequency is $f = 1/X = 0.2$ cycle/mm, and all harmonics are integer multiples of this fundamental frequency (Fig. 6.7A). Suppose now that we leave the function $g(x)$ unchanged within each cycle, but double the period, and hence halve the fundamental frequency (Fig. 6.7B). Since

$$c_n = \frac{(1 - e^{-X})\left(1 - i\dfrac{2\pi n}{X}\right)}{X\left[1 + \left(\dfrac{2\pi n}{X}\right)^2\right]} \tag{6.62}$$

each harmonic will have about half the amplitude and be located half the distance along the frequency axis (Fig. 6.7B). As the period lengthens, the spectral lines become more and more closely packed. As the period extends to infinity, the individual lines blur into a continuous

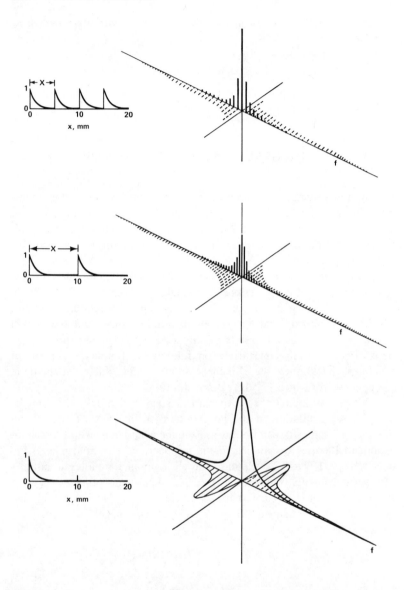

**FIGURE 6.7:** Extending the period $X$ of a periodic function moves its spectral lines closer and closer together until, as $X$ approaches infinity, the spectral lines blur together to form a continuous spectrum, which is the function's Fourier transform.

spectrum (Fig. 6.7C), which is the *Fourier transform* of the nonperiodic function.

To repeat this procedure mathematically, we begin with the Fourier series for a function $g_T(t)$ with period $T$. From (6.42)

$$g_T(t) = \sum_{n=-\infty}^{\infty} c_n e^{2\pi i n t/T} \tag{6.63}$$

and from (6.50)

$$c_n = \frac{1}{T} \int_{-T/2}^{T/2} g_T(t) e^{-2\pi i n t/T} \, dt \tag{6.64}$$

Substitute from (6.64) into (6.63):

$$g_T(t) = \sum_{n=-\infty}^{\infty} \left[ \frac{1}{T} \int_{-T/2}^{T/2} g_T(t) e^{-2\pi i n t/T} \, dt \right] e^{2\pi i n t/T} \tag{6.65}$$

The increment in frequency $f$ between the $n$th and $(n+1)$th harmonic frequencies $f_n$ and $f_{n+1}$ is

$$\Delta f = f_{n+1} - f_n = \frac{n+1}{T} - \frac{n}{T} = \frac{1}{T} \tag{6.66}$$

Substitute this result and $f_n = n/T$ into (6.65):

$$g_T(t) = \sum_{n=-\infty}^{\infty} \left[ \int_{-T/2}^{T/2} g_T(t) e^{-2\pi i f_n t} \, dt \right] e^{2\pi i f_n t} \, \Delta f \tag{6.67}$$

Now define

$$G_T(f) = \int_{-T/2}^{T/2} g_T(t) e^{-2\pi i f t} \, dt \tag{6.68}$$

in which case (6.67) becomes

$$g_T(t) = \sum_{n=-\infty}^{\infty} G_T(f_n)e^{2\pi i f_n t} \Delta f \tag{6.69}$$

where $f_n$ is the left-hand point of the $n$th $\Delta f$ interval. Now let $T \to \infty$. $\Delta f = 1/T \to 0$, and if $g(t)$ satisfies the Dirichlet condition and $\int_{-\infty}^{\infty} |g(t)|\, dt$ is finite, the infinite sum in (6.69) approaches the *Fourier integral*:

$$g(t) = \int_{-\infty}^{\infty} G(f)e^{2\pi i f t}\, df \tag{6.70}$$

Equation (6.68) approaches the *Fourier transform*:

$$G(f) = \mathcal{F}\{g(t)\} = \int_{-\infty}^{\infty} g(t)e^{-2\pi i f t}\, dt \tag{6.71}$$

Equations (6.70) and (6.71) represent the Fourier integral and transform in terms of the cycle frequency $f$. One often encounters the equivalent integrals written in terms of the radian frequency $\omega$. Since $\omega = 2\pi f$, $df = d\omega/2\pi$, and (6.70) and (6.71) become

$$g(t) = \frac{1}{2\pi} \int_{-\infty}^{\infty} G(\omega)e^{i\omega t}\, d\omega \tag{6.72}$$

and

$$G(\omega) = \mathcal{F}\{g(t)\} = \int_{-\infty}^{\infty} g(t)e^{-i\omega t}\, dt \tag{6.73}$$

respectively.

The function $g(t)$ in the *time* (or other independent variable) *domain* contains the exact same information as its Fourier transform $G(f)$ or $G(\omega)$ contains in the *frequency domain*. Equations (6.69) and (6.71) give the function as the sum over all frequencies of its spectrum, and (6.70) and (6.72) say that its spectrum is the sum of contributions from the function at all times.

As an example, let us compute the Fourier transform of $g(x) = u(x)e^{-x}$, shown in Figure 6.7C. From (6.71):

$$G(f) = \int_{-\infty}^{\infty} u(x)e^{-x}e^{-2\pi ifx}\, dx = \int_{-\infty}^{0} 0\, dx + \int_{0}^{\infty} e^{-x}e^{-2\pi ifx}\, dx \tag{6.74}$$

$$= \frac{1}{-(1 + 2\pi if)} e^{-(1+2\pi if)x}\Big|_{0}^{\infty} = \frac{1}{1 + 2\pi if} \tag{6.75}$$

$$= \frac{1 - 2\pi if}{1 + (2\pi f)^2} \tag{6.76}$$

As with the Laplace transform, there are extensive tables of Fourier transforms available, and a corresponding set of theorems (discussed below) which permit finding transforms without evaluating the integral in (6.71). Unlike the Laplace transform, however, the Fourier transform has a distinct physical meaning: it represents the signal's spectrum. This fact helps interpret the results of Fourier analysis in physical terms and gives physical meaning to many of the theorems we will develop.

## PROBLEM SET 6.3

Find the Fourier transforms of the following functions. Plot the real and imaginary parts as a function of frequency.

1. $1/2[u(t) - u(t - 2)]$
2. $[u(t) - u(t - 2)]$
3. $2[u(t) - u(t - 1/2)]$

4. $g(t) = \begin{cases} -t & -1 \leqslant t < 0 \\ t & 0 \leqslant t < 1 \\ 0 & \text{otherwise} \end{cases}$

5. $g(t) = \begin{cases} -2t & -1/2 \leqslant t < 0 \\ 2t & 0 \leqslant t < 1/2 \\ 0 & \text{otherwise} \end{cases}$

6. $\delta(t)$

## FOURIER TRANSFORMS OF PERIODIC FUNCTIONS

We cannot compute the Fourier transform of a periodic function directly because, since they go on forever, they contain infinite energy, i.e., $\int_{-\infty}^{\infty} |g|\, dt$ is not finite. To compute a transform, we must modify the function to make it eventually die out, and hence have finite energy and a transform, then we must examine the limit this transform approaches as the function dies out less and less slowly. This approach is not new to us, since we used it to define the Laplace transform of the unit impulse (Eq. 4.122 ff.). Since the unit impulse was not of exponential order, we could not compute its Laplace transform directly, so we defined the limit of a sequence of Laplace transformations of progressively stronger finite pulses which approached the impulse $\delta(t)$ to be $\mathscr{L}\{\delta(t)\}$. We will use a similar procedure to define Fourier transforms for periodic functions. As examples, we will show that the Fourier transforms of a constant and of a cosine function consist of impulses. This result should not be surprising since we think of the Fourier transform as a spectrum. A constant (Fig. 6.8A) has all its infinite total energy concentrated at a single frequency (zero), so its spectrum consists of an impulse at the origin (Fig. 6.8B). Similarly, $\cos 2\pi f_0 t$ has half its (infinite total) energy as impulses (spectral lines) at $+f_0$ and half at $-f_0$. The Fourier transform of a periodic signal is a series of impulses of magnitude $c_n$ at the $n$ harmonics.

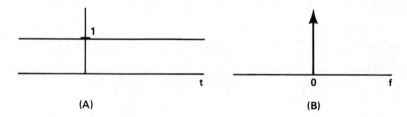

(A)                                                (B)

**FIGURE 6.8:** A constant has all its (infinite) energy concentrated at a single frequency (zero), so its spectrum consists of a single impulse at $f = 0$.

Let $p(t, \tau)$ be a function, called the convergence factor, for which $\lim_{\tau \to 0} p(t, \tau) = 1$ and $\lim_{|t| \to \infty} p(t, \tau) = 0$ when $\tau \neq 0$. Figure 6.9A shows one such function, $p(t, \tau) = e^{-\tau|t|}$. It equals one when $t = 0$, dies off as $t$ moves away from zero, and approaches unity for all values of $t$ as $\tau \to 0$. Therefore if we multiply the periodic function $g(t)$ (Fig. 6.9B) by $p(t, \tau)$ it will no longer be periodic (Fig. 6.9C), so we can compute the Fourier

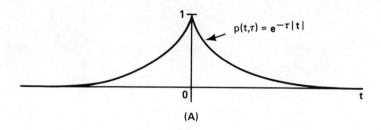

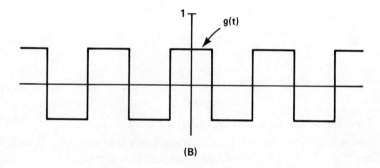

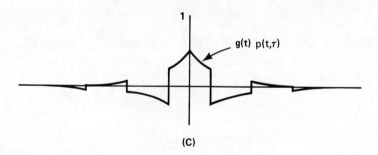

**FIGURE 6.9:** We multiply a periodic function (B) by the convergence factor (A) to obtain a nonperiodic function (C) which has a Fourier transform.

transform as outlined in the previous section. Since $\lim\limits_{\tau \to 0} p(t, \tau)g(t) = g(t)$, we define*

$$\mathscr{F}\{g(t)\} = \lim_{\tau \to 0} \mathscr{F}\{p(t, \tau)g(t)\} \qquad (6.77)$$

To find $\mathscr{F}\{1\}$, let $g(t) = 1$ in (6.77) and let $p(t, \tau) = e^{-\tau|t|}$.

$$\mathscr{F}\{1\} = \lim_{\tau \to 0} \int_{-\infty}^{\infty} e^{-\tau|t|} \cdot 1 \cdot e^{-2\pi ift} \, dt \qquad (6.78)$$

$$= \lim_{\tau \to 0} \left[ \int_{-\infty}^{0} e^{\tau t} e^{-2\pi ift} \, dt + \int_{0}^{\infty} e^{-\tau t} e^{-2\pi ift} \, dt \right] \qquad (6.79)$$

$$= \lim_{\tau \to 0} \left[ \frac{1}{\tau - 2\pi if} e^{(\tau - 2\pi if)t} \Big|_{-\infty}^{0} - \frac{1}{\tau + 2\pi if} e^{-(\tau + 2\pi ift)t} \Big|_{0}^{\infty} \right]$$

$$(6.80)$$

To evaluate the first term in (6.80) we must evaluate $\lim\limits_{t \to -\infty} e^{(\tau - 2\pi if)t}$. Knowing that the absolute value of a function can be no smaller than zero, and that $e^{(\tau - 2\pi if)t} = e^{\tau t}(\cos 2\pi ft - i \sin 2\pi ft)$ we investigate

$$0 \leqslant \lim_{t \to -\infty} |e^{(\tau - 2\pi if)t}| = \lim_{t \to -\infty} |e^{\tau t}(\cos 2\pi ft - i \sin 2\pi ft)|$$

$$= \lim_{t \to -\infty} |e^{\tau t}| \cdot |\cos 2\pi ft - i \sin 2\pi ft|$$

$$= \lim_{t \to -\infty} |e^{\tau t}| \cdot \lim_{t \to -\infty} |\cos 2\pi ft - i \sin 2\pi ft|$$

$$\leqslant \lim_{t \to -\infty} |e^{\tau t}| \cdot 1 = 0 \qquad (6.81)$$

---

* As with our definition of $\mathscr{L}\{\delta(t)\}$ as 1, a rigorous proof that the steps we follow are correct requires generalized function theory. Therefore, we will simply outline the proofs.

because $\tau$ is positive. Thus $|e^{(\tau - 2\pi i f)t}| \to 0$ as $t \to -\infty$; therefore $e^{(\tau - 2\pi i f)t}$ must also approach zero as $t \to -\infty$. Similar logic shows that $e^{-(\tau + 2\pi i f)t} \to 0$ as $t \to \infty$, and (6.80) becomes

$$\mathscr{F}\{1\} = \lim_{\tau \to 0} \left[ \frac{1}{\tau - 2\pi i f}(1 - 0) - \frac{1}{\tau + 2\pi i f}(0 - 1) \right] = \lim_{\tau \to 0} \frac{2\tau}{\tau^2 + (2\pi f)^2}$$

(6.82)

Figure 6.10 shows $2\tau/[\tau^2 + (2\pi f)^2]$ for decreasing values of $\tau$. As $\tau$ decreases, this function becomes a sharper and sharper pulse. Does it approach the unit impulse as $\tau \to 0$?

To prove that it does, we must show that $\mathscr{F}\{1\}$ equals zero everywhere but at $f = 0$ where it is undefined, and that $\int_{-\infty}^{\infty} \mathscr{F}\{1\} df = 1$. Equation (6.82) shows when $f \neq 0$, $\mathscr{F}\{1\} = 0$, but when $f \neq 0$, $\mathscr{F}\{1\} = \lim_{\tau \to 0} 2/\tau$, which is undefined. Thus $\mathscr{F}\{1\}$ meets the first criterion for being a unit impulse. Next, evaluate $\int_{-\infty}^{\infty} \mathscr{F}\{1\} df$ (using Formula 25 from Appendix B):

$$\int_{-\infty}^{\infty} \mathscr{F}\{1\} df = \int_{-\infty}^{\infty} \lim_{\tau \to 0} \frac{2\tau}{\tau^2 + (2\pi f)^2} df$$

$$= \lim_{\tau \to 0} \frac{2\tau}{\tau} \tan^{-1} \frac{2\pi f \tau}{\tau} \Big|_{-\infty}^{\infty} = 2\left(\frac{1}{4} - - \frac{1}{4}\right) = 1$$

(6.83)

regardless of $\tau$. Thus, $\mathscr{F}\{1\} = \delta(f)$.

Note that we defined the unit impulse function with (6.82) rather than a square pulse as we did in Chapter 5. One can define $\delta$ as the limit of a sequence of any of a number of functions which rapidly increase at the origin and approach zero as one moves away from the origin. The key idea is that the function changes so fast that its exact form is unimportant. To show that $\mathscr{F}\{\cos 2\pi ft\} = 1/2\delta(f + f_0) + 1/2\delta(f - f_0)$, we will use yet another function to motivate $\delta(f)$.

To find $\mathscr{F}\{\cos 2\pi f_0 t\}$, we note that $p(t, \tau) = e^{-2\pi\tau^2 t^2}$ meets our requirements to be a convergence factor and $e^{-2\pi\tau^2 t^2}\cos 2\pi f_0 t$ has a Fourier transform (Fig. 6.11). Thus, as before, we define

$$\mathscr{F}\{\cos 2\pi f_0 t\} = \lim_{\tau \to 0} \mathscr{F}\{e^{-2\pi\tau^2 t^2} \cos 2\pi f_0 t\}$$

(6.84)

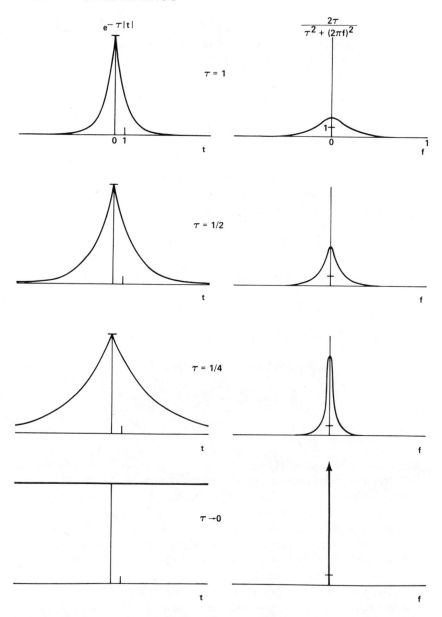

**FIGURE 6.10:** As $\tau \to 0$, $e^{-\tau |t|} \to 1$ for all values of $t$, and its Fourier transform (spectrum) shows more and more energy concentrated over a progressively narrower and narrower range of frequencies.

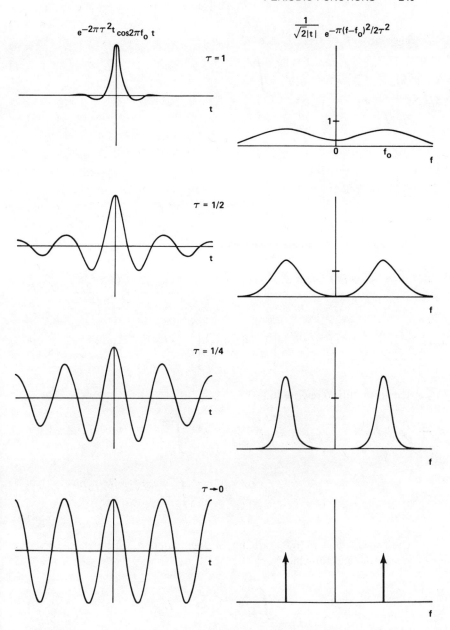

**FIGURE 6.11:** As a modified cosine function dies out less slowly, its spectrum contains energy over a progressively narrower frequency range.

Since $\cos 2\pi f_0 t = (e^{2\pi i f_0 t} + e^{-2\pi i f_0 t})/2$

$$\mathcal{F}\{e^{-2\pi\tau^2 t^2} \cos 2\pi f_0 t\} = \frac{1}{2} \int_{-\infty}^{\infty} e^{-2\pi\tau^2 t^2} (e^{2\pi i f_0 t} + e^{-2\pi i f_0 t}) e^{-2\pi i f t} \, dt$$

$$\tag{6.85}$$

$$= \frac{1}{2} \int_{-\infty}^{\infty} \left( e^{-2\pi\tau^2 [t^2 + ti(f-f_0)/\tau^2]} \right.$$

$$\left. + e^{-2\pi\tau^2 [t^2 + ti(f+f_0)^2/\tau^2]} \right) dt \tag{6.86}$$

Now complete the square in each exponent:

$$\frac{\tau^2 + ti(f \pm f_0)^2}{\tau^2} = \frac{t^2 + ti(f \pm f_0)^2}{\tau^2} - \frac{(f \pm f_0)^2}{4\tau^4} + \frac{(f \pm f_0)^2}{4\tau^4} \tag{6.87}$$

$$\frac{t^2 + ti(f \pm f_0)^2}{\tau^2} = \left[ \frac{t + i(f \pm f_0)}{2\tau^2} \right]^2 + \frac{(f \pm f_0)^2}{4\tau^4} \tag{6.88}$$

Use this result to rewrite (6.86):

$$\mathcal{F}\{e^{-2\pi\tau^2 t^2} \cos 2\pi f_0 t\} = \frac{1}{2} e^{-\pi(f-f_0)^2/2\tau^2} \int_0^{\infty} e^{-2\pi\tau^2 [t+i(f-f_0)/2\tau^2]^2} \, dt$$

$$+ e^{-\pi(f+f_0)^2/2\tau^2} \int_0^{\infty} e^{-2\pi\tau^2 [t+i(f+f_0)/2\tau^2]^2} \, dt \tag{6.89}$$

The two integrals in (6.89) are the *Gaussian function*, which appears often in statistics and for which*

$$\int_{-\infty}^{\infty} e^{-ax^2} \, dx = \sqrt{\frac{\pi}{a}} \tag{6.90}$$

* A normally distributed random variable with mean $\mu$ and standard deviation $\sigma$ has a probability density given by the Gaussian function (bell-shaped curve)

$$p(x) = \frac{1}{\sigma\sqrt{2\pi}} e^{-(x-\mu)^2/2\sigma^2}$$

So (6.89) equals

$$\mathscr{F}\{e^{-2\pi\tau^2 t^2}\cos 2\pi f_0 t\} = \frac{1}{2}\left[\frac{1}{\sqrt{2}\,|\tau|}e^{-\pi(f-f_0)^2/2\tau^2}\right.$$

$$\left. + \frac{1}{\sqrt{2}\,|\tau|}e^{-\pi(f+f_0)^2/2\tau^2}\right] \quad (6.91)$$

To verify that the two expressions in (6.91) approach impulses located at $f_0$ and $-f_0$ as $\tau \to 0$, we again look at their value as $\tau \to 0$ and examine the area under the curve. Let $x = (\sqrt{\pi}/2)(f-f_0)/|\tau|$ in the first term in square brackets in (6.92). Then as $|\tau| \to 0, x \to \infty$,

$$\lim_{\tau \to 0} \frac{1}{\sqrt{2}\,|\tau|}e^{-\pi(f-f_0)^2/2\tau^2} = \lim_{x \to \infty} \frac{1}{\sqrt{\pi(f-f_0)}}xe^{-x^2} \quad (6.92)$$

when $f \neq f_0$. Since $e^x = 1 + x + x^2/2 + \ldots > x$ and since $x$ is positive,

$$0 \leqslant \lim_{x \to \infty} xe^{-x^2} < \lim_{x \to \infty} e^x e^{-x^2} = \lim_{x \to \infty} e^{-(x^2-x)} = 0 \quad (6.93)$$

When $f = f_0$, $\displaystyle\lim_{\tau \to 0} \frac{1}{\sqrt{2}\,|\tau|}e^0$ does not exist. Hence

$$\lim_{\tau \to 0} \frac{1}{\sqrt{2}\,|\tau|}e^{-\pi(f-f_0)^2/2\tau^2} = \begin{cases} 0 & f \neq f_0 \\ \text{undefined} & f = f_0 \end{cases}$$

$$(6.94)$$

meets the first requirement for an impulse. Now, examine

---

Since the probabilities of all possible events must add up to 1

$$\int_{-\infty}^{\infty} p(x)\,dx = 1$$

The reader should be able to derive (6.91) from this observation.

$$\int_{-\infty}^{\infty} \lim_{\tau \to 0} \frac{1}{\sqrt{2}\,|\tau|} e^{-\pi(f-f_0)^2/2\tau^2}\, df = \lim_{\tau \to 0} \int_{-\infty}^{\infty} \frac{1}{\sqrt{2}\,|\tau|} e^{-\pi(f-f_0)^2/2\tau^2}\, df$$

$$(6.95)$$

This integrand is also the Gaussian function (Eq. 6.90), so

$$\int_{-\infty}^{\infty} \lim_{\tau \to 0} \frac{1}{\sqrt{2}\,|\tau|} e^{-\pi(f-f_0)^2/2\tau^2}\, df = \lim_{\tau \to 0} \frac{1}{\sqrt{2}\,|\tau|} \sqrt{\frac{\pi 2\tau^2}{\pi}} = 1$$

$$(6.96)$$

Thus

$$\lim_{\tau \to 0} \frac{1}{\sqrt{2}\,|\tau|} e^{-\pi(f-f_0)^2/2\tau^2} = \delta(f) \qquad (6.97)$$

and (6.84) becomes

$$\mathscr{F}\{\cos 2\pi f_0 t\} = \frac{1}{2}\,[\delta(f - f_0) + \delta(f + f_0)] \qquad (6.98)$$

This limiting process (Fig. 6.11) reflects the fact that as the cosine wave goes on for longer and longer times, more and more energy appears in a narrower and narrower band of frequencies. In the limit, the (co)sinusoid goes on forever and there is infinite energy stored at its frequency $f_0$.

## PROBLEM SET 6.4

1. Show that $\mathscr{F}\{\cos 2\pi f_0 t\} = 1/2[\delta(f + f_0) + \delta(f - f_0)]$. (Hint: Use $1/|\tau|e^{-\pi\tau^2 t^2}$ as the convergence factor where $\tau \to 0$, and note that $\int_{-\infty}^{\infty} e^{-ax^2}\, dx = \sqrt{\pi/a}$.)
2. Find $\mathscr{F}\{\sin 2\pi f_0 t\}$.
3. Show that the Fourier series is a set of impulses, i.e., that a periodic function has an impulsive spectrum.

## DERIVATION OF THE LAPLACE TRANSFORM*

We used the Laplace transform to solve initial value problems which often involved constant or periodic functions. One could also use the Fourier

* This section may be skipped without affecting an understanding of the remaining material.

transform to solve these problems by completing the limiting process which we just used to find $\mathscr{F}\{1\}$ and $\mathscr{F}\{\cos 2\pi f_0 t\}$. However, there is no real need to compute this limit to transform functions into alternative forms that make it easier to solve differential equations. We will now derive the Laplace transform and inverse Laplace transform from the Fourier transform and integral.

We begin with the Fourier transform

$$\mathscr{F}\{g(t)\} = \int_{-\infty}^{\infty} g(t)e^{-i\omega t}\, dt \qquad (6.99)$$

and the Fourier integral

$$g(t) = \frac{1}{2\pi} \int_{-\infty}^{\infty} \mathscr{F}\{g(t)\}e^{i\omega t}\, d\omega \qquad (6.100)$$

Assume $g(t) = 0$ for $t < 0$ and, to assure that we can compute a transform, multiply $g(t)$ by the convergence factor $e^{-at}$, $a > 0$. From (6.99):

$$\mathscr{F}\{e^{-at}g(t)\} = \int_{-\infty}^{\infty} e^{-at}g(t)e^{-i\omega t}\, dt = \int_{0}^{\infty} g(t)e^{-(a+i\omega)t}\, dt$$

$$(6.101)$$

Let $s = a + i\omega$ in (6.101) to obtain the Laplace transform:

$$\mathscr{F}\{e^{-at}g(t)\} = \int_{0}^{\infty} e^{-st}g(t)\, dt = \mathscr{L}\{g(t)\} \qquad (6.102)$$

Thus the Laplace transform is simply the Fourier transform of a function times the convergence factor $e^{-at}$.

The formula for the inverse Laplace transform follows from the Fourier integral. Substitute from (6.101) into (6.100):

$$e^{-at}g(t) = \frac{1}{2\pi} \int_{-\infty}^{\infty} \mathscr{F}\{e^{-at}g(t)\}e^{i\omega t}\, d\omega \qquad (6.103)$$

But $\mathscr{F}\{e^{-at}g(t)\} = \mathscr{L}\{g(t)\}$, and since the integral in (6.103) does not depend on $t$, we can multiply both sides by $e^{at}$ and take this factor inside the integral sign:

$$g(t) = \frac{1}{2\pi} \int_{-\infty}^{\infty} \mathscr{L}\{g(t)\}e^{(a+i\omega)t}\, d\omega \qquad (6.104)$$

Since $s = a + i\omega$, $d\omega = ds/i$ and the limits of the integral change to integrating from $s = a - i\omega$ to $s = a + i\omega$,

$$f(t) = \frac{1}{2\pi i} \int_{a-i\omega}^{a+i\omega} \mathscr{F}(s)e^{st}\, ds \qquad (6.105)$$

the inverse Laplace transform.

We have constructed the Laplace transformation through our attempt to build a Fourier transform with a built-in convergence factor. Since $s$ is a complex quantity, unlike $\omega$ or $f$ which arise in the Fourier transform, direct evaluation of (6.105) requires a technique from the calculus of complex variables, called contour integration. However, we have already constructed a table of Laplace transforms without evaluating (6.105) directly and have used this relative of the Fourier transform to significantly decrease the amount of work required to solve linear ordinary differential equations.

## SOME COMMON FOURIER TRANSFORMS AND THEIR SYMMETRIES

As with the Laplace transform, there are extensive tables of Fourier transforms, but unlike the Laplace transform, the Fourier transform can be pictured as a spectrum and hence is much more amenable to intuitive understanding than the Laplace transform. Figure 6.12 combines an abridged table of Fourier transforms with their graphical equivalents. A study of this figure will suggest many important symmetries of Fourier transforms of real functions. The real part of the Fourier transform is always symmetric about the axis, and the imaginary part is always symmetric about the origin. Functions symmetric about the vertical axis have real Fourier transforms; functions symmetric about the origin have imaginary transforms. A function is its transform's transform, i.e., $g(t) = \mathscr{F}\{\mathscr{F}\{g(t)\}\}$.

For brevity, we define:

*An* even function *is one which is symmetric about the vertical axis, i.e., one for which $f(-x) = f(x)$.*

*An* odd function *is one which is symmetric about the origin, i.e., $f(-x) = -f(x)$.*

For example, $\cos x$ is even, $\sin x$ is odd, and $u(x)$ is neither even nor odd.

With this new terminology, we can summarize our observations about the symmetry of Fourier transforms as follows:

1. Transforms of real functions always have even real parts and odd imaginary parts.
2. Transforms of even functions are real.
3. Transforms of odd functions are imaginary.

These conclusions follow directly from the complex representation of the Fourier series which we used to motivate the Fourier transform and integral. Since

$$c_n = \begin{cases} \dfrac{1}{2}(a_n - ib_n) & n > 0 \\[2mm] \dfrac{1}{2}a_0 & n = 0 \\[2mm] \dfrac{1}{2}(a_{|n|} + ib_{|n|}) & n < 0 \end{cases} \tag{6.106}$$

the real part of $c_n$ equals the real part of $c_{-|n|}$; it is an even function. The imaginary part of $c_n$ equals minus the imaginary part of $c_{-|n|}$; it is an odd function. Since this relationship does not change as we take the

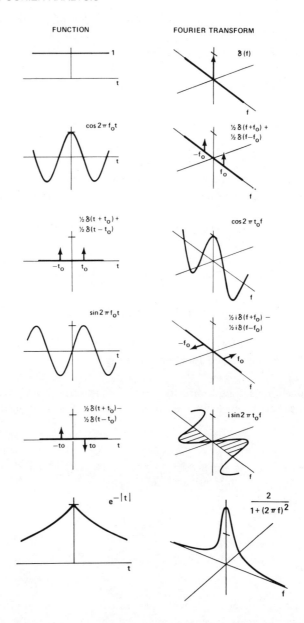

**FIGURE 6.12:** Graphical table of functions and their Fourier transforms. The short marks indicate a value of 1. The vertical plane in the transform space represents the real part of the Fourier transform, and the horizontal

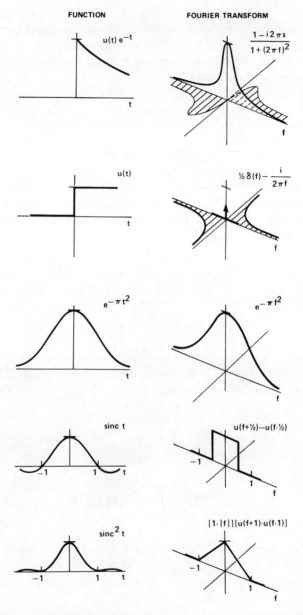

plane represents the imaginary part. (Adapted from *Fourier Transforms and Their Applications* by R. N. Bracewell. Copyright 1965 by McGraw-Hill, Inc. Used with permission of McGraw-Hill Book Company.)

limit to obtain the Fourier integral and transform from the Fourier series, the evenness and oddness of the real and imaginary parts remain unchanged. Since $b_n = 0$ for even functions and $a_n = 0$ for odd functions, we obtain, respectively, pure real and pure imaginary transforms by applying the same logic as above.

Likewise, the fact that $c_n$ and $c_{-n}$ are complex conjugates leads directly to the fact that $G(f)$ and $G(-f)$ are complex conjugates. Conjugation does not change a complex variable's magnitude:

$$|G(f)| = |G(-f)| \qquad (6.107)$$

Hence the power spectrum $|G(f)|^2 = G(f) \cdot \overline{G}(f) = G(f) \cdot G(-f)$ is an even function of frequency. However, conjugation does reverse the phase angle in the polar representation of a function. Specifically, if

$$G(f) = |G(f)|\, e^{i\phi} \qquad (6.108)$$

then

$$G(-f) = \overline{G}(f) = |G(f)|\, e^{-i\phi} \qquad (6.109)$$

Finally, the fact that a function's Fourier transform is also its Fourier integral follows from these symmetry properties and the Fourier integral and transform symmetries:

$$G(f) = \int_{-\infty}^{\infty} g(t)e^{-2\pi ift}\, dt$$

$$\qquad (6.110)$$

$$g(t) = \int_{-\infty}^{\infty} G(f)e^{2\pi ift}\, dt$$

The reader is urged to study Figure 6.12 and, if necessary, find the related Fourier series, until the properties seem reasonable.

## BASIC PROPERTIES OF THE FOURIER TRANSFORM

We will now develop theorems about the Fourier transform that emphasize its physical interpretation as a spectrum. In addition to showing that the Fourier transform is a linear transformation and that the convolution of functions is equivalent to multiplying their Fourier transforms (spectra), we will show that one can compute the power in a signal from either the signal itself or its spectrum, that compressing or shifting the time scale "twists" the signal's spectrum, and that differentiating a signal attenuates the low-frequency components of a spectrum and amplifies its high-frequency components.

We begin with the theorem

*The Fourier transform is a linear transformation. If $\mathscr{F}\{f(t)\} = F(f)$, $\mathscr{F}\{g(t)\} = G(f)$, and $\alpha$ and $\beta$ are constants, then $\mathscr{F}\{\alpha f(t) + \beta g(t)\} = \alpha F(f) + \beta G(f)$.*

In other words, the Fourier transform obeys the superposition principle and scaling a signal magnitude scales the magnitude of its spectrum by the same factor (Fig. 6.13A) and the spectrum of the sum of two signals is the sum of the two signal spectra (Fig. 6.13B). (Prove it.)

To show that the frequency response functions we developed in Chapter 5 are the Fourier transform of the impulse response, we will need this theorem:

*The Fourier transform of the convolution of two functions is the product of their transforms, and the Fourier transform of a product is the convolution of their transforms.*

$$\mathscr{F}\{f(t) * g(t)\} = \mathscr{F}\{f(t)\} \cdot \mathscr{F}\{g(t)\} \qquad (6.111)$$

and

$$\mathscr{F}\{f(t) \cdot g(t)\} = \mathscr{F}\{f(t)\} * \mathscr{F}\{g(t)\} \qquad (6.112)$$

Equation (6.111) follows in the same way that we proved the analogous theorem for the Laplace transform (Eq. (5.54)) and (6.112) follows from (6.111) and the symmetry of the Fourier transform $\mathscr{F}\{\mathscr{F}\{f(x)\}\} = f(x)$. (To prove this, let $f = H(f) = \mathscr{F}\{h(x)\}$ and $g = K(f) = \mathscr{F}\{k(x)\}$ in (6.111), and use the symmetry property.)

Often the power of a signal is proportional to the square of its magnitude. For example, electrical power is proportional to the square of the current and mechanical kinetic energy is proportional to the square of the velocity. One could compute the signal's total power by summing the contributions over all times or frequencies. This logic led to *Rayleigh's theorem:*

(A)

(B)

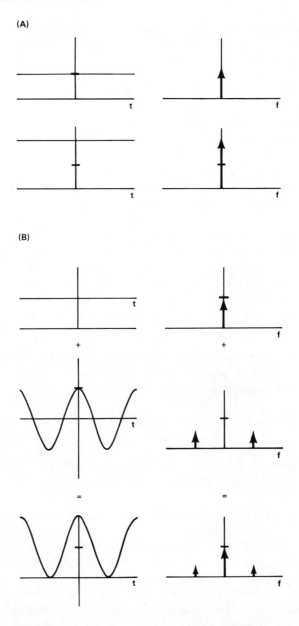

**FIGURE 6.13:** The Fourier transform is a linear transformation: doubling a signal doubles its spectrum (A), and adding two signals corresponds to adding their spectra (B).

*The integral of a function squared equals the integral of the magnitude of its spectrum squared: if $\mathscr{F}\{g(t)\} = G(f)$, then*

$$\int_{-\infty}^{\infty} [g(t)]^2 \, dt = \int_{-\infty}^{\infty} |G(f)|^2 \, df \qquad (6.113)$$

Thus Rayleigh's theorem states that one can find the total power in a signal by finding the contribution at each time and summing over all times or by finding the contribution at each frequency and summing over all frequencies. This result follows from the convolution theorem:

$$\int_{-\infty}^{\infty} [g(t)]^2 \, dt = \int_{-\infty}^{\infty} g(t) \cdot g(t) e^{-2\pi i f_0 t} \, dt \qquad f_0 = 0 \qquad (6.114)$$

$$= \mathscr{F}\{g(t) \cdot g(t)\} \qquad f_0 = 0 \qquad (6.115)$$

$$= G(f_0) * G(f_0) \qquad f_0 = 0 \qquad (6.116)$$

Since

$$G(f) = \overline{G}(-f) \qquad (6.117)$$

we can write (6.116) as

$$\int_{-\infty}^{\infty} [g(t)]^2 \, dt = G(f_0) * \overline{G}(-f_0) \qquad f_0 = 0 \qquad (6.118)$$

$$\int_{-\infty}^{\infty} [g(t)]^2 \, dt = \int_{-\infty}^{\infty} G(f) \cdot \overline{G}(f - f_0) \, df \qquad f_0 = 0 \qquad (6.119)$$

Since $f_0 = 0$

$$\int_{-\infty}^{\infty} [g(t)]^2 \, dt = \int_{-\infty}^{\infty} G(f) \cdot \overline{G}(f) \, df = \int_{-\infty}^{\infty} |G(f)|^2 \, df$$

(6.120)

The function $|G(f)|^2$ is called the *power spectrum* associated with the signal $g(t)$ (Fig. 6.14). Remember that we refer to the Fourier transform $G(f)$ as simply a spectrum. $|G(f)|^2$ is simply a generalization of the power spectrum we defined based on the Fourier series with (6.61). In that case, we took the power at the $n$th harmonic frequency to be the square of the amplitude of the sinusoid at that frequency, $A_n^2$. $|G(f)|$ is the magnitude of the spectrum at frequency $f$, so $|G(f)|^2$ is the square of the amplitude at that frequency. Earlier, we observed that while the coefficients of the Fourier series, $A_n$ and $\psi_n$, contain enough information to reconstruct the signal, the power spectrum $A_n^2$ defined by (6.61) does not because the power spectrum contains no information about the phase of the different harmonics. Likewise, while the spectrum $G(f)$ contains all information necessary to reconstruct the original function, the power spectrum $|G(f)|^2$ does not; it contains no information about the phase at any frequency. Thus while each signal determines a power spectrum uniquely, many different signals can produce the same power spectrum. Often, however, the power spectrum associated with a signal contains all the information one needs. For example, in trying to decide whether or not a transducer has an adequate frequency response to reproduce a signal, one needs only to know that there are no important spectral components beyond the transducer's cutoff frequency. The power spectrum answers this question.

In addition to the squared values of a signal, the need arises to sum the product of two variables (e.g., force times velocity). A proof analogous to Rayleigh's theorem yields the *power theorem*:

If $\mathscr{F}\{g(t)\} = G(f)$ and $\mathscr{F}\{h(t)\} = H(f)$

$$\int_{-\infty}^{\infty} g(t)\,h(t)\, dt = \int_{-\infty}^{\infty} G(f)\,H(f)\, df \qquad (6.121)$$

As one compresses the time scale, the frequencies which comprise the spectrum of a given waveform increase because the function changes

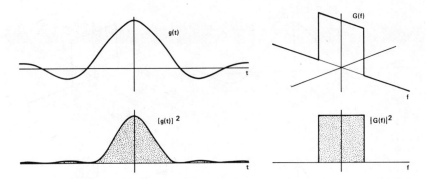

**FIGURE 6.14:** Rayleigh's theorem states that the areas under $[g(t)]^2$ and $|G(f)|^2$ are the same. It is the mathematical embodiment of the fact that whether the total power in a signal is computed by summing contributions over time or over frequency, one obtains the same result.

value in shorter absolute times (Fig. 6.15). The *similarity theorem* describes this phenomenon:

> *If $\mathcal{F}\{g(t)\} = G(f)$, then the Fourier transform of $g(at)$ is $G(f/a)/|a|$ if $g(t)$ is not periodic and contains no impulses, and $G(f/a)$ otherwise.*

If $g(t)$ is not periodic and contains no impulses,

$$\mathcal{F}\{g(at)\} = \int_{-\infty}^{\infty} g(at)e^{-2\pi ift}\, dt = |a|^{-1} \int_{-\infty}^{\infty} g(at)e^{-2\pi i(f/a)at}\, d(at)$$

$$= \frac{G\left(\dfrac{f}{a}\right)}{|a|} \tag{6.122}$$

As one member of the transform pair expands horizontally, the other not only contracts horizontally but grows vertically in order to keep the enclosed area constant (Fig. 6.15). The result for periodic functions follows from the limiting process used to define the Fourier transform of impulses and periodic functions. To see why impulses and periodic functions do not change magnitude with time scale changes, recall that $\mathcal{F}\{\cos 2\pi f_0 t\} = 1/2\delta(f+f_0) + 1/2\delta(f-f_0)$ regardless of $f_0$. Expanding or shrinking the time scale is equivalent to decreasing or increasing the frequency of the cosine function by the same factor and hence moves

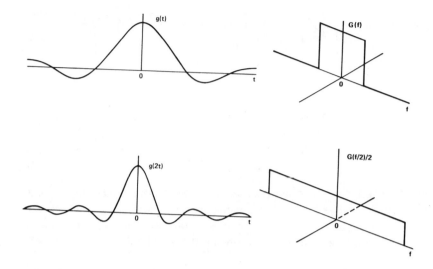

**FIGURE 6.15:** Compressing the time scale by half means that the function changes value more quickly, so its spectrum covers a higher frequency range.

the two impulses which represent its spectrum closer to or farther from the axis without changing their magnitude (Fig. 6.16).

To investigate what happens as we shift a function along the time axis, first examine what happens to $\cos t$ as we shift it along the axis. Since its magnitude remains constant, the magnitude of the spectrum should not change, but its phase should. $\mathscr{F}\{\cos t\}$ consists of two impulses of magnitude $1/2$ located at $\pm 2\pi$ sec$^{-1}$ (radians/sec) (Fig. 6.17A). If we shift this function by $\pi/2$ radians, it becomes equal to $\sin t$, whose Fourier transform is given by two impulses, one at $+2\pi$ sec$^{-1}$ and one at $-2\pi$ sec$^{-1}$, but now in the imaginary plane (Fig. 6.17B). Another $\pi/2$ shift yields the function $-\cos t$, whose Fourier transform is two negative real impulses (Fig. 6.17C). Another $\pi/2$ shift produces $-\sin t$ and twists the two impulses another $\pi/2$ radians (90°). The two impulses rotate in opposite directions: shifting a function is equivalent to twisting its Fourier transform. The amount of this twist depends on the frequency of the spectral component under consideration.

Consider the function

$$g(t) = \cos 2\pi t + \frac{1}{2}\cos \pi t \qquad (6.123)$$

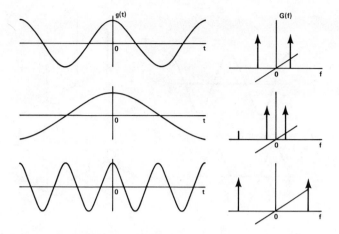

**FIGURE 6.16:** Expanding or compressing the time scale of a periodic function shifts the impulses which comprise its spectrum toward or away from zero frequency without changing their magnitude.

as a sum of two cosines of periods 1 and 2 sec respectively (Fig. 6.18A and B). Shifting this function by 0.5 sec in the positive direction produces

$$g(t - 0.5 \text{ sec}) = \cos 2\pi(t - 0.5 \text{ sec}) + \frac{1}{2}\cos \pi(t - 0.5 \text{ sec}) \quad (6.124)$$

$$g(t - 0.5 \text{ sec}) = \cos (2\pi t - \pi) + \frac{1}{2}\cos \left(\pi t - \frac{\pi}{2}\right) \quad (6.125)$$

The 0.5 sec shift produces a phase shift of $\pi$ radians in the fast cosine, but only $\pi/2$ in the slow cosine (Fig. 6.18C), since 0.5 sec represents a greater fraction of the first cosine's period. If we shift $g(t)$ by another 0.25 sec we obtain

$$g(t - 0.75 \text{ sec}) = \cos 2\pi(t - 0.75 \text{ sec}) + \frac{1}{2}\cos \pi(t - 0.75 \text{ sec}) \quad (6.126)$$

$$= \cos 2\pi t - \frac{3\pi}{2} + \frac{1}{2}\cos \pi t - \frac{3\pi}{4} \quad (6.127)$$

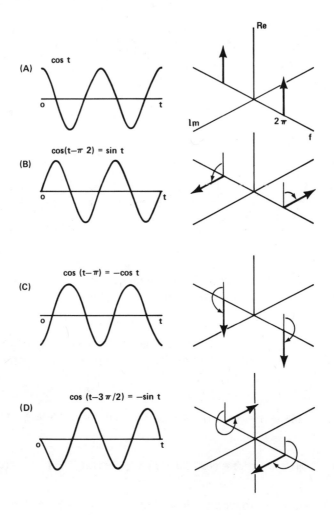

**FIGURE 6.17:** Shifting a function is equivalent to twisting its Fourier transform.

shown in Figure 6.18D. The shift does not change each component's frequency or amplitude but rather its phase, and the change in phase increases in proportion to the frequency. Hence for a positive shift of $\tau$ along the axis, the phase change in the spectral component of frequency $f$ is $\tau f$ cycles or $2\pi\tau f$ radians. Thus, the higher the frequency, the greater the change in phase angle, since the absolute shift $\tau$ occupies a greater

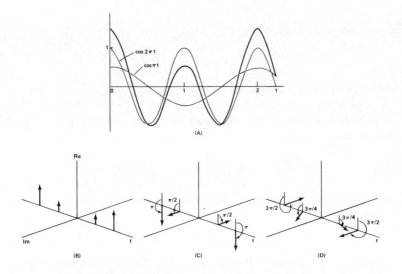

**FIGURE 6.18:** Shifting a function in time is equivalent to subjecting its Fourier transform to a uniform twist.

fraction of the period $T$ $(=1/f)$ associated with each spectral component. Since multiplying a complex function by $e^{-i\phi}$ changes the phase by $\phi$ radians, it should not be surprising that the *shift theorem* states:

*If $\mathscr{F}\{g(t)\} = G(f)$, then $\mathscr{F}\{g(t - \tau)\} = e^{-2\pi i \tau f}G(f)$*

This theorem follows directly from the definition of the Fourier transform:

$$\int_{-\infty}^{\infty} g(t - \tau)e^{-2\pi ift}\, dt = \int_{-\infty}^{\infty} g(t - \tau)e^{-2\pi if(t-\tau)}e^{-2\pi i\tau f}\, d(t - \tau)$$

$$= e^{-2\pi i\tau f} \int_{-\infty}^{\infty} g(t - \tau)e^{-2\pi if(t-\tau)}\, d(t - \tau)$$

$$= e^{-2\pi i\tau f} G(f) \qquad\qquad (6.128)$$

Since

$$|e^{-2\pi i\tau f}G(f)| = |e^{-2\pi i\tau f}| \cdot |G(f)| = |G(f)| \qquad (6.129)$$

shifting a signal does not change its power spectrum.

One often undertakes Fourier analysis to define specifications for a transducer to measure rates of change. How does differentiating a signal change its spectrum?

*If $\mathscr{F}\{g(t)\} = G(f)$, $\mathscr{F}\{g'(t)\} = 2\pi i f G(f)$*

This theorem follows from the definition of the Fourier transform and the derivative:

$$\mathscr{F}\{g'(t)\} = \int_{-\infty}^{\infty} g'(t)e^{-2\pi ift}\,dt = \int_{-\infty}^{\infty} \lim_{\Delta t \to 0} \frac{g(t + \Delta t) - g(t)}{\Delta t} e^{-2\pi ift}\,dt$$

$$(6.130)$$

$$= \lim_{\Delta t \to 0} \frac{1}{\Delta t}\left[\int_{-\infty}^{\infty} g(t + \Delta t)e^{-2\pi ift}\,dt - \int_{-\infty}^{\infty} g(t)e^{-2\pi ift}\,dt\right]$$

$$(6.131)$$

Applying the shift theorem to the first integral,

$$\mathscr{F}\{g'(t)\} = \lim_{\Delta t \to 0} \frac{1}{\Delta t}[e^{2\pi i\Delta tf}G(f) - G(f)] \qquad (6.132)$$

$$= \lim_{\Delta t \to 0} \frac{G(f)}{\Delta t}\left[1 + 2\pi i\Delta tf + \frac{(2\pi i\Delta tf)^2}{2!} + \ldots - 1\right]$$

$$= 2\pi if\,G(f) \qquad (6.133)$$

Since taking the derivative of a function multiplies its transform by $2\pi if$, we see that differentiation changes the phase of the resulting signal. But more important from a practical point of view, it enhances higher frequencies, attenuates lower frequencies, and suppresses any zero-frequency component (constant). Hence one must generally have transducers with higher cutoff frequencies than the signal itself, to measure rates of change accurately.

These theorems form the basis for using the Fourier transform to manipulate data mathematically. However, for our purposes their key significance lies in the fact that they predict how various operations change the spectrum associated with a waveform, and hence the requirements necessary to measure and analyze it.

## FREQUENCY RESPONSE IS THE FOURIER TRANSFORM OF THE IMPULSE RESPONSE

We will now show that the frequency response amplitude ratio $R(f)$ and phase lag $\phi(f)$ introduced in Chapter 5* to describe a linear time-invariant process simply represent the amplitude and phase as a function of frequency of the Fourier transform of the impulse response. A linear time-invariant process with impulse response $h(t)$ responds to the input $g(t)$ according to the convolution integral (5.12):

$$y(t) = \int_0^t g(t)h(t - \tau)\, d\tau \qquad (6.134)$$

Take Fourier transforms of both sides of (6.134) and apply the convolution theorem to obtain

$$Y(f) = G(f) \cdot H(f) \qquad (6.135)$$

in which $G(f)$ and $Y(f)$ are the input and output spectra respectively, and $H(f)$ is the Fourier transform of the impulse response:

$$H(f) = \mathscr{F}\{h(t)\} = |H(f)| e^{-i\theta(f)} \qquad (6.136)$$

To verify that $|H(f)| = R(f)$ and $\theta(f) = \phi(f)$, we examine the response to the sinusoidal input $g(t) = \sin 2\pi f_0 t$.

The input spectrum is

$$\mathscr{F}\{\sin 2\pi f_0 t\} = G(f) = \frac{i}{2}\, [\delta(f + f_0) - \delta(f - f_0)] \qquad (6.137)$$

* Chapter 5 used radian frequency, $\omega$; here we use cycle frequency, $f$. One can easily convert the results from one form to another with the relationship $\omega = 2\pi f$ since 1 cycle = $2\pi$ radians.

and the output spectrum will be $H(f) \cdot G(f)$, so

$$y(t) = \mathscr{F}^{-1}\{Y(f)\} = \mathscr{F}^{-1}\{H(f)\,G(f)\} = \int_{-\infty}^{\infty} H(f)\,G(f)e^{-2\pi i f t}\,df$$

(6.138)

$$y(t) = \int_{-\infty}^{\infty} |H(f)|\,e^{-i\theta\,(f)}\,\frac{i}{2}\,[\delta(f+f_0) - \delta(f-f_0)]\,e^{-2\pi i f t}\,df$$

(6.139)

Because of the unit impulse's sampling property,

$$y(t) = \frac{i}{2}\left[|H(-f_0)|\,e^{-i\theta(-f_0)}\,e^{-2\pi i f_0 t} - |H(f_0)|\,e^{-i\theta(f_0)}\,e^{2\pi i f_0 t}\right]$$

(6.140)

Since $H(f) = \bar{H}(-f)$, $|H(f_0)| = |H(-f_0)|$, and $\theta(f_0) = -\theta(-f_0)$, we can use these relationships to simplify (6.140):

$$y(t) = |H(f_0)|\cdot\left[\frac{1}{2i}\left(e^{i(2\pi f_0 t - \theta(f_0))} - e^{-i(2\pi f_0 t - \theta(f_0))}\right)\right] \quad (6.141)$$

$$= |H(f_0)|\,\sin\,(2\pi f_0 t - \theta(f_0)) \tag{6.142}$$

Thus the response to a unit sinusoid of frequency $f_0$ is another sinusoid of the same frequency but of amplitude $|H(f_0)|$ and lagging behind the original sinusoid by $\theta(f_0)$ radians, the amplitude and phase angle of which depend on the frequency $f_0$. This is precisely the way we defined the frequency response function $R(f)$ and $\phi(f)$ in (5.28). Thus $|H(f)| = R(f)$, $\theta(f) = \phi(f)$ and the frequency response is the Fourier transform of the impulse response.

$$\mathscr{F}\{h(t)\} = H(f) = |H(f)|\,e^{-i\theta\,(f)} = R(f)e^{-i\phi(f)} \quad (6.143)$$

The plots of amplitude ratio and phase angle as a function of frequency are simply one way to represent the Fourier transform analogous to Figure 6.6B.

Equation (6.135) provides one basis for empirically predicting the response of a device to an input. We must experimentally determine the device's frequency response $H(f)$ by subjecting it to sinusoidal inputs, and measure the amplitude ratio and phase lag between the output and input. Next we compute the input signal's spectrum (Fourier transform) either electronically with a spectral analyzer or mathematically with a digital computer.* After completing these two steps, we know the frequency response $H(f)$ and input spectrum,

$$G(f) = \mathscr{F}\{g(t)\} = |G(f)| e^{-i\psi\,(f)} \tag{6.144}$$

$$Y(f) = G(f) \cdot H(f) = |G(f)| e^{-i\psi\,(f)} \cdot |H(f)| e^{-i\psi\,(f)} \tag{6.145}$$

$$Y(f) = |G(f)| \cdot |H(f)| e^{-i(\psi + \theta)} \tag{6.146}$$

At each frequency, the amplitude of the output spectrum equals the product of the input spectrum's amplitude and the amplitude ratio, and the phase equals the sum of the input phase lag and device-induced phase lag.†

Thus all characterizations of linear time-invariant phenomena contain the same information. The step response is the impulse response's derivative, the frequency response is its Fourier transform, and the transfer function is its Laplace transform. One can also obtain the frequency response function by putting a $s = 2\pi i f$ (or $i\omega$) in the transfer function. All these characterizations can in theory be used to describe any linear process; the problem under study generally determines the most appropriate characterization. For example, to describe a drug with linear pharmacokinetics, one would administer a bolus (to find the impulse response) or a constant infusion (to find the step response), rather than attempting to administer the drug at a sinusoidal rate (to find the frequency response). In contrast, one can often simply generate a sinusoidal function to find an electronic device's frequency response. All these approaches are equivalent, and the choice depends solely on the experimental and interpretive convenience, not on the underlying theory.

---

* Most computer facilities have library programs for this purpose, which incorporate numerical methods to speed computation and more accurately estimate the Fourier transform than one would obtain by directly computing  the integrals which arise directly from the theoretical treatment.

† Plotting the amplitudes on a logarithmic scale speeds this analysis, because the multiplication becomes addition.

## PROBLEM SET 6.5

1. Plot the spectrum of the result obtained by passing the aortic pressure wave shown in Figure 6.4 through the two catheters whose frequency response is plotted in Figure 5.19.
2. Plot the resulting output signal using the results of Problem 1 above.
3. Find and plot the frequency response functions of systems with the following impulse responses:

   a. $\delta(t)$
   b. $e^{-t}$
   c. $e^{-t/10}$
   d. sinc $t$
   e. sinc $2t$
   f. sinc $10t$

4. Plot the spectrum of the unit step function.
5. Plot the spectrum of the step response of each system in Problem 3.

## THE IDEAL TRANSDUCER

What is the ideal transducer? Obviously, it must be one that accurately converts and transmits a measurement. In the language of this chapter, its frequency response magnitude (amplitude ratio) should always equal 1, and its phase lag 0. In this ideal case, the frequency response is

$$H(f) = |H(f)|\,e^{-i\phi} = 1e^0 = 1 \tag{6.147}$$

and the signal will pass through the device unaltered. This ideal device, of course, does not exist. Fortunately, however, we can content ourselves with the requirement that the transducer need only have acceptable characteristics over the range of frequencies which contribute significant power to the input signal. All the important components should pass through with similar amplitude changes, and their phases should remain in the correct relationship. In short, an acceptable transducer has *adequate bandwidth, amplitude linearity,* and *phase linearity.* A transducer is specified in terms of these often interrelated properties.

To study the significance of each of these factors, let us examine the response of hypothetical devices to a step input. Our table of Fourier transforms shows that

$$\mathscr{F}\{u(t)\} = \frac{1}{2}\delta(f) - \frac{i}{2\pi f} \tag{6.148}$$

The step function is an attractive test signal because it is easy to generate and contains high-frequency components because of its sudden initial change and low-frequency components because it lasts forever.

*Bandwidth* refers to the range of frequencies the transducer will pass without substantially distorting the signal. Figure 6.19 shows how devices with various bandwidths transmit a step function. (We assume zero-phase change, and do not display phase.) An ideal filter with infinite bandwidth transmits the step precisely (Figure 6.19A). If the transducer responds only to high frequencies (Fig. 6.19B), it accurately reproduces the initial sudden change but fails to show an indefinitely sustained output, since the low-frequency components fail to pass through. The higher the cutoff frequency, the more quickly the output dies away (Fig. 6.19C), because there are fewer low-frequency components. The infinite energy stored at zero frequency is necessary to sustain the signal forever, so any transducer which does not pass this component will not sustain a constant output. Such a transducer acts as a *high-pass filter*, because it filters out the low-frequency components of a spectrum, but passes its high-frequency components. Next, suppose that the transducer passes low frequencies but fails to transmit the high frequencies (Fig. 6.19D). Since the transducer passes the low-frequency components, it accurately reproduces a constant part of the step, but not the initial sudden change which produced the high-frequency components. The lower the cutoff frequency, the more slowly the output signal approaches its final value (Fig. 6.19E). Transducers with this type of frequency response act as *low-pass filters* because they pass the signal's low-frequency components, but suppress its higher frequencies. Finally, a transducer which passes neither low nor high frequencies (Fig. 6.19F) acts as a *band-pass filter*. Since it passes neither the low- nor high-frequency components, it reproduces neither the initial sudden change nor the constant value that the step input signal exhibits. The necessary bandwidth characteristics depend on the spectra of signals one wishes to measure and the desired accuracy of the measurement.

The transducer should have a bandwidth which includes the frequency range in which possible input signals will have significant power. Of course, what constitutes "significant power" depends on the accuracy requirements in following sudden or very slow changes in the signal, as well as how much money one is willing to spend. For example, a solid-state manometer-tipped catheter provides a much wider bandwidth, and hence a more accurate measurement of ventricular pressure, than does a fluid-filled catheter. But it is more delicate, expensive, and difficult to insert.

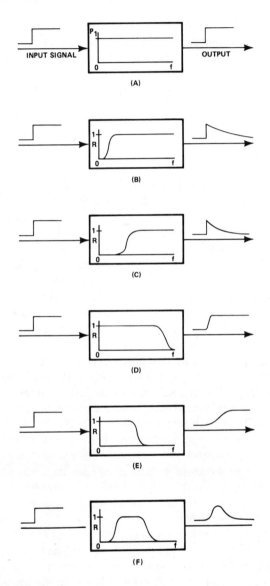

**FIGURE 6.19:** A step function is often used to test a transducer because a step contains components of all frequencies. The high frequencies arise from the initial sudden change and the low frequencies arise from the fact that the step lasts forever. Thus a transducer that does not pass low frequencies will not show that the step lasts forever, while the transducer that fails to pass high frequencies does not show the sudden change.

The second requirement, *amplitude linearity*, means that over the bandwidth all components of the spectrum are transmitted with the same amplitude ratio regardless of their frequencies or amplitudes.* We have already discussed this feature of frequency response at length and need not repeat it here.

Finally, *phase linearity* follows from the need to have all components of the spectrum transmitted in such a way as to leave the relationship between individual components unaffected. As we noted above, the ideal situation would be one in which there was no time lag in the transmission of the signal from the input to output transducer, and as we also noted, this situation is physically impossible. The problem becomes one of specifying how much delay there should be so that the components of the spectrum emerge from the transducer with the correct relative phases. The *shift theorem* we discussed earlier in this chapter tells how to meet this requirement. It stated that if $\mathscr{F}\{g(t)\} = G(f)$, then

$$\mathscr{F}\{g(t - \tau)\} = e^{-2\pi i \tau f} G(f) \qquad (6.149)$$

Now suppose we pass $g(t)$ through a transducer with frequency response

$$H(f) = 1 \cdot e^{-2\pi i \tau f} \qquad (6.150)$$

This transducer induces a phase lag in proportion to the frequency (with $\tau$ being the constant of proportionality), and produces an output signal with the same shape as the input, $g(t)$, but delayed by an amount $\tau$, $g(t - \tau)$.

In the case of a transducer which exhibits damped resonance, such as a fluid-filled catheter or other mechanical system, the transducer should be selected so that its natural frequency (and hence resonant peak) occurs beyond the important frequencies in the input spectrum. Otherwise components near the resonant frequency will seem much more important than they are (see Fig. 5.21). The fact that a device may resonate does not preclude its use, so long as the necessary bandwidth remains far enough below the resonant frequency. If we select a damping ratio of 0.71, there is no resonance and the phase shift changes linearly below the natural frequency $f_n$ (Fig. 6.20). With this damping ratio, there is little phase distortion, but there is about 5% overshoot in its step response and about $1/2f_n$ (seconds) rise time (Fig. 6.21). One could decrease the overshoot by increasing the damping, but this slows down response (rise time). Conversely, the rise time can be hastened at the expense of overshoot by

---

* As long as the transducer remains linear in the sense that superposition applies, the amplitude ratio will by definition be independent of input amplitude.

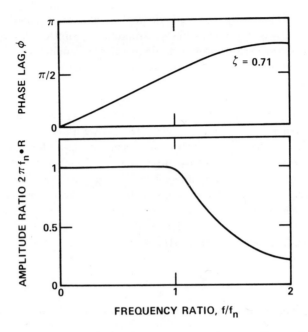

**FIGURE 6.20:** With a 0.71 damping ratio, one obtains a linear phase shift over frequencies below $f_n$ and no resonance.

decreasing the damping ratio. Typically, one sets the damping ratio at about 0.65.

In summary, the ideal transducer depends on a tradeoff of response speed, accuracy, and cost, but the three key steps in choosing a transducer are the specification of a bandwidth which includes the important part of the input signal, assuring that the amplitude ratio remain constant over the bandwidth, and assuring that the phase lag as the signal passes through the transducer be a linear function of frequency so that the spectral components will emerge in the proper phasic relationship.

## PROBLEM SET 6.6

1. Plot the step response of a fluid-filled catheter with $K/(\rho L) = 2$ volt/mmHg sec$^2$, $\omega_n = 30$ sec$^{-1}$, and $\zeta = 0.05, 0.1, 0.2, 0.3, 0.5, 0.8,$ and 1.0. Plot the overshoot as a function of rise time and settling time.
2. Repeat Problem 1 for a catheter with $\omega_n = 15$ and 60 sec$^{-1}$.

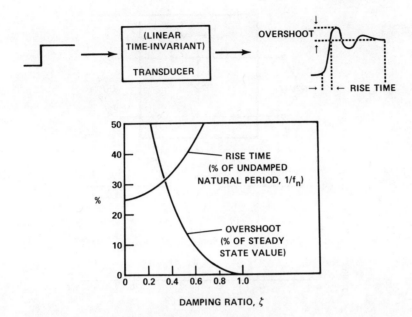

**FIGURE 6.21:** One can describe a damped second-order process, such as a fluid-filled catheter, in terms of its rise time and overshoot. Decreasing damping shortens the rise time (speeds the response), but at the expense of more overshoot. Since $\zeta \simeq 0.7$ produces a reasonably linear phase shift, $\zeta = 0.65$ is often selected as a compromise damping ratio which provides good phase linearity, rapid response, and small overshoot.

## FILTERS

Filters differ from transducers only in their goal. Where a good transducer passes as much of a signal as possible, a good filter selectively blocks parts of the signal. For example, building wiring often induces a 60 Hz signal (noise) in sensitive electronic instruments, which obscures the true signal. Thus the instrument often includes a rejection (or notch) filter to suppress the 60 Hz component of the input spectrum (Fig. 6.22). Often random noise in a signal generally dominates the spectrum at higher frequencies, so it is common to pass the signal through a low-pass filter which eliminates these high-frequency noise components before continuing to process the signal (Fig. 6.23).

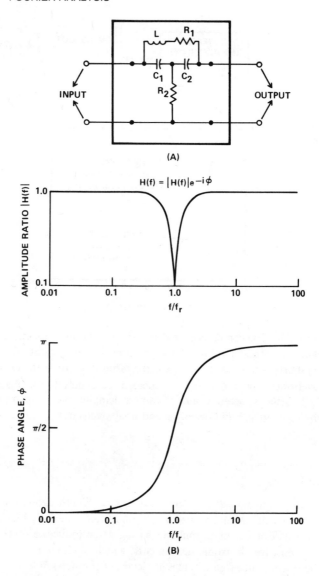

**FIGURE 6.22:** (A) This arrangement of electrical elements, called a *Bridged-T Network*, can be used to reject a narrow band of frequencies around $f_R$. (B) The frequency response for the bridged-T network depends on the values for the resistors, capacitors, and inductor in the network. (For more details, see G. E. Valley, Jr., and H. Wallman, *Vacuum Tube Amplifiers.* Chapter 10: "Frequency-Selective Networks." New York: McGraw-Hill, 1948.)

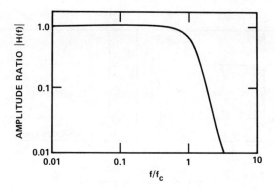

**FIGURE 6.23:** A hypothetical low-pass filter. The amplitude ratio remains 1 until the *corner frequency* $f_C$, then quickly drops toward zero. The corner frequency is the frequency at which $|H(f)| = 0.5$.

One can also use filters to suppress or compensate for resonance introduced in another part of the system, such as when one measures pressure using a fluid-filled catheter, where the noise near the resonant frequency has enough power to amplify the noise to the point where it distorts the output signal. One can avoid this problem by passing the output from the pressure transducer through a low-pass filter with a cutoff frequency below the resonant frequency of the catheter and above the highest component of the pressure signal (Fig. 6.24). The same arguments and intuition we have developed about the frequency response of transducers and their effect on a signal apply to filters. The difference between a filter and a transducer lies in the reason for passing the signal through the device: transducers serve to change the nature of a signal with as little effect on the spectrum as possible, whereas filters are designed to suppress selected parts of the spectrum and pass others, generally for the purpose of removing noise or artifacts.

From a practical point of view, there are two types of filters: analog and digital. Analog filters are physical devices, usually electronic (e.g., Fig. 6.22) or mechanical, through which the signal must pass. Once installed, the laws of physics which underly their transfer functions provide the filtering action. One can also mathematically filter a signal by using a digital computer, giving users precise control over the filter characteristics and freeing them from the problems of component variability and the need for building the physical device. Indeed, some digital filters cannot be physically constructed.

In a digital filter, it is more convenient to work in the time than the

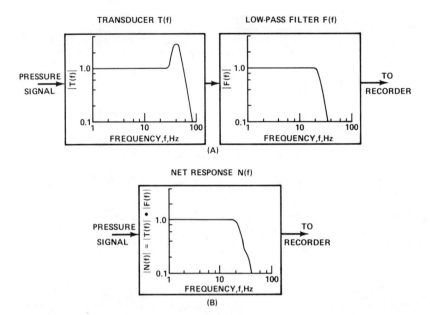

**FIGURE 6.24:** Suppose we wish to measure a pressure signal by using a fluid-filled catheter with the frequency response in (A). We know from prior analysis that the first 15 Hz of the pressure signal contain all the information we need for acceptable measurements, and that the signal contains substantial noise at frequencies up to 50 Hz. Since the pressure transducer resonates at 40 Hz, the resulting signal will be very noisy. To suppress this noise, we pass the transducer's output signal through the low-pass filter with the frequency response shown in (A) to suppress frequencies above 20 Hz. The resulting net frequency response (B) shows that we have effectively removed the resonance.

frequency domain, so rather than thinking in terms of a filter with the transfer function $H(f)$ acting on the input spectrum $G(f)$ to produce the output spectrum $Y(f)$ according to

$$Y(f) = H(f)G(f) \qquad (6.151)$$

we transform (6.151) back to the time domain and filter the signal $g(t)$ by convolving it with the filtering function $h(t)$:

$$y(t) = \int_0^t g(t)h(t - \tau)\,d\tau \qquad (6.152)$$

Figure 6.25A shows the frequency response of an ideal low-pass filter.

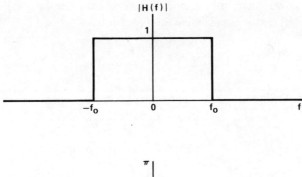

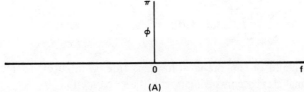

(A)

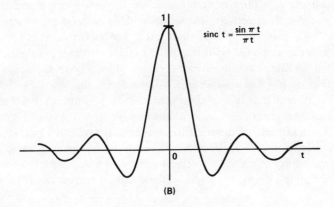

(B)

**FIGURE 6.25:** (A) An ideal low-pass filter passes all components below $f_0$ with no phase change, and rejects all higher-frequency components. (B) The function has a transform (spectrum or frequency response, depending on whether it represents a signal or impulse response) like that shown in (A).

It passes unchanged all frequencies between $+f_0$ and $-f_0$ and rejects everything else, and does not change any component's phase. In fact, the ability to filter with no phase lag is another advantage of digital filters.* It can be shown that the inverse transform of this function equals $\sin 2\pi f_0 t / 2\pi f_0 t$, so we shall define this function as

$$\text{sinc } t = \frac{\sin \pi t}{\pi t} \qquad (6.153)$$

called the *filtering* or *interpolating function.* Figure 6.25B shows that

$$\text{sinc } 0 = 1$$

$$\text{sinc } n = 0 \qquad n = \text{nonzero integer}$$

$$\int_{-\infty}^{\infty} \text{sinc } t \, dt = 1$$

Thus one could obtain the ideal low-pass filter with cutoff frequency $f_0$ for the signal $g(t)$ by convolving it with the sinc function

$$y(t) = \int_{-\infty}^{\infty} g(t) \text{ sinc } 2f_0(t - \tau) \, dt \qquad (6.154)$$

In summary, a filter is simply a device through which one passes a signal in order to selectively remove undesirable components of its spectrum. Analog filters are electro-mechanical devices constructed so as to have frequency responses with the desired effect on the input signal. One is limited to filter characteristics which are physically realizable by the interaction of physical components. Alternatively, the signal can be filtered by storing it in a digital computer, then performing the filtering operations mathematically with a function such as the sinc function, which accomplishes the desired filtration even if one could not actually build an electro-mechanical device with such a frequency response. The following section examines the effects of filters on actual pressure waves recorded during a diagnostic cardiac-catheterization procedure.

## SPECTRAL ANALYSIS OF BLOOD PRESSURE WAVEFORMS

To illustrate spectral analysis and show how it helps specify transducer bandwidth, we will examine human left ventricular, right ventricular, and

---

* This is not to say that the result appears instantly; the computer requires time to complete the convolution in (6.152). It does not, however, introduce any phase distortion in the signal.

pulmonary artery wedge pressure power spectra. We will first discuss the power spectra, then study how filtering affects them and their signals.* In our case study, let us say that we measured the pressure signal $p(t)$ every 0.01 sec (sampled at 100/sec = 100 Hz) for 10 seconds, then computed its Fourier transform $P(f) = \mathscr{F}\{p(t)\}$ and associated power spectrum $|P(f)|^2$ with a digital computer.

Figure 6.26 shows the left ventricle pressure wave with its power spectrum. The pressure varies regularly, with a frequency equal to the

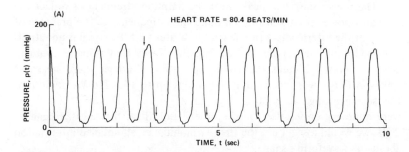

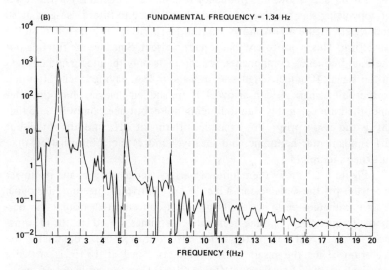

**FIGURE 6.26:** Human left ventricular pressure signal and its associated power spectrum. Since the signal is nearly periodic, the power is concentrated around the harmonic frequencies computed from the average heart rate (dashed lines).

* A. Lawrence Spitz did the computer analysis.

average heart rate, 80.4 beats/min (= 80.4 cycles/min = 1.34 cycles/sec = 1.34 Hz). A close study of Figure 6.26A reveals that each pulse is not a precise duplicate of the others and that the interpulse interval is not precisely constant. In other words, the pulse train is not strictly periodic, so one cannot expect its spectrum (Fourier transform) or its power spectrum to consist only of impulses at the harmonic frequencies. However, since the pressure wave is nearly periodic, we expect power to be concentrated near the harmonics. In Figure 6.26B the power spectrum associated with the pressure signal indeed exhibits this behavior.

The power spectrum peaks near the harmonic frequencies reflect the fact that power is concentrated around these frequencies. The presence of power at the intermediate frequencies indicates that the signal is not strictly periodic and that random noise is present. Notice that at higher frequencies, the noise obscures the power spectrum, although there are small spikes in the power spectrum at harmonics up to 14.8 Hz. We could pass this signal through an 8–10 Hz low-pass filter and feel confident that we were removing only noise. On the other hand, if we filtered this signal at 2 Hz, we would lose all but the first harmonic, i.e., all detailed information about the waveform's shape.

Figure 6.27 shows the frequency response of a digital filter (the result of convolving sinc $t$ with $e^{-t^2/2}$) which was used to filter this signal at 10 and 2 Hz.* Figure 6.28A shows that the 10-Hz filter has little effect on the waveform. This is not to say that it has no effect. Since we are filtering out the high-frequency components, we eliminate only the most rapid changes in the signal. (Compare Figures 6.26A and 6.28A, paying special attention to the points marked with arrows.) These sudden changes which the filter smoothed are ostensibly due to random noise, but one cannot be sure that this is the case a priori. For example, filtering at 2 Hz smooths out all but the fundamental harmonic, but clearly removes more information than just the random noise.

Figure 6.29 shows the pulmonary-artery wedge pressure and its power spectrum for the same person. Like the left ventricular pressure, this signal is approximately periodic, so its power is concentrated around the harmonic frequencies which the heart rate determines. By 10 Hz, the information in the signal has pretty much died out, and noise dominates the spectrum. Thus the result of filtering this signal at 10 Hz is virtually identical to the original signal (Fig. 6.30A). One can again assert confidently that such a filter removes only the noise.

---

* For computational reasons, it is better to use this filtering function than simply to use sinc $t$. Chapter 7 discusses the differences between digital computer arithmetic and real arithmetic.

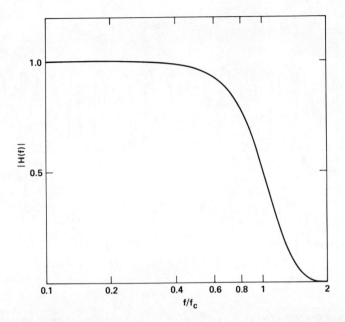

**FIGURE 6.27:** Frequency response of the digital filter obtained by convolving $e^{-t^2/2}$ with sinc $t$. The corner frequency $f_C$ is the frequency at which the amplitude ratio equals $1/2$, and is used to identify the filter.

Unlike the ventricular pressure spectrum, however, there are two spikes in the power spectrum below the 1.34 Hz fundamental harmonic. These two spikes, at 0.3 Hz (18 $\text{min}^{-1}$) and 0.6 Hz, represent the slow variation in pressure due to the effects of respiration, and can be seen clearly after filtering the signal at 2 Hz to remove all but the fundamental harmonic of the contraction-induced pressure wave. If we had filtered the signal at 1 Hz, we would have seen only the pressure variation due to respiration changing the pressures inside the chest cavity. That such changes appear here but not in the left ventricular power spectrum is due to the fact that the left ventricle, being a thicker organ which develops more pressure, is less sensitive to small changes in intrapleural pressure that come with respiration.

Figures 6.31 and 6.32 show pressure and power spectra for the right ventricle which exhibit the same characteristics we have already discussed: power concentrated near the harmonics which the heart rate determines, and two low-frequency components which reflect the first two harmonics of respiratory-pressure variation. At higher frequencies, the spectrum flattens out, indicating that random noise dominates.

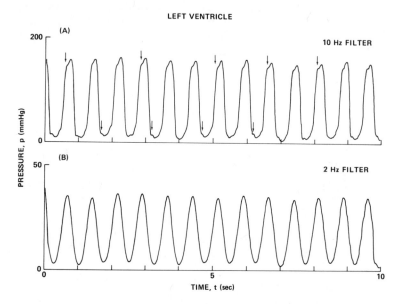

**FIGURE 6.28:** The effect of filtering the left ventricular pressure signal in Figure 6.26A with (A) a 10-Hz, and (B) 2-Hz filter whose frequency response appears in Figure 6.26B.

Often one wishes to differentiate a signal. For example, Figure 6.33A shows the left ventricular pressure, $p(t)$, measured in a dog with an implanted solid-state pressure transducer, and its derivative, $dp/dt$. A comparison of the pressure signal and its derivative reveals two things: the derivative changes value much faster than the original signal and hence contains significant power at higher frequencies, and the derivative signal is much noisier than the original signal. Our analysis explains both phenomena.

We showed that differentiating a signal was equivalent to multiplying its spectrum (Fourier transform) by $2\pi i f$; thus it multiplies its power spectrum by $|2\pi i f|^2 = 4\pi^2 f^2$. Such multiplication eliminates the zero-frequency (constant) component of the spectrum and amplifies the higher harmonics. Figure 6.34 shows the power spectrum of the derivative of the left ventricular pressure wave in Figure 6.26. Notice that significant peaks occur at higher frequencies than the original power spectrum, indicating that power has been shifted to higher frequencies. Thus to measure $dp/dt$ accurately, one must have a transducer with a greater bandwidth than

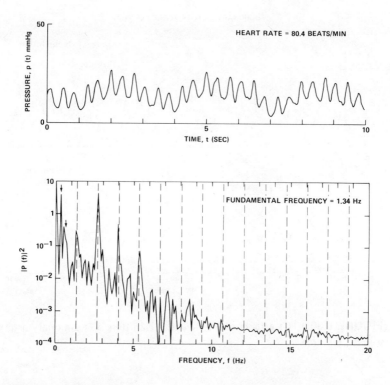

**FIGURE 6.29:** Human pulmonary artery wedge pressure and the associated power spectrum. The two spikes noted with arrows are the first two harmonics of the pressure signal component due to respiratory variation.

would be required to measure the signal itself. The fact that the derivative is noisier than the actual signal also follows directly from the power spectra. Whereas the signal to noise power ratio for the actual signal is on the order of $10^4$ for the original signal (for the first few harmonics), it is only about $10^2$ for the derivative. Hence, the derivative is noisier.

Finally, Figure 6.33B shows how inadequate bandwidth of the transducer system can lead to erroneous measurements. Unless one can accurately measure the first eight harmonics of the pressure wave in Figure 6.33A, one will substantially underestimate even peak $dp/dt$, let alone its actual shape. The analysis of a signal's power spectra permits one to determine the bandwidth of transducers and filters which will be needed to measure a signal while rejecting as much noise as possible.

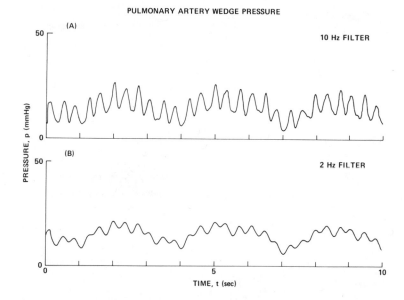

FIGURE 6.30: The effects of 10-Hz and 2-Hz filters on pulmonary artery wedge pressure.

## PROBLEM SET 6.7

1. Plot the spectrum (Fourier transform) of $dp/dt$ for the aortic pressure wave shown in Figure 6.4.
2. Use this result to reconstruct a plot of $dp/dt$ versus time. (Hint: Remember that multiplication by $i = e^{i\pi/2}$ is equivalent to adding $\pi/2$ radians = $90°$ to the phase of a complex number.)
3. Plot the power spectrum of this signal.
4. Plot the $dp/dt$ for the dog aortic pressure signal recorded through the two catheters shown in Figure 5.19.

## ADDITIONAL READINGS

Bracewell, R. N. *Fourier Transforms and their Applications.* New York: McGraw-Hill, 1965.

Bendat, J. S., and Pierson, A. *Measurement and Analysis of Random Data*, Chapter 2, Response Characteristics of Physical Systems, and Chapter

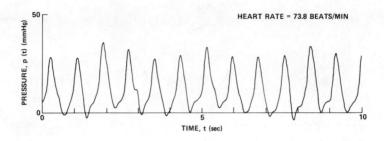

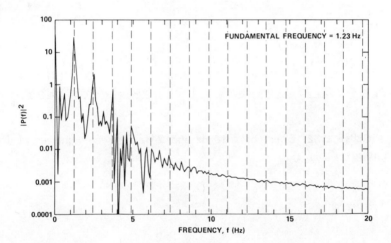

**FIGURE 6.31:** Human right ventricular pressure signal and its associated power spectrum.

3, Mathematical Theory for Analyzing Random Data. New York: Wiley, 1966.

Geddes, L. A., and Baker, L. E. *Principles of Applied Biomedical Instrumentation,* Chapter 14, Criteria for the Faithful Reproduction of an Event. New York: Wiley, 1968.

Gabe, I. T. Pressure Measurement in Experimental Physiology, in *Cardiovascular Fluid Dynamics,* Vol. 1, ed. D. H. Bergel. New York and London: Academic Press, 1972.

Jones, R. W. *Principles of Biological Regulation: An Introduction to Feedback Systems,* Chapter 6, Sinusoidal Signals. New York: Academic Press, 1963.

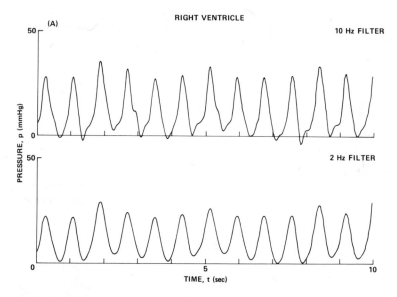

**FIGURE 6.32:** Effect of a 10-Hz and 2-Hz filter on right ventricular pressure signal.

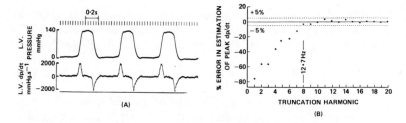

**FIGURE 6.33:** (A) Left ventricular pressure signal measured with a pressure transducer inside a dog ventricle. (B) Adding more and more harmonics permits better and better approximations of peak *dp/dt*. (Adapted with permission from "Pressure Measurement in Experimental Physiology," by I. T. Gabe, in *Cardiovascular Fluid Dynamics, Vol. 1,* ed. D. H. Bergel, Figures 1 and 4. Copyright by Academic Press, Inc. [London] Ltd., 1972.)

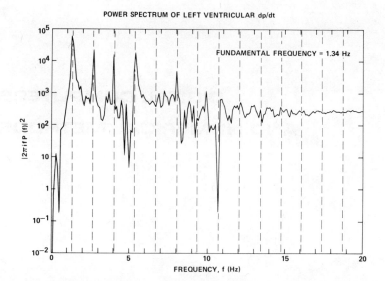

**FIGURE 6.34:** Power spectrum for *dp/dt* of the human left ventricular pressure wave in Figure 6.26. Note that the signal to noise ratio is much higher in this power spectrum than in the power spectrum of the original signal.

# 7

# DIGITAL COMPUTERS
# AND NUMERICAL METHODS

We have developed the mathematical techniques necessary to solve many biomedical problems exactly. These tools, while often adequate, sometimes lack the power to fully solve nonlinear problems. Therefore we must use approximate numerical methods to get an answer. The analytic solutions we have discussed up to this point consist of an equation which holds for all possible values of the parameters of a problem and shows how these parameters affect the solution. We must select values for all parameters before computing a numerical solution, and the solution holds only for that set of parameters. To estimate how the solution depends on the parameters, one must solve the problem many times with different values of the parameters—and even then one may not fully discover how changes in parameter values affect the solution. Therefore, a numerical solution provides much less insight than does an analytic solution. Even so, it is better than no solution at all.

Numerical integration involves the approximation of the area under a curve, and the use of numerical methods to solve differential equations is analogous to the use of approximate methods to solve nonlinear differential equations (Chap. 3, pp. 127ff.). Now we will learn how to take advantage of the speed of digital computers to make much more accurate approximations than we did in Chapter 3. In addition to computing unknown integrals and solutions to differential equations, one often knows the analytical solution to a problem (e.g., drug washout following a bolus), and wishes to find the values of the parameters in this function which best describe a set of measurements. Finding those parameters requires curve fitting.

The speed of digital computers makes all these problems approachable but also introduces another set of potential errors: inherent, truncation, and roundoff errors. *Inherent errors* are errors in the equations being used, or in the data, due to experimental uncertainty. *Truncation errors* arise because the mathematical expressions which form the numerical method only approximate the true solution. *Roundoff errors* are introduced by the fact that computers store only a finite number of digits. These errors propagate as the solution proceeds, and may grow or shrink. For a numerical method to be acceptable, these errors must not grow unacceptably.

Computing costs money, so a good numerical method is economical. This chapter develops a set of simple and accurate numerical methods suitable for many biomedical problems. While naively applying these methods should generally produce accurate results, actually programming them sometimes requires considerable attention to the structure of the computer program and how the computations are performed. In general, the novice should use this chapter as background to select professionally written library programs.

## FLOATING POINT NUMBERS ARE NOT REAL

Loosely speaking, real numbers can be thought of as having an infinite number of decimal places, so that the result of any arithmetic operation on two real numbers equals another real number. In other words, there are no "holes" in the real number system. While one obviously cannot write out those infinite numbers of decimal places, this continuity of available numbers—plus the fact that all computations are carried to an infinite number of digits—assures the existence of limits which define derivatives, integrals, and convergent infinite sums. In contrast to real arithmetic, computers stores and operate on numbers which consist of a finite number of digits, and carry out what is called *floating point arithmetic,* which introduces the problem of roundoff error. To better understand the difference between real and floating point arithmetic—and the problems it brings—we must examine how a computer stores numbers and adds them.

In floating point form, a number is represented by a *fraction f* and an *integer exponent e*. In a computer which does its computations in base $\beta$, it stores the number $x$ as

$$x = f \cdot \beta^e \qquad \text{where } 1 \leqslant f < \frac{1}{\beta}$$

Computers typically use $\beta = 2$, 8, or 16, but for the purposes of illustration we will take $\beta = 10$. For instance, in a hypothetical computer that carries four digits, the floating point representation of 123.4 is $(.1234) 10^3$. Here are some other examples:

| Number | Floating-point representation |
|--------|-------------------------------|
| 5673 | $(.5673) 10^4$ |
| 90013.2 | $(.9001) 10^5$ |
| 0.009235 | $(.9235) 10^{-2}$ |
| 18.3 | $(.1830) 10^2$ |
| -0.7139 | $-(.7139) 10^0$ |

The second example illustrates the first source of roundoff error. Since the computer only carries four digits, it stores 90013.2 as $(.9001) 10^5 = 90010$, introducing an error of 3.2. Another related, but more subtle, problem comes from representing 18.3 as $(.1830) 10^2 = 18.30$, for it suggests that the stored number is accurate to four significant digits instead of the actual three.

Suppose we wanted to add the two floating point numbers 456.7 = $(.4567) 10^3$ and 52.00 = $(.5200) 10^2$. The computer cannot add the fractions as they stand, because the decimal points, represented by the exponents, are not aligned. To align the decimals, the computer shifts the smaller fraction to the right by the number of places equal to the difference of the two exponents. Thus

$$456.7 + 52.00 = (.4567) 10^3 + (.5200) 10^2 = (.4567) 10^3 + (.0520) 10^3$$

$$= (.4567 + .0520) 10^3$$

$$= (.5087) 10^3 = 508.7$$

in this case floating point addition produced the same answer as real addition. This happy situation is, however, not always the case. For example,

$$11110 + 66.66 = (.1111) 10^5 + (.6666) 10^2 = (.1111) 10^5 + (.0006) 10^5$$

$$= (.1111 + .0006) 10^5$$

$$= (.1117) 10^5 = 11170$$

which does not equal the true sum, 11176.66, because some of the digits in the smaller number were shifted out of the computer's storage capacity and lost.* Addition can also lead to a loss of significance. For example,

* Note that these digits were simply dropped, rather than rounded. A few Fortran compilers round in floating point arithmetic, but it is expensive in computer time

$$1112 + {}^-1111 = (.1112)\,10^4 + {}^-(.1111)\,10^4 = (.1112 - .1111)\,10^4$$

$$= (.0001)\,10^4$$

$$= (.1000)\,10^1$$

Even though the true result $(1112 - 11111 = 1)$ is accurate to one significant digit, we must still store four digits, so we must add the trailing zeros. Without seeing the operation that produced it, one could mistake $(.1000)\,10^1$ for 1.000 instead of its true value of 1. Hence another aspect of roundoff error is the loss of significant digits without any simple way to detect this loss.

As a less contrived example, suppose we wish to compute $e^{-5.5}$ using five-place floating point arithmetic.* Most directly, we could begin with the infinite series which defines $e^x$,

$$e^x = 1 + x + \frac{x^2}{2!} + \frac{x^3}{3!} + \frac{x^4}{4!} + \cdots$$

and substitute $-5.5$ for $x$, and continue adding terms until the sum stops changing value (25 terms):

$$
\begin{array}{r}
1.0000 \\
-\;\;5.5000 \\
+15.125 \\
-27.730 \\
+38.129 \\
-41.942 \\
+38.446 \\
-30.208 \\
+20.768 \\
-12.692 \\
+\;\;6.9803 \\
-\;\;3.4902 \\
+\;\;1.5997 \\
\cdot \\
\cdot \\
\cdot \\
\hline
0.0026363
\end{array}
$$

and generally not considered worthwhile. When the number of digits the computer normally carries (usually 7 or 8) is not sufficient, the programmer can use double precision computations (usually 14–16 digits), at the cost of more core storage and execution time.

* This example is from Stegun, I. A., and Abramowitz, M. Pitfalls in computation. *J. Siam* 4 (1956) 207.

This answer contains five digits and is only 36% in error. (To five significant digits, $e^{-5.5}$ = 0.0040868.) Why? The actual computation proceeds by alternately adding and subtracting large (compared to the final answer) numbers which result in relatively small results. In fact, the four most significant digits of all terms greater than 10 have all canceled out. More important, the terms which exceeded 10, being limited to five digits, can only have one digit that contributes to the precision of the final answer. Of course, if we had been dealing with real numbers (an infinite number of decimal places), we would not have had this problem. In fact, had we even worked with ten digits instead of five, we would have obtained an answer accurate to five significant digits. However, carrying more digits is expensive in computer storage and execution time, and we would have run into the same problem again as $x$ became more negative. A more economical approach would be to note that the alternating addition and subtraction leads to loss of significance and devise a way to compute $e^{-5.5}$ which avoids this procedure:

$$e^{-5.5} = 1/e^{5.5} = \frac{1}{(1.0000 + 5.5000 + 15.125 + 27.730 + \ldots)}$$

$$= 0.0040865$$

Computed in this manner, $e^{-5.5}$ differs from the actual value by only 0.007%. This example, then, illustrates both how naively approaching a numerical problem with floating point arithmetic can introduce large errors and how, through thoughtfully casting the computations, these errors can be avoided.

Reliable methods to estimate the roundoff error introduced in floating point arithmetic and how it propagates as the computation proceeds remain incompletely understood. However, numerical analysts have developed some practical suggestions to minimize roundoff errors:*

1. When numbers are to be added or subtracted, work with the smallest numbers first.
2. If possible, avoid subtraction of two nearly equal numbers. An expression containing such a subtraction can often be rewritten to avoid it.

---

* Quoted with permission from Dorn, W. S., and McCracken, D. D. *Numerical Methods with Fortran IV Case Studies*. New York: Wiley, 1972, p. 94. This book contains an excellent discussion of errors and their propagation. See especially Chapter 2, Errors, and Chapter 3, Numerical instabilities and their cure.

3. An expression such as $a(b - c)$ can be written as $ab - ac$, and $(a - b)/c$ can be rewritten as $a/c - b/c$. If there are nearly equal numbers, do the subtraction before multiplying. This step will avoid compounding the problem with additional roundoff errors.
4. When none of the above applies, minimize the number of arithmetic operations.

These guidelines underlie the methods we will now discuss to compute integrals, solve differential equations, and fit curves.

## THE TAYLOR SERIES AND TRUNCATION ERROR

The numerical methods we will develop to estimate the values of definite integrals and the solutions of differential equations begin by approximating the actual function with a simpler one. The basis for selecting these approximating functions and estimating the error they introduce into the calculations can be found by representing the function as an infinite sum called the *Taylor series*. The error which the approximating function introduces is known as *truncation error*, because it arises because we approximate the true function with just the first few terms of an infinite Taylor series.

To motivate the Taylor series, recall that in Chapter 3 (see Fig. 3.30) we used the derivative to approximate a function with a straight line over some small region with the straight line. Figure 7.1 shows that for values of $x$ near $c$,

$$f(x) \simeq f(c) + f'(c) \cdot (x - c) \qquad (7.1)$$

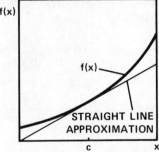

**FIGURE 7.1:** One can approximate a function over a small region near $x = c$ with a straight line tangent to the curve.

The size of the region over which (7.1) reasonably approximates the function depends on how fast the slope is changing, i.e., on the second derivative. To approximate the function over a wider range of values, let us approximate it with a parabola rather than a straight line and use the second derivative to determine the quadratic term:

$$f(x) \simeq f(c) + f'(c) \cdot (x - c) + \frac{1}{2}f''(c) \cdot (x - c)^2 \qquad (7.2)$$

Figure 7.2 shows that Equation 7.2 better approximates the function in Figure 7.1 than does Equation 7.1.

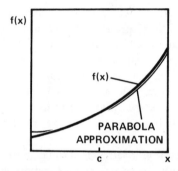

**FIGURE 7.2:** One can approximate a function over a wider range using a parabola rather than a straight line.

This logic leads to the following theorem, which states that any sufficiently smooth function can be represented to an arbitrary degree of accuracy by a power series involving its derivatives, which is called the *Taylor series.*

*If f(x) has n+1 continuous derivatives for $a \leqslant x \leqslant b$ and if $a < c < b$,*

$$f(x) = f(c) + f'(c) \cdot (x - c) + \frac{f''(c) \cdot (x - c)^2}{2!} + \ldots$$

$$+ \frac{f^{(n)}(c) \cdot (x - c)^n}{n!} + R_{n+1}(x) \qquad (7.3)$$

*where*

$$R_{n+1}(x) = \frac{1}{n!} \int_c^x (x - s)^n f^{(n+1)}(s) \, ds$$

$$= \frac{f^{(n+1)}(\xi) \cdot (x - c)^{n+1}}{(n+1)!} \tag{7.4}$$

*and $\xi$ is some number between a and b.* *

The *remainder* term $R_{n+1}(x)$, associated with an $n$th-order Taylor series expression, gives the contribution of terms beyond the $n$th power. This remainder term will help estimate the error we introduce by using a truncated Taylor series to approximate functions in the numerical methods we will develop. We can obtain a more convenient form of the Taylor series by writing it in terms of $h = x - c$, the distance from the point about which we compute the series expansion:

$$f(x) = f(c) + f'(c) h + \frac{f''(c) h^2}{2!} + \ldots + \frac{f^{(n)}(c) h^n}{n!} + R_{n+1}(x)$$

$$\tag{7.5}$$

where

$$R_{n+1}(x) = \frac{f^{(n+1)}(\xi) h^{n+1}}{(n+1)!} \tag{7.6}$$

---

* For example, we find the Taylor series expansion for the function $f(x) = e^x$ about the point $x = 0$.

$$f(x) = e^x \qquad f(0) = 1$$
$$f'(x) = e^x \qquad f'(0) = 1$$
$$f''(x) = e^x \qquad f''(0) = 1$$

$$\vdots \qquad\qquad \vdots$$

Substitute $c = 0$ and from (7.7) into (7.3) to obtain $F(x) = 1 + x + x^2/2! + x^3/3! + \ldots$ . Notice that the Taylor series expansion for $e^x$ is precisely the same infinite sum of powers of $x$ that we used to define $e^x$ in the first place. This situation arises because the power series representation is unique.

As we add more and more terms to the Taylor series expansion for a function, it closely approximates the function over a wider and wider range of values of $x$. Figure 7.3 shows first-, second-, and fourth-order Taylor series approximations to a function. (Figs. 7.1 and 7.2 showed first- and second-order expansions for another function.) Note that as we add terms the truncated series approximates the function over a wider and wider range of values of $x$. In other words, as the order $n$ increases, the remainder decreases. These theoretical and graphical aspects of Taylor series expansions will be of primary interest as we develop practical numerical methods.

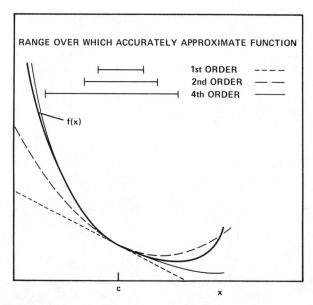

**FIGURE 7.3:** As one adds more terms (increases the order), a Taylor series approximates a smooth function over a wider range of values of the independent variable.

## PROBLEM SET 7.1

1. Carry out the following arithmetic operations in 2, 4, and 6 digit floating point arithmetic:
   a. $123 + 456$
   b. $10001 - 10000$
   c. $(9829 + 2795)/(9829 - 2795) - 1$
   d. $x - x^3/3! + x^5/5!$        $x = 1$

2. The variance of a set of measurements $\{x_i\}$ is defined by the equation

$$s^2 = \frac{1}{n-1} \sum_{i=1}^{n} (x_i - \bar{x})^2$$

where $\bar{x}$ is the mean of the measurements,

$$\bar{x} = \frac{1}{n} \sum_{i=1}^{n} x_i$$

The sum of squared deviations in the definition of $s^2$ can also be written

$$\sum_{i=1}^{n} (x_i - \bar{x})^2 = \sum_{i=1}^{n} x_i^2 - \frac{1}{n} \left( \sum_{i=1}^{n} x_i \right)^2$$

This formula is often used when calculating sums of squares in statistics. Find the variance of the following data using three-place floating point arithmetic:

a. By first finding the mean and using the definition of the variance.
b. By using the sum-of-squares formula.

| $i$ | $x_i$ |
|-----|-------|
| 1 | 3.4 |
| 2 | 3.6 |
| 3 | 4.2 |
| 4 | 4.1 |
| 5 | 3.8 |
| 6 | 4.0 |
| 7 | 3.5 |
| 8 | 4.1 |
| 9 | 3.9 |
| 10 | 3.7 |

Compare these results with each other and the actual variance, 0.0747272727.... What is the percentage error?

3. Repeat Problem 2, using five-digit floating point arithmetic.
4. Why does the first formula provide much more accurate results than the second?

5. Find the Taylor series expansion about $x = 0$ for the functions below. Plot the partial sums obtained by truncating the series after the first-, second-, and fourth-order terms. Plot the actual function on the same sheet, and note how higher-order approximations agree with the time function over a progressively wider range of $x$.

   a. $e^x$
   b. $\sin x$
   c. $\cos x$

6. Repeat Problem 5, expanding each function about $x = \pi$. Plot the first-, second-, and fourth-order expansions as well as the actual functions in the region near $x = \pi$.

7. The definition of $\cos x$ is

$$\cos x = 1 - \frac{x^2}{2!} + \frac{x^4}{4!} - \frac{x^6}{6!} + \frac{x^8}{8!} + \cdots$$

   a. Compute $\cos 3$ approximately, using this eighth-order approximation and three-digit floating point arithmetic.
   b. Compute $\cos 3$, using the mathematically equivalent sum

$$\cos x = 1 - \frac{x^2}{2}\left(1 - \frac{x^2}{4 \cdot 3}\left(1 - \frac{x^2}{6 \cdot 5}\left(1 - \frac{x^2}{8 \cdot 7}\right)\right)\right)$$

   and three-digit floating point arithmetic.

   c. The true value of $\cos 3$ is $-0.9899924966$. The value of the sum computed in 13-digit floating point arithmetic is $-0.9747767857$, providing about a 1.5% truncation error. Compute the percentage errors with methods a and b.

## INTEGRATION

In practice, one often encounters integrals such as $\int_0^1 e^{x^2}\, dx$, which cannot be evaluated analytically, so these integrals must be evaluated using numerical techniques. In addition, one often encounters functions presented in tabular or graphical form, rather than as a mathematical expression. The washout curve for the indicator-dilution measurement of cardiac output we studied in Chapter 2 is one such example. These functions must also be integrated numerically. Numerical methods for computing the value of a definite integral follow from equivalence of the definite integral and the area under the curve. We will examine two popular and accurate numerical techniques for estimating this area. To estimate

$$I = \int_{a}^{b} f(x)\, dx \tag{7.7}$$

we will divide the interval $a \leqslant x \leqslant b$ into $n$ equal subintervals, each $h = (b - a)/n$ wide, approximate $f(x)$ with a simpler function within each subinterval, find the area under the simpler function within each subinterval, and finally, sum the results to estimate $I$.

Figure 7.4 shows one such subinterval, with $f(x)$ approximated by the straight line which connects $f(x_i)$ and $f(x_{i+1})$. The area in the resulting trapezoid approximates the area under $f(x)$ in the subinterval

$$\int_{x_i}^{x_{i+1}} f(x)\, dx \simeq \frac{1}{2} [f(x_i) + f(x_{i+1})] \tag{7.8}$$

Therefore,

$$\int_{a=x_0}^{b=x_n} f(x)\, dx = \sum_{i=0}^{n-1} \int_{x_i}^{x_{i+1}} f(x)\, dx \simeq h \left[ \frac{1}{2} f_0 + f_1 + f_2 + \ldots + f_{n-1} + \frac{1}{2} f_n \right]$$

$$\tag{7.9}$$

This formula, called the *trapezoid rule,* is a *first-order* integration rule because it is equivalent to approximating the function with a first-order Taylor series within each subinterval. In other words, it provides exactly the correct value of the integral of linear functions. Using the remainder

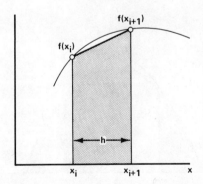

**FIGURE 7.4:** One can approximate the area under the curve (definite integral) with a subinterval using a trapezoid defined by the function values at the end points.

formula, one can show that the truncation error associated with the trapezoid rule is

$$E_T = - \frac{f''(\xi)(b - a)h^2}{12} \qquad (7.10)$$

where $\xi$ is a number between $a$ and $b$.

For example, suppose we wish to estimate

$$\int_0^\pi \sin x \, dx = 2 \qquad (7.11)$$

If we divide the range of integration into two subintervals (Fig. 7.5A),

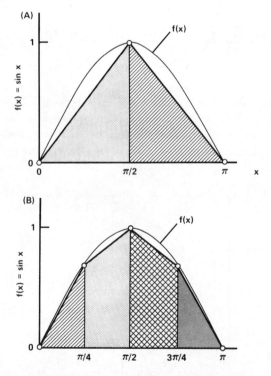

**FIGURE 7.5:** Increasing the number of subintervals increases the accuracy with which the trapezoid rule approximates the definite integral.

we obtain

$$\int_0^\pi \sin x \, dx \simeq \frac{\pi}{2}\left[\frac{1}{2}(\sin 0 + \sin \pi) + \sin \frac{\pi}{2}\right] = \frac{\pi}{2} = 1.570 \quad (7.12)$$

with four subintervals (Fig. 7.5B):

$$\int_0^\pi \sin x \, dx \simeq \frac{\pi}{4}\left[\frac{1}{2}(\sin 0 + \sin \pi) + \sin \frac{\pi}{4} + \sin \frac{\pi}{2} + \sin \frac{3\pi}{4}\right]$$

$$= \frac{\pi}{4}(1 + \sqrt{2}) = 1.896 \tag{7.13}$$

This example and (7.10) show that as we increase the number of subintervals and hence decrease the step size $h$, we could continue to decrease the size of the truncation error. However, since one must consider not only the truncation error induced by the integration formula but also the roundoff error that comes with more arithmetic operations, simply decreasing the step size may not lead to an accurate result. Figure 7.6 shows that as we increase the number of subintervals the truncation error drops, but eventually the roundoff error begins to grow faster than the truncation error falls. Even if roundoff error never becomes substantial, increasing the amount of computation increases the cost of evaluating the integral. Thus, while the trapezoid rule is suitable for some simple problems, we will seek a method which will produce more accurate results without significantly increasing the amount of computation.

Rather than approximating $f(x)$ with a straight line, let us approximate it with a parabola (Fig. 7.7). To develop this approximation, we first divide the interval from $a$ to $b$ into an even number of subintervals, then fit a parabola through each adjacent pair of subintervals. We first select the constants $c_2, c_1$, and $c_0$ in

$$y(x) = c_2 x^2 + c_1 x + c_0 \tag{7.14}$$

to make it pass through $(x_0, y_0)$, $(x_1, y_1)$, and $(x_2, y_2)$ by substituting these values of $x$ and $y$ into (7.14):

$$y_0 = c_2 x_0^2 + c_1 x_0 + c_0 \tag{7.15}$$

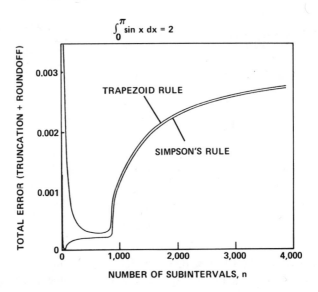

**FIGURE 7.6:** This figure shows the total error in computing $\int_0^\pi \sin x\, dx$. Increasing the number of subintervals (decreasing the step size) decreases the truncation error associated with evaluating an integral, but increases the roundoff error, indicating that there is an optimum step size. This optimum, however, depends on the particular problem and how the computer does floating point arithmetic, and is difficult to find. (Adapted with permission from W. S. Dorn and D. D. McCracken, *Numerical Methods with Fortran IV Case Studies,* Figure 5.7. New York: Wiley, 1972.)

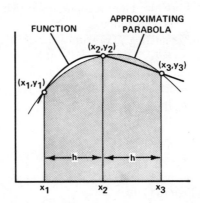

**FIGURE 7.7:** One can approximate the function to be integrated with a parabola.

$$y_1 = c_2 x_1^2 + c_1 x_1 + c_0 \tag{7.16}$$

$$y_2 = c_2 x_2^2 + c_1 x_2 + c_0 \tag{7.17}$$

Equations (7.15) to (7.17) are three linear algebraic equations in the three unknowns $c_2$, $c_1$, and $c_0$. For convenience, take $x_0 = 0$, $x_1 = h$, and $x_2 = 2h$ and solve these equations:

$$c_2 = \frac{1}{2h^2} (y_0 - 2y_1 + y_2)$$

$$c_1 = \frac{1}{2h} (-3y_0 + 4y_1 - y_2) \tag{7.18}$$

$$c_0 = y_0$$

Within these two subintervals, we take

$$\int_0^{2h} f(x)\, dx \simeq \int_0^{2h} (c_2 x^2 + c_1 x + c_0)\, dx = \frac{8}{3} h^3 c_2 + 2h^2 c_1 + 2h c_0$$

$$\tag{7.19}$$

Substitute from (7.18) into (7.19) to obtain *Simpson's rule*:

$$\int_0^{2h} f(x)\, dx \simeq \frac{h}{3} (y_0 + 4y_1 + y_2) \tag{7.20}$$

If we divide the interval from $a$ to $b$ into $n$ subintervals, we find

$$\int_a^b f(x)\, dx \simeq \frac{h}{3} (y_0 + 4y_1 + 2y_2 + 4y_3 + 2y_4 + \ldots + 4y_{n-1} + y_n)$$

$$\tag{7.21}$$

A Taylor series analysis reveals that Simpson's rule is a third-order method. It produces precise answers for integrals for functions up to cubics. From

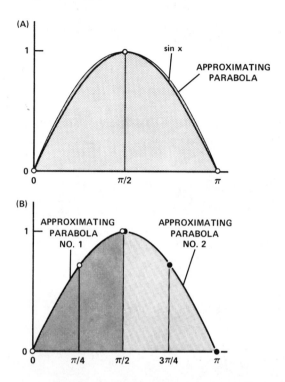

**FIGURE 7.8:** Increasing the number of subintervals makes each parabolic approximation more accurate. In B the curves are closer together than the thickness of the line.

the remainder term, one can show that the truncation error associated with Simpson's rule is

$$E_S = - \frac{f^{(4)}(\xi)(b - a) h^4}{180} \qquad a < \xi < b \qquad (7.22)$$

Since Simpson's rule is a higher-order method than the trapezoid rule for a given step size, we would expect more accurate results. If we apply Simpson's rule to the same integral as we did the trapezoid rule with the same subintervals, we find that for two subintervals (Fig. 7.8A)

$$\int_0^\pi \sin x \, dx \simeq \frac{\frac{\pi}{2}}{3}\left(\sin 0 + 4 \sin\frac{\pi}{2} + \sin \pi\right) = 2.094 \qquad (7.23)$$

and for four subintervals (Figure 7.8B):

$$\int_0^\pi \sin x \, dx \simeq \frac{\frac{\pi}{4}}{3}\left(\sin 0 + 4 \sin \frac{\pi}{4} + 2 \sin \frac{\pi}{2} + 4 \sin \frac{3\pi}{4} + \sin \pi\right) = 2.004$$

(7.24)

it comes much closer to the true value of 2 than did the trapezoid rule, with little added computation. Simpson's rule is far superior to the trapezoid rule for *all* integration problems. It requires only half as many subintervals to obtain a more accurate estimate of the integral than the trapezoid rule (Figure 7.6).

There are many other integration rules, including ones that allow for variable step size to maximize accuracy with a fixed number of subintervals, as well as specialized methods to treat integrals with infinite limits or points at which the value of the integral goes to infinity. Simpson's rule suffices for the vast majority of problems that arise in biomedical applications.

## PROBLEM SET 7.2

Evaluate each of the following integrals using the trapezoidal rule and Simpson's rule with the specified step size, and compute the percentage error.

1. $\displaystyle\int_0^1 x \, dx$                 $h = 1/2$

2. $\displaystyle\int_0^1 x^2 \, dx$               $h = 1/2$

3. $\displaystyle\int_0^1 x^3 \, dx$               $h = 1/2$

4. $\displaystyle\int_0^1 x^4 \, dx$               $h = 1/2$

5. $\displaystyle\int_0^9 \frac{dx}{x}$                $h = 2$

6. $\displaystyle\int_0^9 \frac{dx}{x}$        $h = 1$

7. $\displaystyle\int_0^{10} \sqrt{1 + x}\; dx$        $h = 5$

8. $\displaystyle\int_0^{\pi} \sin 3x\; dx$        $h = 1/4$

9. $\displaystyle\int_0^4 e^x\; dx$        $h = 1$

10. $\displaystyle\int_0^{2\pi} e^x \sin x\; dx$        $h = 1/2$

11. $\displaystyle\int_0^{2\pi} e^x \sin x\; dx$        $h = 1/4$

## DIFFERENTIAL EQUATIONS

We have devoted considerable attention to writing differential equations which describe physiological processes, and have found solutions to most of these equations. Unfortunately, biological problems often involve non-linearities, such as saturation, which lead to nonlinear differential equations that defy analytical solution. To obtain an answer one must resort to numerical methods. We will construct simple numerical solutions to the first-order differential equation

$$y' = f(x,y) \qquad y(x_0) = y_0 \qquad (7.25)$$

then present more accurate related methods without laboring through their derivation. Since one can always replace an $n$th-order differential equation with a set of $n$ first-order differential equations (pp. 6-7), the methods we will develop to treat (7.25) can be extended directly to higher-order equations. We will examine two classes of methods: (a) Runge-Kutta methods, which use the value of the function and slope of the solution curve (determined by the differential equation) to compute the next point; and (b) predictor-corrector methods, in which the next point on the solution curve can be estimated with fewer function evaluations by using a more complex computational technique.

Suppose $y(x)$ is (7.25)'s solution; we can expand $y(x)$ in a Taylor series about the point $x_i$:

$$y(x) = y(x_i) + y'(x_i) \cdot (x - x_i) + \frac{y''(x_i) \cdot (x - x_i)^2}{2!}$$

$$+ \frac{y'''(x_i) \cdot (x - x_i)^3}{3!} + \ldots \qquad (7.26)$$

For $x$ near $x_i$,

$$y(x) \simeq y(x_i) + y'(x_i) \cdot (x - x_i) \qquad (7.27)$$

Now let $x_{i+1} = x_i + h$, where $h$ is the size of a fixed step along the $x$ axis, and replace $y'(x_i)$ with $f(x_i, y_i)$ to obtain

$$y_{i+1} = y_i + h f(x_i, y_i) \qquad (7.28)$$

This formula is called *Euler's method* or the *first-order Runge-Kutta method*. We use the differential equation to find the tangent to the solution curve at each point, then move along this tangent line to estimate the next solution point, and repeat this process until we have obtained the solution over the entire range of interest (Fig. 7.9). The remainder term in the Taylor series tells us that the truncation error associated with (7.28) is

$$E = \frac{y''(\xi)}{2!} h^2 \qquad x_i \leqslant \xi \leqslant x_{i+1} \qquad (7.29)$$

Figure 7.10 shows that the Euler solution to

$$y' = 0.4y \qquad y(0) = 1.0 \qquad (7.30)$$

with $h = 0.5$ develops a sizable total error as $x$ increases. The truncation error from each step propagates to the following steps and rapidly grows. Making $h$ smaller decreases the truncation error according to (7.29), but only as $h^2$ (i.e., halving $h$ decreases the truncation error by 1/4), so that

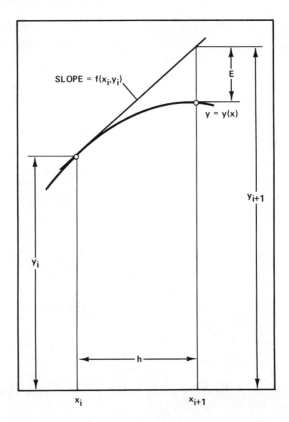

**FIGURE 7.9:** Euler's method for solving a first-order differential equation. *E* is the truncation error.

the step size must be very small in order to obtain accurate results with the Euler method—raising the unfriendly specters of roundoff error and high computing costs. This method is thus unsuitable for most applications.

In our discussion of the Taylor series, we saw that a fourth-order series much better approximated a function than did the first-order series we used to develop the Euler method. By logic similar to that used to develop Euler's method, one can develop a numerical method equivalent to a fourth-order Taylor series, and thus significantly improve accuracy. The intermediate steps are quite involved, but no different in spirit from the process used to develop the Euler method. The resulting *fourth-order Runge-Kutta method* is probably the most popular numerical method for

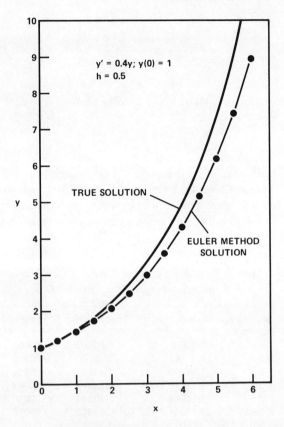

**FIGURE 7.10:** The Euler method uses the differential equation to compute the slope of a line at each step to approximate the solution to the differential equation. Errors can propagate rapidly because the straight line segments often are not a good approximation to the solution function over the range of each step.

solving differential equations today. In fact, it is often referred to as *the* Runge-Kutta method. It is:

$$y_{i+1} = y_i + \frac{h}{6}(k_1 + 2k_2 + 2k_3 + k_4) \tag{7.31}$$

where

$$k_1 = f(x_i, y_i) \tag{7.32}$$

$$k_2 = f\left(x_i + \frac{h}{2}, y_i + \frac{hk_1}{2}\right) \tag{7.33}$$

$$k_3 = f\left(x_i + \frac{h}{2}, y_i + \frac{hk_2}{2}\right) \tag{7.34}$$

$$k_4 = f(x_i + h, y_i + hk_3) \tag{7.35}$$

The truncation error is of the order of $h^5$, so halving the step size decreases truncation error by a factor of 1/32. Table 7.1 shows that, with the same step size which produced poor results with the first-order Euler method, the fourth-order Runge-Kutta method produces very accurate results.

**TABLE 7.1**  Solution to $y' = 0.4y$, $y(0) = 1$ by Fourth-Order Runge-Kutta, with $h = 0.5$

| x | Runge-Kutta Solution | True Solution | Error |
|---|---|---|---|
| 0.0 | 1.00000 | 1.00000 | 0.00000 |
| 0.5 | 1.22142 | 1.22140 | 0.00002 |
| 1.0 | 1.49186 | 1.49182 | 0.00004 |
| 1.5 | 1.82218 | 1.82212 | 0.00006 |
| 2.0 | 2.22564 | 2.22554 | 0.00010 |
| 2.5 | 2.71844 | 2.71828 | 0.00016 |
| 3.0 | 3.32034 | 3.32012 | 0.00022 |
| 3.5 | 4.05552 | 4.05520 | 0.00032 |
| 4.0 | 4.95348 | 4.95303 | 0.00045 |
| 4.5 | 6.05027 | 6.04965 | 0.00062 |
| 5.0 | 7.38990 | 7.38906 | 0.00084 |
| 5.5 | 9.02614 | 9.02501 | 0.00113 |
| 6.0 | 11.02468 | 11.02318 | 0.00150 |

Runge-Kutta has two main disadvantages. First, it requires four function evaluations at each step, and function evaluations are usually the most expensive (in computer time) part of solving a differential equation. Second, it does not provide a good estimate of the truncation error at each step, which could help determine whether the step size is small enough to obtain accurate answers, yet as large as possible to minimize the number of computations. Its accuracy and simplicity, however, make Runge-Kutta one of the most popular methods for numerically solving ordinary differential equations.

A second class of methods, called *predictor-corrector methods*, produces more economical solutions to differential equations because they require fewer function evaluations and permit rational step-size adjustment from one step to the next to minimize the total number of steps. The price for this computational economy is a more complicated computer program. As we did with the Runge-Kutta method, we will develop a simple predictor-corrector method, then simply present analogous but more accurate formulae.* In essence, predictor-corrector methods involve the use of one formula to estimate $y_{i+1}$ in terms of its previous values $(y_i, y_{i-1}, \ldots)$, then using this estimate to compute a more accurate answer.

Compute a first estimate of $y_{i+1}$ with the *predictor*

$$y_{i+1}^{[0]} = y_{i-1} + 2hf(x_i, y_i) \tag{7.36}$$

Figure 7.11A shows this estimate of $y_{i+1}$. The superscript zero indicates that the result is our initial estimate. Geometrically, (7.36) is equivalent to first, finding the tangent line to the solution function at $x_i$ (line $L_1$ in Fig. 7.11A), whose slope is $y_i' = f(x_i, y_i)$, second, drawing a line parallel to it (line $L_1$) through $y_{i-1}$, and third, taking the value of this line when $x_{i+1}$ in order to obtain the first estimate (or prediction), $y_{i+1}^{[0]}$. Given this first estimate, we again use the differential equation to compute the slope at $x_{i+1}, f(x_{i+1}, y_{i+1}^{[0]})$, drawn as line $L_2$ in Figure 7.11B. Now, if we assume that the slope of the solution curve is changing smoothly, the slope of the straight line connecting the true values of $y_i$ and $y_{i+1}$ probably has a slope between the slopes we have computed at $x_i$ and $x_{i+1}$. Therefore, we will estimate the slope of the line connecting $y_i$ and $y_{i+1}$ with the average of these two slopes: $1/2[f(x_i, y_i) + f(x_{i+1}, y_{i+1}^{[0]})]$. This computation is equivalent to finding the line $L_3$ which falls halfway between $L_1'$ and $L_2$ on Figure 7.11B. Given this estimate of the slope of the line connecting $y_i$ and $y_{i+1}$, we estimate $y_{i+1}$ with the *corrector*

$$y_{i+1}^{[1]} = y_i + h \cdot \frac{1}{2}[f(x_i, y_i) + f(x_{i+1}, y_{i+1}^{[0]})] \tag{7.37}$$

Figure 7.11B shows that this computation is equivalent to drawing line $L_3'$ through $(x_i, y_i)$ parallel to $L_3$ and finding the intersection with a vertical

---

* For a thorough discussion of predictor-corrector methods, including computer programs, see Shampine, L. F., and Gordon, M. K. *Computer Solution of Ordinary Differential Equations: The Initial Value Problem*. San Francisco: W. H. Freeman, 1975.

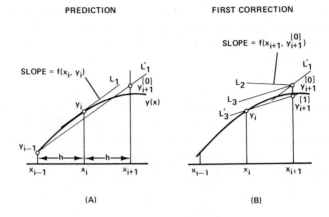

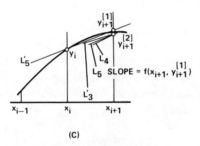

**FIGURE 7.11**: A predictor-corrector method for solving a first-order differential equation; $y(x)$, shown by the heavy line, is the true solution. (Adapted with permission from W. S. Dorn and D. D. McCracken, *Numerical Methods with Fortran IV Case Studies*, Figures 8.6 and 8.7. New York: Wiley, 1972.)

at $x_{i+1}$. Notice that we have greatly improved our estimate of the true answer. To further improve our estimate of the true solution, we again apply the corrector (Fig. 7.11C):

$$y_{i+1}^{[2]} = y_i + \frac{h}{2} [f(x_i, y_i) + f(x_{i+1}, y_{i+1}^{[1]})] \qquad (7.38)$$

Figure 7.11C shows that we have now come very close to the true solution, so we take $y_{i+1}^{[2]} = y_{i+1}$ and step forward to the next point. At each step we use the predictor, then reapply the corrector until successive estimates of the solution change by less than some prescribed tolerance. Experience has shown that this method produces best results when a step size is selected that will produce the final answer after two corrections.

By analyzing the remainder terms of the Taylor series equivalents to the predictor and corrector formulae, one can show that, if $y'''(x)$ remains reasonably constant for $x_{i-1} \leqslant x \leqslant x_{i+1}$, the truncation error after the $k$th correction will be

$$E = \frac{1}{5}(y_{i+1}^{[k]} - y_{i+1}^{[0]})  \qquad (7.39)$$

Thus, unlike the Runge-Kutta method, we have a simple estimate of the error as a by-product of solving the differential equation.

Before we can use a predictor-corrector method, we must "start" it by using a one-step method such as Runge-Kutta to find the base values for the first predictor calculations. Thus, to use our predictor-corrector scheme:

1. Compute the first value $y_1$ from the initial condition $y(0) = y_0$, using Runge-Kutta.
2. Compute $y_{i+1}^{[0]}$ using the predictor

$$y_{i+1}^{[0]} = y_{i-1} + 2hf(x_i, y_i)  \qquad (7.40)$$

3. Apply the corrector

$$y_{i+1}^{[k]} = y_i + \frac{h}{2}[f(x_i, y_i) + f(x_{i+1}, y_{i+1}^{[k-1]})]  \qquad (7.41)$$

repeatedly until the criterion

$$|y_{i+1}^{[k]} - y_{i+1}^{[k-1]}| < \epsilon  \qquad (7.42)$$

is satisfied.
4. Estimate the truncation error with

$$E = \frac{1}{5}(y_{i+1}^{[k]} - y_{i+1}^{[0]})  \qquad (7.43)$$

5. If more than two applications of the corrector are necessary, or if the truncation error is too large, cut the step size (usually in half)

**TABLE 7.2** Comparison of Runge-Kutta and Predictor-Corrector Methods to Solve Ordinary Differential Equations

| | Self-Starting | Computational Efficiency | Truncation Error Estimation | Adjustment of Step | Program Complexity |
|---|---|---|---|---|---|
| Runge-Kutta | Yes | Requires four function evaluations at each point | Difficult | Easy to do, but lack of good estimate of local truncation error makes it difficult to have program automatically change step size | Low |
| Predictor-Corrector | No | By using information about solution at prior points, only requires 2–3 function evaluations at each point | Easy | Available truncation error estimate makes it easy to decide how to vary step size, but then predictor corrector must be restarted with Runge-Kutta | Moderate |

and restart the procedure (with Runge-Kutta) from the last acceptable point. If the truncation error becomes very small, increase (double) the step size and restart the computation.

The method we have developed is a second-order predictor-corrector method. Just as replacing the first-order Euler method with the fourth-order Runge-Kutta method provided more accurate results, in practice we would generally use a fourth-order predictor-corrector combination such as the one which consists of the Adams-Bashford predictor,

$$y_{i+1}^{[0]} = y_i + \frac{h}{24}(55y_i - 59y_{i-1} + 37y_{i-2} - 9y_{i-3}) \qquad (7.44)$$

and the Adams-Moulton corrector,

$$y_{i+1}^{[k]} = y_i + \frac{h}{24}(9y_{i+1}^{[k-1]} + 19y_i - 5y_{i-1} + y_{i-2}) \qquad (7.45)$$

The truncation error associated with each step is approximately

$$E = -\frac{19}{270}(y_{i+1}^{[k]} - y_{i+1}^{[0]}) \qquad (7.46)$$

This method requires three prior values of the solution at each step, so the Runge-Kutta starter must provide the first three steps before the predictor-corrector can be brought into play. A step size should be selected that provides acceptably accurate results while keeping the truncation error within acceptable lines. Thus, this method requires only two function evaluations per step, compared with four for the Runge-Kutta. In summary, predictor-corrector methods require considerably more programming effort than do Runge-Kutta methods, but the reward for this extra effort is a faster, more economical solution. Table 7.2 summarizes the strengths and weaknesses of these two methods.

Thus far we have discussed first-order equations. We will now generalize these results to higher-order equations. Chapter 2 showed how to rewrite a set of $n$ first-order ordinary differential equations as a single $n$th-order differential equation. Given an $n$th-order equation, we must first carry out the reverse process and write it as a set of $n$ first-order equations. For example, we can replace any second-order differential equation with

$$\dot{x}_1 = f_1(t, x_1, x_2) \qquad x_1(0) = x_{10} \qquad (7.47)$$

$$\dot{x}_2 = f_2(t, x_1, x_2) \qquad x_2(0) = x_{20} \qquad (7.48)$$

The solution of these equations with the fourth-order Runge-Kutta method uses relationships analogous to (7.31) through (7.35):

$$x_{1,i+1} = x_{1,i} + \frac{h}{6}(k_{11} + 2k_{12} + 2k_{13} + k_{14}) \qquad (7.49)$$

$$x_{2,i+1} = x_{2,i} + \frac{h}{6}(k_{21} + 2k_{22} + 2k_{23} + k_{24}) \qquad (7.50)$$

where

$$k_{11} = f_1(t_i, x_{1,i}, x_{2,i}) \qquad (7.51)$$

$$k_{21} = f_2(t_i, x_{1,i}, x_{2,i}) \qquad (7.52)$$

$$k_{12} = f_1\left(t_i + \frac{h}{2}, x_{1,i} + \frac{hk_{11}}{2}, x_{2,i} + \frac{hk_{21}}{2}\right) \qquad (7.53)$$

$$k_{22} = f_2\left(t_i + \frac{h}{2}, x_{1,i} + \frac{hk_{11}}{2}, x_{2,i} + \frac{hk_{21}}{2}\right) \qquad (7.54)$$

$$k_{13} = f_1\left(t_i + \frac{h}{2}, x_{1,i} + \frac{hk_{12}}{2}, x_{2,i} + \frac{hk_{22}}{2}\right) \qquad (7.55)$$

$$k_{23} = f_2\left(t_i + \frac{h}{2}, x_{1,i} + \frac{hk_{12}}{2}, x_{2,i} + \frac{hk_{22}}{2}\right) \qquad (7.56)$$

$$k_{14} = f_1(t_i + h, x_{1,i} + hk_{13}, x_{2,i} + hk_{23}) \qquad (7.57)$$

$$k_{24} = f_2(t_i + h, x_{1,i} + hk_{13}, x_{2,i} + hk_{23}) \qquad (7.58)$$

One takes a similar approach in using predictor-corrector methods. Most library subroutines to solve differential equations are written to solve $n$th-order equations.

There are many ways to introduce errors into the computed solution of a differential equation: experimentally measured parameters may be in error, the algorithm introduces truncation error, and the computer introduces roundoff error. These errors propagate through the entire solution. They may die out or increase, depending on the problem, the method of solution, and the computer. If the error does not grow too quickly (i.e., at worst it increases linearly with each step), we say the solution is *stable*. Each of the three potential sources of uncertainty can lead to stability problems. Some differential equations are very sensitive to the exact values of the parameters in them, so small errors in these parameters cause the computed solution to diverge from the true solution. The numerical method itself may cause instability. Predictor-corrector methods sometimes magnify errors for certain step sizes, regardless of the differential equation.* If the step size is taken too large with one-step methods, such as Runge-Kutta, the computed solution will diverge from the true solution (as it did in Figure 7.10). Simply making the step size smaller, however, will not eliminate accuracy problems, because cutting the step size increases the number of computations, and hence the roundoff error. How important roundoff error becomes depends on how the specific computer does floating-point arithmetic and the computer program. Therefore, there must be a step size which leads to small truncation error without causing significant roundoff error. Unfortunately, finding this optimum value is very difficult. However, it does tell that one can make the step size too small. These potential difficulties provide additional reasons for the fledgeling analyst to seek out good library subroutines to solve his differential equations.

## PROBLEM SET 7.3

1. Solve $y' = 0.4y$, $y(0) = 1.0$, using the Euler method with $h = 0.25$. Plot the results from $x = 0$ to $x = 6$ and compare them with Figure 7.10 and Table 7.1.
2. Use Runge-Kutta to solve $\dot{y} = 2y + 1$, $y(0) = 0$ for values of $t$ between 0 and 2, and find the percentage errors by comparison with the exact solution using these step sizes:
   a. $h = 1.0$
   b. $h = 0.5$
   c. $h = 0.25$
   d. $h = 0.1$
3. Use Runge-Kutta to solve $\dot{y} = 2xy + 1$, $y(0) = 0$ for values of $t$ between 0 and 2, using the same step size as in Problem 2. What are the errors?
4. Use the predictor-corrector method summarized in equations (7.40)–(7.43) to solve $\dot{y} = 2xy + 1$, $y(0) = 0$. Select the step size so that the estimated errors stay below 0.5%.

---

* Milne's method, a popular predictor-corrector method developed for hand calculation, produces a growing, oscillatory error and is unsuited for machine calculations.

5. Write $\ddot{x} + 2\zeta\omega_n\dot{x} + \omega_n^2 x = f(t)$, $x(0) = \dot{x}(0) = 0$ as two first-order differential equations.
6. Formulate the equations you would program to use Runge-Kutta with $h = 1$ min to solve for concentration as a function of time after administering a 500 mg dose of a drug followed by a 4 mg/min constant infusion into an individual with these pharmacokinetic parameters: $V = 30$ liters, $k_{10} = 0.02$ min$^{-1}$, $k_{12} = 0.05$ min$^{-1}$, $k_{21} = 0.03$ min$^{-1}$.

## CURVE FITTING

One often has an equation describing experimental data and wishes to use the data to evaluate parameters in the equation. For example, in Chapter 3 we used measured drug plasma concentration following a bolus to estimate the pharmacokinetic parameters in a linear two-compartment model by plotting the result on semi-log graph paper. Often such graphical techniques are not available or, more often, the data contain enough experimental errors to make graphical analysis unreliable. Thus, we wish to develop general methods to fit a given function to a set of measurements.

One generally defines the best-fitting curve as the curve which minimizes the sum of the squares of the difference between the observed value and computed value at each point.* We minimize the sum of squares so that each error contributes a positive increment to the sum and so that large deviations contribute much more than small ones. Thus, the function $f(x)$ which best fits the set of $n$ data points $\{(x_1, y_1), (x_2, y_2), \ldots, (x_n, y_n)\}$ in the *least-squares sense* is that which minimizes the sum

$$Q = \sum_{i=1}^{n} [y_i - f(x_i)]^2 \tag{7.59}$$

We will now see how to use numerical methods to find the set of parameters in a given function to best fit a set of observations in the least-squares sense. Such problems fall into two categories: linear least squares and nonlinear least squares. In linear least-squares problems one can obtain mathematical expressions which uniquely define the best-fitting curve, and the numerical difficulties which one encounters are associated

---

* When the sample variance differs greatly for different points, one obtains better estimates of the fitting parameters by weighting each point's contribution to the sum-squared-error function in inverse proportion to the sample variance at that point. For an example of this procedure, see Glantz, S. A., et al. Age-Related Changes in Ouabain Pharmacology. *Circ. Res.* 39 (1976): 407.

with roundoff error and computational efficiency. Nonlinear least-squares problems—for example, fitting a bi-exponential curve to observed concentration-versus-time data following a drug bolus—generally do not permit unique theoretical location of the best-fitting curve and one uses numerical methods to systematically search for it.

Now, let us formulate and solve the linear least-squares problem. Suppose we wish to fit $f(x)$, a linear combination of $m$ given functions of $x, g_1(x), g_2(x), \ldots, g_m(x)$. Then

$$f(x) = a_1 g_1(x) + a_2 g_2(x) + \ldots + a_m g_m(x) \tag{7.60}$$

in which $a_1, a_2, \ldots, a_m$ are constants, to the set of $n$ data points. Replacing $f(x)$ in (7.59) with (7.60) shows that this curve-fitting problem is one of finding the values of the parameters $a_1, a_2, \ldots, a_m$ which minimize

$$Q = \sum_{i=1}^{n} [y_i - a_1 g_1(x_i) - a_2 g_2(x_i) - \ldots - a_m g_m(x_i)]^2 \tag{7.61}$$

At the minimum $Q$,

$$\frac{\partial Q}{\partial a_1} = 0 = \sum_{i=1}^{n} 2[y_i - a_1 g_1(x_i) - a_2 g_2(x_i) - \ldots$$

$$- a_m g_m(x_i)] [-g_1(x_i)]$$

$$\frac{\partial Q}{\partial a_2} = 0 = \sum_{i=1}^{n} 2[y_i - a_1 g_1(x_i) - a_2 g_2(x_i) - \ldots$$

$$- a_m g_m(x_i)] [-g_2(x_i)]$$

.

.

.

$$\tag{7.62}$$

$$\frac{\partial Q}{\partial a_m} = 0 = \sum_{i=1}^{n} 2[y_i - a_1 g_1(x_i) - a_2 g_2(x_i) - \ldots$$

$$- a_m g_m(x_i)] [-g_m(x_i)]$$

Hence the best $f(x)$ is the one with the values of $\hat{a}_1, \hat{a}_2, \ldots, \hat{a}_m$ that are solutions to

$$[\Sigma g_1^2(x_i)]\,\hat{a}_1 + [\Sigma g_1(x_i)g_2(x_i)]\,\hat{a}_2 + \ldots + [\Sigma g_1(x_i)g_m(x_i)]\,\hat{a}_m$$

$$= [\Sigma y_i\, g_1(x_i)]$$

$$[\Sigma g_1(x_i)g_2(x_i)]\,\hat{a}_1 + [\Sigma g_2^2(x_i)]\,\hat{a}_2 + \ldots + [\Sigma g_2(x_i)g_m(x_i)]\,\hat{a}_m$$

$$= [\Sigma \hat{y}_i g_2(x_i)]$$

$$\hspace{6cm} \text{(7.63)}$$

$$\cdot$$
$$\cdot$$
$$\cdot$$

$$[\Sigma g_1(x_i)g_m(x_i)]\,\hat{a}_1 + [\Sigma g_2(x_i)g_m(x_i)]\,\hat{a}_2 + \ldots + [\Sigma g_m^2(x_i)]\,\hat{a}_m$$

$$= [\Sigma y_i g_m(x_i)]$$

The terms $\hat{a}_1, \hat{a}_2, \ldots, \hat{a}_m$ are the best estimates (in the least-squares sense) of the true values of $a_1, a_2, \ldots, a_m$ in (7.60).

Since the functions $g_1(x), g_2(x), \ldots, g_m(x)$ are given, all the expressions in square brackets in (7.63) are known, and we are left with the problem of solving $m$ simultaneous linear equations in $m$ unknowns. These equations are called the *normal equations* associated with the linear least-squares problem.

This seemingly straightforward problem is fraught with numerical peril! For example, suppose we put $g_1(x) = x$ and $g_2(x) = 1$ in (7.60). We then obtain the straight line

$$y = a_1 x + a_2 \hspace{4cm} \text{(7.64)}$$

with the associated normal equations

$$(\Sigma x_i^2)\hat{a}_1 + (\Sigma x_i)\hat{a}_2 = (\Sigma x_i y_i) \hspace{3cm} \text{(7.65)}$$

$$(\Sigma x_i)\hat{a}_1 + (\Sigma 1)\hat{a}_2 = (\Sigma y_i) \hspace{3cm} \text{(7.66)}$$

One can solve these two equations to obtain

$$\hat{a}_1 = \frac{n(\Sigma x_i y_i) - (\Sigma x_i)(\Sigma y_i)}{n(\Sigma x_i^2) - (\Sigma x_i)^2} \qquad (7.67)$$

and

$$\hat{a}_2 = \frac{(\Sigma y_i)(\Sigma x_i^2) - (\Sigma x_i)(\Sigma x_i y_i)}{n(\Sigma x_i^2) - (\Sigma x_i)^2} \qquad (7.68)$$

Figure 7.12 shows some data that seem to follow a straight line, and Table 7.3 shows that these data, when substituted into (7.67) and (7.68), yield $\hat{a}_1$ = 1.13 and $\hat{a}_2$ = 7.97. Now let us redo these calculations

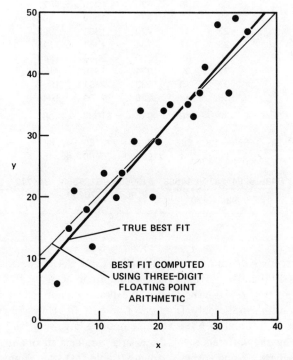

**FIGURE 7.12:** A straightforward solution of the normal equations can lead to significant roundoff errors in even the simple problem of finding the best straight line through a set of data.

**TABLE 7.3**    Real-Arithmetic Calculations for Best-Fit
Straight Line in Figure 7.12

| | $x$ | $y$ | $x^2$ | $y^2$ | $xy$ | |
|---|---|---|---|---|---|---|
| | 3 | 6 | 9 | 36 | 18 | |
| | 5 | 15 | 25 | 225 | 75 | |
| | 6 | 21 | 36 | 441 | 126 | |
| | 8 | 18 | 64 | 324 | 144 | |
| | 9 | 12 | 81 | 144 | 108 | |
| | 11 | 24 | 121 | 576 | 264 | |
| | 13 | 20 | 169 | 400 | 464 | |
| | 14 | 24 | 196 | 576 | 336 | |
| | 16 | 29 | 256 | 841 | 864 | |
| | 17 | 34 | 289 | 1156 | 578 | |
| | 19 | 20 | 361 | 400 | 380 | |
| | 20 | 29 | 400 | 841 | 580 | |
| | 21 | 34 | 441 | 1156 | 714 | |
| | 22 | 35 | 484 | 1225 | 770 | |
| | 25 | 35 | 625 | 1225 | 875 | |
| | 26 | 33 | 676 | 1089 | 858 | |
| | 27 | 37 | 729 | 1369 | 999 | |
| | 28 | 41 | 784 | 1681 | 1148 | |
| | 30 | 48 | 900 | 2304 | 1440 | |
| | 32 | 37 | 1024 | 1369 | 1184 | |
| | 33 | 49 | 1089 | 2401 | 1617 | |
| | 35 | 47 | 1225 | 2209 | 1645 | |
| Sum | 420 | 648 | 9984 | 21988 | 14583 | $n = 22$ |

$$\widehat{a}_1 = \frac{22 \cdot 14583 - 420 \cdot 648}{22 \cdot 9984 - 420^2} = \frac{320826 - 272160}{219648 - 176400} = \frac{48666}{43248} = 1.13$$

$$\widehat{a}_2 = \frac{648 \cdot 9984 - 420 \cdot 14583}{22 \cdot 9984 - 420^2} = \frac{6469632 - 6124860}{219648 - 176400} = \frac{344772}{43248} = 7.97$$

using three-digit floating point arithmetic. Table 7.4 shows that we obtain $\widehat{a}_1 = 1.00$ and $\widehat{a}_2 = 10.2$. These values are in error by 13% and 22% respectively. Figure 7.12 shows that the floating point results produce a line that differs noticeably from the true best fit. How did this arise? Equations (7.67) and (7.68) involve computing large sums and products, then taking the differences of these large numbers to obtain relatively small numbers. If one carries all digits (Table 7.3), this approach poses no problem, but if we carry only three digits, we lose considerable significance and introduce considerable error (Table 7.4). Furthermore, as one adds more parameters and obtains more normal equations, the

**TABLE 7.4**  Three-Digit Floating Point Calculations for Best-Fitting Straight Line for Data in Figure 7.12

| $x$ | $y$ | $x^2$ | $y^2$ | $xy$ |
|---|---|---|---|---|
| $(.300)10^1$ | $(.600)10^1$ | $(.900)10^1$ | $(.360)10^2$ | $(.180)10^2$ |
| $(.500)10^1$ | $(.150)10^2$ | $(.250)10^2$ | $(.225)10^3$ | $(.750)10^2$ |
| $(.600)10^1$ | $(.210)10^2$ | $(.360)10^2$ | $(.441)10^3$ | $(.126)10^3$ |
| $(.800)10^1$ | $(.180)10^2$ | $(.640)10^2$ | $(.324)10^3$ | $(.144)10^3$ |
| $(.900)10^1$ | $(.120)10^2$ | $(.810)10^2$ | $(.144)10^3$ | $(.108)10^3$ |
| $(.110)10^2$ | $(.240)10^2$ | $(.121)10^2$ | $(.576)10^3$ | $(.264)10^3$ |
| $(.130)10^2$ | $(.200)10^2$ | $(.169)10^3$ | $(.400)10^3$ | $(.260)10^3$ |
| $(.140)10^2$ | $(.240)10^2$ | $(.196)10^3$ | $(.576)10^3$ | $(.336)10^3$ |
| $(.160)10^2$ | $(.290)10^2$ | $(.256)10^3$ | $(.841)10^3$ | $(.464)10^3$ |
| $(.170)10^2$ | $(.340)10^2$ | $(.289)10^3$ | $(.115)10^4$ | $(.578)10^3$ |
| $(.190)10^2$ | $(.200)10^2$ | $(.361)10^3$ | $(.400)10^3$ | $(.380)10^3$ |
| $(.200)10^2$ | $(.290)10^2$ | $(.400)10^3$ | $(.841)10^3$ | $(.580)10^3$ |
| $(.210)10^2$ | $(.340)10^2$ | $(.441)10^3$ | $(.115)10^4$ | $(.714)10^3$ |
| $(.220)10^2$ | $(.350)10^2$ | $(.484)10^3$ | $(.122)10^4$ | $(.770)10^3$ |
| $(.250)10^2$ | $(.350)10^2$ | $(.625)10^3$ | $(.122)10^4$ | $(.875)10^3$ |
| $(.260)10^2$ | $(.330)10^2$ | $(.676)10^3$ | $(.108)10^4$ | $(.858)10^3$ |
| $(.270)10^2$ | $(.370)10^2$ | $(.729)10^3$ | $(.136)10^4$ | $(.999)10^3$ |
| $(.280)10^2$ | $(.410)10^2$ | $(.784)10^3$ | $(.168)10^4$ | $(.114)10^4$ |
| $(.300)10^2$ | $(.480)10^2$ | $(.900)10^3$ | $(.230)10^4$ | $(.144)10^4$ |
| $(.320)10^2$ | $(.370)10^2$ | $(.102)10^4$ | $(.136)10^4$ | $(.118)10^4$ |
| $(.330)10^2$ | $(.490)10^2$ | $(.108)10^4$ | $(.240)10^4$ | $(.161)10^4$ |
| $(.350)10^2$ | $(.470)10^2$ | $(.122)10^4$ | $(.220)10^4$ | $(.164)10^4$ |
| Sum $(.420)10^3$ | $(.648)10^3$ | $(.993)10^4$ | $(.217)10^5$ | $(.143)10^5$  $n = 22$ |

$$\hat{a}_1 = \frac{(.220)10^2 \cdot (.143)10^5 - (.420)10^3 \cdot (.648)10^3}{(.220)10^2 \cdot (.993)10^5 - (.420)10^3 \cdot (.420)10^3} = \frac{(.314)10^6 - (.272)10^6}{(.218)10^6 - (.176)10^6}$$

$$= \frac{(.420)10^5}{(.420)10^5} = (.100)10^1$$

$$\hat{a}_2 = \frac{(.648)10^3 \cdot (.993)10^5 - (.420)10^3 \cdot (.143)10^6}{(.220)10^2 \cdot (.993)10^5 - (.420)10^3 \cdot (.420)10^3} = \frac{(.643)10^6 - (.600)10^6}{(.218)10^6 - (.176)10^6}$$

$$= \frac{(.430)10^5}{(.420)10^5} = (.102)10^2$$

numerical difficulties grow quickly. We will not dwell on the numerical problems associated with solving sets of linear algebraic equations, but do caution the reader to seek a library subroutine if he needs to solve more than two or three normal equations.*

It is not necessary that $f(x)$ be a linear function of $x$ to have a linear least-squares curve-fitting problem. For example, one can fit data with

$$y = A_1 e^{a_2 x} \tag{7.69}$$

using linear least squares by replacing $y_i$ with $\ln y_i$ in the normal equations† and letting $g_1(x) = 1$ and $g_2(x) = x$, because

$$f(x) = \ln y = \ln A_1 + a_2 x = a_1 + a_2 x \tag{7.70}$$

Fitting a polynomial is also a linear least-squares problem. If we wish to describe the data with

$$f(x) = a_1 x^2 + a_2 x + a_3 = y \tag{7.71}$$

we simply put $g_1(x) = x^2$, $g_2(x) = x$, and $g_3(x) = 1$ in the normal equations. In sum, fitting a curve defined by a linear combination of any functions of the independent variable leads to a set of linear algebraic equations whose solution yields the values for the curve parameters which produce the best fit to the data. Practical problems arise from roundoff error and questions of computational efficiency, which require careful attention in all but the simplest problems. The mathematical result, however, is precise.

One often wishes to describe a set of data with a function in which the parameters enter nonlinearly—that is, not as simple multipliers in a sum of functions whose values are unknown. In pharmacokinetic applications, we often need to describe the data with the bi-exponential function

$$c(t) = C_1 e^{\lambda_1 t} + C_2 e^{\lambda_2 t} \tag{7.72}$$

---

* Even with only two or three equations, one should use 14–16 digits of precision in order to avoid unpleasant surprises.

† This logarithmic transformation implicitly weights the contribution of each point to $Q$ in inverse proportion to the square of the magnitude of the measured point. In other words, smaller numbers affect the solution more than larger ones. This weighting is appropriate if the data contains a constant percentage error. For more details, see Jacquez, J. A., *Compartmental Analysis in Biology and Medicine*, Chapter 7, System Identification and the Inverse Problem. New York: Elsevier, 1972.

In this case the two parameters $C_1$ and $C_2$ enter the problem linearly and the two parameters $\lambda_1$ and $\lambda_2$ enter nonlinearly. To date there is no universally applicable approach to the problem of fitting a function in which the parameters enter nonlinearly; this is called a *nonlinear least-squares problem*.

In some cases one can write the normal equations and solve them either analytically or through using numerical techniques. In the case where an analytical solution is possible, one only has to contend with the relatively simple problem of formulating the computation in such a way as to avoid the type of roundoff errors we discussed in conjunction with the linear least-squares problem. Solving many simultaneous nonlinear algebraic equations numerically is not especially easy, so unless an analytic solution to the normal equations can be obtained, one does not usually approach a nonlinear least-squares problem by solving the normal equations.

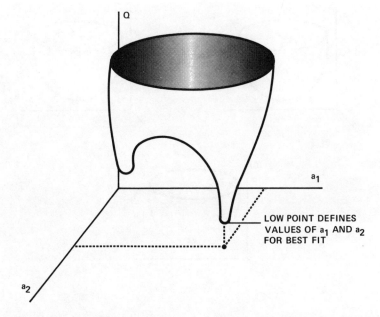

**FIGURE 7.13:** The sum-squared error function $Q$ can be visualized as a surface whose height above the plane defined by the two parameters $a_1$ and $a_2$ in some nonlinear function $f(x)$. (If there are three or more parameters, this surface exists in four or more dimensions, and cannot be drawn, only visualized.) The values of $a_1$ and $a_2$ which minimize $Q$, and hence correspond to the best-fitting curve, are located directly under the lowest point on the surface.

The available numerical methods follow from the idea that, geometrically, the sum of squares defines a surface over a space defined by the parameters associated with the problem (Figure 7.13). The values of the parameters that define the lowest point, where $Q$ is a minimum, define the best-fitting curve. The numerical methods are essentially strategies for searching for this minimum. One of the oldest approaches is the *method of steepest descent*. In essence, one begins with a first guess of the minimum, finds the slope of the sum-squared error surface at that point (using the derivative), then proceeds down along the steepest path a fixed distance, stops, and computes the direction of the next step (Figure 7.14). While this method has the advantage of being straightforward, it often moves toward the solution slowly and is prone to bouncing around the true answer without ever recognizing it (Figure 7.14C).

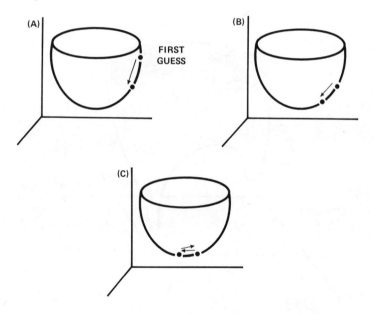

**FIGURE 7.14:** The method of steepest descent begins with a first guess, then uses the derivatives of $Q$ with respect to the parameters to move toward the lowest point on the $Q$ surface. While often a good method far from the minimum, it often fails to recognize the low point on the surface when near it.

In recent years, more sophisticated approaches have been developed, but they too simply attempt to find the bottom of the bowl.* One especially troubling problem in solving a nonlinear least-squares problem is being sure that one *has* the true best fit, the absolute minimum of the sum-squared error surface. Most methods find the minimum point of the valley in which they are started (by the first guess), and there is no way of being sure that there is no deeper valley elsewhere (Fig. 7.15). Thus, one generally should either have an idea of the correct answer before beginning the problem or re-solve it with a variety of first guesses (or both).

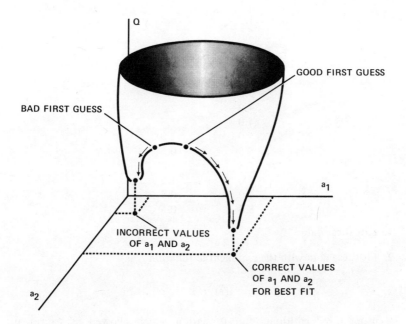

**FIGURE 7.15:** When the Q surface contains more than one valley, an unlucky first guess can lead most—if not all—nonlinear least-squares programs to locate incorrect values of the parameters. Because of this difficulty, it is often prudent to solve nonlinear least-squares problems with a few very different first guesses.

* See, for example, Bard, Y. *Nonlinear Parameter Estimation.* New York: Academic Press, 1974.

## PROBLEM SET 7.4

Suppose one obtains the following data in an experiment:

| $t$ | $z$ |
|-----|-----|
| 0.0 | 11.0 |
| 0.0 | 9.0 |
| 0.5 | 9.0 |
| 0.5 | 7.5 |
| 1.0 | 8.5 |
| 1.0 | 7.0 |
| 1.0 | 5.0 |
| 1.5 | 4.5 |
| 1.5 | 3.5 |
| 2.0 | 5.5 |
| 2.0 | 4.5 |
| 2.5 | 2.0 |
| 3.0 | 3.5 |
| 3.5 | 2.5 |
| 4.0 | 2.5 |
| 4.0 | 1.5 |
| 5.0 | 2.0 |
| 5.5 | 0.5 |
| 5.5 | 1.0 |
| 7.0 | 1.5 |
| 7.0 | 0.5 |
| 8.0 | 0.5 |

1. Plot these data.

2. Fit these data with the exponential function

$$z(t) = Ae^{-kt}$$

using the logarithmic transformation which allowed us to rewrite (7.69) as (7.70).

3. Fit the same data with the parabola

$$x(t) = a_2 x^2 + a_1 x + a_0$$

and plot the results on the same graph.

4. A simple steepest-descent algorithm to solve Problem 2 without taking logarithms is:

a. Guess starting values for $A$ and $k$.

b. Modify the guesses according to

$$A_{i+1} = A_i - h \frac{\partial Q}{\partial A}$$

$$k_{i+1} = k_i - h \frac{\partial Q}{\partial k}$$

where

$$Q = \sum_{h=1}^{22} \left( z_n - A e^{-k t_n} \right)^2$$

and $h$ is a step size (generally less than 1.0).

c. Repeat step b until $|A_{i+1} - A_i| < \epsilon$, and $|k_{i+1} - k_i| < \epsilon$ where $\epsilon$ is a tolerance you choose.

Use this algorithm to solve Problem 2 and plot the results on the same graph as the solution to Problems 2 and 3.

5. Which fit is the "best"?
6. Compute the derivative $dz/dt$ from the results of each problem, and plot this derivative as a function of $t$. What can you say about differentiating empirical equations?

## SUMMARY

This chapter sought not to make you a first-rate computer programmer or numerical analyst, but to introduce the power and limitations of numerical methods available to solve biomedical problems. Unlike the rest of this book, I have not included any specific biomedical examples here, because ones that require computer analysis do so because of their complexity, and little would be gained by developing such problems here only to say that they were solved numerically. (For some good examples of how to formulate such problems, see the books listed in the additional readings.)

Numerical methods bring three sources of potential error. The equations themselves can be highly sensitive to measurement error in the parameters or data, and cause this error to propagate in such a way as to invalidate the solution. Since computers work with a finite number of digits, roundoff error is an ever-present problem, and in poorly conceived computations can grow to such an extent as to produce erroneous solutions. Finally, the numerical methods themselves are often based on local approximations to the true solution, and this truncation error can produce incorrect answers.

While this material will not permit you to write reliable general-purpose computer programs, it should permit you to select library subroutines to intelligently solve the biomedical problems that the rest of this book taught you to formulate.

## ADDITIONAL READINGS

### Numerical Analysis

Bard, Y. *Nonlinear Parameter Estimation.* New York: Academic Press, 1974.

Brent, R. P. *Algorithms for Minimization without Derivatives.* Englewood Cliffs, N.J.: Prentice-Hall, 1972.

Conte, C. S., and C. de Boor. *Elementary Numerical Analysis: An Algorithmic Approach.* New York: McGraw-Hill, 1972.

Dorn, W. S., and D. D. McCracken. *Numerical Methods with Fortran IV Case Studies.* New York: Wiley, 1972.

Forsythe, G. E. Pitfalls in computation, or why a math book isn't enough. *Am. Math Monthly* 27 (1970): 931-956.

Jacquez, J. A. *A First Course in Computing and Numerical Methods.* Reading, Mass.: Addison-Wesley, 1970.

Shampine, L. F., and M. K. Gordon. *Computer Solution of Ordinary Differential Equations: The Initial Value Problem.* San Francisco: Freeman, 1975.

### Examples of Numerical Solutions to Biomedical Problems

Jacquez, J. A. *Compartment Analysis in Biology and Medicine,* Chapter 7: System Identification and the Inverse Problem. Amsterdam, London, and New York: Elsevier, 1972.

Mesarovic, M. D., ed. *Systems Theory and Biology.* New York: Springer-Verlag, 1968.

Talbot, S. A., and Gessner, V. *Systems Physiology.* New York: Wiley, 1973.

# APPENDIX A

## REVIEW OF CALCULUS

FUNCTIONS OF A SINGLE VARIABLE

We begin with the definitions:

1. *A function is a set of ordered pairs,* $\{(x_1, y_1), (x_2, y_2), (x_3, y_3), \ldots\}$, *in which there is one and only one value of y for each x.*
2. *x is the* independent variable *or* argument *of the function.*
3. *y is the* dependent variable *or* value *of the function.*

There can only be a single value of the dependent variable $y$ for each possible value of the independent variable $x$. However, many different values of the independent variable can correspond to a single value of the dependent variable. For example, consider a telephone directory in which any given individual or organization appears only once. The directory comprises a set of ordered pairs of names and telephone numbers, which is a function. Since any individual or organization (the independent variable) appears only once, knowing the value of this independent variable permits one to uniquely determine the corresponding telephone number (the value of the dependent variable). Any two things related this way comprise a function, but for our purposes we will concentrate on functions which relate two physical entities that are described with numbers.

Consider the set of ordered pairs $\{(y_1, x_1), (y_2, x_2), (y_3, x_3), \ldots\}$. Does this set comprise a function with argument $y$ and value $x$? Perhaps. If there is only one value of $x$ for each value of $y$, the set of ordered pairs is a function. On the other hand, if the set associates any value of $y$ with two or more values of $x$, the set is not a function. Suppose that we construct a telephone book listed according to number, not subscriber name. If each individual or organization has a distinct telephone number, this reverse listing comprises a function, because each number is associated with only one name. However, if many people have the same number, the reverse listing associates a given number with more than one name, so the reverse listing then is not a function. When both the sets of ordered pairs $\{(x_1, y_1), (x_2, y_2), (x_3, y_3), \ldots\}$ and $\{(y_1, x_1), (y_2, x_2), (y_3, x_3), \ldots\}$ are functions, we term the second the *inverse function* of the first.

Like our telephone directory, many useful functions consist of a finite number of ordered pairs. However, we will focus on functions in which the independent variable can take on any of an infinite number of values. Thus, rather than tabulate an infinite list of ordered pairs, we seek the *rules* which determine the dependent variable's value from the independent variable's value. In this case, we denote the set of ordered pairs which is the function as $\{(x, y)$ such that $y = f(x)\}$ or, more simply, write $y = f(x)$ or $y = y(x)$ and say that *y is a function of x*. The function $f$ is the rule by which one determines the value of the dependent variable, given a value of the independent variable.

Although some important applications do not require a knowledge of the function's exact form but only that it exhibit certain properties, generally we need to know how the function relates the dependent to the independent variables. A representation of $y = f(x)$ graphically or by an equation (or set of equations) will serve our purposes.

When the function is a set of ordered pairs of numbers, one can display each pair as a point on a graph in which the horizontal coordinate represents the independent variable and the vertical coordinate, the dependent variable. Viewed this way, a graph is simply an analog representation of a table (perhaps with an infinite number of entries). Figure A.1A shows such a representation. For each value of the independent variable $x$ between 0 and 2, the dependent variable $y$ takes on a single value. Notice that this function is only defined for $x$ between 0 and 2; it makes no sense to ask what the function's value is when $x = 3$.

Does the inverse function of the one represented in Figure A.1A exist? We answer this question by reversing the axes in Figure A.1A to obtain Figure A.1B. The resulting relationship is not a function, because there are values for the independent variable (now $y$) which the rule (graph) relates to two different values for the dependent variable (now $x$). Thus $y = y(x)$ does not insure that $x = x(y)$.

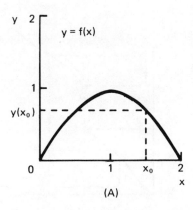
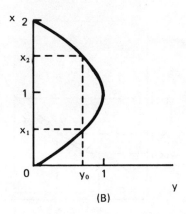

(A)                                    (B)

**FIGURE A.1:** Graph (A) represents a rule which associates a single $y$ with each $x$ between 0 and 2. Each point on the graph represents one of the ordered pairs $\{(x, y)\}$ which comprises the function $f$ with the independent variable $x$ and the dependent variable $y$. Now suppose we wanted to illustrate graphically those $x$ which are associated with each value of $y$ by plotting $y$ as the independent variable on the horizontal axis. The result, graph (B), shows that each value of $y$ between 0 and 1 is associated with two values of $x$. This relationship is not a function, because it fails to associate a *single* value of the dependent variable (now $x$) with each possible value of the independent variable (now $y$). However, by restricting the range of possible values of $x$ we can construct a function from (B). For example, if we add the restriction that $x$ must lie between 0 and 1, we obtain a function, since only one value of the dependent variable is associated with each value of the independent variable.

## CONTINUITY AND LIMITS

Continuity is the most important property of the functions which we will study. Before formally defining continuity, let us examine this concept with graphs. A function $y = f(x)$ is continuous at the point $x = x_0$ if one approaches the same value of $y$ by successively evaluating the function for any sequence of values of $x$ beginning either above or below $x_0$ and moving closer and closer to $x_0$. Consider the function depicted in Figure A.2A. Select an $x$ below $x_0$, evaluate the function at $x_1$, then move $x_1$ closer and closer to $x_0$ and observe the value of $y(x_1)$ which is being approached. Similarly, select an $x_2$ above $x_0$, then repeatedly evaluate $y(x_2)$ as $x_2$

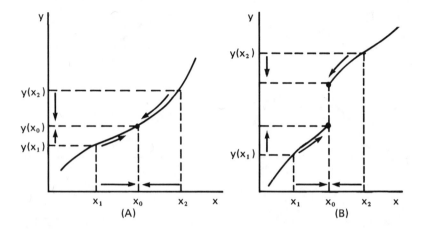

**FIGURE A.2:** (A) A continuous function. As $x$ approaches $x_0$ from either above or below, $y(x)$ approaches $y(x_0)$. (B) A function is discontinuous at $x_0$; $y(x)$ approaches different values as $x$ approaches $x_0$ from above or below.

moves closer and closer to $x_0$. If one obtains the same value of $y$ approaching $x_0$ from both above and below, we say the function is *continuous at $x_0$*.

In contrast, consider the function shown in Figure A.2B. If the two approaches to $x_0$ are repeated from above and below, the same value of $y$ is not approached in both cases. In this case, we say the function is *discontinuous at $x_0$*. Note that a function is continuous or discontinuous at a point; the function in Figure A.2B is discontinuous at $x_0$, but continuous elsewhere (e.g., $x_1, x_2$).

To formally define the concept of continuity, we first examine the concept of a *limit*. Suppose that you begin at one end of a field and move halfway across it. Next, move half the remaining distance to the end, then half of that, again and again. Will you ever reach the end? No. Half the distance before a step always remains after it. With a large enough number of steps you may approach the end as closely as you wish. In mathematical terms we would say that you approach the end of the field as a limit as the number of steps goes to infinity. Thus, the limit of an expression is the value it approaches as the limiting variable approaches some value. To express this mathematically, we write

$$L = \lim_{v \to v_0} g(v) \qquad (A.1)$$

and read "$L$ is the limit of (the function) $g(v)$ as $v$ approaches (or goes to) $v_0$." This notation implies that $v$ can approach $v_0$ from either higher or lower values. We sometimes wish to specify whether $v$ approaches $v_0$ from above or below. In this case, we use the superscript "-" or "+" on the limiting value to denote whether the approach is from below or above:

$$L_1 = \lim_{v \to v_0^-} g(v) \qquad (A.2)$$

and

$$L_2 = \lim_{v \to v_0^+} g(v) \qquad (A.3)$$

Limits do not always exist. For example, both $\lim_{x \to x_0^-} f(x)$ and $\lim_{x \to x_0^+} f(x)$ exist for the function in Figure A.2B (they are the lower and upper points of the discontinuity), yet $\lim_{x \to x_0} f(x)$ does not exist, because one obtains different values for the limit when approaching $x_0$ from above and below. $L = \lim_{N \to \infty} (-1)^N$ where $N$ is the integer is another example of a limit which does not exist. As it increases, $N$ alternates between even and odd numbers, so $(-1)^N$ alternates between $-1$ and $+1$. Thus $L$ does not approach some limiting value as $N$ approaches infinity ($N \to \infty$).

The processes of approaching $x_0$ from above and below used to test for continuity could be rephrased as the definition:

*A function is* continuous *at a point $x_0$ if the limit of the function's value is the same whether approached from above or below*

or

*A function f(x) is* continuous *at $x = x_0$ if and only if*

$$\lim_{x \to x_0} f(x) = \lim_{x \to x_0^+} f(x) = \lim_{x \to x_0} f(x) = f(x_0)$$

$$(A.4)$$

## THE DERIVATIVE

Begin with the function

$$y = f(x) \tag{A.5}$$

and ask, "If the independent variable $x$ is changed by an amount $\Delta x$, how much will the dependent variable $y$ change?" Let us denote this change by $\Delta y$. Then

$$\Delta y = f(x + \Delta x) - f(x) \tag{A.6}$$

Suppose $f(x)$ is the linear relationship

$$y = f(x) = mx + b \tag{A.7}$$

where $m$ and $b$ are constants (see Fig. A.3). Substitute from (A.7) into (A.6) to obtain

$$\Delta y = [m(x + \Delta x) + b] - [mx + b] = m\Delta x \tag{A.8}$$

$$\frac{\Delta y}{\Delta x} = m \tag{A.9}$$

The rate at which $y$ changes with $x$ is a constant equal to the slope of the straight line: the value of $y$ always changes in direct proportion to the change in the value of $x$, with $m$ being the constant of proportionality.

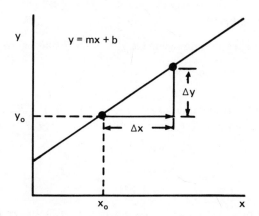

**FIGURE A.3:** For a straight line, the rate at which changes in the independent variable change the dependent variable remains constant, and is equal to the slope of the curve $m = \Delta y/\Delta x$.

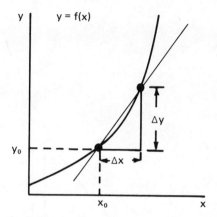

**FIGURE A.4:** The rate at which changes in the independent variable change the dependent variable can be estimated by connecting two points on the graph with a straight line and computing the line's slope.

Now consider the function in Figure A.4. What is the rate of change of $y$ with respect to $x$? In other words, what is the value of the ratio $\Delta y/\Delta x$? One could change $x$ by an amount $\Delta x$, read the corresponding change in $y$, $\Delta y$, off the graph, then compute $\Delta y/\Delta x = m$. This procedure is equivalent to drawing a straight line through the two points $(x_0, y_0)$ and $(x_0 + \Delta x, y_0 + \Delta y)$ and measuring its slope. However, the resulting value of $m$ depends on both $x_0$ and $\Delta x$. The graph shows how the rate of change of $y$ with respect to $x$ depends on $x$'s value. For example, for small values of $x$, a small increment (change) in $x$'s value causes only a small change in $y$'s value, but at larger values of $x$, the same $\Delta x$ produces a larger $\Delta y$. In contrast, the rate of change should not depend on the size of the increment, $\Delta x$. We eliminate this dependence by making the increment smaller and smaller and looking at the limiting value of the ratio $\Delta y/\Delta x$. Figure A.5 shows that as $\Delta x$ gets smaller and smaller, so does $\Delta y$, but their ratio $\Delta y/\Delta x$—the slope of the line connecting the points $(x_0, y_0)$ and $(x_0 + \Delta x, y_0 + \Delta y)$—approaches a limit. This limit is the slope of the line tangent to the curve at $x_0$ and is the instantaneous rate at which $y$ changes with $x$.

We have just computed

$$\lim_{\Delta x \to 0} \frac{\Delta y}{\Delta x} = \lim_{\Delta x \to 0} \frac{f(x_0 + \Delta x) - f(x_0)}{(x_0 + \Delta x) - x_0} \qquad (A.10)$$

Equation (A.10) is the definition of the *derivative*, which is a function that tells the *rate of change* of a function with respect to changes in its

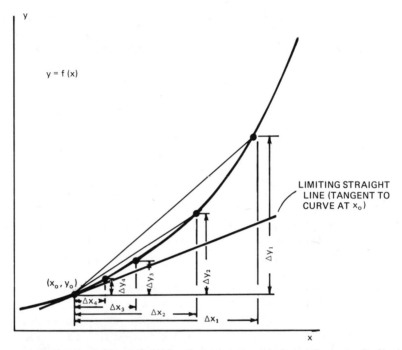

**FIGURE A.5:** As $\Delta x$ approaches 0, $\Delta y$ approaches 0 and the ratio $\Delta y/\Delta x$ approaches the slope of the line tangent to $f(x)$ at $x = x_0$, the derivative.

independent variable. One obtains the derivative of a function by the operation termed *differentiation,* which is denoted by $dy/dx$, $y'(x)$, $y'$, $f'(x)$, $f'$ when $y = f(x)$. A dot usually denotes differentiation with respect to time: if $q = q(t)$, then $\dot{q}(t) = dq/dt$. With our new notation, the definition of the derivative is

$$\frac{dy}{dx} = \lim_{\Delta x \to 0} \frac{f(x + \Delta x) - f(x)}{\Delta x} \qquad (A.11)$$

Suppose $f(x)$ is continuous, then

$$f(x) = \lim_{\Delta x \to 0} f(x + \Delta x) \qquad (A.12)$$

Since $f(x)$ does not depend on $\Delta x$,

$$f(x) = \lim_{\Delta x \to 0} f(x) \qquad (A.13)$$

Equations (A.12) and (A.13) together show that

$$\lim_{\Delta x \to 0} [f(x + \Delta x) - f(x)] = 0 \qquad (A.14)$$

If we consider the opposite case, when the function is discontinuous at point (A.12) and therefore (A.14) does not hold, instead of equaling zero the limit in (A.14) equals the amount of the jump in $y$ at the discontinuity. Thus, the numerator in (A.11) approaches a nonzero number as the denominator approaches zero and as $\Delta x$ gets smaller the ratio grows without bound and therefore the limit, and hence the derivative, does not exist. This proves the theorem

*If a function can be differentiated at a point, it must be continuous at that point.*

Does the converse hold? If a function is continuous, must it be differentiable? No. Recall that for the limit in (A.11) to exist,

$$\lim_{\Delta x \to 0^-} \frac{\Delta y}{\Delta x} = \lim_{\Delta x \to 0^+} \frac{\Delta y}{\Delta x} \qquad (A.15)$$

Now consider the function shown in Figure A.4. When $x = 0$,

$$\lim_{\Delta x \to 0^-} \frac{\Delta y}{\Delta x} = -1 \neq +1 = \lim_{\Delta x \to 0^+} \frac{\Delta y}{\Delta x} \qquad (A.16)$$

Therefore, the limit in (A.11) does not exist and the function is not differentiable at $x = 0$, even though it is continuous. Essentially a function is differentiable if it is continuous and "smooth" in the sense that it has no "sharp corners" such as the one in Figure A.6. More precisely, a function is differentiable when the limit in (A.11) exists.

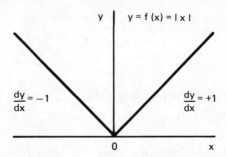

**FIGURE A.6:** An example of a continuous function that is not differentiable at $x = 0$.

## RULES OF DIFFERENTIATION

One could compute the derivative of $y = f(x)$ with respect to $x$ from the definition of the derivative

$$\frac{dy}{dx} = \lim_{\Delta x \to 0} \frac{\Delta y}{\Delta x} = \lim_{\Delta x \to 0} \frac{f(x + \Delta x) - f(x)}{\Delta x} \qquad (A.17)$$

However, rather than evaluating this equation each time we wish to differentiate a function, we can derive rules for differentiating simple functions. These rules allow us to compute derivatives directly, by breaking more complicated functions into collections of simpler ones and then using tabulated rules of differentiation. We now derive the most common differentiation rules and then present others in tabular form. In all cases discussed below, $u(x)$ and $v(x)$ represent differentiable functions.

*Rule 1:* $y = u(x) = x$ $\qquad$ $y' = 1$

Substitute into (A.17):

$$\frac{dy}{dx} = \lim_{\Delta x \to 0} \frac{u(x + \Delta x) - u(x)}{\Delta x} = \lim_{\Delta x \to 0} \frac{(x + \Delta x) - x}{\Delta x}$$

$$= \lim_{\Delta x \to 0} \frac{\Delta x}{\Delta x} = \lim_{\Delta x \to 0} 1 \qquad (A.18)$$

But the constant 1 does not depend on $\Delta x$, so $\lim\limits_{\Delta x \to 0} 1 = 1$ and

$$y' = \frac{dy}{dx} = \frac{dx}{dx} = 1 \qquad (A.19)$$

Thus, *the derivative of a variable with respect to itself is 1.*

*Rule 2:* $y = u(x) = cx$ $\qquad$ $c = constant$ $\qquad$ $y' = c$

Again, substitute into (A.17):

$$y'(x) = \frac{dy}{dx} = \lim_{\Delta x \to 0} \frac{u(x + \Delta x) - u(x)}{\Delta x} = \lim_{\Delta x \to 0} \frac{c(x + \Delta x) - cx}{\Delta x}$$

$$= \lim_{\Delta x \to 0} \frac{c\Delta x}{\Delta x} = \lim_{\Delta x \to 0} c \qquad (A.20)$$

As before, $c$ does not vary with $\Delta x$, so $\lim\limits_{\Delta x \to 0} c = c$, and

$$y'(x) = c \tag{A.21}$$

Thus, *the derivative of a constant times a variable (with respect to that variable) equals the constant.*

*Rule 3: $y = u(x) = c$*      *$c = constant$*      *$y' = 0$*

Since $y$ does not change with $x$, it should not be surprising that

$$y'(x) = \lim_{\Delta x \to 0} \frac{c - c}{\Delta x} = \lim_{\Delta x \to 0} \frac{0}{\Delta x} = 0 \tag{A.22}$$

Thus, *the derivative of a constant (more precisely, a constant function) equals zero.* Note that $\Delta x$ approaches but never *equals* zero; if $\Delta x$ reached zero, the fraction in (A.22) would equal $0/0$, which is a quantity without mathematical meaning.

*Rule 4: $y(x) = u(x) + v(x)$*      *$y'(x) = u'(x) + v'(x)$*

$$\frac{dy}{dx} = \lim_{\Delta x \to 0} \frac{y(x+\Delta x) - y(x)}{\Delta x} = \lim_{\Delta x \to 0} \frac{[u(x+\Delta x) + v(x+\Delta x)] - [u(x)+v(x)]}{\Delta x}$$

$$\tag{A.23}$$

$$= \lim_{\Delta x \to 0} \left( \frac{\Delta v}{\Delta x} + \frac{\Delta v}{\Delta x} \right) \tag{A.24}$$

where $\Delta u = u(x + \Delta x) - u(x)$ and $\Delta v = v(x + \Delta x) - v(x)$. But the limit of a sum equals the sum of the limits,*

$$\frac{dy}{dx} = \lim_{\Delta x \to 0} \frac{\Delta u}{\Delta x} + \lim_{\Delta x \to 0} \frac{\Delta v}{\Delta x} \tag{A.25}$$

and the two limits on the left side of (A.25) define the derivatives $du/dx$ and $dv/dx$:

$$\frac{dy}{dx} = \frac{du}{dx} + \frac{dv}{dx} \tag{A.26}$$

Thus, *the derivative of a sum equals the sum of the derivatives.*

* When all the limits exist.

*Rule 5:* $y(x) = u(x) \cdot v(x)$ $\qquad$ $y'(x) = u(x) \cdot v'(x) + u'(x) \cdot v(x)$

$$y'(x) = \lim_{\Delta x \to 0} \frac{u(x + \Delta x) \cdot v(x + \Delta x) - u(x) \cdot v(x)}{\Delta x}$$

$$= \lim_{\Delta x \to 0} \frac{(u + \Delta u) \cdot (v + \Delta v) - uv}{\Delta x}$$

$$= \lim_{\Delta x \to 0} \left( u \frac{\Delta v}{\Delta x} + v \frac{\Delta u}{\Delta x} + \Delta v \frac{\Delta u}{\Delta x} \right) \tag{A.27}$$

The limit of a sum equals the sum of the limits:

$$y'(x) = \lim_{\Delta x \to 0} \left( u \frac{\Delta v}{\Delta x} \right) + \lim_{\Delta x \to 0} \left( v \frac{\Delta u}{\Delta x} \right) + \lim_{\Delta x \to 0} \left( \Delta v \frac{\Delta u}{\Delta x} \right)$$

$$\tag{A.28}$$

Since the limit of a product is the product of the limits,

$$y'(x) = \lim_{\Delta x \to 0} u \cdot \lim_{\Delta x \to 0} \frac{\Delta v}{\Delta x} + \lim_{\Delta x \to 0} v \cdot \lim_{\Delta x \to 0} \frac{\Delta u}{\Delta x}$$

$$+ \lim_{\Delta x \to 0} \Delta v \cdot \lim_{\Delta x \to 0} \frac{\Delta u}{\Delta x} \tag{A.29}$$

Since $u$ and $v$ do not depend on $\Delta x$,

$$\lim_{\Delta x \to 0} u = u \tag{A.30}$$

and

$$\lim_{\Delta x \to 0} v = v \tag{A.31}$$

From the definition of the derivative

$$\lim_{\Delta x \to 0} \frac{\Delta u}{\Delta x} = \frac{du}{dx} \tag{A.32}$$

and

$$\lim_{\Delta x \to 0} \frac{\Delta v}{\Delta x} = \frac{dv}{dx} \qquad \text{(A.33)}$$

Finally, since $v(x)$ is continuous

$$\lim_{\Delta x \to 0} \Delta v = 0 \qquad \text{(A.34)}$$

Substitute from (A.30) through (A.34) into (A.29) to obtain the rule for differentiating the product $y = uv$:

$$\frac{dy}{dx} = u \frac{dv}{dx} + v \frac{du}{dx} \qquad \text{(A.35)}$$

*Rule 6:*  $y = c \cdot u(x)$ $\qquad c = constant \qquad$ $y' = cu'(x)$

Rather than use the derivative's definition to find $y'(x)$, we begin with $u = u(x)$ and $v = c$ in Rule 5. Then, (A.35) requires that

$$\frac{dy}{dx} = \frac{d(cu)}{dx} = u \frac{dc}{dx} + c \frac{du}{dx} \qquad \text{(A.36)}$$

But Rule 3 says $dc/dx = 0$, so (A.36) becomes

$$\frac{d(cu)}{dx} = c \frac{du}{dx} \qquad \text{(A.37)}$$

Thus, *the derivative of a constant times a function equals the constant times the derivative of the function.*

*Rule 7:*  $y = u(x) = x^n$ $\qquad n \text{ an integer} \qquad$ $y' = nx^{n-1}$

Again use the available rules to evaluate $y'(x)$. Suppose $n = 0$. Then $y = x^0 = 1$ and $y' = 0$ (by Rule 3). Now suppose $n = 1$. Then $y = x^1 = x$ and $y' = 1$ (by Rule 1). For $n = 2$, we set $u = v = x$ in Rule 5, and (A.35), combined with Rule 1, yields

$$\frac{dy}{dx} = \frac{d(x^2)}{dx} = \frac{d(x \cdot x)}{dx} = x \frac{dx}{dx} + x \frac{dx}{dx} = x + x = 2x \qquad \text{(A.38)}$$

Next take $n = 3$. Let $u = x$ and $v = x^2$ and apply Rule 5 again:

$$\frac{dy}{dx} = \frac{d(x^3)}{dx} = \frac{d(x \cdot x^2)}{dx} = x \frac{d(x^2)}{dx} + x^2 \frac{dx}{dx} \qquad \text{(A.39)}$$

Rule 1 and (A.38) with (A.39) yield

$$\frac{d(x^3)}{dx} = x \cdot 2x + x^2 \cdot 1 = 3x^2 \qquad \text{(A.40)}$$

Similarly, this method with $n = 4$ would show

$$\frac{d(x^4)}{dx} = \frac{d(x \cdot x^3)}{dx} = 4x^3 \qquad \text{(A.41)}$$

We could continue this procedure for all $n$ as large as we wished. Comparing the results for $n = 0, 1, 2, 3, 4$ reveals the general rule

$$\frac{d(x^n)}{dx} = nx^{n-1} \qquad \text{(A.42)}$$

We shall not prove it here, but (A.42) applies for any real $n$, including negative values.

The following example illustrates how to use the rules we have just developed:

$$y = 6x^3 + 8x^2 + \frac{1}{x} + 5$$

$$\frac{dy}{dx} = \frac{d}{dx}\left(6x^3 + 8x^2 + \frac{1}{x} + 5\right)$$

$$= \frac{d}{dx}(6x^3) + \frac{d}{dx}(8x^2) + \frac{d}{dx}(x^{-1}) + \frac{d}{dx}(5)$$

$$= 6\frac{dx^3}{dx} + 8\frac{dx^2}{dx} + \frac{dx^{-1}}{dx} + \frac{d5}{dx}$$

$$= 6 \cdot 3x^2 + 8 \cdot 2x^1 + (-1)x^{-2} + 0$$

$$\frac{dy}{dx} = 18x^2 + 16x - \frac{1}{x^2}$$

Make sure you understand the use of each rule.

## THE CHAIN RULE FOR DIFFERENTIATION

Situations commonly arise in which a function's independent variable is itself a function of another variable. A rule called the *chain rule* facilitates the analysis of such problems. It also facilitates the use of the rules of differentiation to differentiate complicated functions. The chain rule states:

*Suppose that y = F(x) and x = f(t) and that F is a differentiable function of x and f is the differentiable function of t. Then*

$$\frac{dy}{dt} = \frac{dy}{dx} \cdot \frac{dx}{dt} \qquad \text{(A.43)}$$

The derivative of $y$ with respect to $t$ equals the derivative of $y$ with respect to $x$ times the derivative of $x$ with respect to $t$. Note that $d/dx$ and $d/dt$ represent the operations "differentiation with respect to $x$" and "differentiation with respect to $t$" respectively, *not dy* divided by $dx$ times $dx$ divided by $dt$. $F$ and $f$ must be differentiable functions for (A.43) to apply; if they are not *both* differentiable at any point, the chain rule fails to hold at that point.

Let us examine the proof of the chain rule to understand its origin and limitations. Suppose

$$z = g(y) \qquad \text{(A.44)}$$

and

$$y = f(x) \qquad \text{(A.45)}$$

then

$$z = g(f(x)) = h(x) \qquad \text{(A.46)}$$

By definition,

$$\frac{dz}{dx} = \lim_{\Delta x \to 0} \frac{h(x + \Delta x) - h(x)}{\Delta x} = \lim_{\Delta x \to 0} \frac{h(x + \Delta x) - h(x)}{\Delta y} \frac{\Delta y}{\Delta x}$$

$$\text{(A.47)}$$

The limit of a product is the product of the limits, so we can rewrite (A.47) as:

$$\frac{dz}{dx} = \lim_{\Delta x \to 0} \frac{h(x + \Delta x) - h(x)}{\Delta y} \cdot \lim_{\Delta x \to 0} \frac{\Delta y}{\Delta x} \tag{A.48}$$

The second limit is the definition of $dy/dx$. To evaluate the first limit, let $\Delta y = f(x + \Delta x) - f(x)$. From (A.46)

$$h(x + \Delta x) - h(x) = z(y + \Delta y) - z(y) \tag{A.49}$$

and since $f(x)$ is continuous, $\Delta y \to 0$ as $\Delta x \to 0$. Therefore, the first limit is

$$\lim_{\Delta x \to 0} \frac{h(x + \Delta x) - h(x)}{\Delta y} = \lim_{\Delta y \to 0} \frac{z(y + \Delta y) - z(y)}{\Delta y} = \frac{dz}{dy} \tag{A.50}$$

Therefore, from (A.48)

$$\frac{dz}{dx} = \frac{dz}{dy}\frac{dy}{dx} \tag{A.51}$$

The following two examples illustrate the use of the chain rule.

1.  $y = x^3 - 3x^2 + 5x - 4 = F(x)$ \hfill (A.52)

$$x = t^2 + t = f(t) \tag{A.53}$$

$$\frac{dy}{dt} = \frac{dy}{dx} \cdot \frac{dx}{dt} \tag{A.54}$$

$$\frac{dy}{dt} = (3x^2 - 6x + 5) \cdot (2t + 1) \tag{A.55}$$

Use $x = f(t)$ to eliminate $x$ from the result:

$$\frac{dy}{dt} = [3(t^2 + t)^2 - 6(t^2 + t) + 5](2t + 1) \tag{A.56}$$

$$\frac{dy}{dt} = 6t^5 + 15t^4 - 15t^2 + 4t + 5 \tag{A.57}$$

We could have eliminated $x$ from $F(x)$ using $x = f(t)$ first, and then differentiated with respect to $t$, to obtain the same result.

2.  $s = e^z$      $z = q^2 - 1$      (A.58)

$$\frac{ds}{dq} = \frac{ds}{dz}\frac{dz}{dq}$$      (A.59)

$$= \frac{ds}{dq} = 2qe^{(q^2-1)}$$      (A.60)

The chain rule also helps evaluate the derivatives of complicated functions. For example, to differentiate $z = e^{x^2}$, let $y = x^2$ and replace $z = e^{x^2}$ with the two equations $z = e^y$, $y = x^2$, then use the chain rule with the seven rules we discussed previously to find

$$\frac{dz}{dx} = \frac{dz}{dy}\frac{dy}{dx} = e^y \cdot 2x = 2xe^{x^2}$$      (A.61)

Table A.1 combines the chain rule with the seven rules of differentiation we derived, as well as some additional useful rules.

Finally, we will examine a useful special case of the chain rule. Given the differentiable function $y = y(x)$, if the inverse function $x = x(y)$ exists and is differentiable, then

$$\frac{dy}{dx} = 1 \Big/ \frac{dx}{dx}$$      (A.62)

This result follows directly by letting $t = y$ in (A.43).

## HIGHER-ORDER DERIVATIVES

Thus far we have discussed differentiable functions and their derivatives. The derivative tells the instantaneous rate of change of a function with respect to the independent variable changes. By definition,

$$\frac{dy}{dx} = f'(x) = \lim_{\Delta x \to 0} \frac{f(x + \Delta x) - f(x)}{\Delta x}$$      (A.63)

But the derivative $f'(x)$ is itself a function of $x$,

$$g(x) = f'(x)$$      (A.64)

When $g(x)$ is differentiable, we can examine its derivative:

$$g'(x) = \lim_{\Delta x \to 0} \frac{g(x + \Delta x) - g(x)}{\Delta x}$$      (A.65)

### TABLE A.1    Rules of Differentiation

| $u = u(x)$    $v = v(x)$    $w = w(x)$    $a = constant$ |
| --- |

$$\frac{d(au)}{dx} = a\frac{du}{dx}$$

$$\frac{d(u + v - w)}{dx} = \frac{du}{dx} + \frac{dv}{dx} - \frac{dw}{dx}$$

$$\frac{d(uv)}{dx} = u\frac{dv}{dx} - u\frac{du}{dx}$$

$$\frac{d\left(\frac{u}{v}\right)}{dx} = \left[v\frac{du}{dx} + v\frac{dv}{dx}\right]/v^2$$

$$\frac{d(u^n)}{dx} = nu^{n-1}\frac{du}{dx}$$

$$\frac{d(e^u)}{dx} = e^u\frac{du}{dx}$$

$$\frac{d(u^v)}{dx} = vu^{v-1}\frac{du}{dx} + u^v \ln u \frac{dv}{dx}$$

$$\frac{d(e^{au})}{dx} = ae^{au}\frac{du}{dx}$$

$$\frac{d(a^u)}{dx} = a^u \ln a \frac{du}{dx}$$

$$\frac{d(\ln u)}{dx} = \frac{1}{u}\frac{du}{dx}$$

$$\frac{d(\log_a u)}{dx} = \frac{1}{u}\log_a e \frac{du}{dx}$$

$$\frac{d(u^u)}{dx} = u^u (1 + \ln u)\frac{du}{dx}$$

From (A.64) and (A.65):

$$g'(x) = \lim_{\Delta x \to 0} \frac{f'(x + \Delta x) - f'(x)}{\Delta x} = f''(x) = \frac{d^2 f}{dx^2} \qquad \text{(A.66)}$$

which is the *second derivative* of $f$ with respect to $x$. The second derivative, the derivative of the derivative, tells how the derivative changes with respect to changes in the independent variable.

For example, consider the parabola $f(x) = x^2$. Then $f'(x) = 2x$ and $f''(x) = 2$. In other words, the parabola's rate of change changes at a constant rate (Fig. A.7).

Differentiability everywhere does not insure that all higher-order derivatives exist at every point. For example,

$$y(x) = \begin{cases} 0 & x < 0 \\[2mm] \dfrac{1}{2} x^2 & 0 \leqslant x \leqslant 1 \\[2mm] x - \dfrac{1}{2} & 1 < x \end{cases}$$

has a first derivative for all $x$, but no second derivative exists when $x = 0$ and 1, because $y'(x)$ is not differentiable at $x = 0$ and 1 (Fig. A.8).

When $f(x)$ is a thrice-differentiable function, we compute the third derivative as

$$f'''(x) = \frac{d^3 f}{dx^3} = \frac{d}{dx}\left[\frac{d}{dx}\left(\frac{df}{dx}\right)\right] \qquad \text{(A.67)}$$

and so on. The *order* of the derivative tells how many times the original function has been differentiated. For example, $f'$ is a first-order derivative, $f'''$ is third-order, and $f^{(n)}$ is $n$th-order. (The function itself is the zeroth-order derivative.)

## LOCATING THE MINIMUM AND MAXIMUM VALUES (EXTREMA) OF FUNCTIONS

Many applications of mathematics require that one locate a function's maximum or minimum value and its corresponding argument. For example, fitting an equation to observed data requires that one minimize

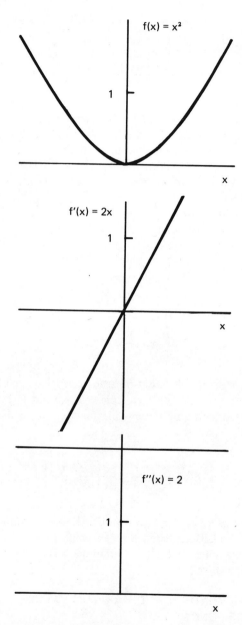

**FIGURE A.7:** The derivative of a function is often another differentiable function. In this case, one can compute the second derivative—the derivative of the derivative. Note that the derivative equals zero, and the second derivative is positive at the parabola's low point.

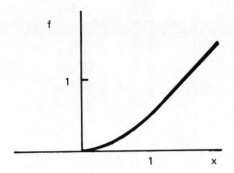

$$f(x) = \begin{cases} 0 & x < 0 \\ \tfrac{1}{2}x^2 & 0 \leqslant x \leqslant 1 \\ x - \tfrac{1}{2} & 1 < x \end{cases}$$

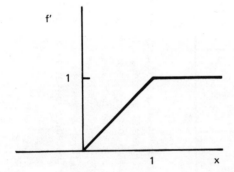

$$f'(x) = \begin{cases} 0 & x < 0 \\ x & 0 \leqslant x \leqslant 1 \\ 1 & 1 < x \end{cases}$$

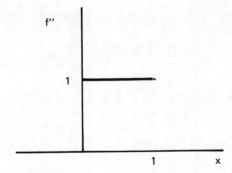

$$f''(x) = \begin{cases} 0 & x < 0 \\ 1 & 0 < x < 1 \\ 0 & 1 < x \end{cases}$$

**FIGURE A.8:** This figure illustrates a function which is differentiable everywhere whose second derivative fails to exist at the two points $x = 0$ and 1 because $f'(x)$ is not differentiable at these points.

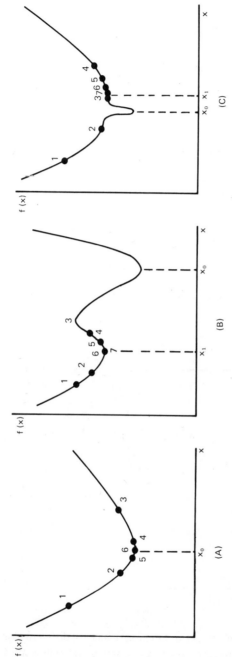

**FIGURE A.9:** Three examples of the use of trial-and-error to locate a function's minimum. The "search rule" being used is stated as: begin with an arbitrary first guess, then move a fixed amount to the right until the function stops decreasing, then take a step midway between the current and last step and evaluate the function again. Continue halving the interval until the function's value decreases by less than a specified tolerance. The numbered points show the locations of these steps. This method works well with the well-behaved (single, broad minimum) function in (A), but fails in cases (B) and (C). In (B) it correctly locates a relative minimum, but gives no indication that this is not the absolute minimum. In (C) the procedure fails to find even a relative minimum. ($x_0$ = actual absolute minimum, $x_1$ = computed minimum.)

some error criterion, such as the sum of the squared differences between predicted and observed points. How does one locate such a minimum (or maximum)?

One procedure would be to evaluate the function at many points over its domain and select the argument which produces the smallest functional value as the location of the minimum. This direct procedure sometimes proves the simplest practical way to locate a well-behaved function's minimum (especially with a digital computer to do the arithmetic), but it fails to give general formulae to deal with the minimization problem. In addition, this procedure is not foolproof. It fails to distinguish relative from overall minima, and can miss the minimum altogether. Figure A.9 illustrates these problems.

In the last section we noted that the derivative's value equals zero at the bottom of a parabola. Can we generalize this property to apply it to any differentiable function? Yes. Let us begin by discussing the function with a minimum in Figure A.10A. To the left of the minimum the function's value is decreasing; hence it will have a negative derivative. To the right of the minimum the function's value is increasing; hence it will have a positive derivative. When the derivative changes from negative to positive, it passes through zero when the function takes on its minimum value. Similarly, the function in Figure A.10B shows that the derivative also equals zero at a maximum point. The condition that the first derivative (where it exists) equals zero, locates *all* relative maxima and minima. Having located these points, the function must be evaluated at each one to locate the *absolute* (or global) maximum or minimum.

Since the derivative equals zero at both the minimum and maximum points (i.e., both extrema), how can one determine which occurs? Figure A.10 shows how the second derivative provides such a test. At a minimum point, the derivative's value will equal zero, but its value is increasing; therefore the second derivative will be nonnegative. At a maximum point, the first derivative equals zero, but is decreasing; so the second derivative will be nonpositive.

We have seen what happens when the second derivative is positive or negative. What if it equals zero? Figure A.11 shows a hypothetical case which reconstructs a function by working backward from the fact that *both* the first and second derivative equal zero. The resulting point on the original function is neither a minimum nor a maximum, but rather a *point of inflection* where the up or down concavity of the curve representing the function changes. Note that the first derivative need not be zero at a point of inflection.

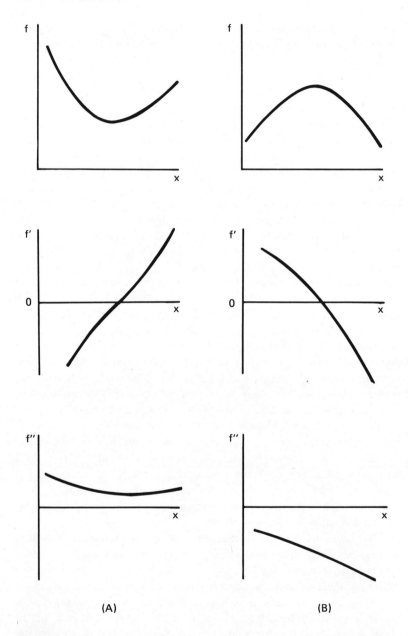

**FIGURE A.10:** The derivative equals zero when a differentiable function achieves an extreme value. The second derivative is positive at a minimum and negative at a maximum.

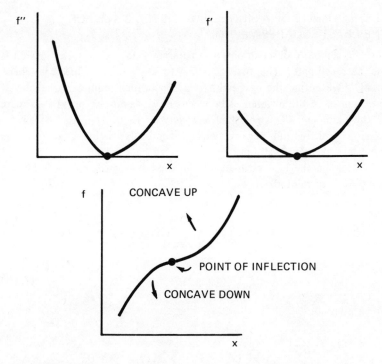

**FIGURE A.11:** The second derivative equals zero at a point of inflection.

The procedure for using derivatives to locate the extrema of the function $f(x)$ is as follows:

1. Compute $f'(x)$ and locate those $x$ for which $f' = 0$.
2. Compute $f''(x)$ at these points to distinguish among relative maxima, relative minima, and points of inflection.
3. Test points where $f$ is not differentiable in order to see if they are relative maxima or minima. In the neighborhood of the point where it fails to exist, the derivative will jump from negative to positive at a relative minimum, and conversely for a relative maximum.
4. If the function is not defined for all values of the independent variable between positive and negative infinity, check the function's values at the ends of the domain.
5. Compute the function's values at each relative maximum or minimum and compare to locate the absolute maximum or minimum.

Graphing the function often speeds this process by showing the steps one can skip.

## BEST ESTIMATE OF A SINGLE PARAMETER BY USE OF
## THE LEAST-SQUARES METHOD

Given a set of $N$ observations of a parameter $\{x_1, x_2, \ldots, x_N\}$, what is the best estimate? The first question to answer is, "What does 'best' mean?" We define the best estimate as that which minimizes the sum of the squares of the differences between the observations and the estimate of the parameter. This so-called *least-squares fit* is often used because it weights positive and negative errors identically, weights larger errors more heavily than small ones, and is easy to handle mathematically.

Let $\hat{x}$ be the best estimate of the unknown parameter. We wish to compute $\hat{x}$ to minimize

$$Q(\hat{x}) = (x_1 - \hat{x})^2 + (x_2 - \hat{x})^2 + \ldots + (x_N - \hat{x})^2 = \sum_{i=1}^{N} (x_i - \hat{x})^2$$

(A.68)

For a minimum

$$\frac{dQ}{d\hat{x}} = \frac{d}{d\hat{x}} \sum_{i=1}^{N} (x_i - \hat{x})^2 = \sum_{i=1}^{N} 2(x_i - \hat{x}) = 0 \qquad \text{(A.69)}$$

$$2\left[ \sum_{i=1}^{N} x_i - \sum_{i=1}^{N} \hat{x} \right] = 2\left[ \sum_{i=1}^{N} x_i - N\hat{x} \right] = 0 \qquad \text{(A.70)}$$

$$\hat{x} = \left( \sum_{i=1}^{N} x_i \right) \Big/ N \qquad \text{(A.71)}$$

The mean of the observations provides the best estimate of the unknown parameter in the least-squares sense.

From the structure of this problem, we can conclude that the single extremal point which $dQ/d\hat{x} = 0$ locates is the absolute minimum. However, we could verify this point by computing

$$\frac{d^2 Q}{d\hat{x}^2} = -2N \qquad \text{(A.72)}$$

Since $Q'' < 0$, we have located a relative minimum, and since only one relative minimum exists for a function defined and differentiable for all $\hat{x}$, we have located *the* absolute minimum.

## THE ANTI-DERIVATIVE

The equation

$$F'(x) = f(x) \tag{A.73}$$

says that *f(x) is the derivative with respect to x of F(x).* We could also use (A.73) to define the *anti-*derivative:

*F(x) is the anti-derivative with respect to x of f(x).*

A function's anti-derivative or *indefinite integral* is derived by a process known as *integration.*

We now prove an important theorem about the anti-derivative's uniqueness:

*If F(x) is an anti-derivative of f(x) with respect to x, then so is F(x) + C, where C can be any constant and is called the constant of integration. Furthermore, F(x) + C describes all anti-derivatives of f(x) with respect to x.*

To prove the theorem, we begin with the hypothesis

$$\frac{dF}{dx} = f(x) \tag{A.74}$$

From the rules of differentiation

$$\frac{d(F + C)}{dx} = \frac{dF}{dx} + \frac{dC}{dx} \tag{A.75}$$

Substitute $dC/dx = 0$ and (A.74) into (A.75), to show that $F(x) + C$ is also an anti-derivative of $f(x)$:

$$\frac{d(F + C)}{dx} = f(x) + 0 = \frac{dF}{dx} \tag{A.76}$$

To show that $F(x) + C$ includes all anti-derivatives of $f(x)$, suppose $F_1(x)$ and $F_2(x)$ are both anti-derivatives of $f(x)$, then

$$\frac{dF_1}{dx} = \frac{dF_2}{dx} = f(x) \tag{A.77}$$

$$\frac{dF_1}{dx} - \frac{dF_2}{dx} = 0 \tag{A.78}$$

$$\frac{d(F_1 - F_2)}{dx} = 0 \tag{A.79}$$

Therefore,

$$F_1(x) - F_2(x) = C \qquad C = \text{constant} \tag{A.80}$$

Thus $F_1(x) = F_2(x) + C$, hence $F(x) + C$ includes all anti-derivatives of $f(x)$.

The constant of integration relates directly to the need for initial conditions in differential equations. Consider the differential equation

$$\frac{dy}{dx} = f(x) \tag{A.81}$$

with the initial condition

$$y(0) = y_0 \tag{A.82}$$

The solution, assuming that one exists, is

$$y(x) = F(x) + C \tag{A.83}$$

where $F$ is the anti-derivative of $f$. Using the initial condition (A.82) to evaluate the constant of integration $C$ in (A.83), we have

$$y(0) = y_0 = F(0) + C \tag{A.84}$$

Equations (A.83) and (A.84) yield the solution to the differential equation (A.81) with the initial condition (A.82), and thus

$$y(x) = y(0) + F(x) - F(0) \tag{A.85}$$

Thus the constant of integration is equivalent to the arbitrary constant which appeared when solving differential equations.

Higher-order differential equations include more derivatives, each of which leads to one constant of integration. Thus there are $n$ derivatives in an $n$th-order differential equation, which give rise to $n$ different constants of integration. In order to determine these $n$ constants, one must specify $n$ initial (or other uniqueness) conditions. To put it in another way, $n$ initial conditions determine the $n$ constants of integration associated with an $n$th-order differential equation.

The following operations are mathematically (although not necessarily operationally) equivalent:

1. Finding the anti-derivative of the function $f$.
2. Integrating the function $f$.
3. Solving the first-order differential equation $y' = f$.

To denote the anti-derivative when $F' = f$, write

$$\int f(x)\,dx = F(x) + C \tag{A.86}$$

and read, "The integral of $f$ with respect to $x$ equals $F(x)$ plus an arbitrary constant of integration, $C$."

## ELEMENTARY RULES OF INTEGRATION AND TABLES OF INTEGRALS

Just as we developed elementary differentiation rules, we can now derive similar integration rules. One can often manipulate complicated functions into a sum of simpler functions, which can then be integrated by using elementary (and other tabulated) rules. In addition to these formal procedures, it is permissible to guess the result of an integration, then check it by differentiation. We will now derive six important elementary rules of integration.

*Rule 1:* $\int du = u + C$      $C = constant$ $\tag{A.87}$

This rule follows directly from the definition of what the integral means as the anti-derivative.

*Rule 2:* $\int a\,du = a\int du$      $a = constant$ $\tag{A.88}$

By the rules of differentiation

$$a\,du = d(au) \tag{A.89}$$

Integrate (A.89):

$$\int a\,du = \int d(au) = au + C = a\left(u + \frac{C}{a}\right) \tag{A.90}$$

But $C/a$ is simply the arbitrary constant $C$ divided by another constant $a$, so we can replace $C/a$ with the equivalent arbitrary constant $c$, then use the definition of the integral to show that

$$\int a \, du = a(u + c) = a\int du \qquad (A.91)$$

Rule 3: $\int (du + dv) = \int du + \int dv \qquad (A.92)$

By the rules of differentiation,

$$du + dv = d(u + v) \qquad (A.93)$$

Integrate both sides of (A.93) and replace the single arbitrary constant with the sum of two arbitrary constants $C_u$ and $C_v$, then use (A.87) to obtain

$$\int (du + dv) = \int d(u + v) = u + v + C = (u + C_u) + (v + C_v)$$

$$= \int du + \int dv \qquad (A.94)$$

Rule 4: $\int e^u \, du = e^u + C \qquad (A.95)$

We verify this rule by differentiating the right side

$$\frac{d(e^u + C)}{du} = e^u + 0 = e^u \qquad (A.96)$$

and noting that the result appears under the integral sign on the left side.

Rule 5: $\int u^n \, du = \dfrac{u^{n+1}}{n+1} + C \qquad n \neq -1 \qquad (A.97)$

Differentiate the right side of (A.97) to show that it is the function being integrated:

$$\frac{d}{du}\left(\frac{u^{n+1}}{n+1} + C\right) = (n + 1)\frac{u^{n+1-1}}{n+1} + 0 = u^n \qquad (A.98)$$

Rule 6: $\int du/u = \ln u + C \qquad (A.99)$

Since the exponential and natural logarithm are inverse functions,

$$e^{\ln u} = u \qquad (A.100)$$

Differentiate (A.100):

$$e^{\ln u} d(\ln u) = du \qquad \text{(A.101)}$$

then use (A.100) to eliminate $e^{\ln u}$ from (A.101):

$$u\, d(\ln u) = du \qquad \text{(A.102)}$$

$$\int \frac{du}{u} = \int d(\ln u) = \ln u + C \qquad \text{(A.103)}$$

by definition of the integral. Notice that Rule 6 fills the gap in Rule 5 when $n = -1$.

In studying the examples that follow, note which rule of integration permits each step. In addition, check the result by differentiating it to see that it is truly the anti-derivative of the expression appearing under the integral sign:

1. $\int 3x^2\, dx = 3\int x^2\, dx = 3 \cdot \dfrac{x^{2+1}}{2+1} + C = x^3 + C \qquad$ (A.104)

2. $\int (2x + 3)^2\, dx \qquad$ (A.105)

Let

$$u = (2x + 3) \qquad \text{(A.106)}$$

then

$$du = 2\, dx \qquad \frac{1}{2} du = dx \qquad \text{(A.107)}$$

Substitute from (A.106) and (A.107) into (A.105) to obtain

$$\int (2x + 3)^2\, dx = \int u^2 \frac{1}{2} du = \frac{1}{2}\int u^2\, du = \frac{1}{2} \cdot \frac{1}{3} u^3 + C \quad \text{(A.108)}$$

Finally, use (A.106) to eliminate $u$ from the result in (A.108):

$$\int (2x + 3)^2\, dx = \frac{1}{6}(2x + 3)^3 + C \qquad \text{(A.109)}$$

3. $\int e^{-t/\tau}\, dt \qquad\qquad \tau = \text{constant} \qquad$ (A.110)

Let

$$u = \frac{-t}{\tau} \tag{A.111}$$

then

$$du = -\frac{dt}{\tau} \qquad -\tau\, du = dt \tag{A.112}$$

Substitute from (A.111) and (A.112) into (A.110) and integrate:

$$\int e^{-t/\tau}\, dt = \int -\tau e^u\, du = -\tau \int e^u\, du = -\tau e^u + C \tag{A.113}$$

then use (A.111) to eliminate $u$ from (A.113)

$$\int e^{-t/\tau}\, dt = -\tau e^{-t/\tau} + C \tag{A.114}$$

4. $\int \sqrt{a + bx}\, dx \qquad a, b = \text{constants} \tag{A.115}$

Let

$$u = a + bx \tag{A.116}$$

then

$$du = b\, dx \qquad \frac{du}{b} = dx \tag{A.117}$$

Substitute from (A.116) and (A.117) into (A.115) and integrate

$$\int \sqrt{a + bx}\, dx = \int \frac{1}{b} \sqrt{u}\, du = \frac{1}{b} \int u^{1/2}\, du = \frac{1}{b} \frac{u^{3/2}}{3/2} + C \tag{A.118}$$

and use (A.116) to eliminate $u$ from (A.118):

$$\int \sqrt{a + bx}\, dx = \frac{2}{3b} (a + bx)^{3/2} + C \tag{A.119}$$

Integrating functions more complicated than simple aggregations of these rules (plus a few more we will develop later) often requires prac-

tice, lots of mathematical tricks, knowledge of similar integrals that indicate how to break the unknown integral into simpler integrals, and clever substitutions. Rather than attempt to compute integrals every time they appear, mathematicians have compiled extensive *tables of integrals* in which the functions to be integrated are indexed by type.*
When confronted with a complicated integral to evaluate, one should consult a table for hints on how to break down and evaluate the parts. Often it is necessary to undertake substitutions to manipulate the function into the form of a tabulated integral.†

To see how to use the table of integrals in Appendix B, evaluate

$$\int (x + 1)(x - 1) \sqrt{x + 1} \, dx \qquad \text{(A.120)}$$

Appendix B contains formulae for integrals of $\sqrt{a + bx}$ and $x^2\sqrt{a + bx}$. We manipulate (A.120) into this form by multiplying the first two terms together and expanding the resulting integral into two integrals:

$$\int (x + 1)(x - 1)\sqrt{x + 1} \, dx = \int (x^2 - 1)\sqrt{x + 1} \, dx$$

$$= \int x^2 \sqrt{1 + x} \, dx - \int \sqrt{1 + x} \, dx$$

$$\text{(A.121)}$$

Use formulae 31 and 33 from Appendix B with $a = b = 1$ to evaluate these two integrals and find

$$\int (x + 1)(x - 1) \sqrt{x + 1} \, dx = 2(5x^2 - 4x - 9) \sqrt{(x + 1)^3}/35$$

$$\text{(A.122)}$$

As a second example, we evaluate

$$\int \frac{t \, dt}{\sqrt{t^2 + 1}} \qquad \text{(A.123)}$$

---

* Appendix B contains a table of integrals.

† When a table does not contain the integral of interest, consult a more extensive table. If that fails, evaluation of your integral may require the numerical methods developed in Chapter 7.

Let $u = t^2 + 1$, then $du = 2t\, dt$ and we can write (A.123) as:

$$\int \frac{t\, dt}{\sqrt{t^2 + 1}} = \frac{1}{2} \int \frac{2t\, dt}{\sqrt{t^2 + 1}} = \frac{1}{2} \int \frac{du}{\sqrt{u}} \qquad \text{(A.124)}$$

Equation (A.124) is of the form $\int u^n\, du$, so

$$\int \frac{t\, dt}{\sqrt{t^2 + 1}} = \frac{1}{2} \int u^{-1/2}\, du = \frac{1}{2} \left[ \frac{u^{1/2}}{1/2} + C \right] = \sqrt{t^2 + 1} + C$$

$$\text{(A.125)}$$

## THE AREA UNDER A CURVE

We shall now discuss the concept of the anti-derivative of a function and the area under the curve which that function defines.

Consider a function $f(x)$ defined for $a \leqslant x \leqslant b$ (Fig. A.12). Define the new function $A(x)$ to be the area under the curve defined by $f(x)$ between $x = a$ and $x$. We approximate $A(x + \Delta x)$ by adding a rectangle of area $f(x)$ high and $\Delta x$ wide to $A(x)$:

$$A(x + \Delta x) \simeq A(x) + f(x) \cdot \Delta x \qquad \text{(A.126)}$$

$$\frac{A(x + \Delta x) - A(x)}{\Delta x} \simeq f(x) \qquad \text{(A.127)}$$

As $\Delta x$ approaches zero, this approximation increases in accuracy. Take the limit of (A.127) as $\Delta x \to 0$ in order to obtain the derivative's definition:

$$\lim_{\Delta x \to 0} \frac{A(x + \Delta x) - A(x)}{\Delta x} = \frac{dA}{dx} = f(x) \qquad \text{(A.128)}$$

The rate at which the area under the curve changes equals the function's local value.

Since according to (A.128) $A(x)$ is the anti-derivative of $f(x)$, we can write

$$A(x) = \int f\, dx = F(x) + C \qquad \text{(A.129)}$$

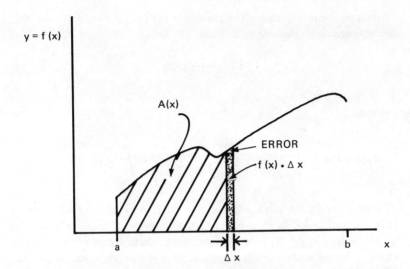

**FIGURE A.12:** $A(x)$ is the area under the curve $y = f(x)$ between $x = a$ and $x$. We approximate $A(x + \Delta x)$ by adding a rectangle of height $f(x)$ and width $\Delta x$ to $A(x)$. The small region marked "error" indicates the difference between the actual $A(x + \Delta x)$ and our approximation. As $\Delta x \to 0$, this error also goes to zero.

To define a value for $C$, observe that $A(a) = 0$, because $A(x)$ represents the area under the curve from $x = a$ to $x$, and *no* area is under the curve from $x = a$ to $x = a$. Substitute this result into (A.129) to show

$$A(a) = 0 = F(a) + C \qquad\qquad \text{(A.130)}$$

$$C = -F(a) \qquad\qquad \text{(A.131)}$$

So

$$A(x) = F(x) - F(a) \qquad\qquad \text{(A.132)}$$

The area under the curve defined by $f(x)$ between $x = a$ and $x$ equals the difference between the anti-derivative of the function evaluated at $x$ and at $x = a$.

Let $x = b$ in (A.132):

$$A(b) = F(b) - F(a) \qquad\qquad \text{(A.133)}$$

To compute the area under the curve $y = f(x)$ from $x = a$ to $x = b$, find the anti-derivative (indefinite integral) of $f(x)$

$$F(x) = \int f(x)\,dx \tag{A.134}$$

evaluate it at $x = a$ and $x = b$, then take the difference. We denote this process:

$$A(b) = F(b) - F(a) = F(x)\Big|_a^b = \int f(x)\,dx\Big|_a^b = \int_a^b f(x)\,dx \tag{A.135}$$

The final expression in (A.135) reads, "the integral of $f(x)$ with respect to $x$ from $a$ to $b$." In it, $a$ is called the *lower limit*, and $b$ is called the *upper limit*, and $\int_b^a f(x)\,dx$ is called the *definite integral*. This integral relates the indefinite integral (anti-derivative) to the area under the curve. The indefinite and definite integrals, while closely related, are not identical. The indefinite integral is a function; the definite integral is a number.

However, it is possible to write indefinite integrals in the form of the definite integral. In this case one also implicitly includes the initial conditions. If

$$\int f(x)\,dx = F(x) + C \tag{A.136}$$

then

$$\int_a^x f(x)\,dx = F(x) - F(a) \tag{A.137}$$

Compare (A.136) and (A.137) to see that $C = -F(a)$. For example, consider the differential equation

$$\frac{dy}{dx} = x^2 \qquad y(0) = 0 \tag{A.138}$$

One could solve this equation by integrating it:

$$dy = x^2\,dx \tag{A.139}$$

$$\int dy = \int x^2 \, dx \qquad \text{(A.140)}$$

$$y + C_y = \frac{1}{2} x^2 + C_x \qquad \text{(A.141)}$$

then using the initial condition to eliminate the two constants $C_y$ and $C_x$:

$$0 + C_y = \frac{1}{2} 0^2 + C_x \qquad \text{(A.142)}$$

$$C_x - C_y = 0 \qquad \text{(A.143)}$$

So that

$$y = \frac{1}{2} x^2 \qquad \text{(A.144)}$$

Alternatively, one could integrate (A.142) between the initial point $(0,0)$ and a general point $(x, y)$:

$$\int_0^y dy = \int_0^x x^2 \, dx \qquad \text{(A.145)}$$

to obtain (A.144) directly:

$$\left. y \right|_0^y = \frac{1}{2} x^2 \left. \right|_0^x \qquad \text{(A.146)}$$

$$y - 0 = y = \frac{1}{2} x^2 - \frac{1}{2} 0^2 = \frac{1}{2} x^2 \qquad \text{(A.147)}$$

Thus it is possible to write *all* integrals in the form $\int_{x_1}^{x_2} f(x) \, dx$. If either $x_1$ or $x_2$ is indefinite, the result is a *function*—an indefinite integral. If both $x_1$ and $x_2$ are fixed, the result is a *number*—a definite integral.

## PROBLEM SET A.1

1. Plot the first and second derivatives of the functions in Figure A.13.

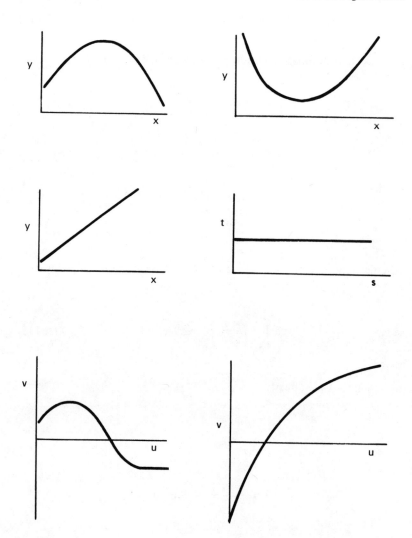

**FIGURE A.13:** Illustration for Problem 1 in Problem Set A.1.

Differentiate the following functions with respect to the dependent variable:

2. $y = x^{-2}$
3. $u = w^5$
4. $V = r^{2/3}$
5. $M = 1/t^3$
6. $A = \sqrt[3]{Q}$
7. $Z = 1/\sqrt{P}$
8. $v = at + b/t + c$   $(a, b, c = \text{constants})$
9. $M = p + qt + rt^2$   $(p, r = \text{constants})$
10. $y = x/(x - 3)$

Compute the second derivatives of the following functions:

11. $y = x^2 + x + 1$
12. $y = mx + b$

Find the local maxima or minima of these functions:

13. $y = x^2 - 3x$                    for $0 \leqslant x \leqslant 5$
14. $v = 1 + 2t + 1/2t^2$       for $-3 \leqslant t \leqslant 3$
15. $U = 1/(2v + 3)$              for $1 \leqslant v \leqslant 3$
16. $y = x^3 - 3x$                    for $-3 \leqslant x \leqslant 3$

Find the anti-derivatives of these functions:

17. $0$
18. $1$
19. $x$
20. $x^2$
21. $mx + b$
22. $ax^3 + bx^2 + cx + d$

23. Sketch a function whose second derivative is always equal to 1 and whose first derivative and magnitude equal zero when the independent variable equals zero.

# APPENDIX B

## TABLE OF INTEGRALS

1. $\displaystyle\int a \cdot f(x)\, dx = a \int f(x)\, dx$

2. $\displaystyle\int (u + v)\, dx = \int u\, dx + \int v\, dx$

3. $\displaystyle\int u\, dv = uv - \int v\, du$

4. $\displaystyle\int x^n\, dx = \frac{x^{n+1}}{n+1} \qquad n \neq -1$

5. $\displaystyle\int \frac{dx}{x} = \ln |x|$

6. $\displaystyle\int e^{ax}\, dx = \frac{e^{ax}}{a}$

7. $\displaystyle\int b^{ax}\,dx = \frac{b^{ax}}{a\,\ln b}$

8. $\displaystyle\int \ln x\,dx = x\,\ln x - x$

9. $\displaystyle\int a^x\,\ln a\,dx = a^x$

10. $\displaystyle\int \frac{dx}{a^2 + x^2} = \frac{1}{a}\tan^{-1}\!\left(\frac{x}{a}\right) \quad = -\frac{1}{a}\cot^{-1}\!\left(\frac{x}{a}\right)$

11. $\displaystyle\int \frac{dx}{a^2 - x^2} = \frac{1}{a}\tanh^{-1}\!\left(\frac{x}{a}\right) \quad = \frac{1}{2a}\ln\frac{a+x}{a-x}$

12. $\displaystyle\int \frac{dx}{x^2 - a^2} = -\frac{1}{a}\coth^{-1}\!\left(\frac{x}{a}\right) \quad = \frac{1}{2a}\ln\frac{x-a}{x+a}$

13. $\displaystyle\int \frac{dx}{\sqrt{a^2 - x^2}} = \sin^{-1}\!\left(\frac{x}{a}\right) \quad = -\cos^{-1}\!\left(\frac{x}{a}\right)$

14. $\displaystyle\int \frac{dx}{\sqrt{x^2 \pm a^2}} = \ln\left(x + \sqrt{x^2 \pm a^2}\right)$

15. $\displaystyle\int \frac{dx}{x\sqrt{x^2 - a^2}} = \frac{1}{a}\cos^{-1}\!\left(\frac{a}{x}\right)$

16. $\displaystyle\int \frac{dx}{x\sqrt{a^2 \pm x^2}} = -\frac{1}{a}\ln\left(\frac{a + \sqrt{a^2 \pm x^2}}{x}\right)$

17. $\displaystyle\int \frac{dx}{a + bx} = \frac{1}{b} \ln (a + bx)$

18. $\displaystyle\int \frac{dx}{(a + bx)^2} = - \frac{1}{b(a + bx)}$

19. $\displaystyle\int \frac{x\,dx}{a + bx} = \frac{1}{b^2} [a + bx - a \ln (a + bx)]$

20. $\displaystyle\int \frac{x\,dx}{(a + bx)^2} = \frac{1}{b^2} \left[ \ln (a + bx) + \frac{a}{a + bx} \right]$

21. $\displaystyle\int \frac{x\,dx}{(a + bx)^n} = \frac{1}{b^2} \left[ \frac{-1}{(n - 2)(a + bx)^{n-2}} + \frac{a}{(n - 1)(a + bx)^{n-1}} \right]$

$$n \neq 1,2$$

22. $\displaystyle\int \frac{x^2 dx}{a + bx} = \frac{1}{b^3} \left[ \frac{1}{2} (a + bx)^2 - 2a(a + bx) + a^2 \ln (a + bx) \right]$

23. $\displaystyle\int \frac{dx}{x(a + bx)} = - \frac{1}{a} \ln \frac{a + bx}{x}$

24. $\displaystyle\int \frac{dx}{x(a + bx)^2} = \frac{1}{a(a + bx)} - \frac{1}{a^2} \ln \frac{a + bx}{x}$

25. $\displaystyle\int \frac{dx}{a + bx^2} = \frac{1}{\sqrt{ab}} \tan^{-1} \frac{x\sqrt{ab}}{a}$

26. $\displaystyle\int \frac{x\,dx}{a + bx^2} = \frac{1}{2b} \ln \left( x^2 + \frac{a}{b} \right)$

27. $\displaystyle\int \frac{x^2\,dx}{a+bx^2} = \frac{x}{b} - \frac{a}{b}\int \frac{dx}{a+bx^2}$

28. $\displaystyle\int \frac{dx}{x(a+bx^2)} = \frac{1}{2a}\ln\frac{x^2}{a+bx^2}$

29. $\displaystyle\int \frac{dx}{x(a+bx^2)^{m+1}} = \frac{1}{2am(a+bx^2)^m} + \frac{1}{a}\int \frac{dx}{x(a+bx^2)^m} \qquad m \neq 0$

30. $\displaystyle\int \frac{dx}{x(a+bx^n)} = \frac{1}{an}\ln\frac{x^n}{a+bx^n}$

31. $\displaystyle\int \sqrt{a+bx}\,dx = \frac{2}{3b}\sqrt{(a+bx)^3}$

32. $\displaystyle\int x\sqrt{a+bx}\,dx = -\frac{2(2a-3bx)\sqrt{(a+bx)^3}}{15b^2}$

33. $\displaystyle\int x^2\sqrt{a+bx}\,dx = \frac{2(8a^2 - 12abx + 15b^2x^2)\sqrt{(a+bx)^3}}{105b^3}$

34. $\displaystyle\int x^m\sqrt{a+bx}\,dx = \frac{2}{b(2m+3)}\left[x^m\sqrt{(a+bx)^3} - ma\int x^{m-1}\sqrt{a+bx}\,dx\right]$

35. $\displaystyle\int \sqrt{x^2 \pm a^2}\,dx = \frac{1}{2}\left[x\sqrt{x^2 \pm a^2} \pm a^2\ln(x+\sqrt{x^2 \pm a^2})\right]$

36. $\displaystyle\int \frac{dx}{\sqrt{x^2 \pm a^2}} = \ln(x+\sqrt{x^2 \pm a^2})$

37. $\displaystyle\int \sqrt{a^2 - x^2}\,dx = \frac{1}{2}\left[x\sqrt{a^2 - x^2} + a^2\sin^{-1}\left(\frac{x}{a}\right)\right]$

38. $\displaystyle\int \frac{dx}{\sqrt{a^2 - x^2}} = \sin^{-1}\left(\frac{x}{a}\right) \quad = -\cos^{-1}\left(\frac{x}{a}\right)$

39. $\displaystyle\int \sqrt{\frac{1 + x}{1 - x}}\, dx = \sin^{-1} x - \sqrt{1 - x^2}$

40. $\displaystyle\int \frac{dx}{\sqrt{a \pm 2bx + cx^2}} = \frac{1}{\sqrt{c}} \ln \left(\pm b + cx + \sqrt{c}\ \sqrt{a \pm 2bx + cz}\ \right)$

41. $\displaystyle\int \frac{dx}{\sqrt{a \pm 2bx - cx^2}} = \frac{1}{\sqrt{c}} \sin^{-1} \frac{cx \mp b}{\sqrt{b^2 + ac}}$

42. $\displaystyle\int \frac{x\, dx}{\sqrt{a \pm 2bx + cx^2}} = \frac{1}{c} \sqrt{a \pm 2bx + cx^2}$

$\qquad\qquad\qquad\qquad \mp \dfrac{b}{\sqrt{c^3}} \ln \left(\pm b + cx + \sqrt{c}\ \sqrt{a \pm 2bx + cx^2}\right)$

43. $\displaystyle\int \frac{x\, dx}{\sqrt{a \pm 2bx - cx^2}} = -\frac{1}{c} \sqrt{a \pm 2bx - cx^2} \pm \frac{b}{\sqrt{c^3}} \sin^{-1} \frac{cx \mp b}{\sqrt{b^2 + ac}}$

44. $\displaystyle\int \sin x\, dx = -\cos x$

45. $\displaystyle\int \cos x\, dx = \sin x$

46. $\displaystyle\int \tan x\, dx = -\ln \cos x$

47. $\displaystyle\int \cot x\, dx = \ln \sin x$

48. $\displaystyle\int \sec x\, dx = \ln\,(\sec x + \tan x) = \ln\,\tan\,\left(\frac{\pi}{4} + \frac{x}{2}\right)$

49. $\displaystyle\int \csc x\, dx = \ln\,(\csc x - \cot x) = \ln\,\tan\,\frac{x}{2}$

50. $\displaystyle\int \sin^2 x\, dx = -\frac{1}{2}\cos x \sin x + \frac{1}{2}x = \frac{1}{2}x - \frac{1}{4}\sin 2x$

51. $\displaystyle\int \sin^3 x\, dx = -\frac{1}{3}\cos x\,(\sin^2 x + 2)$

52. $\displaystyle\int \sin^n x\, dx = -\frac{\sin^{n-1} x \cos x}{n} + \frac{n-1}{n}\int \sin^{n-2} x\, dx$

53. $\displaystyle\int \cos^2 x\, dx = \frac{1}{2}\sin x \cos x + \frac{1}{2}x = \frac{1}{2}x + \frac{1}{4}\sin 2x$

54. $\displaystyle\int \cos^3 x\, dx = \frac{1}{3}\sin x\,(\cos^2 x + 2)$

55. $\displaystyle\int \cos^n x\, dx = \frac{1}{n}\cos^{n-1} x \sin x + \frac{n-1}{n}\int \cos^{n-2} x\, dx$

56. $\displaystyle\int \sin x \cos x\, dx = \frac{1}{2}\sin^2 x$

57. $\displaystyle\int \sin mx \cos nx\, dx = -\frac{\cos\,(m-n)x}{2(m-n)} - \frac{\cos\,(m+n)x}{2(m+n)}$

58. $\displaystyle\int \sin mx \sin nx\, dx = \frac{\sin\,(m-n)x}{2(m-n)} - \frac{\sin\,(m+n)x}{2(m+n)}$     $m^2 \neq n^2$

59. $\displaystyle\int \cos mx \cos nx \, dx = \frac{\sin(m-n)x}{2(m-n)x} + \frac{\sin(m+n)x}{2(m+n)x} \quad m^2 \neq n^2$

60. $\displaystyle\int x \sin x \, dx = \sin x - x \cos x$

61. $\displaystyle\int x^m \sin x \, dx = -x^m \cos x + m \int x^{m-1} \cos x \, dx$

62. $\displaystyle\int x \cos x \, dx = \cos x + x \sin x$

63. $\displaystyle\int x^m \cos x \, dx = x^m \sin x - m \int x^{m-1} \sin x \, dx$

64. $\displaystyle\int \frac{\sin x}{x} \, dx = x - \frac{x^3}{3 \cdot 3!} + \frac{x^5}{5 \cdot 5!} - \frac{x^7}{7 \cdot 7!} + \frac{x^9}{9 \cdot 9!} \cdots$

65. $\displaystyle\int \frac{\cos x}{x} \, dx = \ln x - \frac{x^2}{2 \cdot 2!} + \frac{x^4}{4 \cdot 4!} - \frac{x^6}{6 \cdot 6!} + \frac{x^8}{8 \cdot 8!} \cdots$

66. $\displaystyle\int \log x \, dx = x \ln x - x$

67. $\displaystyle\int x \log x \, dx = \frac{x^2}{2} \ln x - \frac{x^2}{4}$

68. $\displaystyle\int xe^{ax} \, dx = \frac{e^{ax}}{a^2} (ax - 1)$

69. $\displaystyle\int x^m e^{ax} \, dx = \frac{x^m e^{ax}}{a} - \frac{m}{a} \int x^{m-1} e^{ax} \, dx$

70. $\displaystyle\int \frac{e^{ax} \, dx}{x} = \ln x + \frac{ax}{1!} + \frac{a^2 x^2}{2 \cdot 2!} + \frac{a^3 x^3}{3 \cdot 3!} + \ldots$

71. $\displaystyle\int \frac{dx}{a + be^{px}} = \frac{x}{a} - \frac{1}{ap} \ln (a + be^{px})$

72. $\displaystyle\int e^{ax} \cdot \sin px \, dx = \frac{e^{ax}(a \sin px - p \cos px)}{a^2 + p^2}$

73. $\displaystyle\int e^{ax} \cdot \cos px \, dx = \frac{e^{ax}(a \cos px - p \sin px)}{a^2 + p^2}$

# APPENDIX C

## BASIC PROPERTIES OF COMPLEX NUMBERS AND FUNCTIONS

Most of this text deals with functions with real arguments and values, but understanding some of the material, especially Fourier transforms, requires a knowledge of the basic properties of complex numbers and their functions. We say that $z$ is a *complex number* if

$$z = x + iy \qquad (C.1)$$

in which $x$ and $y$ are real numbers and $i = \sqrt{-1}$, and that $x$ is $z$'s *real part*, $Re(z)$, and $y$ is $z$'s *imaginary part*, $Im(z)$. Two complex numbers are *equal* if and only if both their real and imaginary parts are equal.

The rules for addition, subtraction, multiplication, and division which follow treat $z$ as a polynomial in $i$. Recall that $i^2 = -1$. Then, if $z_1 = x_1 + iy_1$ and $z_2 = x_2 + iy_2$,

$$z_1 + z_2 = (x_1 + iy_1) + (x_2 + iy_2) = (x_1 + x_2) + i(y_1 + y_2) \qquad (C.2)$$

$$z_1 - z_2 = (x_1 + iy_1) - (x_2 + iy_2) = (x_1 - x_2) + i(y_1 - y_2) \qquad (C.3)$$

$$z_1 z_2 = (x_1 + iy_1)(x_2 + iy_2) = x_1 x_2 + i(x_1 y_2 + x_2 y_1) + i^2 y_1 y_2$$

$$= (x_1 x_2 - y_1 y_2) + i(x_1 y_2 + x_2 y_1) \qquad (C.4)$$

$$\frac{z_1}{z_2} = \frac{(x_1 + iy_1)}{(x_2 + iy_2)} = \frac{(x_1 x_2 + y_1 y_2)}{(x_2^2 + y_2^2)} + \frac{i(x_2 y_1 - x_1 y_2)}{(x_2^2 + y_2^2)} \tag{C.5}$$

The result for division follows by long division of the two polynomials in $i$. We shall soon discover an easier way to complete such division.

The commutative, associative, and distributive laws for addition and multiplication all hold for complex variables:

$$z_1 + z_2 = z_2 + z_1 \tag{C.6}$$

$$z_1 z_2 = z_2 z_1 \tag{C.7}$$

$$(z_1 + z_2) + z_3 = z_1 + (z_2 + z_3) \tag{C.8}$$

$$(z_1 z_2)z_3 = z_1(z_2 z_3) \tag{C.9}$$

$$z_1(z_2 + z_3) = z_1 z_2 + z_1 z_3 \tag{C.10}$$

Perhaps the most useful way to visualize the complex number $z = x + iy$ is as a point $(x, y)$ in the two-dimensional *complex plane*, of which one axis represents the real part of $z$ and the other axis represents the imaginary part of $z$ (Fig. C.1A). This geometric interpretation naturally leads to the *polar form* of the complex number, for as Figure C.1B shows, we could also locate the point $z$ by its distance from the origin $r$ and the angle $\theta$ the line connecting $z$ with the origin makes with the real axis.

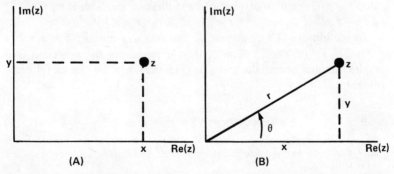

**FIGURE C.1:** Rectangular and polar forms of the complex number $z = x + iy = r \cos \theta + ir \sin \theta = re^{i\theta}$.

Since

$$x = r \cos \theta \tag{C.11}$$

and

$$y = r \sin \theta \tag{C.12}$$

$$z = x + iy = r \cos \theta + ir \sin \theta = r(\cos \theta + i \sin \theta) \tag{C.13}$$

Chapter 3 showed that

$$\cos \theta + i \sin \theta = e^{i\theta} \tag{C.14}$$

so (C.13) becomes

$$z = x + iy = re^{i\theta} \tag{C.15}$$

the polar form of the complex number $z$. Thus $r = \sqrt{x^2 + y^2}$ is $z$'s *magnitude*, *absolute value*, or *modulus*, and $\theta$ is its *phase angle* or *argument*.

$$\frac{y}{x} = \frac{r \sin \theta}{r \cos \theta} = \tan \theta \tag{C.16}$$

so $\theta = \tan^{-1}(y/x)$.* In general, the rectangular form of the complex variable proves more convenient for addition and subtraction, while the polar form proves more convenient for multiplication and division. In multiplication, magnitudes multiply and phase angles add. If $z_1 = r_1 e^{i\theta_1}$ and $z_2 = r_2 e^{i\theta_2}$, then $z_1 z_2 = r_1 e^{i\theta_1} r_2 e^{i\theta_2} = r_1 r_2 e^{i(\theta_1 + \theta_2)}$.

By definition, the *conjugate* of the complex number $z = x + iy = re^{i\theta}$ is $\overline{z} = x - iy = re^{-i\theta}$. The conjugate represents the reflection of a complex number across the real axis (Fig. C.2), and has the useful property that

$$z\overline{z} = (x + iy)(x - iy) = x^2 + y^2 = |z|^2 \tag{C.17}$$

---

* $\tan^{-1} \theta$ will give two possible values for $\theta$; select the correct quadrant by referring to the signs of $x$ and $y$.

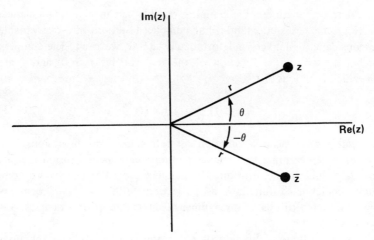

**FIGURE C.2:** Points $z$ and $\bar{z}$ are a complex conjugate pair.

This result proves especially useful for finding quotients, since it permits one to avoid carrying out long division. For example,

$$\frac{z_1}{z_2} = \frac{z_1 \bar{z}_2}{z_2 \bar{z}_2} = \frac{(x_1 + iy_1)(x_2 - iy_2)}{(x_2 + iy_2)(x_2 - iy_2)} = \frac{(x_1 x_2 + y_1 y_2) + i(x_2 y_1 - x_1 y_2)}{x_2^2 + y_2^2}$$

$$(C.18)$$

By convention, one never leaves a complex number in the denominator of a fraction. Conjugation has these properties:

$$(\overline{z_1 + z_2}) = \bar{z}_1 + \bar{z}_2 \qquad (C.19)$$

$$\overline{z_1 z_2} = \bar{z}_1 \bar{z}_2 \qquad (C.20)$$

$$\overline{\left(\frac{z_1}{z_2}\right)} = \frac{\bar{z}_1}{\bar{z}_2} \qquad (C.21)$$

$$\bar{\bar{z}} = z \qquad (C.22)$$

Complex functions of a complex variable can involve mathematical questions that are quite subtle, but complex functions of a real variable are considerably simpler, and fortunately are all we need. The complex number $z = x + iy$ is a function of the real variable $t$, if $x$ and $y$ are real-valued functions of $t$:

$$z = z(t) = x(t) + iy(t) \qquad (C.23)$$

One can picture such a function as a line in three dimensions, one dimension representing the independent variable, one dimension the real part of $z$, and one dimension the complex part. For clarity, we commonly depict such functions as projections in the real and complex planes rather than as a three-dimensional curve. (For examples, see Figure 6.12).

$z$ is a continuous function of $t$ if $x$ and $y$ are continuous functions of $t$. If $x$ and $y$ are differentiable functions of $t$,

$$\frac{dz}{dt} = \frac{dx}{dt} + i\frac{dy}{dt} \qquad (C.24)$$

If $x(t)$ and $y(t)$ are integrable,

$$\int z(t)\, dt = \int x(t)\, dt + i\int y(t)\, dt \qquad (C.25)$$

is the sum of the areas under the real and imaginary projections of the curve $z(t)$.

# APPENDIX D

## TABLE OF LAPLACE TRANSFORM PAIRS*

| $F(s)$ | $f(t) \qquad t \geqslant 0$ |
|---|---|
| 1. $1$ | $\delta(t)$ |
| 2. $\dfrac{1}{s}$ | $1$ or $u(t)$ |
| 3. $\dfrac{1}{s^2}$ | $t$ |
| 4. $\dfrac{1}{s^n}$ | $\dfrac{1}{(n-1)!}\, t^{n-1}$ $\quad n$ is a positive integer |
| 5. $\dfrac{1}{s}e^{-as}$ | $u(t-a)$ |
| 6. $\dfrac{1}{s}(1-e^{as})$ | $u(t) - u(t-a)$ |
| 7. $\dfrac{1}{s+a}$ | $e^{-at}$ |
| 8. $\dfrac{1}{(s+a)^n}$ | $\dfrac{1}{(n-1)!}\, t^{n-1}e^{-at}$ $\quad n$ is a positive integer |
| 9. $\dfrac{1}{s(s+a)}$ | $\dfrac{1}{a}(1-e^{-at})$ |

* Adapted from *Feedback Control System Analysis and Synthesis* by J. J. D'Azzo and C. H. Houpis. Copyright 1966 by McGraw-Hill, Inc. Used with permission of McGraw-Hill Book Company.

| $F(s)$ | $f(t)$ | $t \geqslant 0$ |
|---|---|---|

10. $\dfrac{1}{s(s + a)(s + b)}$    $\dfrac{1}{ab}\left(1 - \dfrac{b}{b - a}e^{-at} + \dfrac{a}{b - a}e^{-bt}\right)$

11. $\dfrac{s + \alpha}{s(s + a)(s + b)}$    $\dfrac{1}{ab}\left[\alpha - \dfrac{b(\alpha - a)}{b - a}e^{-at} + \dfrac{a(\alpha - b)}{b - a}e^{-bt}\right]$

12. $\dfrac{1}{(s + a)(s + b)}$    $\dfrac{1}{b - a}(e^{-at} - e^{-bt})$

13. $\dfrac{s}{(s + a)(s + b)}$    $\dfrac{1}{a - b}(ae^{-at} - be^{-bt})$

14. $\dfrac{s + \alpha}{(s + a)(s + b)}$    $\dfrac{1}{b - a}[(\alpha - a)e^{-at} - (\alpha - b)e^{-bt}]$

15. $\dfrac{1}{(s + a)(s + b)(s + c)}$    $\dfrac{e^{-at}}{(b - a)(c - a)} + \dfrac{e^{-bt}}{(c - b)(a - b)} + \dfrac{e^{-ct}}{(a - c)(b - c)}$

16. $\dfrac{s + \alpha}{(s + a)(s + b)(s + c)}$    $\dfrac{(\alpha - a)e^{-at}}{(b - a)(c - a)} + \dfrac{(\alpha - b)e^{-bt}}{(c - b)(a - b)} + \dfrac{(\alpha - c)e^{-ct}}{(a - c)(b - c)}$

17. $\dfrac{\omega}{s^2 + \omega^2}$    $\sin \omega t$

18. $\dfrac{s}{s^2 + \omega^2}$    $\cos \omega t$

19. $\dfrac{s + \alpha}{s^2 + \omega^2}$    $\dfrac{\sqrt{\alpha^2 + \omega^2}}{\omega}\sin(\omega t + \phi)$    $\phi = \tan^{-1}\dfrac{\omega}{\alpha}$

20. $\dfrac{s \sin \theta + \omega \cos \theta}{s^2 + \omega^2}$    $\sin(\omega t + \theta)$

21. $\dfrac{1}{s(s^2 + \omega^2)}$    $\dfrac{1}{\omega^2}(1 - \cos \omega t)$

22. $\dfrac{s + \alpha}{s(s^2 + \omega^2)}$    $\dfrac{\alpha}{\omega^2} - \dfrac{\sqrt{\alpha^2 + \omega^2}}{\omega^2}\cos(\omega t + \phi)$    $\phi = \tan^{-1}\dfrac{\omega}{\alpha}$

23. $\dfrac{1}{(s + a)(s^2 + \omega^2)}$    $\dfrac{e^{-at}}{a^2 + \omega^2} + \dfrac{1}{\omega\sqrt{a^2 + \omega^2}}\sin(\omega t - \phi)$    $\phi = \tan^{-1}\dfrac{\omega}{a}$

24. $\dfrac{1}{(s + a)^2 + b^2}$    $\dfrac{1}{b}e^{-at}\sin bt$

24.* $\dfrac{1}{s^2 + 2\zeta\omega_n s + \omega_n^2}$    $\dfrac{1}{\omega_n\sqrt{1 - \zeta^2}}e^{-\zeta\omega_n t}\sin\omega_n\sqrt{1 - \zeta^2}t$

* $[(s + a)^2 + b^2]$ and $[s^2 + 2\zeta\omega_n s + \omega_n^2]$ are equivalent; to change from the former notation to the latter, put $\omega_n = \sqrt{a^2 + b^2}$ and $\zeta = a/\sqrt{a^2 + b^2}$ or $a = \zeta\omega_n$ and $b = \omega_n\sqrt{1 - \zeta^2}$.

| $F(s)$ | $f(t)$        $t \geqslant 0$ |
|---|---|

25. $\dfrac{s + a}{(s + a)^2 + b^2}$     $e^{-at} \cos bt$

26. $\dfrac{s + \alpha}{(s + a)^2 + b^2}$     $\dfrac{\sqrt{(\alpha - a)^2 + b^2}}{b} e^{-at} \sin(bt + \phi)$     $\phi = \tan^{-1} \dfrac{b}{\alpha - a}$

27. $\dfrac{1}{s[(s + a)^2 + b^2]}$     $\dfrac{1}{a^2 + b^2} + \dfrac{1}{b\sqrt{a^2 + b^2}} e^{-at} \sin(bt - \phi)$     $\phi = \tan^{-1} \dfrac{b}{-a}$

27.* $\dfrac{1}{s(s^2 + 2\zeta\omega_n s + \omega_n^2)}$     $\dfrac{1}{\omega_n^2} - \dfrac{1}{\omega_n^2\sqrt{1 - \zeta^2}} e^{-\zeta\omega_n t} \sin(\omega_n\sqrt{1 - \zeta^2}\, t + \phi)$ $\phi = \cos^{-1} \zeta$

28. $\dfrac{s + \alpha}{s[(s + a)^2 + b^2]}$     $\dfrac{\alpha}{a^2 + b^2} + \dfrac{1}{b} \sqrt{\dfrac{(\alpha - a)^2 + b^2}{a^2 + b^2}}\, e^{-at} \sin(bt + \phi)$

$\phi = \tan^{-1} \dfrac{b}{\alpha - a} - \tan^{-1} \dfrac{b}{-a}$

29. $\dfrac{1}{(s + c)[(s + a)^2 + b^2]}$     $\dfrac{e^{-ct}}{(c - a)^2 + b^2} + \dfrac{e^{-at} \sin(bt - \phi)}{b\sqrt{(c - a)^2 + b^2}}$     $\phi = \tan^{-1} \dfrac{b}{c - a}$

30. $\dfrac{1}{s(s + c)[(s + a)^2 + b^2]}$     $\dfrac{1}{c(a^2 + b^2)} - \dfrac{e^{-ct}}{c[(c - a)^2 + b^2]}$

$+ \dfrac{e^{-at} \sin(bt - \phi)}{b\sqrt{a^2 + b^2}\,\sqrt{(c - a)^2 + b^2}}$

$\phi = \tan^{-1} \dfrac{b}{-a} + \tan^{-1} \dfrac{b}{c - a}$

31. $\dfrac{s + \alpha}{s(s + c)[(s + a)^2 + b^2]}$     $\dfrac{\alpha}{c(a^2 + b^2)} - \dfrac{(c - \alpha)e^{-ct}}{c[(c - a)^2 + b^2]}$

$+ \dfrac{\sqrt{(\alpha - a)^2 + b^2}}{b\sqrt{a^2 + b^2}\,\sqrt{(c - a)^2 + b^2}}\, e^{-at} \sin(bt + \phi)$

$\phi = \tan^{-1} \dfrac{b}{\alpha - a} - \tan^{-1} \dfrac{b}{-a} - \tan^{-1} \dfrac{b}{c - a}$

32. $\dfrac{1}{s^2(s + a)}$     $\dfrac{1}{a^2}(at - 1 + e^{-at})$

33. $\dfrac{1}{s(s + a)^2}$     $\dfrac{1}{a^2}(1 - e^{-at} - ate^{-at})$

34. $\dfrac{s + \alpha}{s(s + a)^2}$     $\dfrac{1}{a^2}[\alpha - \alpha e^{-at} + a(a - \alpha)te^{-at}]$

* See footnote on preceding page.

| $F(s)$ | $f(t)$ | $t \geqslant 0$ |
|---|---|---|

35. $\dfrac{s^2 + \alpha_1 s + \alpha_0}{s(s + a)(s + b)}$

$\dfrac{\alpha_0}{ab} + \dfrac{a^2 - \alpha_1 a + \alpha_0}{a(a - b)} e^{-at} - \dfrac{b^2 - \alpha_1 b + \alpha_0}{b(a - b)} e^{-bt}$

36. $\dfrac{s^2 + \alpha_1 s + \alpha_0}{s[(s + a)^2 + b^2]}$

$\dfrac{\alpha_0}{c^2} + \dfrac{1}{bc} [(a^2 - b^2 - \alpha_1 a + \alpha_0)^2$

$+ b^2(\alpha_1 - 2a)^2]^{1/2} e^{-at} \sin(bt + \phi)$

$\phi = \tan^{-1} \dfrac{b(\alpha_1 - 2a)}{a^2 - b^2 - \alpha_1 a + \alpha_0} - \tan^{-1} \dfrac{b}{-a}$

$c^2 = a^2 + b^2$

37. $\dfrac{1}{(s^2 + \omega^2)[(s + a)^2 + b^2]}$

$\dfrac{\left(\dfrac{1}{\omega}\right) \sin(\omega t + \phi_1) + \left(\dfrac{1}{b}\right) e^{-at} \sin(bt + \phi_2)}{[4a^2\omega^2 + (a^2 + b^2 - \omega^2)^2]^{1/2}}$

$\phi_1 = \tan^{-1} \dfrac{-2a\omega}{a^2 + b^2 - \omega^2} \qquad \phi_2 = \tan^{-1} \dfrac{2ab}{a^2 - b^2 + \omega^2}$

38. $\dfrac{s + \alpha}{(s^2 + \omega^2)[(s + a)^2 + b^2]}$

$\dfrac{1}{\omega}\left[\dfrac{\alpha^2 + \omega^2}{c}\right]^{1/2} \sin(\omega t + \phi_1)$

$+ \dfrac{1}{b}\left[\dfrac{(\alpha - a)^2 + b^2}{c}\right]^{1/2} e^{-at} \sin(bt + \phi_2)$

$c = (2a\omega)^2 + (a^2 + b^2 - \omega^2)^2$

$\phi_1 = \tan^{-1} \dfrac{\omega}{\alpha} - \tan^{-1} \dfrac{2a\omega}{a^2 + b^2 + \omega^2}$

$\phi_2 = \tan^{-1} \dfrac{b}{\alpha - a} + \tan^{-1} \dfrac{2ab}{a^2 - b^2 + \omega^2}$

39. $\dfrac{s + \alpha}{s^2[(s + a)^2 + b^2]}$

$\dfrac{1}{c}\left(\alpha t + 1 - \dfrac{2\alpha a}{c}\right) + \dfrac{[b^2 + (\alpha - a)^2]^{1/2}}{bc} e^{-at} \sin(bt + \phi)$

$c = a^2 + b^2$

$\phi = 2 \tan^{-1}\left(\dfrac{b}{a}\right) + \tan^{-1} \dfrac{b}{\alpha - a}$

40. $\dfrac{s^2 + \alpha_1 s + \alpha_0}{s^2(s + a)(s - b)}$

$\dfrac{\alpha_1 + \alpha_0 t}{ab} - \dfrac{\alpha_0(a + b)}{(ab)^2} - \dfrac{1}{a - b}\left(1 - \dfrac{\alpha_1}{\alpha} + \dfrac{\alpha_0}{a^2}\right)e^{-at}$

$- \dfrac{1}{a - b}\left(1 - \dfrac{\alpha_1}{b} + \dfrac{\alpha_0}{b^2}\right)e^{-bt}$

# APPENDIX E

## SOLUTIONS TO PROBLEMS

*Set 2.1*

1. First
2. Second
3. First
4. Third
5. Second
6. $\ddot{x}_1 - 2\dot{x}_1 - x_1 = 0$     $x_1(0) = x_{10}$     $\dot{x}_1(0) = x_{10} + x_{20}$
7. $\ddot{x}_1 - 2\dot{x}_1 + x_1 = 0$     $x_1(0) = x_{10}$     $\dot{x}_1(0) = x_{10} - x_{20}$
8. $\ddot{c} + (k_{12} + k_{21} + k_{10})\dot{c} + k_{12}k_{10}c = k_{21}\,I/V$

    $c(0) = c_0$

    $\dot{c}(0) = I/V - (k_{12} + k_{10})c_0$
9. $y''' - y'' = x$     $y(0) = 1$     $y'(0) = 0$     $y''(0) = 0$
10. $\ddot{x}_1 - 2\dot{x}_1 + x_1 - x_1^2 = 0$     $x_1(0) = x_{10}$     $\dot{x}_1(0) = x_{10} + x_{20}$

*Set 2.2*

6. $y(t) = c(e^t - e^{-t})/2$
7. a.   1.5 min
   b.   1.5 hr
   c.   7.2 min
   d.   17.3 hr

8. $\tau = 50$ min; yes; $V = 100$ ml/kg, $k = 0.02$ min$^{-1}$
9. No.
12. Put all derivatives equal to zero and solve the resulting algebraic equations.

*Set 2.3*

1. $\dot{c}(t) = \dfrac{I}{V} - kc$ $\qquad\qquad\qquad c(0) = \dfrac{B}{V}$

2. $c(t) = \dfrac{I}{kV} + \dfrac{1}{V}\left(B - \dfrac{I}{k}\right)e^{-t/\tau}$ $\qquad \tau = \dfrac{1}{k}$

3. $B = Vc_\infty$, $I = kVc_\infty$; both the washout of drug from the bolus and buildup from the infusion have the same time constant.

4. The model should have three compartments; the solution will be the sum of three exponentials.

5. $c_\infty = \dfrac{I}{(k_{10}V)}$

6. a. $\dot{q}_1 = i(t) - (k_{10} + k_{12} + k_{13})q_1 + k_{21}q_2 + k_{31}q_3$ $\qquad q_1(0) = q_{10}$

$\dot{q}_2 = k_{12}q_1 - k_{21}q_2$ $\qquad\qquad\qquad\qquad\qquad q_2(0) = q_{20}$

$\dot{q}_3 = k_{13}q_1 - k_{31}q_3$ $\qquad\qquad\qquad\qquad\qquad q_3(0) = q_{30}$

b. $\dot{q}_1 = i(t) - (k_{10} + k_{12})q_1 + k_{21}q_2$ $\qquad\qquad q_1(0) = q_{10}$

$\dot{q}_2 = k_{12}q_1 - (k_{21} + k_{23})q_2 + k_{32}q_3$ $\qquad q_2(0) = q_{20}$

$\dot{q}_3 = k_{23}q_2 - k_{32}q_3$ $\qquad\qquad\qquad\qquad\qquad q_3(0) = q_{30}$

7. a. $\dfrac{I}{(k_{10}V)}$

b. $\dfrac{I}{(k_{10}V)}$

Drug in = drug out at steady state.

*Set 2.4*

1. $[E]_\infty = E_T$, $[S]_\infty = 0$, $[P]_\infty = S_0$

*Set 3.1*

1. $y(x) = e^{x^2}$

2. $s(t) = \dfrac{a}{b}(e^{bt} - 1)$

3. $s(t) = \dfrac{1}{b} \ln\left(\dfrac{1}{1 - abt}\right)$

4. $y(x) = \sqrt{2 \ln(x + 1)}$

5. $y = \ln\left[(e^{x^2} + 2e^{1/2} - 1)/2\right]$

6. $y = \sqrt{2 - \dfrac{2}{x}}$

7. $m(t)$ is defined implicitly by the equation

$$\ln \frac{m}{m_0} + \frac{m - m_0}{M} = -\frac{R}{M}t$$

if $M \gg m$, the second term on the left side is negligible and we obtain the same solution as before.

8. Let $k = ac$:

   a. $c(t) = \dfrac{1}{\left(\dfrac{B}{V}\right) + at}$

   b. $c(t) = K \dfrac{e^{2Kt/a} - 1}{e^{2Kt/a} + 1}$    where $K = \sqrt{\dfrac{I}{aV}}$

*Set 3.2*

1. $\dfrac{x^2}{2} + 3x + 2y^2 - 4y = c$

2. $x^2y + xy^2 = c$

3. Exact if $a = -b$, in which case the solution is $cy^2 + 2axy + ax^2 = k$.

4. Not exact.

*Set 3.3*

1. Linear
2. Nonlinear
3. Linear
4. Linear
5. Nonlinear
6. Linear
7. Nonlinear
8. Independent
9. Dependent
10. Dependent
11. Independent
12. Independent

*Set 3.4*

3. $2\pi, \pi, c = 2\pi\theta/360°$; $c$ = circumference subtended

*Set 3.5*

1. $\lambda = 2, -2$         $e^{2x}, e^{-2x}$

2. $\lambda = 2, -2$         $e^{2x}, e^{-2x}$

3. $\lambda = 2 + 2i, 2 - 2i$     $e^{(2+2i)x}, e^{(2-2i)x},$

                      or $e^{2x} \cos 2x, e^{2x} \sin 2x$

4. $\lambda = 2i, -2i$       $e^{2ix}, e^{-2ix}$, or $\cos 2x, \sin 2x$

5. $\lambda = -2 + 2\sqrt{5}, -2-2\sqrt{5}$    $e^{(-2+2\sqrt{5})x}, e^{(-2-2\sqrt{5})x}$

6. $\lambda = 0, -1$         $1, e^{-x}$

7. $\lambda = 4, -3$         $e^{4x}, e^{-3x}$

8. $\lambda = 1, -1$         $e^{x}, e^{-x}$

9. $\lambda = 2, 2$          $e^{2x}, xe^{2x}$

10. $\lambda = k$            $e^{kx}$

11. $\lambda = 0, 0, 0$        $1, x, x^2$

*Set 3.6*

1. $y_p(x) = 0$

2. $y_p(x) = e^x$

3. $y_p(x) = -1/3 \sin 2x$

4. $y_p(x) = e^x - 1/3 \sin 2x$

5. $y_p(x) = \dfrac{1}{b}x^2 - \dfrac{2a}{b^2}x + \dfrac{3b^2 - 2}{b^2}$

6. $y_p(x) = 1/730 \cos 3x - 27/730 \sin 3x$

*Set 3.7*

1. $y = \dfrac{[4e^{-x} - 5e^{-2x} + 10 + \cos 2x - 3 \sin 2x]}{10}$

2. $y = \left(\dfrac{K}{k}\right)(1 - e^{-kx})$

3. $y = (1 - 3t)e^{-3x} + (t - 5)$

4. $y = x^2 + 2 \sin x$

5. $x = \dfrac{1}{\omega_0^2 - \omega^2}[(\omega_0^2 - \omega^2 - 1) \cos \omega_0 t + \cos \omega t]$

6. $x = \cos \omega_0 t + \left(\dfrac{t}{2\omega_0}\right) \sin \omega_0 t$

7. $y = \dfrac{[e^x(3 \cos x + 4 \sin x) - 3e^{-x} - 10xe^{-x}]}{25}$

8. $x = 0$

9. $V = \dfrac{B}{(C_1 + C_2)} = 111 \text{ ml/kg}$

$$k_{10} = \frac{(C_1 + C_2)}{\tau_f \tau_s \left( \dfrac{C_2}{\tau_f} + \dfrac{C_1}{\tau_s} \right)} = 0.16 \ \text{min}^{-1}$$

$$k_{12} = \frac{-C_1 C_2 \left( \dfrac{1}{\tau_f} - \dfrac{1}{\tau_f} \right)^2}{C_1 + C_2 \left( \dfrac{C_2}{\tau_f} + \dfrac{C_1}{\tau_s} \right)} = 0.23 \ \text{min}^{-1}$$

$$k_{21} = \frac{-\left( \dfrac{C_2}{\tau_f} + \dfrac{C_1}{\tau_s} \right)}{(C_1 + C_2)} = 0.045 \ \text{min}^{-1}$$

10. $B = c_\infty V$ and $I = c_\infty k V$

11. $\dfrac{B}{V}$

*Set 3.8*

1. $E(t) = \dfrac{PK}{\rho L} \left[ \dfrac{1}{\omega_n^2} - \dfrac{1}{\omega_n^2 \sqrt{1 - \zeta^2}} \, e^{-\zeta \omega_n t} \sin \left( \omega_n \sqrt{1 - \zeta^2} \, t + \phi \right) \right]$

where $\phi = \cos^{-1} \zeta$ and $P = 15$ mmHg. For the numbers in this problem, $E(t) = [4.2 - 5.9 e^{-t/7.6 \ \text{msec}} \sin (134 \ \text{sec}^{-1} t + 0.8)]$ mv.

2. $E(t) = \dfrac{K}{\rho L} \left[ P_0 + \dfrac{\Delta P}{\omega_n^2} - \dfrac{\Delta P}{\omega_n^2 \sqrt{1 - \zeta^2}} \, e^{-\zeta \omega_n t} \sin \left( \omega_n \sqrt{1 - \zeta^2} \, t + \phi \right) \right]$

where $P_0 = 5$ mmHg and $\Delta P = 15$ mmHg. For this problem, $E(t) = [5.6 - 5.9 e^{-t/7.6 \ \text{msec}} \sin (134 \ \text{sec}^{-1} t + 0.8)]$ mv.

3. $3 \zeta \omega_n$

4. $R(\omega) = \left[ \omega_n^2 \sqrt{\left[ 1 - \left( \dfrac{\omega}{\omega_n} \right)^2 \right]^2 + 4 \zeta^2 \left( \dfrac{\omega}{\omega_n} \right)^2} \right]^{-1}$

*Set 3.9*

1. $b$ (or $-b$)

2. $\dot{c} = -abc$

3. $c(t) = c_0 e^{-abt}$

4. $c(t) = \ln [(e^{c_0} - 1)e^{-abt} + 1]$

*Set 4.1*

1. $\dfrac{5}{s^2} + \dfrac{3}{s}$

2. $\dfrac{a}{s^2} + \dfrac{b}{s}$

3. $\dfrac{2}{s^3} + \dfrac{2}{s^2} + \dfrac{1}{s}$

4. $\dfrac{7}{(s - 2)}$

5. $\dfrac{c_0}{\left(s + \dfrac{1}{\tau}\right)}$

6. $\dfrac{1}{(s^2 + 1)}$

7. $\dfrac{A\omega_n \sqrt{1 - \zeta^2}}{(s^2 + 2\zeta\omega_n s + \omega_n^2)}$

8. $\dfrac{B(s \cos \phi + \omega \sin \phi)}{(s^2 + \omega^2)}$

9. $\dfrac{n!}{s^{n+2}}$

10. $\dfrac{n!}{s^{n+2}}$

11. $\dfrac{t^2}{2}$

12. $e^{3t} \sin 2t$

13. $e^{-t} + 2e^{-3t}$

14. $20 \sin 5t$

15. $2e^{-6t} \cos t - e^{-t}$

*Set 4.2*

2. $2e^{-t} + e^{-2t}$

3. $\sin t + \cos t$

4. $(t + 4)e^{-t/2}$

5. $e^t \sin 4t + e^{-2t}$

6. $1 + 2e^{-2t} + 3e^{-3t}$

*Set 4.3*

1. a. 20 min

4. $E(t) = \dfrac{P_0}{\omega_n \sqrt{1 - \zeta^2}} e^{-\zeta \omega_n t} \sin (\omega_n \sqrt{1 - \zeta^2} \, t)$

For the specific numbers in this problem, $E(t) = 745e^{-t/7.6}$ msec $\sin (134t)$ mv.

*Set 4.4*

1. $x_1(t) = \dfrac{[(2x_{10} + x_{20})e^{-t} - x_{20}e^{-t}]}{2}$

2. $x_1(t) = \dfrac{[(2x_{10} - x_{20})e^t + x_{20}e^{-t}]}{2}$

3. $y(t) = 1 + t$

4. a. $\dot{g} = P\delta(t) - k_A g$ \qquad $g(0) = 0$

$\dot{c} = \dfrac{k_A g}{V} - k_M c$ \qquad $c(0) = 0$

$g$ mass of drug in gastrointestinal tract, $c$ = concentration of drug in blood, $V$ = volume of distribution of blood compartment.

b. $c(t) = \dfrac{k_A P}{V(k_M - k_A)} (e^{-k_A t} - e^{-k_M t})$

## Set 4.5

1. a. $c(t) = \left(\dfrac{Bk}{2V}\right) te^{-kt}$

b. $c(t) = \left(\dfrac{I}{2kV}\right)(1 - e^{-kt} - kte^{-kt})$

## Set 5.1

2. a. $e^{-2t}$

b. $te^{-t}$

c. $e^{-2t} - e^{-3t}$

d. $1/2 \sin 2t$

e. $1/8(1 - e^{-4t} - 2e^{-2t})$

f. $\dfrac{1}{\omega_n\sqrt{1 - \zeta^2}} e^{-\zeta\omega_n t} \sin (\omega_n\sqrt{1 - \zeta^2}t)$

3. a. $1/2(1 - e^{-2t})$

b. $(1 - e^{-t} - te^{-t})$

c. $1/6(1 - 3e^{-2t} + 2e^{-3t})$

d. $-1/4 \cos 2t$

e. $1/8[t + 1/4e^{-4t} + e^{-2t} - 5/4]$

f. $\dfrac{1}{\omega_n^2} - \dfrac{1}{\omega_n^2\sqrt{1 - \zeta^2}} e^{-\zeta\omega_n t} \sin (\omega_n\sqrt{1 - \zeta^2}t + \phi) \qquad \phi = \cos^{-1}\zeta$

The step response is the integral of the impulse response.

4. Each solution is of the form $y(t) = x(t) - (t - 1) \cdot x(t - 1)$, where $x(t)$ is the solution to the corresponding part of Problem 3.

5. $y(t) = AB[\omega e^{-t/\tau} + (1/\tau) \sin \omega t - \omega \cos \omega t]/[(1/\tau)^2 + \omega^2]$

*Set 5.3*

2. $\dfrac{4}{\pi}\left[\sin t + \dfrac{1}{6}\sin(3t - \pi/8)\right]$

3. $y(t) = \dfrac{(\sin \omega_n t - \omega_n t \cos \omega_n t)}{2\omega_n^2}$

4. $\zeta = 0.3, \omega_n = 15$ Hz

*Set 5.4*

1. $H(s) = \dfrac{V(s)}{E(s)} = \dfrac{1}{(s + a)}$

2. $H(s) = \dfrac{Y(s)}{F(s)} = \dfrac{1}{(3s^2 + 2s - 1)}$

3. $H(s) = \dfrac{X(s)}{G(s)} = \dfrac{2(2s + 1)}{(s^3 + s - 5s + 2)}$

4. $H(s) = \dfrac{Y(s)}{X(s)} = 2$

5. $H(s) = \dfrac{E(s)}{P(s)} = \dfrac{\dfrac{K}{(\rho L)}}{s^2 + 2\zeta\omega_n s + \omega_n^2}$

6. a. $H(s) = \left(\dfrac{C(s)}{I(s)}\right) = \dfrac{s + k_{21}}{V[s^2 + (k_{12} + k_{21} + k_{10})s + k_{10}k_{21}]}$

7. a. $H(s) = \dfrac{\dfrac{K}{(\rho L)}}{(s^2 + 2\zeta\omega_n s + \omega_n^2)(s + a)}$

   b. $H(s) = \dfrac{1}{(s^2 + 12.6s + 3944)(s + 50)}\ \dfrac{\text{volt}}{\text{mmHg}}$

   g. When $a$ is low, the recorder prevents the higher frequency components of the signal from being recorded. When it is just below the catheter's resonant frequency, it compensates by eliminating the resonant peak. When $a$ is large, the recorder has no practical effect on the signal.

8.  a.  $Y(s) = H(s) \cdot I(s)$

    b.  $\dfrac{Y(s)}{I(s)} = \dfrac{H(s)}{(1 + H(s))}$

9.  a.  $(1 - e^{-t})/2$ without feedback; $(1 - e^{-t/(2/3)})/3$ with feedback.

    b.  $(2 - 3e^{-t} + e^{-3t})/6$ without feedback; $(1 - e^{-2t} - 2te^{-2t})/4$ with feedback.

    c.  $$\dfrac{1}{\omega_n^2}\left[1 - \dfrac{1}{\sqrt{1 - \zeta^2}}\, e^{-\zeta\omega_n t}\, \sin\left(\omega_n\sqrt{1 - \zeta^2}\, t + \phi\right)\right]$$

    where $\phi = \cos^{-1}\zeta$, $\omega_n = 2$ and $\zeta = 0.1$ with no feedback, and $\omega_n = \sqrt{5} \simeq 2.24$ and $\zeta = \sqrt{5}/25 \simeq 0.089$ with feedback.

10.  The response speeds up and changes steady-state response.

11.  $\dfrac{Y(s)}{I(s)} = \dfrac{H(s)}{(1 + G(s) \cdot H(s))}$

12.  a.  $(1 - e^{-t/\tau})/2$ where $\tau = 4/3$, $2/3$, $2/11$ for $G = 0.5$, 2, and 10, respectively.

    b.  $$\dfrac{1 + \left(\sqrt{2} - \dfrac{1}{2}\right)e^{-(2+\sqrt{2}/2)t} - \left(\sqrt{2} + \dfrac{1}{2}\right)e^{-(2-\sqrt{2}/2)t}}{2}$$

    $$\simeq \dfrac{1 + 0.91e^{-t/0.36} - 1.91e^{-t/0.77}}{2}$$

    when $G = 0.5$ and

    $$\dfrac{1}{\omega_n^2}\left[1 - \dfrac{1}{\sqrt{1 - \zeta^2}}\, e^{-\zeta\omega_n^2 t}\, \sin\left(\omega_n\sqrt{1 - \zeta^2}\, t + \phi\right)\right]$$

    where $\phi = \cos^{-1}\zeta$ with $\omega_n = \sqrt{5} \simeq 2.2$ and $\sqrt{13} \simeq 3.6$ and $\zeta = 0.91$ and $0.55$ for $G = 2$ and 10, respectively.

    c.  Same form of response as 9c, with $\omega_n = 2.1$, 2.4, and 3.7 and $\zeta = 0.095, 0.083$, and $0.054$ for $G = 0.4$, 2, and 10, respectively.

    d.  The response speeds up and becomes more oscillatory. Note that increasing the feedback gain in part (b) actually changes the qualitative nature of the response from an exponential to a damped oscillation. Increasing the gain too high can make the system unstable.

*Set 6.1*

1. a. $2\pi$

   b. $\dfrac{2\pi}{3}$

   c. 1

   d. $\dfrac{1}{2}$

   e. $\dfrac{1}{2}$

3. a. $y(t) = (4/\pi)(\sin t + 1/3 \sin 3t + 1/5 \sin 5t + 1/7 \sin 7t + \ldots)$ in both representations.

   b. $y(t) = (4/\pi)(\pi/4 + \sin t + 1/3 \sin 3t + 1/5 \sin 5t + 1/7 \sin 7t + \ldots)$ in both representations.

   c. $a_n = \begin{cases} 1/4 & n = 0 \\ -2/(\pi n)^2 & n \text{ odd} \\ 0 & n \text{ even} \end{cases}$     $b_n = (-1)^{n+1}/(\pi n)$

   $A_n = \begin{cases} 1/4 & n = 0 \\ \sqrt{(\pi n)^2 + 4}/(\pi n)^2 & n \text{ odd} \\ 1/\pi n & n \text{ even} \end{cases}$

   $\psi_n = \begin{cases} 0 & n = 0 \\ \pi & n \text{ even} \\ \cos^{-1} 2/\sqrt{(\pi n)^2 + 4} & n \text{ odd} \end{cases}$

*Set 6.2*

2. $c_0 = \dfrac{1}{\pi^2}$, $c_n = c_{-n} = \begin{cases} 1/[2(n-1)(n+1)] & n \text{ even} \\ 0 & n \text{ odd} \end{cases}$

4. See Table E.1.

*Set 6.3*

1. $\dfrac{[\sin 4\pi f + i(\cos 4\pi f - 1)]}{4\pi f}$

2. $\dfrac{[\sin 2\pi f + i(\cos 3\pi f - 1)]}{2\pi f}$

3. $\dfrac{[\sin \pi f + i(\cos \pi f - 1)]}{\pi f}$

4. $\dfrac{[\pi f \sin 2\pi f + \cos 2\pi f - 1]}{(\pi f)^2}$

5. $\dfrac{[\pi f \sin \pi f + \cos \pi f - 1]}{(\pi f)^2}$

6. 1

*Set 6.4*

2. $\left(\dfrac{i}{2}\right) [\delta(f + f_0) - \delta(f - f_0)]$

*Set 6.5*

1. See Table E.1.

3. a. $\mathscr{F}\{\delta(t)\} = 1$ $\qquad$ $R(f) = 1$ $\qquad$ $\phi(f) = 0$

   b. $\mathscr{F}\{e^{-t}\} = \dfrac{1 - i2\pi f}{1 + (2\pi f)^2}$ $\qquad$ $R(f) = \dfrac{1}{\sqrt{1 + (2\pi f)^2}}$

   $\phi(f) = \tan^{-1} 2\pi f$

   c. $\mathscr{F}\{e^{-t/10}\} = \dfrac{1 - \dfrac{i\pi f}{5}}{1 + \left(\dfrac{\pi f}{5}\right)^2}$ $\qquad$ $R(f) = \dfrac{1}{\sqrt{1 + \left(\dfrac{\pi f}{5}\right)^2}}$

   $\phi(f) = \tan^{-1}\left(\dfrac{\pi f}{5}\right)$

   d. $\mathscr{F}\{\text{sinc } t\} = u\left(f + \dfrac{1}{2}\right) - u\left(f - \dfrac{1}{2}\right)$ $\qquad$ $R(f) = 1 - u\left(f - \dfrac{1}{2}\right)$

   $\phi(f) = 0$

**TABLE E.1** Tabulated Solutions to Some Problems in Chapter 6

| Problem Set Problem Number | | 6.2 4 | 6.5 1 | | | | 6.7 1 | | 6.7 2 |
|---|---|---|---|---|---|---|---|---|---|
| | | | Good Catheter | | Bad Catheter | | | | |
| $n$ | $f_n$ (Hz) | $A_n^2$ (mmHg$^2$) | $A_n$ (mmHg) | $\psi_n$ (rad.) | $A_n$ (mmHg) | $\psi_n$ (rad.) | $A_n$ (mmHg) | $\psi_n$ (rad.) | $A_n^2$ (mmHg$^2$) |
| 0 | 0.0 | 5560 | 74.5 | 0.00 | 74.5 | 0.000 | 0.0 | -1.57 | 0 |
| 1 | 0.6 | 116 | 10.7 | 3.76 | 10.7 | 3.76 | 40.5 | 2.19 | 1640 |
| 2 | 1.2 | 80.6 | 8.97 | 2.41 | 8.97 | 2.41 | 67.6 | 0.839 | 4580 |
| 3 | 1.8 | 15.9 | 3.99 | 1.00 | 4.00 | 1.00 | 45.1 | -0.564 | 2040 |
| 4 | 2.4 | 4.04 | 2.01 | 0.372 | 2.11 | 0.372 | 30.3 | -1.19 | 918 |
| 5 | 3.0 | 9.21 | 3.03 | 5.73 | 3.33 | 5.73 | 57.2 | 4.16 | 3270 |
| 6 | 3.6 | 5.19 | 2.28 | 3.99 | 2.62 | 3.99 | 51.5 | 2.42 | 2660 |
| 7 | 4.2 | 0.106 | 0.327 | 4.20 | 0.392 | 4.20 | 8.62 | 2.63 | 74.4 |
| 8 | 4.8 | 2.20 | 1.48 | 2.91 | 1.85 | 2.91 | 44.7 | 1.34 | 2000 |
| 9 | 5.4 | 1.86 | 1.36 | 0.489 | 1.77 | 0.48 | 46.3 | -1.08 | 2140 |
| 10 | 6.0 | 0.123 | 0.352 | 3.08 | 0.458 | 3.08 | 13.2 | 1.51 | 176 |
| 11 | 6.6 | 1.29 | 1.13 | 5.97 | 1.51 | 5.97 | 47.1 | 4.40 | 2220 |
| 12 | 7.2 | 0.60 | 0.779 | 3.48 | 1.05 | 3.48 | 35.2 | 1.91 | 1240 |
| 13 | 7.8 | 0.375 | 0.613 | 5.77 | 0.828 | 5.77 | 30.0 | 4.20 | 902 |
| 14 | 8.4 | 0.744 | 0.863 | 2.85 | 1.18 | 2.85 | 45.5 | 1.27 | 2070 |
| 15 | 9.0 | 0.216 | 0.465 | 6.01 | 0.651 | 6.01 | 26.2 | 4.44 | 691 |
| 16 | 9.6 | 0.277 | 0.527 | 2.17 | 0.748 | 2.17 | 31.7 | 0.606 | 1010 |
| 17 | 10.2 | 0.261 | 0.511 | 5.63 | 0.741 | 5.63 | 32.7 | 4.05 | 1070 |
| 18 | 10.8 | 0.0384 | 0.196 | 2.15 | 0.284 | 2.15 | 13.3 | 0.582 | 176 |
| 19 | 11.4 | 0.0870 | 0.295 | 4.91 | 0.435 | 4.91 | 21.1 | 3.34 | 446 |
| 20 | 12.0 | 0.0538 | 0.232 | 1.95 | 0.348 | 1.95 | 17.4 | 0.379 | 305 |

**TABLE E.1** (conclusion)

| Problem Set Problem Number | | 6.2 4 | 6.5 1 | | | | 6.7 1 | | 6.7 2 |
| | | | Good Catheter | | Bad Catheter | | | | |
| $n$ | $f_n$ (Hz) | $A_n^2$ (mmHg$^2$) | $A_n$ (mmHg) | $\psi_n$ (rad.) | $A_n$ (mmHg) | $\psi_n$ (rad.) | $A_n$ (mmHg) | $\psi_n$ (rad.) | $A_n^2$ (mmHg$^2$) |
|---|---|---|---|---|---|---|---|---|---|
| 21 | 12.6 | 0.0201 | 0.142 | 5.14 | 0.213 | 5.14 | 11.2 | 3.57 | 126 |
| 22 | 13.2 | 0.0125 | 0.112 | 1.14 | 0.179 | 1.14 | 9.28 | -0.425 | 86.2 |
| 23 | 13.8 | 0.0174 | 0.132 | 4.89 | 0.211 | 4.89 | 11.4 | 3.32 | 130 |
| 24 | 14.4 | 0.00221 | 0.047 | 0.662 | 0.082 | 0.662 | 4.25 | -0.909 | 18.0 |
| 25 | 15.0 | 0.00689 | 0.083 | 4.88 | 0.146 | 4.88 | 7.82 | 3.31 | 61.1 |
| 26 | 15.6 | 0.00068 | 0.026 | 5.76 | 0.052 | 3.76 | 2.54 | 4.19 | 6.49 |
| 27 | 16.2 | 0.00336 | 0.058 | 4.70 | 0.122 | 4.70 | 5.90 | 3.13 | 34.8 |
| 28 | 16.8 | 0.00048 | 0.022 | 6.02 | 0.047 | 6.02 | 2.32 | 4.44 | 5.39 |
| 29 | 17.4 | 0.00044 | 0.021 | 5.33 | 0.047 | 5.33 | 2.29 | 3.76 | 5.27 |
| 30 | 18.0 | 0.00036 | 0.019 | 5.81 | 0.047 | 5.81 | 2.14 | 4.24 | 4.61 |
| 31 | 18.6 | 0.00102 | 0.032 | 5.12 | 0.096 | 5.12 | 3.74 | 3.55 | 13.9 |
| 32 | 19.2 | 0.00053 | 0.023 | 5.38 | 0.087 | 5.23 | 2.77 | 3.81 | 7.69 |
| 33 | 19.8 | 0.00090 | 0.030 | 5.36 | 0.113 | 5.21 | 3.73 | 3.79 | 13.9 |
| 34 | 20.4 | 0.00058 | 0.024 | 5.71 | 0.089 | 4.91 | 3.07 | 4.14 | 9.46 |
| 35 | 21.0 | 0.00063 | 0.025 | 5.69 | 0.093 | 4.89 | 3.29 | 4.12 | 10.8 |
| 36 | 21.6 | 0.00048 | 0.022 | 5.86 | 0.068 | 4.26 | 2.98 | 4.29 | 8.91 |
| 37 | 22.2 | 0.00058 | 0.024 | 5.49 | 0.067 | 3.79 | 3.34 | 3.92 | 11.2 |
| 38 | 22.8 | 0.00058 | 0.024 | 5.59 | 0.065 | 3.79 | 3.43 | 4.02 | 11.8 |
| 39 | 23.4 | 0.00044 | 0.021 | 5.47 | 0.055 | 3.57 | 3.08 | 3.90 | 9.53 |
| 40 | 24.0 | 0.00044 | 0.021 | 5.83 | 0.052 | 3.63 | 3.16 | 4.26 | 10.0 |

e. $\mathscr{F}\{\text{sinc } 2t\} = \frac{1}{2}\left[u\left(\frac{f+1}{2}\right) - u\left(\frac{f-1}{2}\right)\right]$

$R(f) = \frac{1}{2}\left[1 - u\left(\frac{f+1}{2}\right)\right]$        $\phi(f) = 0$

f. $\mathscr{F}\{\text{sinc } 10t\} = \frac{1}{10}\left[u\left(\frac{f+5}{10}\right) - u\left(\frac{f-5}{10}\right)\right]$

$R(f) = \frac{1}{10}\left[1 - u\left(\frac{f+5}{10}\right)\right]$        $\phi(f) = 0$

4. $\mathscr{F}\{u(t)\} = \frac{1}{2}\delta(f) - \frac{i}{2\pi f}$

$$R(f) = \begin{cases} 1 & f = 0 \\ \dfrac{1}{2\pi f} & f > 0 \end{cases} \qquad \phi(f) = \begin{cases} 0 & f = 0 \\ \dfrac{\pi}{2} & f > 0 \end{cases}$$

*Set 6.7*
1. See Table E.1.
2. See Table E.1.

*Set 7.1*

1. a. $(.57)10^3 = 580$        $(.5790)10^3 = 579.0$        $(.57900)10^3 = 579.000$

   b. $(.00)10^5 = 0$    $(.0000)10^5 = 0$

   $(.000010)10^5 = (.100000)10^1 = 1.00000$

   c. $(.06)10^1 = (.60)10^0 = 0.60$   $(.0794)10^1 = (.7940)10^0 = 0.7940$

   $(.07947114)10^1 = (.79471140) = .79471140$

   d. $0.90, 0.9170, 0.91666670$

2. a. $(.733)10^{-1} = 0.0733$

   b. $(-.001)10^3 = -1$ (an impossible number!)

3. a. $(.74233)10^{-1} = 0.074233$

   b. $(.00076)10^2 = 0.076$

4. The second formula requires subtracting two large numbers to obtain a relatively small one. Since we only carry a fixed number of digits, the truncation errors lead to a loss of significance. (Note that if one is

willing to accept the additional work and expense of carrying more
digits, the second formula does provide accurate results. The larger the
$X_i$ or greater the number of measurements, however, the less reliable
the first formula.)

5. a. $e^x = 1 + x + \dfrac{x^2}{2!} + \dfrac{x^3}{3!} + \dfrac{x^4}{4!} + \ldots$

   b. $\sin x = x - \dfrac{x^3}{3!} + \dfrac{x^5}{5!} - \dfrac{x^7}{7!} + \ldots$

   c. $\cos x = 1 - \dfrac{x^2}{2!} + \dfrac{x^4}{4!} - \dfrac{x^6}{6!} \ldots$

(Compare these results with the power series used to define them in
Chapter 3.)

6. a. $e^x = e^\pi \left[ 1 + (x - \pi) + \dfrac{(x - \pi)^2}{2!} + \dfrac{(x - \pi)^3}{3!} + \ldots \right]$

   b. $\sin x = -(x - \pi) + \dfrac{(x - \pi)^3}{3!} - \dfrac{(x - \pi)^5}{5!} + \dfrac{(x - \pi)^7}{7!} - \ldots$

   c. $\cos x = -1 + \dfrac{(x - \pi)^2}{2!} - \dfrac{(x - \pi)^4}{4!} - \dfrac{(x - \pi)^6}{6!} + \ldots$

7. a. 0.025

   b. -0.98

   c. 1%, 103%

*Set 7.2*

1. Actual: 0.5000        Trapezoid: 0.5000 (0% error)
   Simpson: 0.5000 (0%)

| | | |
|---|---|---|
| 2. 0.3333 | 0.3750 (13%) | 0.3333 (0%) |
| 3. 0.2500 | 0.3125 (25%) | 0.2500 (0%) |
| 4. 0.2000 | 0.1406 (30%) | 0.2083 (4%) |
| 5. 2.1972 | 2.4635 (12%) | 2.2773 (3%) |
| 6. 2.1972 | 2.2734 (3%) | 2.2100 (0.6%) |
| 7. 23.6552 | 23.0390 (3%) | 23.5243 (0.6%) |
| 8. 1.3333 | 1.3408 (0.6%) | 1.2641 (5%) |
| 9. 53.5982 | 57.9919 (8%) | 53.8638 (0.5%) |
| 10. -267.2458 | -167.3013 (37%) | -223.0684 (17%) |
| 11. -267.2458 | -240.3518 (10%) | -264.7020 (0.9%) |

*Set 7.3*

1. $y(6) \simeq y_{24} = 9.8497$

2. a. Value at $t = 2$: 24.0000 (10%)
   b. Value at $t = 2$: 26.4016 (1.5%)
   c. Value at $t = 2$: 26.7615 (0.1%)
   d. Value at $t = 2$: 26.7978 (0.005%)

   Exact solution: 26.7991

3. a. 37.9167
   b. 45.9394
   c. 47.8878
   d. 48.1495

5. $\dot{x} = y$ $\qquad\qquad\qquad x(0) = 0$

   $\dot{y} = f(t) - 2\zeta\omega_n y - \omega_n^2 x \qquad y(0) = 0$

6. Let $c$ = concentration in central compartment, $q$ = mass of drug in outer compartment.

   $\dot{c} = -0.07 \ \text{min}^{-1} \ c - 0.001(\text{liter-min})^{-1} \ q + 133 \ \text{mg}/(\text{liter-min})$

   $\dot{q} = 1.5 \ \text{liter/min} \ c - 0.05 \ \text{min}^{-1} \ q$

   The starting (initial) conditions are $c(0) = 16.67 \ \text{mg/liter}$
   $$q(0) = 0$$

   The Runge-Kutta equations are

   $c_{i+1} = c_i + 0.1667 \ \text{min} \ (C_1 + 2C_2 + 2C_3 + C_4)$

   $q_{i+1} = q_1 + 0.1667 \ \text{min} \ (Q_1 + 2Q_2 + 2Q_3 + Q_4)$

   where

   $C_1 = -0.07c_i - 0.001q_i + 0.133$

   $Q_1 = 1.5c_i - 0.05q_i$

   $C_2 = -0.07\left(c_i + \dfrac{C_1}{2}\right) - 0.001\left(q_i + \dfrac{Q_1}{2}\right) + 0.133$

   $Q_2 = 1.5\left(c_i + \dfrac{C_1}{2}\right) - 0.05\left(q_i + \dfrac{Q_1}{2}\right)$

$$C_3 = -0.07\left(c_i + \frac{C_2}{2}\right) - 0.001\left(q_i + \frac{Q_2}{2}\right) + 0.133$$

$$Q_3 = 1.5\left(c_i + \frac{C_2}{2}\right) - 0.05\left(q_i + \frac{Q_2}{2}\right)$$

$$C_4 = -0.07(c_i + C_3) - 0.001(q_i + Q_3) + 0.133$$

$$Q_4 = 1.5(c_i + C_3) - 0.05(q_i + Q_3)$$

*Set 7.4*

2. $A = 7.21$ $\qquad$ $k = -0.324$

3. $a_2 = 0.231$ $\qquad$ $a_1 = -2.86$ $\qquad$ $a_0 = 9.47$

6. Don't do it!

*Set A.1*

2. $y' = -2x^{-3}$

3. $u' = 5w^4$

4. $v' = \dfrac{2}{3r^{-1/3}}$

5. $M' = \dfrac{-3}{t^4}$

6. $A' = \dfrac{1}{3Q^{-2/3}}$

7. $Z' = \dfrac{-1}{2P^{-3/2}}$

8. $v' = a - \dfrac{b}{t^2}$

9. $M' = q + 2rt$

10. $y' = (x - 3)^{-1} + x(x - 3)^{-2} \cdot 1 = \dfrac{1 - x(x - 3)}{(x - 3)^2} = \dfrac{1 + 3x - x^2}{(x - 3)^2}$

11. $y'' = 2$

12. $y'' = 0$

13. $x = \dfrac{3}{2}$

14. $t = -2$

15. No extreme exists.

16. $x = 1$

17. $C$

18. $x + C$

19. $\dfrac{1}{2}x^2 + C$

20. $\dfrac{1}{3}x^3 + C$

21. $\dfrac{1}{2}mx^2 + bx + C$

22. $\dfrac{1}{4}ax^4 + \dfrac{1}{3}bx^3 + \dfrac{1}{2}cx^2 + dx + C$

# INDEX

Absolute maximum or minimum. *See* Extrema, absolute
Absolute value, of a complex number, 384
Acceleration, 31
Adams-Bashford predictor, 319
Adams-Moulton corrector, 319
Additivity, definition, 62
Amplitude linearity
  definition, 273
  need for, 272
Amplitude ratio
  computed from impulse response, 270
  definition, 191
  for second-order system, 195
  in frequency response, 193
  in terms of frequency ratio, 196, 197
Amplitude, of harmonic in Fourier series, 227
Analog filter. *See* Filter, analog
Anti-derivative, 361
Aortic pressure
  harmonic decomposition, 227-228
  measured through catheter, 202-204
  of dog, 204
Aortic valve, area, 44, 45
Area under the curve

indicator-dilution method to measure flow, 40-41
numerical integration, 302
relationship to integral, 368-370
Argument
  of a function (*def.*), 335
  of complex number, 384
Arrhythmia, 105
Assumptions
  linearization, 129
  need for, 1
  scrutiny of, 4, 133

Band-pass filter, 273
Bandwidth
  adequacy of, 272
  definition, 273
  required to measure derivative, 286-287, 290
Bell-shaped curve, 250n
Bernoulli equation
  assumptions for, 41
  derivation, 41-43
Bi-exponential decay
  appearance on semi-log plot, 2, 27, 101, 103
  curve fitting, 104, 328

Mary Hurtado and Edward Stokes helped prepare this index.

|            |                                   |
|-----------:|-----------------------------------|
| Designer:  | Michael Bass                      |
| Compositor:| Trendwestern                      |
| Printer:   | Braun Brumfield                   |
| Binder:    | Braun Brumfield                   |
| Text:      | MTSC Press Roman                  |
| Display:   | Photo Typositor Microgrammic Bold Extended |
| Cloth:     | Joanna Arrestox B 21500           |
| Paper:     | 50lb. P&S Offset Vellum           |